> A daughter's memoir of her mother evolves beautifully into a narrative of the sweeping changes in women's lives in the twentieth century.

*O*ur Revolution, vivid and rich, reads like a nineteenth-century novel as we follow the love story of a woman and her family through the twentieth-century civil rights, antiwar, and feminist movements. Born into Boston society in 1923, Jenny Moore rebelled by going to college and later emerged as a writer. At twenty-one, she married Paul Moore, a decorated war hero who became Bishop Paul Moore, and joined him in a socially radical ministry. Eventually, they had nine children. "Everything was just starting," Jenny protested—meaning a new independent life inspired by the women's rights movement—when she was diagnosed with cancer at fifty.

Jenny bequeathed her eldest daughter her unfinished writing, and there Honor Moore finds the mother whose loss had long haunted her. *Our Revolution* is a gripping account of two women navigating the twentieth century and a daughter's story of the mother who shaped her life as an artist and a woman.

Brittany Ambridge for Domino

HONOR MOORE is the author of *The Bishop's Daughter*, a National Book Critics Circle Award finalist; *The White Blackbird*, a *New York Times* Notable Book; and three poetry collections. A professor at the New School, she lives in New York City.

OUR REVOLUTION

ALSO BY HONOR MOORE

MEMOIR

The Bishop's Daughter

The White Blackbird

POETRY

Red Shoes

Darling

MEMOIR

Editor

Poems from the Women's Movement

Amy Lowell: Selected Poems

The New Women's Theatre

The Stray Dog Cabaret:
A Book of Russian Poems (with Catherine Ciepiela)

TRANSLATOR

Revenge by Taslima Nasrin

OUR REVOLUTION

•

A MOTHER AND DAUGHTER AT MIDCENTURY

HONOR MOORE

W. W. NORTON & COMPANY
Independent Publishers Since 1923

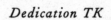

Dedication TK

CONTENTS

Author's Note

My mother's writings and what she says are rendered in *italics* to distinguish them. Source notes follow the text.

OUR REVOLUTION

Prologue: A Bequest

IT WAS A CATASTROPHE, HER SUDDEN DEATH, A BREAK IN THAT STREAM of birthday celebrations and Christmases, disruption of the ever-renewing sequence of photographs—little girls in bright-colored coats, little boys in red overalls, photo-ready smiles, with her, with our father. She would get home first with us, not standing with him at the church door as people left, as he shook their hands or embraced them. Or maybe she hadn't gone to the morning service, had gone only to midnight mass the night before, waited till we were all in bed then filled the stockings, eaten Santa's cookies leaving crumbs, and later, as they sat with friends drinking and laughing, had asked someone please to drink half Santa's glass of milk. The stockings were nylon, the ones with runs she saved for the purpose. She wrapped every present in bright tissue and put it in a stocking so that all she had to do was replace the empties hung from the mantelpiece with the full ones she'd been stuffing for weeks. Eventually there were nine of us, but her diligence did not waver. Sometime after I reached my teens, she began to use pantyhose.

Is that her I see now, walking across the meadow outside my window, the ground-length white coat, white hair, chin raised, winter sun at her face? And then her face turns to me, dark blue eyes, the look that contains all I do not know. It's the Christmas I am sixty-seven, and I am leafing through photographs, her letters, the unfinished writing she left me in her will. Or: it is a Christmas in the early 1950s, and I am coming down the stairs, maybe six years old, and she is standing there, dancing, singing, *I saw Mommy kissing Santa Claus, underneath the mistletoe last night.*

If she were alive now, she would be almost ninety.

The low December sun has settled on the winter yellow of the meadow in the New Hampshire studio where I am writing. The pines are green dulled to black, and spattered close to me at the foot of a stone wall is what remains of the snow; through the pines, another building.

In a photograph of her taken at a party some years before the accident, she wears a sleeveless white brocade sheath, quite short since it's 1971, is standing in the corner of the room at a party, her smile ablaze. Yes, her death was a catastrophe, each of her children thrown into individual sorrow, into our lives, now without the attentiveness of her companionship. She bought a blue suede dress to wear when she visited President Kennedy. When he was killed she passed the dress to me, and it was stolen from the college costume shop where I had taken it to be altered. I'm sorry, they said, as if what I had lost was only a dress. There is a woman in white coming toward me along the narrow road. She is taller than I am and she has black hair. I can't make out her face. These past days that word *catastrophe*, and in my imagination a blank of forgetfulness. The woman in white walking toward me on the winter road, the woman dancing at the foot of the stairs Christmas morning, the woman in white glistening in the corner of a room at a party, her black hair tangling on the white pillow of a deathbed.

I have some of the photographs I took of the Christmas after she died: Patience, my youngest sister then eleven, in the Lanz flannel nightgown given her by our mother the Christmas before; Marian, born sixth and seventeen, also in a Lanz nightgown, an expectant look on her face, as if our mother had not died, as if she were in the room with us, about to say one of those things she'd say that would send all of us off into gales of laughter. "Peel me a grape," when someone asked her to do something he could perfectly well do himself. For a few years she'd been ordering seven nightgowns, keeping one, sending one to each of her six daughters. She loved inventing traditions—identical Easter dresses when we were just three girls, identical yellow terry cloth bathrobes when we were six children, for all of us, even herself and our father: Pop arranged us on the porch one summer afternoon—Mom with Marian, then a baby, on her lap—set the camera on a chair, ran back around to join us before the minute was up.

It is January 1970, and she's been to Boston to visit her mother, bedridden and now living in an apartment high above the Public Garden. Not as difficult as usual, she was thinking, her mother now almost eighty, not quite as dangerous now that drugs controlled the mania that once had her calling everyone on the Eastern Seaboard, giving lobster dinners for thirty in the Tremont Street high-rise two-bedroom, the depression that turned her silent and monosyllabic for weeks at a time. Just two hours with her mother, lunch with her mother's lawyer, a visit with her second daughter who is in her second year at Radcliffe.

On the Eastern shuttle home to Washington, she runs into an old friend from Boston. She's known Bob Amory forever, though not well—the odd dinner party the years in Washington, in the past, debutante parties and the like, long ago; those miscellaneous Boston weekends during the war. At the baggage claim, he offers her a lift from the airport, and she hesitates. She'd looked forward to the taxi, a half hour of calm before she found herself back in her life, with her children, her husband. But why refuse, really? Whenever she's outside time like this, quiet and freedom of mind seem inexhaustible, and that's what she wants now, freedom of mind. But she doesn't want to be rude, and so she accepts. It's afternoon; sun glistens off the Potomac, gleams through the trees in Rock Creek Park. And it's January! She still can't get over the climate here, so beneficent, almost tender.

They drive up Massachusetts Avenue, past the embassies. Talk of Boston, of this one and that one—there are still so many Boston people in Washington, "Harvard types" she knew so well who'd come here to work in the Kennedy administration, mutual friends whose families go back in New England history, as hers does, and his. Now they are on the quiet street, and she will be home in minutes, the children rushing to the door when they hear the jangle of the gold bangles on her arm—a gift from her husband each time she has a child. She is relishing this evening, this city she has so loved, where they have lived for six years, where she has had the luxury of time with her children, where, all the children now in school or moved out, she has come into the beginnings of a new, singular self. Though she doesn't want to be corny, that's really how she thinks of it. One book published, a new one underway. She'd even tried to talk to her mother about it, the book on aging. But her mother, hair dyed light brown, expertly made up even to spend the day in bed—it was that or a wheelchair—was in one of her silent periods and had just looked at her.

"Hello, Mumma."

"Hello, Jenny."

Now Bob pauses the VW at a stop sign, and then they are in the intersection, and from nowhere there's a jolt, a sudden crashing swerve. She is thrown forward. When her eyes open, she is still sitting there in the passenger seat of Bob Amory's Volkswagen Beetle. Something has hit them, but he is still there too, the back and forth light falling back to stillness, but not the same stillness. A car hit them and Bob can't open the driver's door. She too is unharmed she realizes, though she was pitched forward, felt something like a fist in her stomach.

But it was nothing, thank God.

She was not wearing a seat belt, and the car that hit them had run the stop sign, she now realizes. It was invisible until it hit them. Hard to believe still that Bob was unhurt, and she, well, it must have been the gearshift stick. She feels its mark there, an indentation. The police come and an ambulance and then someone drives her home. She greets the children, embraces her husband. She takes a bath, she tells Paul about running into Bob Amory, about how the car was invisible until it hit them, that she is fine, fine, just a little ache there, she puts her hand at her mid-abdomen. As if she had been punched in the stomach.

Then they are getting dressed to go out. At first it's just the slight stomachache and then pain so piercing, she collapses onto their bed. Unbearable. She'd better not go out, but you go ahead Sweetie. He calls an ambulance and of course he stays with her. When they get to the hospital they take her right into surgery.

She is forty-six years old and the mother of nine children, six still at home, the oldest twenty-four, the youngest seven. She is tall with dark blue eyes and black hair. Her husband Paul, an Episcopal bishop in Washington and an activist in the civil rights and peace movements, has just been elected bishop of New York. A year or so earlier she'd published a book, about living and working with the poor when she and Paul were young; since the run-up to the book, she's also been writing for the *Washington Post*—occasional features, about who's on the train to New York for a peace demonstration, about the poor here in the District of Columbia, about Dorothy Day, the *Catholic Worker* activist, a lifelong friend. If she isn't wearing jeans and a tennis top, she dresses in vivid colors, though she has no time to shop and orders almost everything from catalogues. She loves to laugh, to make people laugh, is always at the center of a group of friends. She is a seeker, and, one of her daughters will say decades later, a truth teller. Soon the family will leave Washington and move to New York City; she'd flown up to Boston to see her mother after a visit to New York to look at schools for the children.

On the operating table they found her abdomen filled with blood.

I was living in New York when the telephone call came, standing in the dim, shabby living room of the apartment I had sublet. She had taken the shuttle alone back from Boston, my father said, had accepted a ride from an old Boston friend in his Volkswagen Beetle. A car had run a stop sign, hitting them broadside, and she'd been thrown forward onto the gearshift stick. Dressing for dinner, she'd felt sick, then sicker. An ambulance had taken her to the Washington Hospital Center. They saved a third of her liver, cut away the rest.

Is she okay?

I don't know.

For days it is not certain that she will live. Her husband rushes back and forth to the hospital, friends gather, the children wait for news. Shadows and bits of light, drugs that remove her from herself, hours on the operating table with no certain outcome. Outcome still uncertain when an item about the accident and her injuries appears in the *Post*. But when she writes about the accident later, she says she had no doubt she would get well. *I never thought for one instant that my strength would be permanently impaired.* Days after the surgery, she leaves intensive care for a capacious room in the luxury wing of the hospital. Flowers and get-well messages flood in. Catastrophe of near-death soon passes, replaced by the catastrophe of recovery, of what-will-happen-now. The surgeon, who is German, tells her about the damage, that seven-tenths of her liver has been removed. Perhaps it is true, what they say about precision and Germans.

The surgeon has a thin bony head, a long face, and warm, penetrating eyes.

Taking a kind of inventory, she introduces herself: Nine children, five of them by natural childbirth; for exercise, I play tennis. I have a strong body.

The liver regenerates, he tells her. It is the only human organ that can. Actually, she appreciates the precision.

Black and white tiles on the kitchen floor. She loves that kitchen and also the teakettle that the senator gave her, Senator McCarthy, who had come so close to winning the New Hampshire primary on an anti-war platform that President Johnson had decided not to run again. They played tennis Monday mornings and sometimes he came to tea, often bringing poems he has written or a poem by someone else that he reads to her, for instance the one by Yeats that begins,

When you are old and gray and full of sleep
And nodding by the fire, take down this book,
And slowly read, and dream of the soft look
Your eyes had once, and of their shadows deep . . .

She turns in her bed, thinking of him, of how she loves the poem, how sweet those mornings are, the teakettle he brought her once as a present she thinks of again, and now pain jolts through her belly. "Jesus!" she yelps, pushing the button for the attendant. Gene had given her the book of Yeats poems and she'd put it in the bookcase, painted semigloss white, the colors of book jackets vivid against the white. The nurse arrives and gives her a pain shot. There are the kids' summers to plan, and what they'll do after school these weeks she's in the hospital. Well, it's pretty much under control, and she thinks about them. George at the piano playing rock music, his friends the band; how easily Marian, fourteen, took to chess; Danny at the playground with all his friends; Rosie living with a Navajo family, a special program of her boarding school in Arizona; Susanna playing with her friend Jack, collecting snakes; and Patience number nine. She must ask Georgia to be sure to clean out the refrigerator. She must make a list for Mr. Johnson, the carpenter—Patience needs a bookshelf in her room. And the party in New York to meet Paul's new clergy—what was the date? And then the five or ten people she has to write *before I do another thing*.

"Hello, darling." She looks up, and her oldest daughter walks into the room.

I can barely hear her voice, but because I know so well how she talks, I understand what she says. Even in real life, she sometimes looks so vague it is hard to understand how she does all she does. No letter left unanswered, no present unthanked-for. She wrote letters every day, short notes or long letters on yellow legal pads. I'm holding her hand now, and she's alive. Does she know how scared I was? Does she know I love her? All those letters! To her children in college, her friends in faraway places, to friends in Washington whom she wants to thank or speak to in a special, intimate way. I sit there for a while, holding her hand. It's so strange to be holding my mother's hand, for her to allow me to hold her hand, even want me to hold her hand. She was always so busy, and shy I realize, even with me. Soon she is asleep, breathing with some difficulty. Then a young doctor comes in, and she opens her eyes, those dark blue eyes, the black lashes on her cheek.

"How are we doing today?" I watch the young doctor's bright, enthusiastic face, and I watch my mother.

"I had to ask for another shot," she says in a voice I have never heard, a voice that is hers, speaking for her own self, somehow separate from everyone else, from me. I am thinking that I love my mother.

"That's normal," the enthusiastic doctor says, making a note on his clipboard. "This is my oldest daughter."

I look at him and smile. "How do you do—"

"You've got a great mom!"

I would have said "a great mother. I don't like it when people use *mom* as a noun like that, and what does he know anyway, about this woman.

He turns and leaves the room.

When she is alone again, she turns in her bed, forgetting I am still there.

Like a punch in the gut, in the lower gut. Would this have happened if she had taken a taxi? Was it intuition that made her hesitate when Bob Amory offered a lift?

Later, when she starts to leave her husband, a rumor will circulate among people who barely know her that the man who gave her a ride home that day was her lover. He was not, but it was true she had fallen in love with a man other than her husband, had found herself admitting to herself that her marriage wasn't working, even telling her oldest daughter, who responded by writing her an enraged letter. "What makes you think this is *your marriage?*" was my complaint, my particular fury directed at her use of the singular pronoun. But then Paul was elected bishop of New York, and their troubles faded in the excitement—she won't leave him after all. They had both worked for this, his life ambition, to bring the social activism they'd conceived of together to New York, the city where they fell in love and dreamed of their future.

She will recover, quickly, and they will move the family together one last time. *I have a strong body.* In the will she writes as soon as she is able, she leaves Bob Amory a small painting, so that he will not feel responsible about having driven the car that almost killed her. Even in the will's revision, which she executes two years later when she has cancer, she leaves him that painting, still wishing to assuage any guilt he might have about having driven the car that caused the injury that made her vulnerable to what finally did kill her.

The woman who comes to me in dreams is not my real mother. Or she is my real mother now and has been since she appeared in that bright green field. I was twenty-seven and she had not yet died, but she would within weeks. The green of the field was so vivid. Usually in dreams, there is no color, and she does not speak clearly to me, though her voice can come to me now in daylight—if I'm vacuuming, for instance. *Life is too short,* she says, one of those phrases of hers; *Can't you get someone to help?* It's not exactly her voice but the movement of her voice, and the expression, the slight irony that tells me there are other things to which I might apply myself, which is strange, since in life she was always telling me to neaten up my room.

My mother collected relics of the female past, framed embroideries of Victorian paeans to motherhood, stitched samplers and the like, which she hung in the downstairs bathroom or on the way up the stairs, right next to photographs of my father marching with Martin Luther King, or of herself posing with some of the street kids she worked with in Jersey City. She liked the irony. She was a bishop's wife and mother of nine who didn't look the part, who wore bright colors and net stockings. The prize of the collection was a print Currier and Ives published in 1850 called *Life and Age of Woman.* Because it hung on the wall of my mother's bedroom during the last months of her life, I had a lot of time to puzzle over it, over what stage she had reached and what lay ahead for me.

Woman's life begins in her mother's arms, and one step up the arch with stairs, she's a girl with a doll, two steps and she's marriageable, holding an embroidery hoop. Next she's a bride, hair streaming to her waist, then a young mother with an infant. At the apex stands the matron in her prime, wearing black, a white tea towel over her arm. This is the last we see of woman standing fully upright and the last of her "crowning glory," as all four women on the descent—holding keys on a ring, bending over a cane, knitting, rocking—wear white ruffled caps that cover their hair. This life cycle had nothing to do with me; this was 1973 and I wore my hair down, nearly to my waist. Would I even enter into marriage, an institution of which, after three years of consciousness-raising, I was increasingly skeptical?

My mother rarely wore black and would have framed the tea towel, but otherwise she was certainly as upright and confident as the matron at the top of that pyramid. If she dies, I thought to myself, she will never have to get old like the crone in the rocker whose nose almost touches her chin. My mother came of age nearly a hundred years after the print was published, at the end of World War II. At twenty-one, she threw in her lot with a Marine hero bound for the Episcopal ministry, and for the next seventeen years was enthusiastically and almost always pregnant, while always dreaming of doing "something else." She may have been born into those Currier and Ives proscriptions, but for her generation those ideas were as quaint as black bombazine, as bygone as Whistler's mother, for God's sake! My mother dreamed of an old age, free of all of us and onto a future all her own. Her life would not descend from a central height of maternal satisfaction, but would rise further, making another arc, and another—a double, even a triple rainbow.

"Everything was just starting." She said that soon after she was diagnosed with the cancer that killed her.

It was the accident really that changed everything, or started the change, all those hours in bed, days then weeks, all that time to think. At first she had just suspected it and quickly dismissed the idea, then certainty took hold, and she became sure that her husband was being unfaithful to her. "Their marriage was over in 1968," my brother Paul said recently; "I knew that then." What he did not know and what she came to believe was that his infidelities had been with men. Shocking, but it explained everything. But even when she told him in 1969 that she wanted to leave their marriage, she did not raise the subject of homosexuality. Why not? "She thought he was the most tormented man she had ever known," one of the three friends in whom she confided told me decades later. She did not confront my father, and she never told any of us children what she knew. Later, we knew vaguely that at a certain point she began to have other relationships, but we did not know about the painful negotiations she and my father had, the agreement between them that each would see other people. She had three great loves who were all men. He had relationships with at least three women, and also, simultaneously, with men.

Everything was just starting.

Eighteen months after the accident, my parents moved together to New York City. Too soon; she became exhausted, broke down. A year later, in late 1971, she finally moved back to Washington with the five of her children still at home, and my father commuted two days a week, a process of separation beginning, a new house, a new garden. And she was writing again. The day after her fiftieth birthday, on March 12, 1973, having felt overtired for weeks, she went to the hospital for tests. There were malignant tumors in her colon and liver, the latter inoperable. She died almost exactly six months later.

What, exactly, was just starting?

While her youngest child was in nursery school, my mother had written *The People on Second Street*, a memoir about leaving a privileged life to work with my father at a mission church in downtown Jersey City just after the war; it came out in 1968 and sold more than 25,000 copies. She had become increasingly active in civil rights and against the war in Vietnam; the summer of 1968 she was at the Democratic convention in Chicago, in the crowd tear-gassed outside the Hilton Hotel. The week she was diagnosed and operated on to remove the tumor from her colon, she was admitted to a master's program in fiction writing at Johns Hopkins. She suspended acceptance, and still in pain and dazed from anesthesia, she began to write about her life from the vantage point of her almost certain death. In early convalescence, she dictated; then she wrote by hand. When she again became unable to write by hand, she dictated, In her will,

she left me those unfinished pages, fragments of memoir, and other manuscripts. I was to develop those pages as I saw fit.

I was twenty-seven and a graduate school dropout, writing poems that
were satiric, angry, and feminist. I was just beginning to publish. I was
honored by her bequest, but also confused. Was I to put my own work
aside? How was I to do her work and my own? Over the years, from
time to time, I would look through the boxes of her writing—yellow
legal pads, stories or fragments written on them; multiple copies of memoir fragments in typescript; an almost finished play, but also handwritten college short stories, broken binders of course notes from college. I
remembered her telling me what her friend and teacher had said about
the memoir pages: "We'll get it into print." But there hadn't been time
to finish.

As the daughter of a living mother, I had been rebellious and confused.
Not knowing how to do otherwise, I had rationed expressions of my love,
even as we worked our way into a new, adult relationship. In the months
after her death, I wrote my way out of grief in poems about her; all that
held-in feeling broke into a writing voice that I now recognize was the
first utterance of the writer I would become—no longer a daughter. I
developed these poems into a play called *Mourning Pictures*, which was
produced a year after her death, on Broadway. That I was to develop my
mother's writing was crowded from my mind—I carried the boxes with
me from dwelling to dwelling, always carefully placing them at the back
of a closet.

In the 1990s, I published *The White Blackbird*, a book about my mother's mother, who was a painter. Thirty years after my mother, my father
died, and I wrote *The Bishop's Daughter*; I and my siblings had learned of
his secret bisexual life, and in the book I integrated that revelation into the
story of my relationship with him. As I wrote about my father, memory
loosened images of my mother, and a sense of her as a woman began to
cohere. She had died at fifty years old, and I was now in my sixties, almost
twenty years older than she had ever been. I began to see my fifty-year-
old mother as young, to get a sense of her as a woman, by which I mean

a person. Who would she be if I wrote about her now? Who would I be? I looked up the will. Implicit in the bequest was my mother's recognition that I had a self, a self she saw clearly enough to entrust with the life she had not lived to have, which was the life I have lived, the life of a writer. It was time to pull the pages of her writing from their cartons and read them more carefully than I had as a grieving daughter in my twenties. It was time to get to know my mother.

I

Fretwork

1.

A YOUNG WOMAN IS HOLDING A FLOWER. SHE IS SMILING, NOT THE CON-
trived smile of someone sitting for a photograph, but a wide-open smile.
She has black hair just to her shoulders and a widow's peak and pale white
skin, and she is wearing a dress made of cotton with big checks on it,
open at the neck. A young woman in a checked dress smiling, black hair
swept away from her face with a barret. She is looking at the photographer, a tall man with light brown hair who is being silly and makes her
laugh. She is posing in front of granite, and nothing of the world is visible except a woman in a dress smiling, a vast wall of granite behind her,

creased and wavy. The photograph is black and white, and she is holding the flower up, as if it is a cigarette; but it seems to be a flower, let's say a marigold.

I like to think of this young woman holding a flower, laughing at the man taking a picture of her, and wearing an everyday shirt dress with two buttons undone at the neck. I wonder what she's thinking, so I zoom the photograph, one of several of her I have scanned into my computer, and I see that her smile is flirty and that what she holds is not, after all, a marigold, not even a flower, but a pair of glasses, which I recognize because one of the things I know about this woman is that she rarely wore her glasses in a photograph, that when she was photographed wearing glasses, she was in a hurry, not posing but living. In this photograph, though, she is posing, looking absolutely adorable, smiling at her husband, because by now the tall almost gawky boyish man is her husband, and she is holding her glasses to the side, so you get all of her, looking at you with eyes I know are blue.

I chose this picture to begin because although she is being photographed and is therefore in the company at least of the photographer, who is her husband, she looks free, and I don't think of her as being free. I'm pretty sure that by the time this photograph was taken, she was already a wife and the mother of one or two children, and that her dreams were attached to them and to her husband. But in the photograph, it looks as if her dreams are her own, as if what attaches her to others is held aside, like the pair of glasses I first took for a flower. I don't want to attach any significance to the wall of granite behind her. She doesn't look confined; as I said, she looks free. I think that if I had been the photographer, if I had been her husband, I too would have said, hold it Jenny! Let me get your picture there, right there in front of that big rock.

She had such glossy, thick hair, he said. Even though Evans Woollen is white-haired now, I see the shock of light brown hair across his broad forehead and he is the man I knew as a child, still has that sudden shy laugh. He was a young architect, in his own firm in Indianapolis, where we moved when I was eleven and my mother was thirty-four. Now, at a café in the Museum of Modern Art, we are eating lunch, and he is eighty-two; when I first knew him, he was twenty-nine.

"At a dinner party," he said when I asked how he and his wife had met my parents. He was introduced to my mother first: "and immediately we were having a real conversation." I was now taking notes. "Jenny was unusual in that way. Distinct," he said. "She would begin talking and you felt that a good deal had been dispensed with and that you were talking to someone whom you had known for a long time. I liked her immediately—and the feelings deepened."

A flicker of feeling at the edges of his mouth.

"She had such glossy, thick hair," he said again.

I have had conversations resembling this one with several men, none of whom actually had love affairs with my mother.

Writing now, I am looking out the window in a place where Jenny never was—a piece of the ocean, a mountain beyond that is only some-times visible. It's nearly the end of the growing season, a few purple blossoms, some yellow leaves sprinkled on concrete, a rainy day that will brighten up by four, a dense roof of clouds that will break, leaving, incredibly, some blue.

I open one of the bankers boxes and lay my mother's manuscripts on the floor. On a typed page of memoir dated July 6, 1973, I find this fragment:

Was I conceived in love, and if so, what does that mean? And if not—in what pain, or need, or out of what fright, in what loneliness or lust did my mother and father come together?

It's composed on a typewriter on that crispy corrasable bond from the 1970s. I decide that when I quote her writing or exact speech, I will always use italics:

For I must begin there, where I began, she wrote.

How to find her as a baby? Another photograph? And then, a memory: Large, simply framed, pastel in sweeps of green, blue, and sepia line, a baby is taking a nap. I don't remember ever not looking at that drawing. I looked at it before I had a word for *drawing* or for anything, before I knew a drawing could be "of" or "by" someone. Later, when I knew about *by* or *of*, I didn't ask who had done the drawing or who it was of, and so a silence formed around it, which I entered whenever I stood and looked up at it. I don't know if my not asking was pride (I was the oldest; I was supposed to know everything) or a trait my situation as a child required—the house always too noisy to ask such a quiet question. And so, for many years, I drew no conclusion as to the artist or the subject. I only vaguely knew that my mother's mother had once been an artist; Margarett, as she was called more often than Grandma, rarely visited—she was mostly in mental hospitals for what was later diagnosed as manic-depressive illness, what is now called bipolar disorder. Not one painting of hers ever hung in any place we lived.

By the time I determined that Margarett, my mother's mother, had made the beautiful drawing, it was a matter of faith that she was a source of pain to my mother, such a source of pain that my mother saw her only on occasional short visits she made to Boston. As for the identity of the subject, it didn't occur to me that a mother whose daughter harbored such hurt could possibly picture her daughter the way this artist had—therefore it never crossed my mind that my mother was the sleepy happy baby in the picture. I even wondered if the drawing might be of me, since my father always said that as a baby my eyes squinted and the eyes of the baby in the picture did that. It was not until much later, maybe not until the reading of my mother's will, that the drawing was identified, and I realized the baby was my mother, Jenny.

Memoir pages:

> *My father, his eye over the years trained by my mother's eye for beauty, she over the years aware but unaffected by his ways of kindness; he, always moral but occasionally swindled by the world, she amoral, but cheated by the mores of her time; he, the reconciler of conflict, she without judgement of anything save perfection (beauty)*

*or the lack of it. Patience had married impatience, the selfless with
the self-obsessed.*

They married in 1920, and a year later their first daughter, Margarett,
called Margie, was born. They named my mother, born fifteen months
later, Jenny after Margarett's mother. As was the custom, Margarett
passed the infant to a baby nurse and returned to her feverish sketching,
her pastels and watercolors, and to the vast studio at the center of the
house, where she worked on sculpture. Outdoors, with a staff of garden-
ers, she expanded the gardens, planting rare trees and flowering shrubs.
In January, Jenny was ten months old, and Margarett was pregnant again,
with twins. When Jenny turned one, Margarett, pregnant, was outdoors
supervising the planting of an arbor vitae hedge to enclose the new swimming pool, and there are photographs of my grandfather, Shaw, posing
with a shovel after digging a flower bed. Soon, from his mother's estate, a
flatbed truck would transport "the music room" where the èmigrè musi-
cian Emma Eames had played the piano. The modest outbuilding was
placed on a hill out of sight of the house; this would be Margarett's new
studio—soon to have four children under five, she could no longer work
in the house.

The former studio, which you went into when you entered the house,
now became an enormous two-story living room, hung with paintings,
purchased or inherited—Picabia, Morisot, Cassatt, Renoir, eventually Gauguin—and adorned with sculpture first by Degas and later, as
Margarett turned to Modernism, by Calder and Zadkine. By the end of
spring 1925, an octagonal tower rose at the corner of the old saltbox, a
guest room on its second floor—its ceiling of mirrors that Margarett had
aged by leaving them outdoors all winter. In September, when twin boys
named Shaw and Henry (called Harry after Shaw's brother) were born,
Jenny was eighteen months old. Two weeks before Jenny's third birthday,
when Margie was four and the twins not yet two, the first of nine one-
woman shows Margarett had in six years opened at the Kraushaar Galleries in New York City.

"What is the first thing you remember?" my mother asks herself, writing those close-to-death pages.

When she was in her late forties, she began to see a psychiatrist. She wanted to come to terms with her new independent life, but also with a childhood she described as *rarefied* and also very lonely. She was close to her father—by then decades into a long, happy second marriage and a new family—but she dreaded her mother. No longer painting or drawing, bedridden from a succession of strokes, her bipolar illness controlled by drugs, Margarett was unpredictable—charming, loving, seductive on one visit, volatile and cruel the next.

Once (it was 1972) one of my brother's friends was experimenting with astrology and offered my mother a reading, and so, on a visit, she asked her mother the time of day she was born. "I can't possibly remember," Margarett said. "But I do remember what time I gave birth to two boys."

"Can you believe it?"

My mother was incredulous and hurt telling the story, but also amazed at the demonic accuracy of the blow. Margarett was certainly not unconscious of her daughter's situation, of the new life she was then beginning as an independent woman, as a writer; she also knew that women's liberation was in the air. The new feminism's emphasis on bonds between women was what had inspired my mother to reconcile with Margarett, whom she admired for having pursued a career as an artist. Also: *"I don't want to go to my grave hating her."*

We are on the telephone and she is telling me she's just had the "most extraordinary" experience. She'd just gotten home after a *"very intense"* session with her *shrink*—while talking about her childhood, she'd found herself an infant, *"right at my mother's breast!"* I'd never heard her say "my mother" before; usually Margarett was Mama (pronounced "Mumma") or, as we children called her, Grandma Kean (pronounced "Cane"). Hearing my mother use the phrase "my mother" suggested seriousness I couldn't parse, as into my imagination came not an infant nursing, but my mother, a woman in her late forties, in her house in Washington, D.C., telephone in hand, and Margarett in her apartment above Boston Common, pink bedclothes tumbling, a woman in her eighties, fully and perfectly made up, hair dyed a careful brown: that daughter at that mother's naked breast.

"Wow," I think I said.

Nothing in my own therapy sessions had taken me back that far—I was not breast fed—the practice was out of fashion when I was born; my mother began breastfeeding with number five—and though I considered myself, at twenty-five, a grown woman, it's clear to me now that I was too young to understand what such a memory might cost a woman like my mother. *Right at my mother's breast!* Am I only imagining her voice was tinged with horror? For my mother, as for other women of her generation and class, psychotherapy at midlife was a way to make a transition from old repression to new freedom, but uttering the word *breast* to describe her mother's naked breast broke a taboo; it seemed so unbefitting her tongue that when she said it, she exclaimed it, as if by infusing the syllable with appalled surprise, she could still pass muster as the gentlewoman she had been raised to become.

I, on the other hand, was in women's liberation where use of a word for any formerly hidden female body part was a triumphant peeling away of an old, imprisoning carapace. My mother wanted to be part of our movement, single woman that she was now becoming, albeit with nine children in an era before anyone ever combined the words *single* and *mom*, so in this phone call, she was making common cause with me. This adult phase of our relationship was still new. I remember the weight of the black telephone receiver in my hand, a sense of her still weakened by the accident that had taken her so close to death, the diminution of her strength that had culminated in a depression that landed her in a psychiatric ward and precipitated, it seemed to me, her separation from my father. I wanted her confidences, but I was wary of her vulnerability.

But listening now in memory, I can also hear awe in her voice—*my mother's breast!*—awe at this late reassurance she might once have lain in a mother's arms, that the mother whom she'd always found so difficult had been, if only briefly, a source of nourishment, even tenderness.

2.

The little girl is dancing, whirling so fast she can barely see; and then she can see, all the colors, Mama's paintings, the pink of the brocade that hangs at the end of the huge living room, how the light comes in from the ceiling, the square shape of the window spinning so it's a pinwheel. Papa is laughing and so is Mama, and because she spins like this, Jenny's nickname is Dizzy. She doesn't know what makes her whirl. She gets a little laughing look on her face and then something inside her starts to spin and so she starts to spin with it, soon as fast as the top the twins have that whirls so fast a dot of red becomes a stripe, or like egg whites when the cook beats them that are gooey transparent syrup, but as she beats get whiter, then become puffy little mountains of foam and white and light. Spinning, the girl feels herself become foam too, full of air, her dress whizzing into paleness and then nothing, and when she slows down she still feels her head spinning; then, as if there's a surface inside her head rocking like water in a bowl on a boat, she sees tiny sparkles that look like needles and feel as if they are pecking at the dark, and then she's slowing down, all the colors still and everyone talking, but she has a cone of quiet all to herself.

In a home movie made a few years later, you first see her at a distance climbing onto her bicycle; when you see her again, she's doing a handstand on the handlebars, one foot on the seat, the other leg high in the air behind her, like a ballerina in an arabesque. She is ten years old, but she is not a ballerina, as she makes clear in one of the childhood essays I find in my file boxes:

> I was a young Spartan boy hardy and strong and very excited. I was going to the Olympic games for the first time. Chariot racing was the first sport and one of my favorites. I had always secretly hoped to be a charioteer some day, although such sports were not favored in Laconia, my native town, where men travel by means of their own legs.

In the home movie, her hair is not just short but cropped short and she wears jodhpurs and black riding boots to her knees, and the bike is coasting fast. One, two, three. . . . Astonishing! She stays that way for eight whole seconds before she speeds out of the frame. Later, she's on her horse, Me Too, taking a first jump over a double fence, a second over a triple fence. She's wiry and intent, and I watch her take nine jumps, bent forward on the horse, cantering to the fence, and easily taking it. Me Too refuses just once, but forcefully the small girl turns the big horse and quickly takes the jump again. She became a champion.

On the first page of the battered scrapbook are pasted results of that summer's horse shows at the Myopia Hunt Club in Hamilton, Massachusetts; on the list of winners: Sears, Forbes, Tuckerman, McKean. In the enclave of families who summered in large houses near the seashore north of Boston, the surnames of one's friends were those of one's parents' friends, one's grandparents' friends, even one's great-grandparents' friends, a thread that might extend back to the passenger lists of the *Arbella* or the *Mayflower*. This genealogy came to embarrass my mother, who, by the time I knew her, had come to see her privilege as unjust, a wounding separation from other people. "McKean children star in saddle," reads a clipping, and out slips an eight-by-ten glossy, Jenny McKean on Me Too, Patsy Keough, her riding teacher, black-haired and handsome, holding her harness. It's Labor Day 1933 and Jenny is ten and a half and has just won three ribbons.

The stables were gone by the time I first visited Prides, as the house where my mother grew up was called, the house with the gardens and the rare trees, the house in Beverly with the octagonal tower. The name was short for "Prides Hill Kennels." Like many of his friends, Jenny's father bred dogs. You have a whippet, a King Charles or a miniature boxer for the house, but in the kennels resides a bitch of your breed with her recent litter and a few "examples"—the most charming puppy goes to one of the children. I can't help considering all that breeding a displacement of some eugenic impulse: Clip the ears, dock the tail. Are the markings just right?

Shaw had bred wire-haired fox terriers while he was still at Harvard; then, through Harpo Marx, the story goes, he discovered Afghan hounds and bred the first in America. He gave Jenny a dark brown one called Loppy—she's shown with him in newspaper photographs, silver cup in her hand, captions giving the winner's official name, Bad Shah of Ains-dart. When my grandfather bought Prides as a law student, he named it Prides Hill Kennels, after his mother's grand house in the neighboring town of Prides Crossing. When he divorced Margarett in 1947, he left her the house, the stables, and the kennels. In a fit of revenge and panic about money, she had the stables and kennel torn down. By then she'd stopped painting and as she once told me, "turned to horticulture," but the gardens she imagined for the site of the razed buildings were never realized, and that part of the place became overgrown. Doing research years after she died, I once poked through a dump there and found rotting sketchbooks, months of canceled checks, a white plaster angel with just one wing.

What happened to the other wing? Had the white plaster once been painted? I have been returning to the past all my life, it seems, recovering such lost fragments. That's what we dig for, isn't it? Find the wing, glue it back, and you have it whole—evidence of what was once real, evidence that the house in sight of this dump was once filled with flowers and paintings, children racing in and out of big rooms, one little girl your mother.

A literary party in New York, 2010: A woman my age with straight blond hair and glasses with chic black rims is walking toward me. I do not know her. "So happy to meet you," she said, "at last," introducing herself.

"How do you do," I answer. Her name is Susan. She has read my books, she says, and we have a mutual friend. She names the friend. She has something to tell me about my mother, she says.

"My mother?"

I had expected a conversation about the friend.

"Yes, your mother."

Years ago, she says, while she was on retreat at a Catholic monastery on the New Jersey shore, the retreat leader, a monk, aware she was a novelist, asked if she knew Honor Moore. He had followed my work, he said, and was "very proud" of me. For Susan, because she was a writer, the fact that this monk was a reader was a "sign"—but why, she wondered, was he proud of Honor Moore's writing, of anyone's writing?

The monk had grown up on the North Shore, as the string of seashore towns north of Boston are called. He had worked as a stable boy, Susan continued, "for your grandparents in Beverly, Massachusetts." That was how he'd known my mother as a girl, and why he'd read *The White Blackbird*, the book I'd written about Margarett.

"Rip Collins was his name," Susan said. "Like the pitcher." For a second I was disoriented, rattled. I knew nothing of baseball, and out of context like this, an entirely new fact about my mother feels like adhesive pulled from the skin. But Susan was a novelist intent on her story, and as she told it, I remembered that on one of our few trips together to the place where my mother grew up, we'd visited the stables where she took riding lessons with Pat Keough. But I had never heard of any stable boy or anyone named Rip Collins.

"He talked a lot about your mother," Susan said.

Why, I'm wondering?

Father Rip, she continues, had "piercing" blue eyes and white hair, "the bright white that black hair turns with age." My mother's coloring, I was thinking. As a child he'd nearly died of pneumonia, and when he was twelve, he declared a vocation to follow his brother into the Redemptorist order, which ministered to the poor. Until Rip left for the monastery at sixteen, he had worked at Prides.

Because I never saw the stable, I'm free to imagine it: shingled and gray, room for five or six horses, maybe as many as ten, for riding and work. It was 1920 when Margarett and Shaw and an architect began to turn the modest seventeenth-century dark clapboard saltbox into something like a Florentine villa. Horses were still used for light farming tasks like plowing—I've seen pictures taken before my mother was born of horses pulling a plow at Prides, clearing land for the acres of garden and lawn.

My mother and Rip Collins were fifteen when they met, I calculate. My mother didn't talk much about her riding. It was only that time she took me to Pat Keough's stable and someone there told me what a "great rider" she had always been that I began to picture her grooming her horse, maybe even mucking out a stall. On the first of her memoir pages, I find this:

I ride my brown horse through the woods, the stones and brush untouched by the years of not seeing them, the smell of sweat and hair on her withers heavy and wet on my hands, my thighs slightly chafed, tensed with the strength of her body beneath me.

Into this scene now strides Rip Collins, fifteen years old. Let's say he already had the charisma that drew Susan to him at the retreat, and that soon the two black-haired kids became friends.

"He said he fell deeply in love with her," Susan calmly stated.

"In love with her?"

"*Deeply* in love with her," she repeated. "I kept asking him what happened, and he said, 'I could always make her laugh.' "

"That's all?"

"That's all he would say, and no one would tell me more after he died," she said. "You know, it wouldn't do for a priest to have a romantic history." What is another man of God doing in my mother's life?

I think of my mother as the teenager I have always imagined—not laughing but looking solemn, and then I think of my youngest sister's delicious laugh, which breaks everything open, and I give that laugh to my mother, the girl who now turns toward a boy with black hair and blue eyes like hers, in a fit of giggles. Suddenly my sense of her as a girl opens up. Will I ever learn everything about her?

"I kept after him," Susan is saying, "because then I read *The White Blackbird*, and we talked quite a lot about Boston in those days. Finally, all he would say was, 'Nothing *could* happen.' "

"Nothing *could* happen?" I repeated.

"I asked him why," Susan said. And he said, "Because 'she was of a different class.' "

A different class? Now my mother had become something out of D. H. Lawrence. Since the life of her desire was one of the most mysterious things about her, I loved the appearance of a boy not of her "class," and I began to think of her in a way I never had before, as a woman whose erotic choices were constrained by social position. But why do I think only of the limitation on her desire? She probably had more freedom in the matter than a sixteen-year-old stable boy bound for the priesthood. Rip Collins would never have declared himself to Jenny McKean, much less kissed or touched her. All their erotic exchange was subsumed in the care of the horses, the grooming of shiny flanks, I was thinking, the smell of hay and oats and sweat. Would Jenny McKean even have noticed? Even have imagined Rip Collins "deeply in love" with her? And anyway, what would "deeply in love" have meant in the 1930s to a boy of fifteen from a big Boston Irish family, a boy pledged to the monastery? But half a century later, he remembered Jenny McKean and also his feeling.

Now the image of my mother as a girl polishing tack and mucking stalls is not so lonely, since Rip Collins was probably mucking stalls right along with her or standing next to the horse, taking her hand as she mounts, perhaps even going out riding with her on one of the other horses, across the road to the Prince place, way back into the woods and past the meadows where there's a view of the sea. *If I were in any way discouraged*, my mother wrote in one of those deathbed fragments, *I'd spend my time with dogs and horses.*

I saw her ride only once. The years we lived in Jersey City, I rode seriously when we spent weekends at Hollow Hill, my father's family's "gentleman's" farm in New Jersey. Along bridle paths, miles into the woods, I would ride Mademoiselle, a dark bay mare, and Christy, the Scottish groom, would ride Jackson, a big chestnut gelding. But once on a misty, cloudy afternoon, my mother decided to ride too, my mother who I knew had been a riding champion at my age. Maybe if she likes riding here today, I thought, she'll come on weekends and we can ride together, long green rides, have meandering talks as we walk the horses through forest, as we canter across meadows.

In my memory of that day, she was wearing jodhpurs, which I'd never seen her wear, and she didn't talk much. She was very polite to Christy as he helped her mount Mademoiselle, and I watched her walk the horse into the field with the jumps as Christy held and then closed the gate. She planned to ride the entire course, and since I had jumped just once or twice, I was curious to watch. I listened to the hooves on the grass and saw her take one then two jumps, but then she was no longer on the horse—

she was there and then not there. I saw Christy leap toward the gate and open it and suddenly my mother was walking toward us, her glasses in her left hand (they'd fallen off). She laughed and said something embarrassed, and Christy walked toward her. When they came through the gate, I hugged her. "I'm so glad my glasses didn't break," she said.

3.

Whenever my mother had a new baby, she would send a few of us away for a week or two. Once, when I was about five, I was sent to Prides to stay with Margarett—I barely knew Grandma Kean, and I was confused when the cook and maid acted as if they had known me forever. I must purposely have been given the room under the eaves, but no one told me that was where my mother and her sister Margie had slept as children. Our entire house in Jersey City could easily have fit into the giant living room, which I compared to a church: very high ceilings, shafts of light falling into shadow, the room a landscape of odd furniture and wonderful things that I identified only much later—a wooden giraffe by Alexander Calder big enough for a child to ride on, small bronze horses by Degas; a loaf of bread painted by Derain, a small Renoir called *Coco* of a boy with blond hair.

That week I was often alone with Grandma, outdoors with men digging, watching her decide where to plant a new tree on the lawn that was as big as a park. One day she gave me a pile of construction paper and taught me to paste them into pictures. "Collages," she said, "like Matisse." I didn't know who that was, and I was too scared to ask. Another morning my hair was carefully combed, parted, and pulled up into ribbons, and a photographer arrived. I had never seen a camera so big or a photographer who pulled a black hood over his head. Why was Grandma having so many pictures taken of just me? She and the photographer talked about everything—just how I stood, which way I turned my head, held my hands. In the eight-by-tens I still have, I'm no older than five—in

Margarett's bedroom, the rocking horse I ride a skinny miniature of the huge horses on the wall behind me that she says were painted by an artist called De Chirico; me looking up at a portrait of my mother dressed like a princess in a painting by George Luks—"my teacher," Grandma says; me avid at cutting and pasting as she looks on.

Some part of my imagination was set loose by the mysteries of that house. Being photographed alone rather than with my siblings, all the paintings, the strange furniture, my grandmother's deep voice and the way she called me "dahling." For me this represented freedom, a new way of seeing; but for the child my mother had been, the perpetual shadows of that house brought on disquiet, a discomfort of the soul. In her own houses, every surface was painted white. She hung bright colors on the walls, and curtains she often made herself let the sun pour in.

In the memoir pages she dictated at the end of her life, she attempts to describe her feeling of displacement: *Failing to find a structure in which I could comfortably be a little girl in the fretwork of my mother's collection of antiques, Impressionist paintings, and Dutch tulips . . . I was a boy wanting to throw a ball like my brothers, climb like them.* She's captured that moment just before puberty when tomboy girls balk at social control. *Fretwork. Fret*: to be peevish, irritated, something that gnaws at you—in the Viking language it's the word for "monsters eating"; later it can mean "to eat one's heart out." But *fretwork* is what my mother writes—from the old French for "trellis work"; and later, in Chaucer, a woman wears a "golden frette" to hold her hair in place. Fretwork—lines that interlock, a net that imprisons. Did my mother ever consider her mother's sense of incarceration? When Jenny was five, Margarett turned from pale pastel and watercolor to oil, and with it came a new rebellious intensity. Paintings in oil, bright, piercing, expressionistic, usually of a single confrontational figure or face, and the line drawings—witty, poignant, at their best uncanny—were bringing Margarett Sargent the beginning of real worldly success. That she had small children and an abundance of house guests and visiting relatives seemed to inspire her—they were often new subjects. In the newspaper she and her siblings "published," Jenny portrays her mother, starting with her apprenticeship to Gutzon Borglum, later famous for Mount Rushmore, and the Ashcan school painter, George Luks:

> *Margarett Sargent took up sculpturing at an early age. Mr. Gut-*
> *zon Borglum taught her, but she hated him and still does hate him.*
> *Though she was a sculptor at that time, she did some good watercolor*
> *painting. Mr. George Luks taught her too and she likes Mr. Luks.*
> *After a long time, she moved to Prides Crossing and married Quincy*
> *Adams Shaw McKean. Every winter she moved into town and got*
> *children. She does very good painting and paints people best.*

When Jenny was eight, Margarett's sixth New York show opened; when Jenny was nine, her seventh show at the Arts Club of Chicago, an important Modernist venue. Later that year she had a one-woman exhibition at the Harvard Society for Contemporary Art, in galleries above the Coop in Harvard Square. The society also showed Alexander Calder, who performed his circus one night in the McKean's living room—a party for grown-ups, but the children were allowed to stay up. In the memoir fragments, my mother never mentions her mother's paintings, and not one of them hung in our house.

Of her father's work, she knew little—*his business ventures, alternating success and failure were never clear. I decided at some point that if discussions of money were vulgar, so must be the details of the workaday life, so I never asked questions—what my father 'did' was part of the sea of the unknown. I remember phone calls from his broker, Bert Good, a name belying the impression I always had that the trade they discussed in undertones was bad. I watched Papa's face each time he came back to the table. The expression varied—but its communication to me was always "You are preserved from my troubles, my concerns and my successes." I think now that he must have thought me disinterested, when in truth I yearned to know all I could about a man so handsome and so kind.*

Did my mother know the extent of his troubles? That shortly after marrying Margarett, Shaw lost all his money in a bad business venture, to live thereafter on stipends from his mother, Marian? That story comes accompanied by another: that over decades, he paid back his investors. Papa had what my mother called the McKean nose and she inherited his eyes, dark blue, deep-set, and sparkling. Handsome in a bespoke suit with chalk stripes and a silk checkered tie, he's smiling in a black and white photograph taken at a party—a man who loved to laugh, beautifully dressed and drawn to art. In another photo, he's caught mid-stride in an autumn field in a tweed hunting jacket, his long gun uncocked, pointed downward. "Huntin' shootin' kind of guy," I was told more than once, though in my memory he seems too elegant to have his pastimes described in gerunds without the final *g*. In autumn he traveled with business friends to the Carolinas to shoot pheasant and quail, in the spring to Canada to fish for salmon—also golf and fly fishing for a few weeks in summer, when the entire family decamped to Vermont and a rundown farmhouse that Margarett filled with country antiques and quilts. The house was situated in Dorset, a town away from the Equinox Hotel and its eighteen holes. After a day at golf, Shaw would cook outdoors, fish he'd caught or steak and potatoes, as he had in northern Michigan as a young man, when he did a stint at the Calumet and Hecla copper mines developed by his grandfather Quincy Shaw and great-uncle Alexander Agassiz. The mines produced untold wealth in the late nineteenth century, when every telephone and electrical connection required copper, refreshing the fortunes of many old Boston families. I was always told that before income tax was instituted in 1913, Shaw's mother Marian had an income of a million dollars a year.

Marian's adored her—when she came to Prides, they kept her there by sticking *her white kid gloves to glistening amber flypaper thinking she could not possibly leave without their limp elegance once more pulled and smoothed onto her small capable hands*, my mother wrote. *She treated it as a new joke every time.* When Jenny was in her teens, Marian confided details of her "brilliant" marriage to Henry Pratt McKean of Philadelphia: the *terror of her wedding night*, her new husband *locking the bedroom door and chasing her, totally ignorant of sex she said, and fearful of his drunkenness.* For ten years she was *brutalized in bed, ostracized for her Unitarianism by the arrogant Episcopalians of Philadelphia, where not to believe in the Father, Son*

and Holy Ghost, was social as well as theological heresy. After her divorce
Marian returned to Boston, set up in a house at 13 Commonwealth Avenue, and married a *nobody her relatives whispered* named Malcolm Graeme
Haughton, *who nursed a blond handlebar moustache, twisted its antenna-like
waxed ends, and wore enormous tweed overcoats with fur collars even when
indulging in his favorite game, curling—aiming huge disks to particular spots
of ice followed by sweeping the ice with brooms—a kind of polar checkers.*

It was to Grandma's house that the McKeans went for *intermina-
ble command-performance Sunday lunches* with Shaw and Agassiz aunts,
uncles, and cousins and often some of the European émigré musicians
Marian helped financially—Emma Eames, the pianist; Serge Koussev-
itsky, conductor of the Boston Symphony, and his wife Olga. I remember
Grandma Haughton as a tall presence in gray shadowy light, her white
hair coiffed into a swirl; she had a declarative way of pronouncing my
name. I learned that her grandfather was Louis Agassiz, the Swiss émigré
biologist, only my first week at Radcliffe when the publicity office had me
photographed for a press release announcing the freshman class included
a descendant of the college's founder, Elizabeth Cary Agassiz, the scientist's Bostonian second wife. The widowed Louis Agassiz had crossed the
Atlantic to lecture at Harvard in 1846 and remained in the United States
with his three children—Alexander became a scientist and then developed the copper mines; Ina married the financier Henry Higginson, a
cousin of the Thomas Higginson who was the radical writer and Emily
Dickinson's correspondent, and a founder of the Boston Symphony; and
Pauline married Quincy Shaw. If she'd been alive when I learned these
details, I'd have asked my mother if she thought she resembled her black-
haired, elegant great-grandmother Pauline Shaw who, to recover from
a depression she suffered after her marriage, became a philanthropist.
She supported with both money and her presence the kindergartens her
friend Elizabeth Peabody established for poor children in Boston and
later contributed critical resources to the campaign for woman's suffrage,
especially in the West, as an ally of her friend, the Boston feminist Lucy
Stone. My mother believed that Marian was embarrassed that her mother
was a "Lucy Stoner," but in Pauline's papers at the Schlesinger Library

of Women's History, I found Marian's grateful correspondence with her mother's suffragist comrades.

Marian *hated* Margarett—*the cheek offered for my mother's kiss, Jenny wrote, seemed covered with a film of distance rather than the white powder with which she feathered her face each morning after the corset strings were tightened.* There was some justification for her aversion as Margarett and Shaw's marriage deteriorated; but, my mother wrote, Marian eventually mellowed: *Many years later, when she was very old, she wrote me that she had had to realize that it was not the specific woman but the son's wife she detested because my father's second marriage—serene and stable—gave rise to the same anger.*

4.

The schoolroom, separated from the main house by an arch and standing next to the swimming pool, was described in a showy newspaper account as having four small desks and walls hung with Margarett's watercolors. At one end was a curtain that could be pulled open for the plays the children put on, costumes from trunks in the attic, and a large table where they edited and published the *Prides Hill Gazette*—there little Shaw reviewed Jenny's portrayal of Macbeth: "She had a good costume and her acting was marvelous." In 1933, via *Prides Hill Press*, Jenny and her siblings published *The Onion River Anthology, with apologies to Edgar Lee Masters*, each verse ventriloquizing a member or friend of the household: the housekeeper, Mary McLellan: *My hard hard work / My lengthy days / The children and their fussy ways;* Walsh the chauffeur: *I'll bet you a dollar / I'll beat the light.*

When Margie was five and Jenny three, a young woman of nineteen named Catherine Nearly arrived to be their "governess." They named her Senny, and she stayed a dozen years. It was she who dressed the girls, ate with them either with or without their parents, accompanied them to skating and riding lessons, and taught their lessons until her brother John, a Harvard graduate student, arrived two years later when Jenny was five. Jovial and bright and a graduate of Exeter and Dartmouth, John Neary made Margarett's dream for her children possible. She herself had been tutored with two cousins until she went to the Winsor School in Boston, where the lessons never held her attention. As they grew older, the children wanted to go to actual schools, but Margarett wanted them to have an education centered on Latin and Greek "as children did abroad." Their isolation bred in Jenny an enduring longing to be *normal*.

Almost every year, Margarett and Shaw went to Europe for several weeks, and by the time Jenny was ten, she was writing them letters in Latin, about, for instance, Senny taking them to a play based on *Alice in Wonderland*. *"Laetae sumus 'Alicia in Terra Mira,' vidiemus duobus, diebus."* John had them translating Caesar—*Soon we are coming to Ariovistus. We like him because he is very brave and noble,* Jenny wrote of the Gaulish general. When the twins were nine, Jenny wrote, *Dear Mama, Isn't it marvelous! The boys are beginning Latin. I think it will help them with their French and English.* "Madame" came twice a week to teach them French. In her letter that week, Senny wrote that she was giving the girls a history exam on the Civil War.

On her own, Jenny was reading Helen Keller's *The Story of My Life*— *very interesting*—and "Kubla Khan"—*I really adore it, especially this part*—"Then reached the caverns measureless to man, / And sank in tumult to a lifeless ocean." She sped through *Heidi* and *Quo Vadis* and then turned to her parents' library. *I read in gulps, skipping great chunks of childhood literature because I found more I could understand in books for adults—grown-ups at least, were often strange. My mother and father never stopped me from reading anything—except that* Lust for Life *mysteriously and permanently disappeared from its shelf in the library. It had always been in the same spot, with* Chrome Yellow *by Aldous Huxley and* Crisis *by Winston Churchill.*

By 1935, when Jenny was eleven, the children knew what a poem was and were writing them. Researching a paper at Harvard, John Neary saw drafts of Dickinson and Milton and in a note to Margarett and Shaw with a sheaf of the children's poems, written on "a rough, blustering fall afternoon, with a sort of melancholy dominant, and some of Jen's seem almost Emily Dickinson to me," he wrote. "Of course none of them sprang full-fledged, like Minerva, from the brain of Jove." He had advised "sufficient reflection" before choosing a word and offered "a little imaginative baiting now and then." Surely he explained simile and metaphor as he read them poems by others. Did Jenny mimic Amy Lowell's "The Pike"—"Thick and silver-sheened in the sunshine"—when she wrote *a stream-lined pickerel / Leapt at a fly?* Some of the poems were free verse, some couplets or quatrains. "Perhaps you might have preferred them without a reworking," John wrote Margarett, "but so little that is really fine has been written that way. I saw the manuscript of "Lycidas" the other day at Widener and was shocked to find no single line virginal—not even 'flames in the forehead of the morning sky.' "

When my mother told me about her childhood, she never described writing poems, just her parents' fights and scenes at the dinner table: *Horrible shouting, slammed doors.* It was hard to put that description together with "Grandma Kean," who wrote me long poetic letters, and "Grandpa Kean," whom I knew as dignified and reserved. As I came to know Margarett's painting in my twenties, saw how the faces of the "mostly people" she painted seemed to express her own anguish, her own irony and predicament. Part of her condition was genetic: she was afflicted with a disposition toward depression going back for generations in her own family, a mother given to periodic depression, one brother a suicide, her older sister hospitalized, a second brother "not quite right." Margarett's condition coexisted with vivid beauty, intelligence, and talent; so, in the 1940s before any cultural consciousness or diagnosis of bipolar disorder, she mystified everyone and her illness went untreated. Those who loved her marveled at her brilliance; those whom she wearied considered her selfish.

"I think for years Papa just thought she was a lush," Margie said.

When they were little, the sisters weren't sure what afflicted their mother, so they used images. It was as if a glaze came over her eyes, so that when she looked at you, she didn't seem to see you, I remember Margie explaining. They learned to put up with her irritation and impatience, but when she drank to rein in her mania, she became peculiar, outrageous, or even cruel.

Margie primped and posed for her mother's painting, while Jenny became a crack student and a virtuoso of bicycle and horseback. As a rider, she got her mother's applause but also her rivalry—Margarett had been a girl rider herself, but never with Jenny's success. After Jenny won the three blue ribbons at ten, Margarett took up riding again, signed them up for a parent-child event without even telling her. "Why?" I asked Margie; "Why would she do that?" "Just plain competition," Margie answered. I heard the story from others as well, their voices tense with disbelief. Jenny was not unaware, writing a poem that year: *Color of envy / Picture of threat / Glance of jealousy / Hue of Hatred*. In her grown-up handwriting in felt-tip marker on a torn bit of stationery, I find this about her childhood: *I kicked my dog, I tore at my fingernails*. But also this, written as a child to her mother, away in Paris: "I adore you and I love you; I hope you had a nice sleep last night and dreamed good things." It was Senny who guided such correspondence. My mother never used the word *governess* to describe her, only said she did not know what would have *become of* them without her.

If I had not visited Senny and met her brother John the summer I was seven, I would have taken my image of "governess" from Charlotte Brontë, an unhappy young woman down on her luck, and imagined her brother, the "tutor," as effete and always dressed in tweeds, or drunk and irresponsible like Charlotte's brother Branwell. Senny was efficient and pretty, with shining eyes, even though she seemed "old" because she wore her honey-colored hair pulled back in a bun. She was in her forties then, single and living by herself in a small house on the kind of street in a small town where children played, sun shone through green leaves, and people had pots of petunias and geraniums on their front porches. For my two weeks there, I slept in a room with a window that looked out on the backyard, the house entirely quiet except for the sound of the doorbell or an occasional car driving by.

In the morning, Senny and I sat at a small table and had breakfast, just toast and eggs, or maybe cereal. "What would you like for breakfast?" she would say. Of course she took me swimming at Singing Beach, where she took my mother and her siblings when they were little. "Listen," Senny said, "to what the sand does when you walk," and I did, and it squeaked with each scuff of my bare foot. After a swim, we'd have a delicious sandwich on the club porch and Senny would charge everything to Grandma. One morning she took me to the big bright room at Manchester Memorial, the public school where she taught second grade. John had a "tutoring school" for a few years after the war and now he was in advertising, but Senny stayed with teaching. When she died young, Manchester declared the schools closed and five hundred attended her funeral.

Sometimes Senny and I had supper at John's house, where we sat around eating spaghetti with his wife and sons, everyone laughing and talking. I'm not sure I exactly knew that John Neary had been my mother's teacher. "He gets such a charge out of your daughter," Senny wrote my mother. One night we cooked lobsters over a fire on the beach, and on the fourth of July we went to fireworks, which I had never seen before. I remember John and the boys calling out the names of the fiery pinwheels that burst into gigantic flower in explosions all over the sky, and I am certain, though I've never seen one since, that the last firework flung an American flag across the sky that blazed red, white, and blue until it sputtered and scattered, its final sparkles falling into the ocean.

At Senny's, the two of us sitting in her small living room with John and his wife Ann, I watched television for the first time, intent as "General Eisenhower" was nominated for president. Unconscious of anything but the warmth of the Nearys, their Boston Irish accents rowdy as the night turned cool, I cheered along as they exclaimed over the man it seemed certain would be the next president. I do not remember the speech in which "Ike" urged Americans "to join up" and proclaimed us "now at moment in history when, under God, this nation of ours has become the mightiest temporal power and the mightiest spiritual force on earth." When I got home, I learned that another man, Adlai Stevenson, was also "running" for president and that my parents wanted him to win—he was, I learned, something called an egghead, which meant he liked to read like my mother did and was not a soldier like Eisenhower. I boasted an Eisenhower button until I overheard my mother laughing on the telephone, "Honor came home from the Nearys saying, 'I Like Ike.' "

My mother became a Democrat the first time she voted in 1944, putting herself at cross purposes with her father. She grew up, *navigating a house divided—against the man in the White House, for the man in the White House. Senny was Irish—the Irish suffered in the Depression—Roosevelt was the savior after the Depression—and therefore Senny and John were Democrats. My father hated Democrats, Roosevelt in particular—looked down on the Irish and wondered about the Depression in a different way than I did, hearing tales of lines of starving men, and old people selling apples.* Among my mother's papers was a handwritten political autobiography, which begins with *a Nabokovian memory combining the warm brown texture—smell of the paneled wall of a New England house, the steam rising from scrambled eggs, and my father's declarative phrase, "Herbert Hoover won, Al Smith lost." Somehow the ring of dispassion sounded contrived to my five year old ear. Around Boston, the Irish were the PROBLEM, the Irish were Catholic, and Al Smith was one of THEM.* Did my grandfather not consider that the man and woman he entrusted with his children's education were Irish? Not to mention the cook and the laundress; the women who served their food; the men who worked with their dogs and horses, mowed their lawn, weeded the garden, and chauffeured their cars?

My mother got the irony: *I sensed in a childish fashion that the contradictions were something I would have to understand and even deal with—my first awareness of injustice. When I was nine (1932), I learned that a new president Franklin Roosevelt had betrayed the old school tie (whatever that was) by dealing with something called a Depression when banks close. I imagined enormous doors swinging shut, people suffering, and I saw my father's grim face.* All of this made her *extremely self-conscious* about how her family lived and about not going to a real school—she would not keep her own children at home. *People who went to school knew how to talk like grown-ups and learned a middle-of-the road kind of politics out of books that would reconcile my father with the Irish—and inspire John Neary to tell us more about Calvin Coolidge than that his son had died of a blister on his foot when he was ten. John, Jenny made clear, was, at the very least, bored with wordless Coolidge; his enthusiasms were for livelier personages like Sacco and Vanzetti.*

Sacco and Vanzetti reside for me in a haze of the past, but the trial for murder of the two immigrants, a shoemaker and a fishmonger, stretched from 1921 until 1927, widening rifts between the political right and left, capital and labor, Brahmin and immigrant Boston and also dividing more broad-minded Brahmins from others. To the right, Nicola Sacco and Bartolomeo Vanzetti were suspect foreigners and wild anarchists; to the left, they were hardworking immigrants unjustly accused, the trial a travesty. The judge, Webster Thayer, was a conservative—"I'll get them good and proper," he declared. The judge's name was familiar to my mother—the Thayers were her people, Bostonians like the McKeans were Bostonians.

As the years of appeals went on, thousands marched all over the world—Barcelona, Rome, London, Paris, even Beijing. Writers like Edna St. Vincent Millay and John Dos Passos marched for them, and Felix Frankfurter of the Harvard Law School—a Viennese immigrant, a Jew, and later a Supreme Court justice—argued for a new trial in the very Bostonian *Atlantic*. The rage and argument, he believed, blurred the facts of the case. In response, Thayer appointed an "outside" committee— Abbott Lawrence Lowell, the president of Harvard; a retired judge; and only one non-Brahmin, the president of MIT. This committee ruled against the defendants, and in spite of convincing new evidence, the Massachusetts Supreme Judicial Court denied a motion for a second trial. Justice Oliver Wendell Holmes, an old man by then and part of the McKean's social circle on the North Shore, signed the Supreme Court writ denying the defendants' final appeal. The men were executed in August 1927.

By the time my mother was writing about her childhood, she knew firmly where she stood in the struggle for social justice in America. She was only four years old when the men were executed, but Sacco and Vanzetti come into her memory as she considers her political development. *My father never mentioned them that I can remember,* she wrote, *clearly finding their guilt unquestionable, their appearance unseemly and any mention of their fate unnecessary. John Neary, on the other hand, anti-Establishment and an Irish raconteur, thought of politics in terms of good guys and bad guys, the peddler and the fish monger were done in by the lousy system—you've got to know the story, he seemed to be telling me, and remember it for the rest of your life.* Remember it for the rest of your life: so vivid was John Neary's telling that it was not until her late teens that my mother realized there was any other position on the Saccio and Vanzetti verdict. *I inquired of my father if he agreed with John—and he, believing in no position other than his own, threw back his head and laughed as if I had no head at all.* Right then, my mother made a decision never again to talk to her father about *political things.*

5.

I am picturing my mother as girl of twelve sitting at her desk in the Prides schoolroom. There is a sheet of blank paper, a bottle of ink, and she is bent over the paper, holding her pen. *Ink,* she writes, *is the most splendid thing to use with a pen on paper. On the floor or on the table it's wicked. On the tablecloth it's worse. Mostly it's better to keep it in a bottle.* It may be "better" to keep the ink in the bottle, but today she will not. She is holding a pen, and she believes herself a poet.

I had no idea. Only a decade after her death did I take a look at the loose-leaf notebook of the poems the children had written for John Neary. Only decades after that did I see that my mother's poems were actual poems. When my first was accepted for publication, she complimented me again and again, but she never told me she'd written poems as a child. Did she even remember?

I want to imagine how she feels as she writes, a fresh page on the small desk, the pen in her hand. I think of her dreaming and seeing, seeing hills, and all the hills she sees are thick with trees; but because today she is a poet, she believes it is her privilege and her task to alter what she sees, so she strips the trees away—you can't see the forest for the trees—makes one hill bare, unprotected, a blank, and writes a first line: *On a bare hill . . .*

The manuscript before me was typewritten before it was sent off to her parents, so it is impossible to make out whether Jenny pauses to consider the hill before she writes again:

> On a bare hill
> three trees,

She chooses to leave space after *three trees* so that one's imagination may rest in the open space after the comma. I recognize that quiet waiting, listening for the sound of those two words—*three trees*—how double sets of double *e*'s make long sounds, so what you hear is *ee* then *ees*, the *s* leading to another *s*, until something offers the word *sway*, and within *sway*, a long *a*—and then, to extend your pleasure, you add *–ing*:

> On a bare hill
> three trees,
> swaying

What happens now? What about letting an *–ing* displace the *way* in *sway*? Yes!

> On a bare hill
> three trees,
> swaying and singing

And the trees have nearly come to life, as each time she writes a poem, she herself comes to life, a life solitary and more vivid than the ordinary, even though the others see just Jenny bent over her desk, writing.

It is early spring, and as she dips the pen again in ink, she hears from outdoors actual wind, the tiny sound of a twig knocking against another twig, branch against branch. Or she is just making up the wind, the short *i*'s within *hill* and *sing* resounding, as, to her amazement, comes *bickering*, what the married couple she and her sister invent every night are always doing:

in the wind
bickering

And women do it too—not the kind of woman she wants to be, but jealous, silly women and girls in dressing rooms before a dance, powdering their faces. But now, as she listens, the sound lightens, opens into light repartee, exchange that scampers, trips, and alights:

three trees
swaying and singing

in the wind
bickering, bantering

Through dressing room walls, she can actually see them: girls—no, *trees*, the *three trees* becoming girls, women—all of whom she now sees on a dance floor as, again, she dips her pen, hears it scratch, swoosh along on the good thick paper and her ear, alive with desire for that short *i*—*hill*, *-ing, sing, wind, bicker*—prevails and she chooses it again, writing not *swoosh* but *swish*:

in the wind
bantering, bickering
as they swished—

Now her trees are dancers dressed to whirl, and because her ear remembers the *-er* in *bicker* and *banter*, she writes

As they swished their skirts

What a delight, how a skirt makes the tree a girl, a woman—Daphne returning human from the tree Apollo turned her into, coming into the mind of this girl at the desk in Massachusetts, who is deep in her poem—

One in taffeta, she is called Elm

so deep in her poem, there is more than one dancer, summoned by the *m* that ends *Elm*; her name is *Maple*:

On a bare hill
Three trees
Swaying and singing
In the wind
Bantering, bickering
As they swished their skirts
One in taffeta, she is called Elm
One in velvet, Maple is she . . .

Now within the poet's dream, I see the three trees multiplied as if by mirrored walls, skirts swishing, *Elm* and *Maple* waiting, so that the entrance of the third tree, *Pine*, is rather startling:

Pine was in tweeds,

at first just a contrast to taffeta and velvet until, with a dip of the pen, the poet announces a gentleman, and, still hearing the twirl of *ir* in skirt, writes

Pine was in tweeds as he flirted with Elm.

There is no break after *Maple*, no pause whatsoever, just a tiny echo of the *ck* from *bicker*:

Maple, neglected

and, because *Maple* stands in for the poet, she is allowed dignity, the consolation of hands, of folding them; and, rolled out as ballast vowels, the calm and serenity of the poem's final words:

THREE TREES

On a bare hill
Three trees—
Swaying and singing
In the wind
Bickering, bantering
As they swished their skirts.
One in taffeta; she is called Elm,
Another in velvet; Maple was she;
Pine was in tweeds as he flirted with Elm
And Maple, neglected
Just folded her hands.

Is it too easy to identify *Pine* with Papa, imagine the tweeds her father's? *Elm* dressed in taffeta, with whom he flirts, Mama or Margie? And *Maple, neglected*, the poet alone with herself?

It seems to me that Jenny must often have *folded her hands* and entertained herself with the inner voice recorded in her poems. Rain in summer? *A soft wet kiss— / it gave as it fell / On the primrose's / head.* A storm: *Old woman with a scrawny head / Horribly howling her hates.* This quatrain: *He was caught / And put in jail / Because he tore / His mother's veil.* This is the Jenny John Neary called "elfish," who declared herself *a boy, wanting to throw balls like her brothers*, tear her mother's veil, expose what she does not ordinarily see in the mother who disappears, reappears, then disappears again. "For we think back through our mothers if we are women," Virginia Woolf wrote, which is what, at twelve, Jenny McKean does in another poem, disguising and transforming what she knows:

The moon so quietly lifted her head
That no one saw her rise from the dead.
Gradually she loosed her smile on the world
Like a silver sail so gently unfurled;
Soon she tired and her smile did subside.

Slowly she lowered like the evening tide,
And took her repose on a cloudy bed
And everyone knew that again she was dead.

Dead to her is what her mother was those days she spent in her darkened bedroom. The sisters had a way of signaling their mother in that condition: *Mama is languid again.*

In Vermont the summer Jenny was six and Margie seven, the twins four, "she cried all the time." Even Margie did not know specifics when I interviewed her in the 1990s for *The White Blackbird*, only assumed it the onset of their mother's mental illness. When I wrote the book I knew that Lewis Galantière, writer and American translator from the French, was among Margarett's throng of admirers—but the image was comic: he'd spent at least one summer in Vermont walking up and down the road "shouting her name." But as I researched this book, an e-mail arrived out of the blue from Galantière's biographer revealing Margarett's relationship with his subject had been "quite an affair."

When I opened the e-mail attachment, the familiar handwriting crossed my screen, Margarett's characteristic use of hyperbole to obscure direct feeling—"the flowers came in like a snowstorm in Bois, so softly, so clingingly, so *fatally* and so *solemnly*. Freesia and lilies." She was returning a letter of his—"best destroyed by you or treasured by you." It seems there had been talk of their being together, of her leaving Shaw: "You have so much at stake," Galantière wrote, "that I shiver sometimes with fright of what I should be depriving you of if the storm broke. . . . I resent your ties, I want them broken, but I don't want you to bleed when they break. I want you to be freed by the rotting of the rope around your wrists not by the knife."

But Margarett was not to be "freed" and the affair had cooled by the fall. Galantiere eventually came to understand her as "a sick soul," any urge to choose happiness "complicated," he wrote in a journal, "by her sense of failure in love and her feeling of deep inferiority,—at least of deep-seated uncertainty about her own painting." But he didn't understand: How she could pull away when she'd said he'd taught her "all she knew of sexual pleasure." His assessment leaves behind Margarett's Victorian context: She had "a terror of happiness and accomplishment; a panic seizes you when you approach the frontier of either." The only cure in his view was psychoanalysis—she should take the children and the governess and go paint for a year in Europe: "There is Ferenczi in Budapest, Schmidt in Lausanne, Ernest Jones in London."

As adults Jenny and Margie knew Margarett was mentally ill, but they had no idea anyone had presented her with options for treatment when they were children. They also knew that their mother had lovers, but were less conscious of the men than of the women, who came to stay at Prides for weeks at a time and of whom she painted her most striking portraits. Chief among them when they were children was Isabel Pell, who, as "Cousin Pell" appeared in the children's *Onion River Anthology*: *I can't live for things that aren't / I must live for things that are / —the thing I really live for / Is my black enameled car.* When I questioned Margie about her mother's bisexuality, she was as direct as my mother was later; but while Margie enjoyed the glamor of these occasional visitors, my mother found her mother's lesbianism threatening, warning me about it when I expressed a desire to go to Radcliffe, close to where her mother lived in Boston.

She had no qualms about announcing her most public affair, and the man she chose was not a sophisticated writer but a Bostonian businessman. At a dance one winter evening in 1935, she takes the first glass of champagne passed to her, says hello to this one and that one, takes a second a third; then sometime during the evening, her desire conjures a man with blond hair whom she barely knows. Harry Snelling was "attractive to women," Margarett's brother later sniffed, as if it were an insult. Snelling and his wife were friends of friends, but tonight his wife is not with him. He and Margarett leave the party in his car, drive to Boston, check into the hotel "purposely not the Ritz." It's not clear how many days they spend there, but long enough for friends to pass, point up at the offending windows. They begin to make plans, they will live "abroad," she tells her friends. She tells her brother Dan, her confidant since childhood, that she will marry this man and begin again, that she will be a good wife, a better mother. "Are you with me?" "No," he replied.

Neither her brother nor her daughters considered that by then, Margarett, for the first time in a decade, had no scheduled exhibition. She had been a working artist since her early twenties, and making had always been part of her emotional and psychic metabolism. Now that piece of her was on the loose, and, aware of it or not, everyone close to her felt the aftershocks of that loss.

6.

In the ceiling of the studio where I am writing, there is a skylight that tilts open, insects kept out by a Velcro-edged screen. It is August, and for days, I have noticed a mosquito here and there, and this morning, after a cold night, I see rips in the screen, a straight slit and also a more complicated tear caused it seems by the corner of the window. I must have pulled it open too far. How long had the slit been there? How long the snarled gash made by the skylight's sharp corner? With Margarett's very public affair came a snarl in the fretwork. "We knew something was wrong," Margie said of herself and Jenny. My mother was dead before we could have a conversation about Harry Snelling—Margarett survived her by five years. Amazingly, it was Margarett herself who gave me the details of the affair. I was visiting her one evening when she was in her eighties, and over smoked salmon and red wine, she began a story; I did not understand what she was talking about until years later: "He came to the hotel! 'Him or me!' " she said, apparently quoting Shaw's ultimatum, "Can you imagine?"

I should have noticed the snarl, the corner-shaped gash in the neat fabric—had it happened yesterday or this morning? It looks violent, like the hacking of a knife, as Margarett's gesture must have seemed—quick exit from the dance floor, the humiliation of her husband. Did she even think of her children? Margie is growing into a young woman, Jenny can still make everyone laugh but she is also increasingly curious, observant, solemn. The boys can hardly stay still. But the slits in the screen are almost invisible, as if inflicted by a knife so razor thin, the break in the weave: who notices weakness when everything is in balance?

Immediately, Shaw and Senny move with the children to his mother's; there is no need to explain as they "adore" Grandma, nothing more fun than staying at her house. It does not take terribly long for Harry Snelling to go back to his wife. He telephones their mutual friends, the Robbs: "Margarett is very upset." And the Robbs go over to Prides, find her threatening to jump from a window. A day or two later, Margarett and Shaw meet with his mother. Marian suggests a trip abroad "to save the marriage."

Once the bargain is struck, passage is booked for late May, Shaw and the children and Senny move back into the house, and it's not long before the forty trunks are packed. On May 29, 1935, the family, along with Senny, set sail on the *Bremen*. They intend to stay three months but do not return until nearly a year later when the German invasion of the Rhineland makes Europe too dangerous. What did my mother, then twelve, know about the trip? Had her mother become even more remote? Once, late in her life, my mother wrote me this: *I'm sorry that I had so little time for you.*

For how many generations has that *so little time* been passed down?

Laid out on the coffee table are pictures of my mother's childhood, of Margarett's childhood, black and white photographs of children near barns and mansions, in gardens and swimming pools, the generations sometimes mixed up, so that until I look closely I can't tell whether a likeness is of me or my mother or her mother. Here's a photo smaller than a postage stamp, of Margarett as a schoolgirl in 1909, a curious blend of my mother and me, a dash of sister or cousin—she's less inward than any photograph of my mother at that age, more confident than I have ever looked, at least to myself. How has a miniature glimpse survived an entire century?

Trying to identify an architecture in the relation between a daughter and her mother, I am in search of a photograph of Jenny and Margarett alone together, comparable to the one of me as a little girl with my young mother, or a close-up that exposes what Jenny was feeling about her mother when she was twelve, the spring when "something happened" and forty trunks were packed and an ocean liner took them all "abroad." Much of the time Margarett herself was the photographer, so that, in snapshots in which Jenny stands apart from her siblings, she may also be edging away from her mother's gaze, trying to evade her mother's power. Even in family portraits taken by a professional photographer whose visual will governs, I see that Jenny often finds a way to look as if she would rather not be there, in contrast to the smile of her older sister who seems ready to receive the world.

I find no photograph of Jenny alone with Margarett to add nuance to what I know; except for that glimpse in memory of her mother's breast in psychotherapy in her late forties, my mother told me nothing of closeness with her mother, only of difficulty. Tenderness and security came from her father, in the form of his gruff attention, his bedtime stories, his constancy. To these circumstances, Jenny had responded by becoming the "Spartan boy," a tomboy as Margarett had, and as I would when I played handball with my brother and his friends in Jersey City or galloped the pavement on my imaginary horse.

On my bedroom wall there is an ink drawing on the back of a piece of stationery that Margarett made of Jenny at about five; she's at the table in Vermont, wearing a cardigan sweater, not a tomboy in pants but a little girl in a dress, looking quite solemn, tranquil even. But there's also a portrait I have in storage. Margarett's paintings of her children were usually small but this is two by five feet, of Jenny bare-armed blue overalls, sitting on a red chair, one of her father's fox terriers at her feet. Her hair is full, black and wild, an orange hair ribbon above her right ear. Is the slightly startled look on Jenny's face directed at the painter, her mother? Is the artist able to see and allow what the mother cannot? I'm wondering if my mother ever had a moment when Margarett looked at her in a way she understood as real love, if real love can be located in the depth an imagination can bring to an instant, rather than in endurance and variation through time.

The McKeans landed at Southampton where "Hardy," a British chauffeur with a Cockney accent awaited them with a car. Advertised as a linguist, he often stumbled, speaking French instead of German. This caused a bit of a panic when they crossed into Germany for the winter Olympics at Garmisch, where they had seats, courtesy of German business friends of Shaw's, right across from Hitler's at the final turn of the bobsled run. My uncle Harry, one of the twins, recalled a sense of foreboding in the atmosphere of Olympic festivity, gangs of brownshirts marching in formation, shovels on their shoulders in lieu of the guns proscribed by the Treaty of Versailles. At night the light of torches jolted across the Eibsee, the huge lake that stretched out from the hotel—Margie and Jenny skated there during the day, its surface swept free of snow by men on skates pushing huge brooms.

For a religion class in college, my mother framed as "demonic" worship the closing ceremony in the stadium:

> I was twelve, but the intensity of my impressions has not changed—
> or so it seems as I recall it . . . The spectators and participants gathered in the dark semi-circle of the ski stadium. All eyes were turned in the direction of a mountain which rose from the opening of the semicircle. This area was soon illuminated by huge torches held aloft in the hands of black hooded skiers speeding down the mountain toward a jump. I remember especially the contrast between the wild streaming of the orange torches and the snowy air; the eeriness when the flames rose over the obstacle, to come down a moment later, flickering in a salute to the leader as the weird figures slid to a stop in vast parade. The drama was heightened as the peculiar silence of mountainous outdoors swelled into the triumph of thousands of German voices singing "Deutschland, Deutschland, Uber Alles."

Margie's memory of those seats is tinged with comedy, Shaw madly shooting photos of the führer and his companions across the bobsled run, only to find afterward that he had left the lens cap on: sarcasm from Marga-rett, shrieks of laughter from the children—"Oh Papa, how could you!!!"

Jenny did not photograph at the Olympics, but she left a scrapbook—haunted black and whites of castles and coves, small churches and walls, fields of sheep, cows grazing, her brother Shaw tiny at Stonehenge. Mar-gie kept a diary; her commentary is vivid with quick flashes of atmo-sphere and character, as in "Lunch at Lady Dracks' house. Four girls, one boy. Her Ladyship promptly remarks on my size. One would think I was a pet giraffe. Most unpleasant." Or "The cathedral was lovely gothic architecture. Filled with boy scouts and queer very old ladies." And this: "Jenny looks like a drowned rat. Something should be done about her hair." Monopoly, new then, was the game, and, no matter where they were when it rained, the four children played game after game: "Shaw being slowly bankrupt. Harry gloating. Jenny making casual remarks, causing fistfights. Senny shushing from bathroom next door."

For the first weeks, the family settled at Bournemouth, where the girls skated in the professional rink, instructed by Willy Frick, who coached them at the Boston Skating Club. Later, in London, they'd meet the skat-ing star Sonja Henie, whom Margie found the "most stupidly catty per-son I ever saw" as she had "nothing good to say" about Maribel Vinson, the American champion who was the girls' idol in Boston. After Bour-nemouth, they moved to Plymouth by the sea, taking up residence in a house owned by Shaw's "Aunt Nancy." Now Lady Astor, the former Nancy Langhorne of Virginia had first married Marian's brother, Robert Shaw; in a few years, she would become hostess to the notorious Clive-den set, which supported Chamberlain's appeasement of Hitler. But now Lady Astor was a heroine: in 1919, she became the first woman member elected to the British parliament, winning with the slogan: "If you can't get a fighting man, take a fighting woman." She never turned up at Plym-outh, but later in London, she took the twins into Parliament, through the members' entrance, and on a tour.

At her house in Plymouth, the McKeans were well attended to: "for lunch and supper / we eat on our plums raw cream," Margie wrote; "you'll find them in a dream." Some days they picnicked at lunch, and each night

Margarett pulled out the guidebooks. Jenny's snapshots place them at the ruins of Corfe Castle, built by William the Conqueror in the eleventh century, and Abbotsbury Castle, where she photographed the swans. In London they stayed at Brown's Hotel. Senny took them to lunch at "Hungaria" near Piccadilly, and gypsy violinists played "Dark Eyes," as Jenny "wiggles all over." At the zoo, Jenny photographed Margie riding an elephant, and a giraffe much taller than the wall he stood behind.

I've heard many times how Margarett was in a museum: how she would point and exclaim over a certain passage in a painting, a juxtaposition of color, a cropping of image, how deeply she understood the quattrocento from her year in Florence as a girl. Now I find that one day in London she took Jenny to the National Gallery. I picture her, dressed in pale linen, with her long-legged twelve-year-old daughter, the two of them leaning into the Botticelli nativity: small flecks of gold—the holy family in a stable cut into the side of a stony hill, the infant naked and awake on a white cloth on the ground. Mary is the tallest person in the painting, her head so close to the ceiling she cannot straighten or stand up, and the kneeling shepherds barely reach her waist. Joseph, too, is preternaturally large, crouched, head in his hands. I imagine Margarett pointing out the disparities in size, the trees behind the stable, beyond their dark trunks, a golden light—can it be heaven? But the stable is a cave—how can there be an opening at the back of a cave?

Let Jenny be drawn in, exclaim over the angels, twelve of them, dancing in a circle within the gold dome of heaven, above the blue sky. And look, Margarett says, pointing out a crack in the rocks at the lower left of the canvas: a tiny devil, driven by the sacred event back into the underworld—and there's another, impaled on a stick. "Mama and Jenny came home," Margie wrote that day, "having been at the National Gallery and St. Paul's Cathedral saying they'd never had such a good time!" In Jenny's scrapbook is her snapshot of the approach to the cathedral dome, and in a sketchbook Margarett declares, "Victorious happiness with Margie and Jenny. Everything is easy now—everything is evolvable—everything is worthwhile." For her forty-third birthday a month later,

Jenny gave her mother watercolors, "From your second eldest child /
Colors which are somewhat wild."

In a photograph Jenny took on their last stop, in Biarritz. Here, her
mother is dressed in a light color that reads white, white shoes too, and
a white hat that shades her forehead. Margarett is looking straight at her
daughter, whom I imagine standing in front of her, camera to her eye,
taking in her mother, who has lowered her sketchbook to her knee for
just that moment, pencil in her hand. Everyone always said that Margarett was beautiful, and here she certainly is, legs crossed, ankles slender.
Jenny has her for the moment she snaps the photograph, has at last the
undivided attention of her glamorous mother.

II

The Diana Cup

1.

I WANT TO SEE JENNY ON THE RETURN FROM EUROPE, AT FOURTEEN NO longer a girl or half a matched set of sisters: Margie was now wearing such garments as a pink evening dress with "sequined stars"; Jenny would rather head out to the stable and Me Too, taking along her Afghan Loppy, whose dark coat matches her almost black hair. He pleases her, especially when she takes him into the ring and he wins all those blue ribbons, silver cups, including a best in show—he's as sprightly in photographs as she is, sprightly when he follows her riding Me Too *through the woods, the smell of sweat and hair on her withers, my thighs slightly chafed and tense, the spring of her body beneath me.*

Cantering, even galloping through the woods, crackling breakage of twigs, blurring landscape, sound of hooves sharper on earth and stones than on meadow. It's after Europe that Rip Collins comes onto the stable staff, begins to fall for the daughter of the house. Is it her idea, or Pat Keough's, that she run The Myopia ladies race on Armistice Day? Compete with women a decade older—"ladies in hunt costume, who are members of, or subscribers to, a recognized hunt." You had to be fourteen to enter the four-and-a-half furlough race, run for the honor of having "Jenny McKean" engraved on a silver cup, named for Diana—goddess of the hunt, known for her communication with animals, one of three goddesses sworn not to marry.

Jenny had not ridden in the ten months abroad, had not been athletic there except for skating in Bournemouth, so that, except for games of Monopoly, her determination to win, *to be seen*, had been restrained for a year. The day of the race was overcast, the November air was cool, and spectators milled about as the riders gathered at the start line of the course set out along the Ipswich River, grooms quietly saddling, pulling at reins and tack. Jenny wore tall boots, jodhpurs and riding coat, her hair obscured beneath a hard black velvet cap. Mama, Papa, Senny, Margie, and the twins were there, the crowd all in raincoats and umbrellas against the threat of rain. Pat Keough helped Jenny mount—the smell of horse and leather, dampness of New England autumn air, and Jenny is breathing it in.

Four-and-a-half furlongs was barely half a mile, but the rain was pouring down in torrents as the riders neared the finish, Jenny first, bent forward, the familiar encouragement of Me Too beneath her, her legs hard against the saddle. Margie sent me an old clipping, a photo caption identifying Jenny as the winner: It was an especial triumph, for Miss McKean was by far the youngest rider, with her fourteen years." I had looked at the battered eight-by-ten glossy for years, not knowing why Pat Keough looked proud and Jenny so stunned, why sweat slathered Me Too's flank. She'd won a race! I'm amused that one of the women she defeated was

Katherine Winthrop, competitor in doubles at Wimbledon and nationally ranked tennis player, who in less than a decade would marry Shaw McKean and become Jenny's stepmother.

Margarett did not resume painting, and any possibility for change glimpsed in Europe was illusory—she was soon drinking again. After Christmas that year, Senny took the girls to Lake Placid for a month of skating instruction at the all-weather rink built for the 1932 Olympics, and Margarett paid them an unexpected visit: "I have decided to become a Catholic," she announced. Her brother Dan had converted after returning from France and the war, where he drove an ambulance at the Somme and fought in the American offensive at Cantigny, and though Margarett would joke she'd converted to "shock Boston," she was in fact desperate to get help in a world without Alcoholics Anonymous, accessible therapy, or antidepressants. No one took her conversion seriously. The girls paid no attention—just another phase– and Shaw only wanted to be sure his children would not be compelled to become Catholic. That spring Margie and Jenny took their father to lunch at the Ritz to talk about their mother—she was drunk all the time and even when she was not, she was no wife to him—they wanted him to divorce her. He could not, he explained. No Massachusetts court would grant a father custody, and he would not abandon them. When my mother told me this story, the idea that anything would ever go wrong with my parents' marriage was beyond my imagination, as was the idea that I or any of my siblings would be sent away to school. For my mother, though, boarding school was an escape from her painful family, the beginning of a new life.

Miss Madeira's in Greenway, Virginia, near Washington, D.C., was for girls the academically rigorous equivalent to Groton and St. Paul's, schools where Sargent and Shaw sons had prepared for Harvard. Its athletic program included riding; for a fee, one's horse was boarded at the school's stable and an extra hundred dollars purchased tuition for an exacting equestrian program. The school had opened in 1906 in two townhouses on Dupont Circle, then a short walk from open country: "I have always believed exercise and time outdoors an important counterbalance to education of the intellect if Madeira is to remain 'strong in her girls,' " the school's founder, Lucy Madeira, wrote.

All four children left home at once. The twins went to Fay School in Massachusetts, where their father had gone, and Margie, prevented by the war from going to Florence as her mother had, enrolled in the French School on Park Avenue in New York. My mother's choice was unique; no other woman in her family had gone to boarding school with the intention to prepare for college. Did Shaw McKean know that the legendary Miss Madeira was, as *Time* magazine put it, "a New Dealer" who taught a bible class that enlightened her students about the conditions of the poor? Poor herself and the daughter of a Union Civil War veteran, Lucy Madeira spent her early childhood on a farm in West Virginia, until her parents moved to Washington in 1882 to enroll their four children in the "excellent" public schools the capital offered white children. After her husband died of tuberculosis contracted in Confederate prisons, Selina Madeira opened a boardinghouse where her daughter Lucy cleaned and waited on tables. Lucy nonetheless excelled in high school, and at a time when few working-class girls went to college, attended George Washington University (founded 1821) until a family friend who had gone to Vassar (founded 1865) persuaded local alumnae to give her $200 a year for tuition and expenses—scholarships did not yet exist. At Vassar Lucy wore secondhand clothes until she got a new dress for her graduation in 1896—as the Madeira Centennial volume declares, "lack of material things never dampened Lucy's spirits."

After graduation, she taught, but soon decided to start her own school: "I needed to make more money," she wrote, understanding a paltry teacher's salary would not house and feed her mother and younger sibling. Charismatic and hardworking, Lucy soon attracted financing from parents of close Vassar friends, and "Miss Madeira's School" opened with a class of fifteen girls. At the time, the District of Columbia was a small city; but by the 1920s the city had grown, and Miss Madeira, now married, began to dream of moving her school to the countryside. In 1926 her husband purchased 210 acres across the Potomac in Greenway, Virginia, with a spectacular view of the river, and she managed, despite the crash of 1929, to raise money for the design and construction of a new campus.

My mother never told me much about Miss Madeira or the school's history or philosophy—it was, at the time, progressive, even feminist, in its outlook. The usual "women's seminary" design accommodated all school functions under one roof, to allow strict monitoring of the girls' movements, but Lucy Madeira's belief that students should be independent and self-governing prompted her to discard that mode of design. Growing up poor and working attracted her to the ideas of John Dewey, who believed that a successful education was a synthesis of a student's experience of life and her intellectual training. The new Madeira campus, its buildings neo-colonial and grouped around a central space, reflected the idea that a young woman could move from place to place, on her own. The campus was built in a remarkably short time by the construction company that had just completed the Lincoln Memorial and the Folger Shakespeare Library. For its construction, Miss Madeira attracted supporters like Dean Acheson, Roosevelt's secretary of state, and Eugene Meyer, owner of the *Washington Post*, who sent his three daughters there. But she did not see her school as a place only for the education of an elite; private education should model what public education might become in the future—small classes, rigorous instruction, attention to each student. Dewey's belief in the value of involving each student in her own education was replacing ideas of learning by rote: "The work of each pupil is planned with reference to her particular tastes, abilities and future plans," read the school catalogue, and to encourage individual achievement, students were dressed in uniforms, there was no honor roll, and each girl was graded on her participation in student government.

Jenny, given credit for the Nearys' instruction in English, History, Latin, Greek, Algebra, and Biology, entered the school as a first-semester junior in 1938. She was fifteen-and-a-half and had never been to an actual school. Even so, a teacher wrote in her records, Jenny McKean "fit right in," but her grades suggest the fit took a while: B's and C's; barely an A until the end of her second year. Not, apparently, for lack of study—"In her work, she is conscientious, earnest, and diligent," her teachers wrote and she has "a good quicksilver mind." She would graduate twelfth in a class of fifty-three. Faculty of long standing were often single women whose master's degrees and doctorates had not found them university jobs—my mother studied English with Miss Coyle, who had done her graduate work at Yale, and history with the wildly popular Millicent Rex, who had a doctorate in British history from Columbia—of her classes, a graduate wrote, "facts and imagination soared and learning was like mercury." Lucie Dediu, third in her class at the Sorbonne, taught French, along with two Parisian sisters, Annette and Marie Berault de St. Maurice.

At Madeira my mother began the life of the mind that would sustain her, the life of her own she was dreaming for herself every time she looked away in family photographs. "We began to have separate lives," Margie said. "We went to different schools, had different friends, and different interests." In Jenny's yearbook photo, it's not the life of the mind that one sees; she has an almost sultry expression, a shiny pageboy to her shoulders, and dark lipstick: *the most glamorous* it says beneath; *I'm an old smoothie* . . . lyric of a song written for Ethel Merman, which continues, "You're an old softie you're an old meanie."

"It was pathetic!" Debbie Solbert, a class ahead of my mother, exclaimed of social life at Madeira, "everyone dressed up Saturday night, but there were no boys!" Single-sex dances were time honored at all-girl schools; when Margarett was at Miss Porter's, she kept a diary of "crushes" punctuated by exclamation points when a girl accepted her invitation to the weekend dance, though the school was close enough to New Haven that Yale boys took the train up and lurked on the street outside. Even thirty years later, no such loiterers attended Madeira girls. "We were so desperate!" Debbie said, "we leaned out dormitory windows to watch for delivery boys!" Aside from the all-girl dances and soda in the recreation room, the only distractions were occasional trips into town for shopping or for visits to the Washington Zoo, where the girls spent the night in the "dreary" apartment of Miss Glazbrook, the chaperone. Debbie did not remember ever going away for the weekend, but in a flurry of Google searching I found, in the social pages of a West Virginia paper, "Jenny McKean" among the guests at a classmate's weekend house party.

2.

I didn't understand at the time why my mother was so excited when I got into Radcliffe. I was having lunch at school, but she couldn't wait. She piled the kids into the station wagon and sped the few blocks to my high school, where she crashed past the school policeman, my littlest siblings in a throng behind her, and made her way into the cafeteria, waving a white envelope and shouting, "You got in!" "You got in!"

For me, born into a privileged family after the war, college was simply what a girl did after high school. My mother never told me that she was the first woman in her family to go to college, but here is the history: When her paternal great-grandmother Pauline Agassiz was of college age, Vassar was barely in existence; Mount Holyoke, founded as a girls' seminary, was twenty years from certification as a college; and Oberlin, coed and racially integrated, was far off in Ohio. Had college been more available, it's possible Pauline would have wanted to be educated; she started a school for her children. Any educational aspirations of my mother's grandmothers—Pauline's daughter Marian and Margarett's mother Jenny Hunnewell, both born into extreme wealth—seem to have been blocked by obligations of privilege, reproduction, and marriage. A generation later, Margarett's bookish older sister Jane was accepted at Radcliffe but did not enroll. It was she, however, who persuaded their parents to send her rambunctious and brilliant younger sister to the rigorously academic Miss Porter's School in Connecticut: Margarett was the first woman in her family to seek education beyond secondary school. A year in Florence, where she studied Renaissance Italian art history, inspired her to become an artist, making her the first woman in her family to have a profession. Always, Margie said, Mama wanted us "to have a career."

My mother's Madeira transcript and the school's warm recommenda-tion—"quicksilver mind"—was sent both to Smith and Vassar. I don't know if Smith admitted her, but once when we talked about "college," she suggested I might want to think about this women's college, where the students lived in "houses," not dormitories—that seemed wonderful to her, small groups of intelligent women living together in a noninstitutional space. But she never recommended Vassar, where she enrolled in autumn 1940, one of 370 freshmen who represented thirty-three states and the District of Columbia, Hawaii, and seven foreign countries—England, Poland, Canada, Puerto Rico, Argentina, Columbia, and Chile. Some chose Vassar because of its international reach, others were attracted by its distinguished history as an institution for the superior education of women, and still others chose it because it had a professional theater pro-gram and a famous English department that emphasized writing. When my mother applied, the college's most famous graduate was the poet Edna St. Vincent Millay, whose life and career were the stuff of myth.

Every girl with literary leanings right down into my generation knew Millay's poem "Renascence": "The world stands out on either side / No wider than the heart is wide; / Above the world is stretched the sky,— / No higher than the soul is high." We also knew the poet's story, that her dream had been to leave hardscrabble Maine for college, and that the only college she ever dreamed of was Vassar. But how did she do it? Her single mother Cora Millay made a living as an itinerant weaver of hair and was in love with poetry, Shakespeare, and stories. In cold weather, when her three daughters were not running wild outdoors, they wandered through books, put on plays, recited poems in the high-toned English she taught them, and were soon writing their own poems. Sixty years later, when I met the poet's sister Norma, then in her eighties, she greeted me in a trained theatrical voice reminiscent of Eva Le Galliene or Katharine Cor-nell. Cora was given to presenting her daughters; one summer afternoon in 1912, at a tea held on a hotel veranda overlooking the ocean, "Vincent," as Edna was known, stood and, as always from memory, recited her poem "Renascence."

Already, the critic Louis Untermeyer wrote, her voice "had the sound of an ax on fresh wood,—hearing her percussive recitation, one would never have known she was barely five feet tall with an intent angelic face, the luminous nimbus of her curly red-blond hair." Transfixed by the girl was a YWCA executive, Miss Caroline Dow, who in no time at all had Cora's permission to host her daughter in New York for a year of study at Barnard to prepare for college. Vincent arrived at Grand Central with her hair in pigtails, wearing a broad-brimmed hat, looking much younger than her twenty years. Miss Dow set about outfitting her protégée—a white silk umbrella, black satin pumps with "big rhinestone buckles," a gray chinchilla coat "with a rolled collar." Vincent was soon writing home of nights at the opera, afternoon tea with the poet Sara Teasdale ("we talked & talked"), and the attentions of mesmerized literary men, some young, some not. Miss Dow offered her charge to Smith and Vassar, and Vincent chose Vassar; her tuition was raised, and with the support of Henry Noble MacCracken, the activist president, Millay, at twenty-one, became the school's most famous freshman. Underprepared but undaunted, she boasted she'd master German in a term, and she did. Famously, she acted, wrote songs, operas, and poems, and recited rafts of Shakespeare.

My mother introduced me to Millay, presenting me with a copy of "Renascence," and from my mother I first heard the name Mary McCarthy, whose literary Vassar generation succeeded Millay and preceded Jenny. McCarthy and her classmate Elizabeth Bishop scoffed at Millay's poems, and when the undergraduate quarterly turned down their writing, they launched a new journal—"to startle the college and kill the traditional magazine," wrote Bishop. The editors of *Con Spirito*, which also included Muriel Rukeyser, submitted anonymously; their contributions, McCarthy wrote, were placed "unsigned, on a wooden chair to be read and argued over" at meetings that took place at a local speakeasy.

The campus was fresh with radical ideas. The great theater director Hallie Flanagan, responsible for the school's new theater program and major, had done away with tableaux vivants and bad Shakespeare. She was staging productions based on ideas she'd absorbed in Europe as the first female recipient of a Guggenheim Fellowship: the directors Meyerhold, Stanislavski, and Piscator; the playwrights Luigi Pirandello, Lady

Augusta Gregory; and the designer Edward Gordon Craig were her inspi-
rations. A production of Euripides' *Hippolytus*, in the original Greek, was
her first offering; decades later, Mary McCarthy, a harsh critic, remembered it as the most extraordinary theater event she'd ever seen. On
leave from Vassar and with a budget of $7,000,000 ($105 million in 2018)
from Roosevelt's WPA, Flanagan launched the Federal Theatre Project,
which employed 12,500 theater people across the country and in New
York City offered performances at reduced admission to 350,000 people
a week: "Living Newspapers," inspired by Piscator, a "voodoo" *Macbeth*
produced in Harlem with black actors, and a *Pinocchio* that inspired the
young Walt Disney, all directed by Orson Welles, then in his twenties.
By the time the House Un-American Activities Committee shut it down
in 1939, Flanagan's effort had brought more than 2,700 plays to thirty
states. Too much progressive content, the congressmen complained; and
besides, its director had traveled in Russia!

When Jenny arrived in fall 1940, the campus of brick and limestone still
evoked nineteenth-century tranquility. The senior class still wove a daisy
chain for graduation, as they had since the college was founded eighty-
five years earlier by Matthew Vassar, a brewer interested in women's education. Responsible for the modernist ferment was the president Henry
MacCracken who, with the great C. Mildred Thompson, had transformed
the college from its seminary origins into a twentieth-century college
with a rigorous academic curriculum and a national presence. On the day
my mother arrived on campus in September 1940, MacCracken was at the
University of Pennsylvania Bicentennial giving a speech on the tolerance
of religious difference, drawing on his knowledge of what was happening
to Jews in Germany.

My mother became an English major, entering a department formed by
the vision of Laura Johnson Wylie—one of the first women to receive a
PhD from Yale—a Vassar graduate who'd taught at the college from 1895
until 1921. Her legacy was a course of study that, blending the disciplines
of writing critically and creatively, emphasized a student's relationship
to literature as both a reader and writer. When my mother arrived, the
English chair was Helen Sandison, mentor to both Mary McCarthy and

Elizabeth Bishop, and her English professor was the only teacher I ever heard her mention, Richard A. E. Brooks, the lone man in the department cadre of powerful women.

Old photographs of Stone, where my mother lived, show small rooms furnished with iron-framed single beds, wooden desks, and faux Windsor chairs; a Yale banner often held pride of place on the wall, and girls dressed in skirts and blouses. My mother soon met Ruth du Pont ("Dupy"), who had gone to Foxcroft. Who else was on the corridor? Years later when my mother was deep into her life and I was beginning mine, I interviewed to become the press agent at a theater in the Berkshires. "Call me at five o'clock," the producer Lyn Austin, a cheerful woman in her forties, told me as I left her Broadway office. I did so, from a gas station on the Merritt Parkway on my way back to Yale where I was a first-year theater management student at the drama school. "Don't let me down," she said, offering me my first paid job. "I had to fight to get you; the board wanted some dreary old guy."

"I won't," I certainly replied, leaning against the glass wall of the phone booth, looking down at my black-and-white spectator pumps.

"And I have something to ask you," she said. "I went to Vassar with a girl named Jenny McKean, who married Paul Moore. Are you her daughter?" Lyn was the nickname of Evelyn P. Austin, and she too had been on that corridor. The three became the core of a group; the college actually encouraged groups, Mary McCarthy tells us in her memoir, *How I Grew* (1987). McCarthy's 1963 novel, *The Group*, was about her college class and, it seems, preserved a piece of Vassar culture.

My mother of course made other friends—Nancy Wright, a friend all her life, and Annabel Toland, who would marry Fred Herter, my father's best friend at St. Paul's School. There was a framed photograph on the wall when I was little of a tall, pretty girl with long blond hair holding a big fish she had just caught: "She was a friend of mine who died," my mother said; sometime later, she would use Annabel Herter to explain to me what suicide meant, telling me that Annabel's brother had been killed in the war, which had made her very sad, that she was "sensitive, very sensitive," and that suicide was actually impossible to explain. One of my mother's classmates remembered that Jenny McKean "always said the right thing" but also that there seemed always to be something going on "underneath." My mother loved her women friends, but I wonder how many she found at Vassar in whom she could confide what went on "underneath"—the discomfort, shame, she called it—about her difficult mother, her parents' fragile marriage.

I always hoped that within the sheaves of her Vassar stories and blue books, I'd find a crack in Jenny's veneer, but I did not. "Non tengo type-writer," she jotted on a Spanish exercise at the top of one of many hand-written pages. She had told me about the English professor she called "Mr. Brooks," and there in red pencil were the kind of respectful and challenging comments I recognize. After decades of writing and of teaching writing to adults, undergraduates, and MFA students, I have a perspicacious eye. If I had been Jenny McKean's teacher, I would have taken note of the force and confidence of her writing, as Mr. Brooks did, providing what we would now call permission. Permission not only for what she wrote and read, but how she saw the world: I remember my own freshman year, a speech at Harvard Law School by Madame Nhu of South Vietnam—in the headlines as much for her very long fingernails as for her role in the country's corrupt and reactionary government; the speech complicated my sense of the war, which so influenced my four years of college.

I don't know how much my mother knew of the world when she entered college. America was still a year from entering the war that so changed the lives of her generation, but Vassar in 1940 was not isolated from the concerns of the moment. On October 23, the student paper, *Vassar Miscellany News,* announced the coming visit of Muriel Rukeyser, the first major Vassar poet since Millay (Elizabeth Bishop would not emerge for decades). Rukeyser had left the college after two years to learn how to fly a plane, which her parents forbade, and her first collection, *Theory of Flight,* had won the Yale Younger Poets Prize and brought her some fame. She'd been to Spain, where she'd witnessed the beginning of the civil war; the experience changed the course of her writing from the literary to what she called "treason against poetic tradition and content": *I do not say forgive to my kindred dead / Only Understand my treason*. I came to know Muriel Rukeyser thirty years later when I was a young poet: the surge of her passion and feminism inspired me when I first heard her read, outdoors on a hillside in the Berkshires, at an event hosted by my mother's Vassar classmate Lyn Austin. I want to believe that my mother and Lyn went to Rukeyser's Vassar reading and heard the poems she declared to a *Miscellany* interviewer were "built of people and economics and science and disease, hope, machinery and water."

Mr. Brooks assigned papers about campus events, and I have Jenny's first—an essay about *Nightmail*, the short 1936 British documentary about the delivery of mail by a train traveling north from London to Glasgow, Edinburgh, Aberdeen. In one click, I have the film—a poem by W. H. Auden is the screenplay, the score is by Benjamin Britten. My mother noted its lack of Hollywood veneer: *There is sweat and stubble on the faces of the workers, the air is heavy with coal dust.* The locomotive is *a stolid, steaming stenographer, puffing hurriedly and guiltily in among his already hard working colleagues,* and she's taken by Auden's railroad rhythms: "Letters for the right, letters to the poor / the shop on the corner, the girl next door." The train is *almost gliding through the foggy valleys, the wooded hills and the green meadows where squirrels quietly scamper . . . the poetry's recited in smooth, low tones, then the rhythm changes to one of thumping speed, and we find the train jolting through the dying manufacturing towns of Northern England, then again the peaceful sweep of landscape.* Listening to the poem, she finds her imagination creating the scenes—*a double enjoyment.*

Not a week passed without a speech on campus. Jenny had met Russian and Polish émigré musicians at her grandmother's Sunday lunches, but no one like the subject of a paper for Mr. Brooks that she titled *Impressions of the World's Greatest Revolutionist*. Angelica Balabanoff, a onetime comrade of Lenin, was in the United States to publicize her memoir. *Tiny and rather squat,* Jenny wrote, *dressed in a long, slightly shabby black dress, loosely knitted lavender shawl over her rather proud little shoulders, Dr.*

Balabanoff gave the impression last night that she would be in command of her audiences wherever she went. It was remarkable, my mother noted, that Balabanoff had survived after she broke with Lenin in 1921 following the notorious slaughter at Kronstadt of sailors who were demonstrating in favor of what we would now call democracy. My mother was struck by the contrast between the speaker's equanimity and the drama of her life, so counter to one's preconceived notions of a revolutionary. That Balabanoff considered her political work *a privilege* and not to her own *merit* deeply impressed my eighteen-year-old mother: *Completely sincere in the presentation of her argument: that the working classes, can, will and must have the upper hand in the world in order to have peace, this Russian socialist . . . did not . . . try to stuff her beliefs down her audiences' throats.*

I remember the fast walks with girls from the dorm on the mile from Radcliffe to Harvard, the nineteenth-century classroom buildings, gigantic and brick, the dusky orange-red of Richardsonian Romanesque Revival, the old trees on the big lawn of the Yard. The lecture halls, the racket of students settling, the bang of wooden seats unfolding and shouted greetings built excitement until a robust male professor arrived, or in a smaller classroom, the young assistant professor slipped in, rustling his papers and beginning an exegesis of Wallace Stevens or John Keats. I had to pay very close attention——a focus that bore little resemblance to how I did homework at my Indiana high school, where I was never directed to acknowledge what lay beneath type on a page or behind the ostensible meaning of what I read. I didn't think to ask my mother what it was like for her those first weeks at Vassar; she had a Phi Beta Kappa key, after all. Instead, I stumbled trying to explain to her during my first vacation home what was happening to me: "I am on a new intellectual plane," I said, which prompted her to lead a torrent of teasing that night around the supper table.

I was too hurt to imagine she might have been thinking back to Vassar and the beginnings of her intellectual and literary passions, that her ridicule might have its source in the sting of her own subsequent choices.

Decades after my mother died, her Vassar class invited me to speak at their fifty-fifth reunion. Pulling into the parking lot, I was struck by the old-growth trees, the green of June against the gloomy red brick of the building to which I had been directed. I'm visualizing my mother at seventeen as I enter the classroom, its fixtures still old-fashioned. I find myself startled by how old my mother's classmates seem, about twenty women in their mid-seventies, among them a few of their spouses. My mother would have been seventy-six; would her hair have gone white?

But I'm thinking of the girl in Mr. Brooks's class, not the seventy-six-year-old, not even the mother I knew. She signed up for English, History, Spanish, and French, courses might have met in this classroom, where I now step to the lectern to read, maybe poems about her but also from *The White Blackbird*, my book about Margarett. And then I speak, I think, about women's education, how Jenny McKean's mother did not go to college and how important Vassar had been to her, how she often spoke of a Mr. Brooks, who had encouraged her writing. But I also mention this: that my first visit to the campus was during the fall of 1969, with fellow dropouts from Yale Drama School, for a dress rehearsal of *The Serpent*, by the Open Theatre, an experimental take on the recent assassinations through the lens of the Book of Genesis.

I remember intensity and actors miming the tongues of snakes. But more vividly, I tell them, I remember a short conversation after the play: "Some women in New York have started something called Women's Liberation," a small dark-haired woman said. We were sitting outdoors, around a table, smoking. She wasn't particularly a friend, so I'm not sure I would remember her at all if her announcement, delivered with no fanfare, had not changed the course of my life, sending me home to New York to seek out the new women's movement. There was a quiet chuckle when I finished the anecdote, a few responses and thank-yous, but no one offered a particular memory of my mother as a girl, or even of Mr. Brooks.

The assignment had been to write down a conversation "as it was heard." But instead Jenny wrote dialogue reported to her by her sister, a moment between Margie and their mother on the trip the two had taken to Peru six months earlier, in the early spring of 1940:

There are wonderful furs in South America.

Honey bears?

Mr. Cross gave me a letter to a man who has a private zoo filled with honey bears . . . but the boat doesn't stop there.

Who's Mr. Cross?

Margie, don't look as though you had unearthed a scandal, Papa knows him very well.

The next day, when Mr. Brooks assigned "the same conversation made real," my mother began with an image of her sister:

On one of the beds lies a young girl. She is on her side, the blue quilt pulled half way over her. Her right hand wearily holds her head and with her left she picks up the Special Delivery letter which she reads with a rather complacent look in her small, gray eyes. Her light brown hair hangs simply to her shoulder and is what she would call "vaguely curled." She has on a simple black street dress and a string of pearls. As she puts the letter back into its large envelope, there is a reserved knock on the door. At that moment a lady backs out of the closet, pulling her magenta taffeta dressing gown tighter around her. She is tall and fairly stout and is one of those about whom people always say "She just couldn't *be thin!" She looks over to the bed with sharp, very blue eyes, but Margie is staring toward the windows, so Mrs. Shaw opens the door herself . . .*

"There are wonderful furs in South America," said Mrs. Shaw. She loved to change the subject.

"Honey bears?" said Margie with almost a glint in her eye.

"Mr. Cross gave me a letter to a man who has a private zoo of honey bears, but the boat doesn't stop there." Mrs. Shaw was disappointed. She had forgotten the boat didn't stop at that town. Her change in emotion corresponded to climbing up something very big then sliding all the way down.

"Who's Mr. Cross?" This time there was a definite glint in Margie's eye.

"Margie, don't look as though you were unearthing a scandal. Papa knows him very well." And Mrs. Shaw smiled to an imaginary audience.

Except for using her father's first name as the family surname, she doesn't invent much as she takes an actual incident in hand to render her way of seeing things and people, in particular her mother: *Her change in emotion corresponded to climbing up something very big then sliding all the way down.* Where will Margarett's emotions be when she returns to Prides, to the room under the eaves—soon to be hers alone because in the fall Margie will marry?

Jenny turns eighteen in March. It's her debutante year, and enough of the tomboy is gone that she loves the dinners and dances in full swing when she gets home. How handsome all the boys have become, boys she hasn't seen since they were all children at Singing Beach! By July, she and her friend Ruthie Robb have fallen in with Bobby Potter and Paul Moore; Ruthie remembered she was always paired with Paul and that Jenny, the youngest and thrilled to be part of something, was definitely "Potter's girl." "The younger set," as they called themselves, were a quartet—Paul and Ruthie the brassy ones, Jenny and Bobby quieter.

"Potter" had a droll sense of humor that emerged from beneath a calm exterior just when you least expected it, and he was kind. "I loved your mother," I remember him saying at a family dinner in the 1980s. He had cancer, and it was the summer before he died. If I'd asked, I might have learned that he had been my mother's first boyfriend; but I was in my early forties, afraid of the certain coming of his death that I saw in his eyes: *The thing with Potter,* Jenny later wrote Paul, *was that he was beautiful.*

Everything was beautiful that "golden" summer of 1941, the four of them dancing to Ruby Newman's orchestra at the Magnolia Casino, drinking martinis, and wandering down the long willow walk to the beach below Rockmarge, the big white Beaux Arts mansion that belonged to Paul's grandmother, keeping ominous news of war just at the edge of consciousness. Jenny found Paul funny and sweet and by his own account her found her "so beautiful." He also drank too much, he admitted: he loved to tell the story of one night that summer when at two a.m. he cracked up a family car in the driveway, of Higgs the butler being awakened by the noise and racing out of the house in his bathrobe, reassuring "young Paul," who drunkenly begged Higgs please "not to tell Mother."

By the end of the summer, Paul was at his family's camp in the Adirondacks, his father teaching him to shoot a rifle, and Potter was back at Harvard. The day after the annual Myopia Labor Day horseshow, the *Boston Globe* society page reported that Jenny, the "dark haired" younger daughter of Mr. and Mrs. Q. A. Shaw McKean and "a pretty debutante" was preparing "to return to Poughkeepsie" later that month, "to continue her studies at Vassar."

But that is not what happened.

<h2 style="text-align:center">3.</h2>

In a chatty late-September letter to Paul, Jenny announced that *since I saw you* she had been *sick* and ensconced in the *Phillips House* at Mass General, the private clinic within the hospital where she was born, where everyone in her family, and everyone her family knew in Boston, endured serious illnesses and medical rites of passage like appendectomies, tonsillectomies, and births. She reveals nothing about why she was there, inventories the *lousy* photographs she's enclosed—*the usual ones of Robb, representing the oldest profession in the world, are the only decent ones.* There had been a barrage of weddings, she tells Paul, who in his own diary was mooning about a girl named Coralie Waring: *I expect to be the only one unmarried upon release from the Phillips House,* she wrote.

"Withdrew, September 1941," is all the Vassar transcript says, and the college kept no records of infirmary stays or reasons for a student's withdrawal. The change of plans was abrupt—Jenny had loved Vassar. She did not have her appendix out, or her tonsils. There was *something wrong* with her eyes.

However impatient my mother might be, I always felt secure in her love, confident there was a family, a home to return to when I began to leave home—that was not true for Jenny. There had been an emergency the spring she was at Vassar—a phone call from the Ritz. Shaw and young Shaw raced into Boston: "Mrs. McKean" would not leave, was sitting there; Mama, Margie reported, "just blasted," unable (unwilling it was thought) to move, other diners long gone, the maître d' said, the waiters wishing to set afternoon tea. Margarett had been "lovely" with Margie on their cruise to Peru the year before, but now, with no children at home and Shaw increasingly leading a separate life, the fretwork had dissolved. When Jenny came home, the house seemed lonely, even dangerous.

I imagine this: On the verge of returning to Vassar, Jenny wakes up, alone in the room under the eaves. She pushes her hair from her eyes and finds herself unable to see. Senny is long gone, and Margie off somewhere with her fiancé, Wally Reed. To whom does my mother turn? "Mama, Papa, something is wrong with my eyes." Or does she make a telephone call? "Margie, oh Margie, something is wrong with my eyes." I have vague memories of my mother talking about her eyes, but I have no details of her "blindness." For how it must feel, I rely on the testimony of a friend who also temporarily lost her sight at eighteen, so blind her mother had to escort her up and down stairs. She felt no pain, she said, it just came upon her one morning, darkness closing in, leaving just a central speck of light.

"What was going on in your life?" I asked my friend. "I was a bit free for the first time," she said. "Had a boyfriend, you know, serious for the first time."

Why did you leave Vassar? I had asked my mother.

Something was wrong with my eyes.

I know that she went blind, temporarily, because eventually she told me so. It was nicotine poisoning, my sister said, which she had heard from Ruth du Pont, but when I asked Ruth about it, she had just turned ninety-two and it was not in her memory that day. Even the usually hyperbolic Internet stops short: to go blind requires much more nicotine than a single person can possibly ingest. "I think we can reject nicotine poisoning," allowed my friend who lectures all over the world on neuroscience. Charcot, Janet, and Freud all articulated theories of hysteria, later called disorder"—paralysis, seizures, spasms, deafness, and blindness that mimic neurological disorders yet refuse to disclose a medical problem to even the most astute physician. Sudden attacks like Jenny's are still mysterious, but recent research has discovered brain changes in those who suffer them. I had thought hysterical blindness arose when one refused to see something, but that is too simple. Such symptoms have long been linked to trauma and degrees of emotional and physical stress, the idea being that for reasons still unknown, a patient, rather than *feeling* the sadness, grief, fear, or rage. It is the trauma itself that shuts down the eyes.

I was twelve or thirteen when my mother told me she had gone blind because she *read too much*. Plausible to me at that age. She always seemed to be reading and, as an obsessed reader myself, I could easily imagine her as a girl, thick glasses on her nose, deep in book after book. But too much for what? Could it be that halfway through the twentieth century there survived the notion that a young woman could damage her health by reading too much? Or was my mother, in telling me the story, simply acknowledging the vulnerability of her eyes, a vulnerability I share? (I got my own thick glasses at eleven.) I remember my mother's nearsightedness as extreme; she looked odd without her glasses, and terror that looked like sadness struck when she mislaid or broke them. Does the unconscious deliver its conversion to the site where you'd feel the most significant loss? If Jenny had been a champion tennis player, might hysteria have paralyzed an elbow or a shoulder? Even as a grown woman, my mother bit her nails to the quick, so I can be fairly certain there was always feeling of which she remained unconscious. It occurs to me now she had the example of a mother who kept intense feeling unexpressed in company, converting forbidden sadness or rage into routes of escape that ultimately cost her a marriage, the love of her children, the expression of her sexuality, and the pursuit of her art. Not surprising that Jenny might have absorbed the power of her mother's suffering and turned it against herself.

I went blind when I was sixteen. I wanted to look beautiful—which in the 1960s one didn't in eyeglasses. "Men never make passes at girls who wear glasses," quoted my mother from Dorothy Parker. It was nowhere written that wanting to be beautiful was a sin; but the Episcopal Church, clear on the existence of sin, was vague on its boundaries. I converted to sin anything that made me feel guilty. It could not be a sin to *be* beautiful, I reasoned, because beauty was close to God. But to *want* to be beautiful when one wasn't born that way? Or to want to be beautiful in order to attract sexual attention? Surely that was sin. I woke up, my eyes burning, couldn't open them: everything was too bright, too shiny; I had worn my contact lenses for twelve hours the day before, and I could not see.

For years I had saved for the contact lenses, babysitting at seventy-five cents an hour to pay half—$87.50, which came to sixty-two hours of babysitting. My mother, finally free of her glasses and triumphant in contact lenses, had suffered while getting used to them. She thought I would give up if I didn't work to pay for them. She had it backward; I resented having to pay for them; they were hard lenses, and I wore them to blindness. Was I taken to an eye doctor? I must have been, because for days my eyes were covered with gauze.

It was early in the summer after my sophomore year in high school, and I remember lying in bed, terrified that I'd never see again. My mother is as strangely absent from this memory as her mother is from the story of her blindness. My father is present, though not with compassion for my terror—would I have admitted I was afraid? I feel him there, next to the bed, hear his voice reading me "The Monkey's Paw," by Edgar Allen Poe. Would the story be scarier, he wondered, if I couldn't see? He was testing his theory, and I was thrilled by the attention. I don't remember being scared of the story, just wishing he'd talk to me about how scared I was that I would never see again—wearing the lenses so long had scratched my cornea. I did not wear them again until I was a freshman in college, more than two years later.

4.

When her sight returned and Jenny was well, Margarett and Shaw gave her a small dinner at Prides as a debutante party. In a photograph taken that night she is talking to her beau Harry Fowler; she's radiant, smiling, bending toward him—the dress has a long white chiffon skirt, and its bodice, cut black velvet over white, has cap sleeves. There was dancing in the great hall, and a photographer from Beverly wandered the party. In early December Harry returned to Prides for the weekend; and on that Saturday, Loppy died, the dog who had accompanied Jenny on her solitary rides, whom she had shown, who'd won all those blue ribbons and silver cups. On Sunday the Japanese invaded Pearl Harbor, and on Monday the United States declared war. Harry Fowler enlisted immediately, in the British army.

In the next months, everything changed. After Christmas the family moved into town, taking a suite at the Copley Plaza—oil was rationed and "the ark at Prides," as Harry called it in a letter from London, was shut down. In May, when the weather warmed up, the family moved back to the country; in July, Jenny answered a letter from Paul Moore: *Contrary to your conception of our existence it has really been very gay around here, at least on weekends when most of what's left of Harvard College come down.* A month earlier Paul had sailed for the South Pacific; since Jenny knew her letter wouldn't reach him till September, she told him the secret news that her best friend since childhood, Sylvia Choate, was any minute going to marry Sandy Whitman. War's requirements were disruptive—leaves canceled, hasty weddings, air-raid drills, young wives awaiting letters or telegrams, and once in a while the staticky voice of a deployed husband or beau along a phone line. There was a compulsion to jam things in before it was too late. One couple, Jenny wrote Paul, were *ensconced* in a house at the foot of the groom's parents' driveway. *I rarely see them because I don't think they ever get out of bed.*

She was working from eight until one every weekday in Boston at Mass General Hospital and staying nights at her grandmother's Boston apartment. On paper she's blasé, wanting to seem older, but the nineteen-year-old sneaks in: there's a new word their friend Wattie Dickerman has introduced: *toto—it has no definition but you would understand exactly what I meant if I said something, say 'last summer's cruise for instance, was completely toto.'* Margie had named her first child Jenny, and she and the baby were often at Prides; Margarett was spending more and more time in New York, and during the winter in Boca Grande, Florida, with Florence Shaw, the woman who had become her lover. Papa had purchased a plant nursery, and when Margarett was inclined, they collaborated on gardens, though really, they were leading quite separate lives. Weekends at Prides, Jenny could escape for tennis at Myopia or for Singing Beach with Sylvia; and the Dickermans were around—Wattie, often called "Tino," had been a classmate of Paul's at St. Paul's and his wife Maisie, who had long honey-blond hair.

In spite of the fun, Jenny was relieved soon to be departing the North Shore. It had, she wrote Paul, *a sense of finality and forced gaiety that leaves me a little cold.* She had been accepted at Barnard College—she refers to it as Columbia—and would live with Connie Bradlee on East 74th Street. *I am rather thrilled* . . . Connie had been a friend of my mother's since they were little girls, and her older brother Freddie was my father's first best friend. Their youngest brother Ben had fallen for Jenny when they were sixteen—he'd taken her to see Bette Davis in *Dark Victory*, the movie in which the heroine goes blind: "I planned to kiss her at the end of the movie," he told me, "but I was crying too hard." Connie was not at college but working at *Vogue*, not just for fun but because she needed to—their family had lost all their money in the crash. The war would bring many of Jenny's friends to New York that fall: two of the Aldrich sisters, Harriet and Mary, would also be at Barnard, and in her English class she'd meet Isabel Russell from Princeton, New Jersey—blond, *always pro-wholesome,* and lots of fun. Two years later, "Zobby" would marry Bobby Potter in San Francisco during the same week Jenny married Paul Moore in New York. The Potters would be my parents' friends all their lives.

An aerial photo of Barnard College taken in the 1940s: Broadway separating the campus from Columbia, the dome of Earl Hall across the street, and open lawn where the library and the Diana (named for the goddess) student center are now. I don't find Jenny in actual photographs of young women taken on campus—wearing skirts and crisp blouses, carrying books, as depicted sixty years later on paperback covers of Mary McCarthy's *The Group* and Rona Jaffe's *The Best of Everything*. There's a Barnard Committee of the British War Relief Society, an International Relations Club, and a Social Service Committee that placed girls as helpers in hospitals and settlement houses, recruited them for refugee work, or sent them to conferences "on the Negro problem and on peace." There are photographs of Barnard girls on campus learning from civil defense officials how to extinguish "incendiary bombs" and in the gymnasium learning first aid. "The mere domestic problem of 'what to feed the dear man,' " declared the yearbook text, "was presented in diet and canteen courses in terms of mass feeding and mobile kitchen units." By spring 1945, the *Mortarboard* writers could afford a little humor about the war: Barnard girls have become "the victims of a manpower shortage. We read newspapers with a more avid interest now, since we all have a personal stake in the battles in the Pacific and on the Italian front. We haunt our mail-boxes for V-Mail letters instead of invitations to college weekends." There's a photograph of a girl's left hand, a diamond on the ring finger: "We've grown accustomed to a new engagement ring every week."

Actual troops resided on campus. In the fall of 1942, Columbia law and graduate students were evicted from their dormitory to make way for three hundred navy midshipmen. "Frankly," wrote a *Barnard Bulletin* reporter, "it must be just a bit disconcerting to be told, practically at the point of a (Navy) gun, that you have to evacuate." In her 1970s "political autobiography" my mother offers a sense of the ethos: *In the early forties, a Columbia department head, in a startlingly loud voice for Morningside Heights, admonished his Barnard College advisees, of which I was one, "Whatever you do, take some courses that will teach you how to live." He was not, by the way, recommending his own lectures, nor did he make any suggestions. I have thought of his charge over the years—and, simple as it sounds, to question whether we accept the intimate connection between how we have learned to live and how we function politically.*

There was a stirring of dread among Jenny's group of friends, a fear that like their parents, they would suffer the sadness of loss in a war they found themselves supporting, but that a prior generation had brought about. They do not yet imagine the reckonings the war will force upon them, how passionately they will come to believe that such a cataclysm must not happen again. Nor can they predict that when "all this" is over, many of them will set out on lives they could not have imagined before the war, lives in a world so drastically altered they will barely recognize it.

The college Jenny McKean entered as a sophomore that fall of 1942 still had elements of boarding school: a required three hours a week of "sports, games, dancing, individual gymnastics and other activities," along with an antediluvian noncredit course on "the importance of effective speech and of voice production." In that course, taught by Professor Cabel Greet, "each student will examine a recording of her own voice and confer concerning her own individual needs." A friend of mine who graduated in the early 1960s cast a perspective on Barnard's speech training: she went to the speech department, she said, and was warmly welcomed when she announced, "I want to speak like them," meaning free of any New York accent, like the girls with blond hair and blue eyes from the Upper East Side, girls who were not, perhaps, as brilliant as she, a graduate of Forest Hills High School in Queens.

Barnard was founded in 1889 twenty years after Vassar and a decade after Radcliffe, its equivalent at Harvard. The force behind the victory after generations of agitation was Annie Nathan Meyer, a socially prominent member of a wealthy New York Sephardic Jewish family, who convinced most of the Columbia trustees when she proposed naming the new college after an outgoing president of the university, Frederick A. P. Barnard. To counter the overwhelming Episcopalian majority of Columbia trustees, Nathan assembled a board that included two Jews (herself and the banker Jacob Schiff), an Episcopal priest who served as chairman, a Catholic, a Unitarian social activist, and Mrs. John D. Rockefeller, who was Baptist. Altogether there were eleven women and eleven men, a group unusually diverse in gender that also departed from tradition in its religious makeup: at the time, social clubs in New York still blackballed Jewish, if not Irish Catholic, aspirants.

Unlike the overwhelmingly Protestant student populations of other women's colleges, Barnard from the beginning was religiously and economically (though not racially) diverse. Enrolled were debutantes who lived at home so they would not miss the New York social season; daughters of Jews and Catholics also attended, as did professionals who could not afford to go to a residential college. A scholarship fund was instituted immediately, and Reverend Arthur Brooks, the Episcopalian chair of the trustees, announced that Barnard was "for women of every class . . . those who are to earn their living and those who are not can meet here, each class, nay better, each woman, helping the other, without patronage, without condescension, without bitterness." The first African American to graduate from Barnard was Zora Neale Hurston in 1928, recruited at the age of thirty-three by Annie Nathan; only after the war were more than one or two blacks admitted; significant diversity would have to wait until the late 1960s.

Very soon after Barnard enrolled its first class, Columbia outgrew its quarters on Madison Avenue, and Seth Low, the president, purchased land on Morningside Heights to build a new campus. The Barnard board acted quickly and decisively: George Arthur Plimpton, a trustee, purchased land adjacent to Columbia at 120th Street and Broadway, and the heiress to Borden Milk provided the funds to build Milbank Hall, whose cornerstone was laid in 1897. In 1900 Columbia granted Barnard the right to hire its own professors so that, virtually from the beginning, students encountered a considerable number of women faculty, unlike their sisters at Radcliffe. By the 1940s, Barnard had been for decades a small, thriving college with an elegant campus whose professors engaged in the national conversation.

Even though the head of the college was effectively its president, she was called the dean. When my mother was at Barnard, that position was held by Virginia Gildersleeve, an 1895 graduate of the college with a doctorate from Columbia. After the war, at President Roosevelt's request, Gildersleeve would be the only woman to participate in the San Fran-

cisco conference at which the UN charter was written. Like Henry Mac-
Cracken of Vassar, Gildersleeve brought her college into the twentieth
century; but she was also one of the last in a tradition of nineteenth-
century academic women—scholarly, childless, unmarried but with an
"intimate" female companion. When Jenny was at Barnard, that companion was Elizabeth Reynard, professor of English, who helped to found the
Navy female corps the WAVES and, as Lieutenant Reynard, coordinated
the campus war effort. Gildersleeve's successor, Millicent McIntosh, with
a husband and five children including a set of twins, would idealize acceptance of the conflicting demands of motherhood and work—a contradiction that would bedevil my mother and women of her generation.

Her first semester, Jenny resumed the subjects she began at Vassar—
Spanish, American History, and English. But she also ventured into
something new, a course in "comparative anthropology" that brought
her into a revolutionary sphere of thinking first offered at Columbia. Her
anthropology professor was Gladys Reichard, one of a group of brilliant
women who received doctorates under the aegis of Franz Boas, a German
Jewish émigré who came to the United States in 1887 to work as a cura-
tor at the Smithsonian and in 1899 accepted a professorship at Columbia.
There he pioneered a new anthropology that broke from the nineteenth-
century white supremacist, racist theory called polygenism promulgated
by, among others, Louis Agassiz—my mother's great-great-grandfather.
Boas's discovery, based on studies of skeletal anatomy, was revolutionary at the time: Cranial shape and size depended on environmental fac-
tors and were not genetic traits; human intelligence did not originate in
anatomy; differences in human beings were determined by culture, which
developed through social interaction. Further, cultural development
itself was not evolutionary, nor was Western culture its apex. Boas's lecture on these ideas at Harvard in 1906 inspired W.E.B. Du Bois; conse-
quently, Boas joined Du Bois and others at the founding conference of the
NAACP in New York in 1909.

Boas's students—including Gladys Reichard, who studied the Navajo
in Arizona—traveled the world, examining cultures not hewing to an
abstract standard, but based on their relation to one another. After teach-

ing at Columbia for almost fifty years, Boas died at the end of 1942; but his influence remained vibrant in the work of Reichard and his other, more famous, female protegees—Ruth Benedict, Margaret Mead, and Zora Neale Hurston. When Jenny came to Barnard, Benedict was a tenured professor at Columbia and Mead was on the staff of the American Museum of Natural History, where Barnard anthropology students went for weekly field trips. In the course description that attracted my mother, Gladys Reichard presented anthropology not merely as the collection of cultural data, but as a way of analyzing and using that data to think about the contemporary world, taking into account "the emotional attitudes determining behavior, the influences of patterns determining lines of thought and action, and the individual and society."

The course would approach a number of issues, beginning with "Problems of race." Early for that issue, I thought, but the *Barnard Bulletin* that fall announced a pamphlet on race that Ruth Benedict, also rejecting polygenism, had cowritten for American servicemen: "The peoples of the earth," it read, "are one family. We all have just so many teeth, so many molars, just so many little bones and muscles—so we can only have come from one set of ancestors no matter what our color, the shape of our head, the color of our hair."

And race was in the news—even though black and white were (until 1948) kept separate in all branches of the service, racial tensions were high. James Baldwin opens his essay *Notes of a Native Son* with an account of a race riot in Harlem in 1942—the streets becoming "a wilderness of smashed plate glass"—and in describing the threat of violence to black recruits in basic training in the South, he observed "that people I know felt a peculiar kind of relief when their sons were being shipped out of the south to do battle overseas." My mother's Boston upbringing had isolated her—the threatening minority on the North Shore was the Irish—and Gladys Reichard's course was the first time she studied and considered race, an issue that would gather force and meaning for her and inform her moral and political thinking for the rest of her life. By the end of 1944, Jenny was reading Lillian Smith's *Strange Fruit*, a novel that culminates in a lynching, and eagerly pushing her husband, Paul Moore—who had been sensitized to "different kinds of people" by his experiences with Jews in the Marines—to rethink his unquestioning bigotry toward African Americans.

Jenny's Barnard English class, "Structure and Style," was a lecture class with both essays and fiction assigned. The professor, Ethel Thornbury, was a single woman in her forties. A visiting professor from the University of Wisconsin, she had studied economics and philosophy and turned to literature in graduate school. She settled on teaching after flubbing a series of office jobs. "I realized I was an intellectual," she said with an amused smile to a *Barnard Bulletin* interviewer, who remarked of Thornbury that "it takes but a leading question from some artful student to set her off on one of her inimitable story-telling jaunts." She was a campus figure, on Friday afternoons giving lectures open to the whole college on the fate of human ideals in wartime. The World War I generation, she believed, had left their children "with nothing in which to believe." Barnard girls should respond "imaginatively" to the present situation, emphasize "philosophical problems, the nature of beauty and the place of the arts in civilization." Women in military service—"WACS and WAVES"—had their place, but if everyone became a welder, the postwar world would be run by "technological monsters." But Thornbury's own life contradicted that caution: she herself spotted airplanes for the Department of Defense, helped take fingerprints for wartime identification cards, and kept a Victory garden at her farm upstate. In a year, when she left Barnard, she would move to Washington to serve as an economist for the Office of Strategic Services (OSS), the agency that after the war became the CIA.

Miss Thornbury's double messages seemed to encourage confusion about womanhood in her student Jenny McKean. Writing an essay on the role of women in war, Jenny acknowledged that *inbred Bostonianism might motivate her distaste for women in the military, even though various feminine services may prove invaluable in the war effort.* But women in uniform was an unpleasant spectacle: *I object to dumpy ladies doing congas on dance floors, in overseas caps cocked at absurd angles. It is inappropriate that blue hooded WAVES should be saluted by strong armed seamen.* She found

more in common with characters in *The Trojan Women*—women imprisoned by the enemy, commenting on a war because they *knew most about it.*

In October the class read *Ethan Frome*, which Jenny adored. She found
Edith Wharton's similes *honest—the most expressive was the way in which*
Mattie "threw back her head when she was amused, as if to taste her laugh
before she let it out." She noted that when Mattie and Ethan were happy, a
winter day was *as clear as crystal, the sunrise burned red in a pure sky, the*
shadows on the ruin of the woodlot were darkly blue, but that when Ethan was
old, crippled, and caring for Mattie, *he seems a part of the mute and melan-*
choly landscape, an incarnation of its frozen woe."

Did Thornbury then ask her students to imitate Wharton? To write,
as Wharton had, a story about a person different from oneself? I have the
story Jenny wrote next, I'm sure remembering summers in Vermont, the
children of the farmer next door, the skinny man who lived in a falling-
down cottage and never spoke. Her protagonist is a boy whose father had
been killed in an accident caused by a hired man named Fred: *In the sum-*
mer, she began, *they ate the vegetables that Fred grew. He wasn't really a hired*
man anymore; he hadn't been paid since Pa was crushed by a tree. Sometimes,
though, Ep got a ride into town and bought store food:

> *The last time he'd been in, he'd bought a newspaper, and he'd read*
> *about Hitler promising his people that Russia would be part of the*
> New Order *before the winter was over. He thought it sounded pretty*
> *fancy. Ep was proud that with the little schooling he'd had, he could*
> *read about Hitler. Ma said it was nine years since the tree fell on Pa,*
> *and he hadn't been to school since then. He quit, so he could sit in*
> *Belle's stall, and brush her up, more than just evenings. But in the*
> *winter, the snow was deep and you might have to wait a whole day*
> *for even a sleigh. Yesterday, Ep had waited, and none came. It was*
> *while he was away, his mare had died.*

Died, he believed, because the day he was in town the hired man had
not given her water. When Jenny described Ep's horse dying, her eyes
faltering, like the twilight beyond the barn doors, was she remembering the

death of Me Too, her own horse? The boy takes extreme revenge and with *the mallet that stood near Belle's stall*, beats the hired man to death and hides him in the barn. *If Hitler could kill fifty people because one of his soldiers was murdered, why should Fred live, who knew Belle would die if she wasn't watered?*

When his mother asks where Fred is at supper time, Ep lies; that night, when he can't sleep, he goes out into the snow. *It took a while, digging in the frozen ground.* After burying Fred, he *looked at the mare a minute before he rolled her into the grave, on her side. The snow crunched under his boots, as he stamped it flat over the graves.* In the morning, he gulped his coffee and left the house saying nothing to his mother, who watched *till he was out of sight*, then took up her broom to sweep, *the only way she could think of to show she knew the boy had done something wrong.*

I read the story as a dream of the end of childhood, a glimpse beneath Jenny's impressions of people unlike herself, and curiosity about mortality, not only the deaths of her dog and horse, but the deaths of human beings by willful violence. There was Hitler at a distance, but might there also be, within some young men, even a boy like Ep, a murderous strain that enables war? Something outside of her understanding that she can barely take in? It's as if she is bringing, close enough for examination, the murder of one older man "for cause" by a younger one. And the burial in snow—is it a nod to what can emerge when snow, which makes everything so beautiful and clear, melts away?

Jenny did not hear the news for a month, but the first war death among her friends occurred within days of her finishing the story of Ep. Rob Fowler, Harvard '41, mortally wounded while firing a torpedo during the second Marine landing at Guadalcanal, died in a field hospital on October 14. He was the brother of Jenny's beau Harry Fowler, and Pat, his wife of six months, was pregnant. Devastated and the concern of all her friends, Pat would go to work for the OSS in London, leaving her baby son behind. "I wanted to do something for the war effort, as Rob had," she told me at ninety-three. She pulls from a bookshelf the Harvard commemorative volume for the class of 1941, and it falls open to a photograph of Rob Fowler. "So handsome," she says. I remember that his son looked like him; in the Adirondacks the summer I was ten, we sneaked a slippery kiss in the dark during a game of prisoner's base.

5.

Whether she was in Boston for the weekend or New York, the names of her young men recurred: Cheston, Aldrich, Potter, Hickox, Bradlee, Challinor. In New York, the "set" maintained a kind of ESP Facebook— marital and deployment news via snippets of conversation picked up at cocktail parties, on the street, by postcard, telegram, letter, at weddings or cocktails or dancing, once in a while on the telephone, which was not yet a medium for extended conversation. There were places in New York where "everyone" went at night: The Maisonette at the St. Regis, the Copacabana, La Rue on 58th Street where there was dinner and dancing from 5:30 p.m. and two orchestras played till four in the morning. The Kretchma Russian Café on West 14th Street was the downtown boundary of their world; the gypsy music was live, the banquettes were red leather, and the lights were low.

She was trying not to go out every night, she wrote Paul, apt to do *four o'clockers* to get papers finished. What time of night did she begin this story?

> *The stairs were bare and made alternately cavernous and creaking sounds as Liz walked slowly up them.*
>
> *She tried hard to be graceful but her black toeless shoes gave her no support and the thin high heels caught on the rough edges of the boards. She kept her hand, with the chipped pink polished nails, on the slim railing, and a patent leather bag hung from her wrist and the side of it where the shine had worn off slurred against the worn wood.*

What was the assignment? Had my mother seen a girl who looked like that walking the street in New York, riding a bus or the subway?

She kicked the door open and flung herself on the unmade iron bed. Her purse clattered to the floor, and the small mirror fell out and broke so you could see the smoked part on the back of the pieces of glass. Mrs. McLellan, who was standing near a small stove, left her stirring.

She turned and looked wearily at her daughter. Liz was lying on her back with her hands behind her head. Her face was pleasant but the blackness around her eyes and the annoyed furrow on her forehead took all attention from what prettiness she had.

It was only when Liz stood up that Mrs. McLellan noticed the bruise on the inside of her daughter's arm. With the sharp mirror fragments still in her hand she sat on the edge of the bed, and tears tumbled onto her already stained apron.

Not again, Liz, she said. And why this time?

Jake says he don't want to marry no harlot, that's what he said, who works part time at Woolworth's and then don't do nothing the rest of the day. Liz touched the bruise on her arm and the pain made the furrow on her forehead even deeper.

"But working at a Five and Dime is no good reason for him to hit you," said Mrs. McLellan.

"It's enough for Jake. In his lunch hour he came into the grill where I was having a beer with a sailor I met at my counter. He didn't do no more than look at the sailor and then he grabbed me by the arm . . ."

Or maybe at the grill in South Station, she'd seen a waitress with bruises around her eyes, or maybe it's just simple—maybe Mrs. McLellan, the housekeeper at Prides, after whom she names her character, had a daughter in a battering marriage. The only other violence in my mother's early writing is an account in a letter to Paul of her mother, drunk, throwing the telephone receiver at her: that she excused—"Poor thing"—even though the receiver hit her and bloodied her lip. And there's something I recognize in the writer's voice—she'll have the same compassion twenty years later when she writes about the sexual vulnerability of young women caught in poverty in *The People on Second Street*, her memoir of Jersey City. Her own love life seemed to be a lot of fun, the pleasure of juggling a raft of admirers.

"When and if Moore comes back, you'll fall in love with him," Wattie Dickerman kept saying, and Margarett teased Jenny about him as well, couldn't understand why she always said she could *never* love Paul Moore. She would soon have the chance; shot through the chest at Guadalcanal, he returned from the South Pacific in late January, weak after three months in a New Zealand hospital, but a war hero: he had (he said) "damn near" died. Jenny and all their friends had read accounts of Paul's heroism in the paper. He had leapt into the river, swimming across, arm around the wounded Marine, a heroic rescue under enemy fire. Having fallen to his knees, he was shot through the chest while still giving orders, and passed out. Later, when he and Jenny were going out, he would tell her about the malaria, fever visions of Japanese charging the foot of his bed, the relief when he was taken by hospital ship to New Zealand. He would be awarded three medals: the Purple Heart, Silver Star, and Navy Cross. Now he was stationed in New York to convalesce and the Marines had him speaking *at factories to inspire munitions workers, and the New York papers, not yet sated with heroics, wrote stories about him.*

Jenny first saw him again with a group of friends: *We all went out, I wondered at you, for from first glance, it seemed war had done nothing more than make you a little more hectic than you were the set summer.*

It was a word they all used, *hectic*. In another generation it evoked the particular fever of tuberculosis, its dictionary alternatives *het up, highstrung, jumpy, uneasy*. Jenny did not yet know Paul suffered episodes of something the two came to call *confusion*, "Combat fatigue," it was called, the World War II version of PTSD: the emotional and psychic aftermath of witnessing violent death, enduring constant gunfire; of escaping death when so many under your command did not—and, in my father's case, the indelible mark on his conscience of having killed a human being. My mother did not then understand—and neither, of course, did he—that this confusion was not temporary; it would return, sudden, even into his sixties—seeing Oliver Stone's *Platoon* in 1988, he had to leave the theater, lean against the lobby wall until he stopped hyperventilating.

On the evening of March 8, their friend Cord Meyer picked Jenny up at her apartment: a drink with Paul Moore at the Copacabana. Cord was just a friend and so was Paul, despite how Dickerman had kidded her, which made her uncomfortable. She still thought of Paul as boyish, not *beautiful* like Potter, maybe because she had first met him when she was twelve the day he brought one of his mother's dalmatians to the kennel trials on the Prides lawn. The Moores were very rich, everyone knew; Bostonians liked to turn up their noses at New York money, in the Moores' case robber baron spoils, raw compared to theirs so much purer—if *pure* meant a hundred years older, laundered of cotton, rum, sugar, slaves. Paul disguised his self-consciousness about being rich, joked he was "waited on hand and foot" at home in Convent, New Jersey. The family's vast riches were his "cross of gold," Bob Potter said when my brother and I asked him about my father and money decades later.

She wore a black velvet dress and dark lipstick, not a trace of tomboy or the wonky Barnard girl given to wearing *college gingham*. She was nineteen, her twentieth birthday in less than a week. I imagine myself into her, five foot nine—taller in the pumps she wears—black hair turned under at shoulder length, dark blue eyes, dark red lipstick, a new color called Raven Red. That is how she looked that night. But when I want a sense of her presence, I think of a Kodachrome photograph my father took then, her swimming, wearing a pale aqua and white two-piece bathing suit. You can see into the pale turquoise water, and she is looking up at the camera, half-smiling. As my mother, she hid that wide-open part of herself; as a girl, she was always working out how much she wanted to let herself be known. I saw her open like that only when I caught her waking from a nap or on the rare occasions when I found her alone, and she looked at me and said, "Hi, sweetie."

"Hi, Paul," she says, a quick embrace as if he were a handsome cousin, and Cord pulls out a chair for her, a gesture I still find romantic. All her life Jenny had tracked her seductive and glamorous mother and a beautiful older sister, and so, in spite of shyness, she knew how to make an entrance.

I see the light-and-shadow gleam of a nightclub bar, glint of dark polished wood and bottles of gin and Scotch, bourbon and vermouth, small bowls of olives and twists of lemon. My long-legged father-to-be is sitting at the table, younger than I ever remember him, the way he looked in a formal photograph in uniform taken before he was wounded, his lips almost bee stung. But he's not in khaki or Marine blue that night, and they are sitting at a table right up front, close enough that Jenny noticed when he *plucked at the chorus girl*, the woman on stage with a standing mic, singing Cole Porter's "I'm in Love with a Soldier Boy."

"I hang around the phone waiting for his buzz
Does it rock me, yes it certainly does . . ."

The famously charming and brilliant Cord, one in a family of two sets of twin boys, had just enlisted in the Marine Reserve, and would be called up in a few weeks. Four months later, in the battle for Guam, he would lose his left eye, and in the battle for Okinawa at the end of the Pacific war, his twin, Quentin, would be killed. But tonight they're downing martinis; Paul asks Jenny to dance and then Cord does—I remember a man's large hand at the base of your back, his first polite question in a voice that sounds delectably fresh because he uses it so seldom. What was the conversation? For tone, I'll take this letter Cord wrote Jenny a few months later: "a good many miles and a good many days have intervened since our last meeting at 4 o'clock in the morning at the corner of 72d Street. The coconut palms here bear little resemblance to the street lights that morning, and even the stars are strange. I should give much for just such an evening again." They're dancing, laughing, and Paul Moore is looking at Jenny McKean, a lanky girl the summer before, now a beauty. He picks up the siphon bottle and shoots her with soda. Hilarity. Nothing serious.

Everything so false, my mother was thinking. Compared to what? I was eleven and there had been a piece in the newspaper about my father's Marine heroism; oblivious, I made the kind of joke we always made at the table, a tease about his bravery, and he left the table. *Go after him*, my mother said. I found him in my parents' bedroom, his hands shaking, between thumb and forefinger the gilt-edged tissue pages of his Bible. He had been sobbing, could not manage to speak as I apologized, also in tears. This was the *confusion*, and my mother knew it well but had kept it hidden from us—the mysterious aftermath of a war that for us was in the distant past.

Four o'clock in the morning Cord wrote, drinking and laughing at the Copa, Jenny and Paul leaving together, Cord having assured Paul he had no designs on Jenny McKean.

In a booth at the Kretchma, she no longer found Paul *false*. They could talk, which they did for hours: *He was terribly tall, very funny, and exceptionally loving*, she wrote decades later in her book. *He took seriously all the events of his life, but himself rather lightly. I was afraid of life . . . and Paul understood.*

He lit her cigarette, he always said. Their hands touched, and they both felt that jolt, what lovers call electricity. Her Chesterfield, his Cartier lighter. *Electricity*, she wrote then, the word he also used, remembering, thirty years later. *Electricity*, when his hand grazed my mother's hand, and they began to fall in love.

This is happening to me, Jenny kept saying to herself, underlining the phrase when she wrote it down.

What else would she have told me about that night if I had been curious enough to ask about it when she was still alive? On the rare occasions I confided a romance, she told me only to keep my power. I was seventeen, a boyfriend hadn't called. *Play hard to get*, she advised. Fine, but what was I to do with my feelings? She didn't say. In those days, her marriage was happy, and she believed she had triumphantly survived her childhood, that she had *exaggerated, painting a picture of a lonely childhood, like one of those tiresome English children who read too much.*

Paul understood. He had a hunger for talking about important things. He was "very close" to his mother, but it was his grandmother he talked with for hours, about her travels to Egypt and Greece, her study of ancient religions, and confided in her his own religious experiences. At St. Paul's School there had been an inspiring chaplain; at sixteen Paul had a conversion experience when he made his first confession and received absolution, the sacrament in which God takes away all one's wrongdoing. Oddly, he didn't really go into detail about God with Jenny. But he told her how strange it felt to be at home where his parents treated him differently now that he had been wounded and decorated for fighting a war, killing a man. He told Jenny *how dishonest this heroism business seemed*, how his mother, who had diligently had his combat letters typed and sent to family and friends, had a way of bursting into tears and hugging him a little too hard; how his father, with whom he was not close and who did not go to church, slipped a note under his bedroom door the first night he was home: "Your faith must have been of great help to you." I doubt he told his parents about Jenny right away, that he felt "closer" to her than to anyone he had ever met; but gradually, it seems, he let them know about her, why he was so often in New York. Which delighted her. *I continued classes in the daytime, and at night we danced, went to parties.*

Sometimes they'd even meet for lunch or when she had a break between classes or exams. Word that Paul Moore and Jenny McKean were an item went an old-fashioned equivalent of viral and facts became muddled— they had already married, the wedding would be in Boston in June. The gossip was so thorough it seemed that only Cord Meyer had not heard what happened after the Copa. He was thousands of miles away, on a Pacific island the censors kept secret. "There are rumors of wars to the West," he wrote Jenny. His mother had sent him "a clipping of Moore's sanctification into Valhalla and a fine thing it is. Have you seen him, Jenny? If you do, kid him about it. . . ."

In the photograph that accompanies laudatory text, a Marine general is pinning a medal on Captain Paul Moore. My father looks as if he's holding his breath.

She was taking six courses, so that, with summer school, she could graduate the following spring. For Thornbury, along with stories, Jenny was at work on a research paper, a criticism of American higher education's incautious rush to join the war effort. Undergraduate enrollments that year had fallen 11 percent among men, 7 percent among women; after Pearl Harbor, graduate school applications had fallen 28 percent—and *in*

September of 1942, there was a shortage of fifty thousand teachers. Barely a week after Pearl Harbor, on December 12, 1941, a new federal program had been announced that would *give education to boys in the service who are equipped for specialized training regardless of their financial status*; they would live *under military discipline at college.*

Like Columbia the year before, Harvard and Princeton had turned over classrooms and accommodations, the beginnings of what after the war became ROTC. Yale made the largest commitment: *the Army Air force will send two thousand air force specialists, six hundred officers as instructors, a medical detachment and MPs to New Haven.* Women's colleges also participated. Vassar decreased the time necessary for a BA to three years, and deans and presidents of women's colleges met with military and industrial leaders to coordinate recruitment of their students and graduates into engineering and scientific programs, some of which had never before admitted women.

In this unquestioning haste to aid the war effort, Jenny saw a threat to the American tradition of liberal education set out by Thomas Jefferson: "It becomes expedient," he wrote, "for promoting publick happiness that those persons whom nature hath endowed with genius and virtue should be rendered by liberal education worthy to receive and able to guard the sacred deposit of the rights and liberties of their fellow citizens." President Roosevelt, on the other hand, believed that while "a liberal education must provide the final answer. College can render a function—service to the cause of lasting freedom." Jenny stood with Wendell Willkie, Roosevelt's 1940 moderate Republican opponent, who believed that conversion of the universities to the war effort—what was called *total war*—was a threat: "The destruction of the tradition of liberal arts at this crisis in our history would be a crime comparable in my opinion to the burning of books by the Nazis." *Some American universities,* Jenny wrote, *must be reserved to prepare the college generation for peace, an international peace.*

The following fall, my mother would turn her own education in a direction influenced by the war effort. Dean Gildersleeve had conceived a new "interdepartmental" major—a student could study the language, literature, customs, religion, and government of a country or region of her choice. Jenny would continue with Spanish and, leaving literature and writing behind, take philosophy, economics, and most exciting, a course in Latin American history. She and her friends looked to a more international consciousness as a solution to the cycle of war; when Cord Meyer returned wounded from Guam, he would embrace World Federalism. Jenny ended her paper with glimmer of how a postwar world might employ the values she believed in. *The French teacher could prepare men and women disqualified from military service to help France. The Chinese teacher can instruct another group to aid China, and so on.* She was certain that liberal education was essential and *could be made practical.* In the phrase *could be made practical* I recognize the beginning of my mother's activism, politics first inspired by John Neary, that combined the practicality of her businessman father with the beliefs of her mother, who as an artist made actual what she imagined.

6.

"Paul and Jenny" was becoming one name. They spent weekends at Hollow Hill, the Moores' farm in New Jersey, and when the weather got warm, at Prides, newly open after a second long winter of wartime oil rationing. At Prides, the guest room where Paul stayed was called the Silk Room, after the blue French silk print on its walls, and they named what they did there *silkrooming.* They listened to a singer named Hildegarde sing "Darling, Je Vous Aime Beaucoup" and visited friends in Newport. *My shell was gone,* Jenny wrote; new in her life is a *feeling that silent or not, someone understands you.* At Hollow Hill, Mrs. Moore put her in "the Modern Room" which had the only double bed in the huge house, and she and Paul kissed there, their reflection in *the mirrored headboard.* They found a hidden place on the farm, near a manure pit—a location they found hilarious—lay on the grass there and talked and talked. At dawn on Mondays, Paul's father (nickname "Sudden") drove her into Manhattan in time for class.

We fell in love, laughing ridiculously, mother wrote in her forties, *and found that knowing each other upset the adolescent logic that whatever happens happens to you alone. Everything we talked about seemed afterwards to be part of both our lives.* In *The People on Second Street*, my mother has them marry in the next sentence, but in real life nuptials were a year and a half away— an eternity. After three months, she began to worry that Paul had not yet said *I love you.* Her father, noticing she and Paul never spent a weekend apart, warned that she was *making herself too available, that man must be a hunter and all that crap every daughter has heard at one time or another.*

It wasn't that Paul had no feeling, he insisted when telling me the story. To say "I love you" meant certain marriage, and although their friends were marrying in droves and he intended to marry, he was not ready. He didn't *dare* say "I love you," but he also didn't *dare* not say it since he didn't know what he'd do without her. Sometimes Jenny almost said it, but a prohibition was in place: as in the fox-trot, the man leads. What's also in play for Paul is that his convalescent leave is almost over, and he can't wait to return to the camaraderie of the Marines, is even eager to fight again. In a letter, he put the conundrum this way: "I was wanting, wanting to find something on getting home, something that would mean home, something that could be felt and known and kissed, that was home. Yes, I was wanting to embrace home and to fully realize that the horror was over. You were that realization."

Play hard to get, I hear my mother saying; but sometime late that spring, she lost patience and one weekend at Prides, put her *cards on the table* and told Paul she was in love with him. She wanted to prove that she was in earnest, not *a faithless little hussy.* He did not tell her that his orders had come through. He had been named commander of the V-12 unit the Marines had set up in Seattle at the University of Washington as part of the wartime education campaign she'd described in her term paper. He was also offered a position at Yale, but he chose Seattle.

Yale offered the comfort of his alma mater, and New Haven was an easy trip by train to and from both Boston and New York, but he decided he preferred the excitement of a new place. With trains commandeered for troops, spotty and expensive telephone service, and sparse civilian air travel, Seattle might have been another planet, but it was also closer by a continent to combat, and far from his feelings for Jenny McKean and hers for him. "Two people could not go on without something happening," he later wrote her, the "something" being marriage.

He told Jenny his plans late one July evening. They were entwined in a *sofa scene*—she had cooked him supper and now he was telling her he had been posted to Seattle, that he was leaving for two weeks training in Quantico, Virginia, the next day, then bound for Seattle.

How to render her shock, the devastation of his announcement. She tried to be rational. Why not choose New Haven? He had his argument, which she considered a lie. Hadn't she noticed that their *closeness* had *vanished*? It was just fear, she argued. The conversation went on for hours. When we talked about *the practical side of things*—after she declared herself—*I could not be natural*—*I had to explain my silence and explaining it, I became boring.* Trying to get him to change his plans was of course futile. She hummed out loud as if trying to drown him out, beat weakly at his chest with her fists. After he finally left, she was in a fury, *screaming bloody murder*, she wrote him later.

Her roommate Connie, sound asleep, woke up, came into her room, listened; let's say she brought a cool washcloth and placed it on her friend's forehead, sitting at the edge of her bed until Jenny finally fell asleep.

By the time Paul left the apartment, he was building a case: "Propinquity; fun; bodies; a naturalness and a pleasantness; a delightful continuity of seeing things together and knowing all of another for a few months," is how he belittled their romance in his first letter. "There was a fault of ignorance on my side, a fault of naiveté on yours."

Naive? The accusation enraged her, as did the accompanying tautology: "Perhaps I was ignorant of your naiveté and you of my ignorance."

The morning after, she gave a scheduled report in Spanish, then left class early to spend the afternoon with her brother Shaw, who happened to be in New York. She told him everything, and he reminded her what Papa had said about her making herself too available. Which still made her furious. He was just protecting you, Shaw told her.

In the story she'd written about Liz, the girl's bruise was not the consequence of what a man said or did not say, but of something he did. Now Jenny had her own bruises, her own story, and she turned to writing it. Should the first letter to Paul be tough? Something like *Steer away from women, Paul, you might break someone else's heart?* Ha ha! No, she wanted to write as the Jenny he had fallen for—could she do that and be honest? On the other hand, she wanted to shock him as he had shocked her, *to hurt him or anyone* because her pain felt *so physical*. The next night, she and Connie went out with George Cheston and her old beau David Challinor, and she flirted *like a wild thing*. In the days that followed she continued to *do crazy things with Challinor—listening to waltzes in a music store booth,—yesterday drinking mint juleps at the Stork and tea dancing . . . to see if it would soothe the raw edges, but still nothing means anything and I am going around in circles.*

All of this she wrote to Paul, who wrote back in a voice that made her feel even more alone: "Please write. The relationship need not be strange; and our public, I hope, will understand that 3000 miles and 2 years are too much for even the strongest hearts. And so good bye with a sweet sorrow, and at least for me, the happiness of a dear memory."

He had settled into a new life: "I am officially in the driver's seat of 350 odd college Marines & really getting a bang out of it. You can't imagine what fun it is to get back to work & to have a command, if you want to use a glorified phrase; just the little things like today a kid came into the office and wanted special liberty to see his sick wife. Asked what the matter was; OBVIOUSLY she was going to have a baby."

Jenny replies that she is *not embarrassed to say that tears have been frequent, that I can't sleep, that college has become a thing just to pass the time, that I leave places and people in a hurry for fear that I will show something.* She had always been self-conscious about her temper, not surprising given lifelong training to tell little or—was this what Emily Dickinson meant?—tell "slant" what she felt, anything to get the laugh so you could say, just kidding. But being with Paul had changed that; she no longer regretted being straightforward, even though she believed she did so in a *clinging way that still keeps tormenting me,* feared *that by my display of emotions I stopped something that had not run its true course,* she realized that any other person with a touch of worldliness would not have put their cards on the table as I did. *Naiveté perhaps, but I never imagined that something that seemed so sure—so fine and almost beautiful—would not continue.*

Writing her back, Paul kept to the surface, offering awkwardly drawn cartoon figures, exclamation points, gossip, rather inept flirtatious talk. *Duty* he once spelled "doo-tee." He was feeling terrific, he wrote. The *confusion* he had confided to her was behind him. He pretended that his feelings for Jenny were also behind him—this new self of his in a new place had new "freedom." To my mother the change in his tone felt abrupt and incomprehensible. She wrote Harry Fowler she was seeing Challinor: "You really have captured Chally's heart," Harry replied. She threw herself into her work.

By the end of July, summer school at Barnard was over, and Jenny had A's in Spanish and B's in economics. She was back at Prides—*so prewar*—sitting at the dining table even for lunch, attending dinner parties given by the parents of friends, diving into *sofa scenes* and roof parties with whoever turned up. As for Paul, no matter how hard she tried in letters to get him to acknowledge her side of the story, the lover and confidant she'd so relied on was nowhere in evidence. What she considered intimate exchange he now dubbed "sort of subjective & inverted & rather unhealthy . . . seriously there's no point in worrying the scar tissue, to use a rather nauseous analogy."

In response, Jenny dropped intimacy from her letters, peppering chatty narratives with composed remarks: *Yet I have no regrets.* She suggests he go see *For Whom the Bell Tolls,* in which Ingrid Bergman is even more *emotionée, shameless and has even less pride than me. . . . It was great while it lasted and all boils down to the fact that I happen to feel something you don't.*

When he replied that he was dating a Navy woman, Jenny's response was all debutante snark—*I think you must be getting quite coarse to see so much of a WAVE. How is it with TWO sets of buttons?????* She decided not to answer his next letter, but he persevered. "I'm curious as a feline as to your 2 wk. silence. Granted there's no reason why you *should* write, but I am rather inclined to think you have either found a new lover, died, had more eye-trouble or just have become extremely lazy."

She didn't write.

"At least satisfy my curiosity."

She didn't write.

"Look, you dope, write me a line fairly soon or I'll be more than annoyed." He had no one else to write him from home. How, without her, was he to know what was happening? But Jenny is beyond responding when he tries romance: "Your letters are my life's breath." She hoped news had reached him that she was seeing David Challinor.

7.

Once in the 1960s when we lived in Washington and I came home from college for Thanksgiving, we went for cocktails at the home of old family friends. "Challinors"—I loved how the name sounded, like a knight of the Round Table. There were Challinor children the same ages as some of my brothers and sisters, and I remember sitting in formal chairs, a little awkwardness as we drank and picked at hors d'oeuvres, not the ease I usually felt with my parents' old friends. After my mother died in 1973, I lost touch with the Challinors; but when a close friend of mine married Joan Challinor's nephew in the 1980s, I began to hear about them again: there was always a mild flurry, my friend said, when Jenny Moore's name came up. This friend had come into my life after my mother died, but from the vibration in the room prompted by her name, my friend formed a portrait of Jenny Moore as brilliant, beautiful, alluring, and somehow mysterious. When I began to write about Margarett, this friend told me that David Challinor had things to tell me, memories of "Prides during the war."

It was a late spring day in Washington, and I met David in the offices of the Washington Zoo where, retired, he volunteered as an executive. We commented on the weather; he had rowed on the Potomac that morning, he told me, as he did every morning, and now when I think of him, I think of the river, the distinctive splash of oars in quiet water. If I were writing fiction, I would put myself in a rowboat with him, that sound of oars accompanying our talk, but we spoke in his office.

He announced himself a "WASP Catholic" among Episcopalians and joked about a subcategory: WASC. When he spent weekends at Prides, he told me, he went to early mass Sundays with the "Irish servants"—your grandmother certainly didn't go to early mass, he said, but she was "very much a Catholic," and he talked theology with her: François Mauriac, Jacques Maritain. Now he was in his early seventies, what my mother would have called "wonderful looking"—silvery gray hair, a long narrow face, dark brown eyes, a modest and engaging smile. "I tried to marry Jenny," he said calmly. I had not known this, and of course it explained the awkwardness at cocktails that Thanksgiving, and Mrs. Challinor's response to my mother's name. That declaration is also why I tell this particular story—I am always looking for roads not taken in the bumpy story of my parents' courtship.

David Challinor does not appear in Jenny's life as a serious suitor until 1943, when she flirts with him *like a wild thing* to make Paul Moore jealous. They had "seen something" of each other the year before when Paul Moore was not yet a prospect and David was still at Harvard—her nickname for him then, "Koff," evolved from an earlier one, "Challnikoff." She invited him to Prides for a summer weekend: *I'll meet you at 545 at the Ritz to go to the country.* There was to be a house party; it would be fun. Then, in October, he was in New York, and so was she: *Dear Koff, Name your day, and I will cook you supper.* Joan Challinor needn't have worried: the letters and telegrams David returned to me at the end of his life end abruptly at the beginning of February 1943, a month or so before Jenny began to see Paul Moore, and contain not a syllable of romantic interest.

At this point in my mother's story, her diffidence at the interest of David Challinor argues that she has set marriage to Paul Moore as a goal. She is a woman of her generation, and marriage is what they did. She has no idea the force that leads her so powerfully now will eventually capsize her. I know that she will marry my father, win him in no small part because of who she is in her letters: her humor, her intelligence, and the verve of her argument. She does not see herself as a cog in an economy or a means of reproduction: she and my father marry for love. She will take his name and join his work, which will separate her from her mother, reassure her father, give her a place in the world, and allow her to live in a way she never could have on her own.

But how did one thing lead to another? I want to understand how Jenny McKean became the woman I knew, and so, at this point in the story, I allow myself a lack of foresight about what actually happens. If she were not my mother, where would I begin my research? In her diaries and letters, of course. And if she were a writer, in her fiction.

I return to the story of Liz, to its dynamics:

> *He didn't do no more than look at the sailor and grabbed me by the arm. I told him I was only having a beer, and that the sailor was slovenly, and that I was going to marry no one but him anyways, but he said he had to beat me and I knew he had to.*

I knew he had to. Jenny McKean, it seems, was aware of the dangers and physical power of men, though the man she loved was nothing like, for instance, the man sitting next to her at the café at South Station. *Had breakfast in the station and got the most fantastic goose from a Norwegian sailor—the whole way up as a matter of fact.* She turned away the affront and used the story to taunt Paul Moore. *SO you with your WAVE and me with my Nordic, we get a button scene by hook or by crook.*

The morning after I write that, I dream a woman friend and I are in an old but solid dinghy, rowing out into the ocean, gray and choppy with a bit of white edging the waves, but not too cold: benevolent. The feeling is that we are "out to sea," about to launch into conversation, about everything, about our poems. I don't remember which of us is rowing, and then suddenly we are capsized by some outside force, thrown apart, drawn under, then I am underwater but surfacing, up toward the light like a smooth fish, as if I were still young, and I see my friend in the distance, first underwater with me, then also surfacing, and beyond her, the ocean surface broken by the leaps of dolphins.

Let's say a girl's piece of fiction is a form of dreaming. *I was going to marry no one but him anyways, but he said he had to beat me and I knew he had to.*

I knew he had to. Where are the dolphins? If I were my mother's teacher at Barnard, which I might have been had she lived fifty years later, I would praise her evocative use of detail: *the chipped pink polished nails,* how she has Liz keep hidden *the side of her purse where the shine had worn off.* And then I might have asked if Liz's sailor was actually *slovenly* or if her description was a lie she told so as not to regard herself as a *harlot.* I would praise how, when Liz arrives home, she *kicked the door open and flung herself onto the unmade iron bed.* In the moment she *flung herself,* I felt Liz's body in the air! Such action, such self-possession! But barely three pages later, the story ends with Liz's submission. *I was going to marry no one but him anyways,* she says, which the reader somehow knows matters not at all to a man who beats women.

What happens next to Liz? When does she repair the chips in her pink nail polish? Why don't we see her bruises fade? Does she break up with Jake? Why does Jenny not take us past the truncated, fatalistic, thanks-to-Hemingway ending? How does she know that a woman's momentary interaction with a sailor, that glimpse into another world, must be smartly punished?

Jenny McKean took Paul Moore's abandonment as punishment, a slug in the stomach, morally unquestionable because he was returning to the war effort. The times give her no autonomous nobility of purpose; like the girl who lived the story of Liz, she feels at first that she is without a future, *hurt, going around in circles.* Even college and the world it offers suddenly bore her. The semester is over; no more essays or stories for Alice Thornbury.

Some girls might quickly have dropped out of school, found another beau, and married on the rebound; others might have taken an exciting job or, like Pat Fowler, joined the war effort. But not every girl had raced for and won the Diana Cup. As she had as a little girl when her horse refused a jump, Jenny turned back and again forward, and, as she would have put it, in a phrase she used often, *forged ahead*. She will not accept Paul Moore's sudden blasé denial of the tenderness and passion he had expressed all spring. She will write to him, argue. Jane Austen did not have Anne Elliot write to Captain Wentworth, but Jenny McKean writes, writes, and writes to Captain Moore. Then stops writing him for four weeks, leaving him to dangle and beg.

In the meantime, back at Prides after summer school, she took up riding again. (I remember this so well, that she would "take up" something, a project, return to something she used to do, further work on her tennis game.) She found it *heavenly* to see Pat Keough again. She had almost forgotten how *wise and good* he was, and how *I love to hear him talk*. She thought they'd just canter a little on the first day, but he wasted no time. "Throw your heart to the other side me darlin' and pop that fence!" And so she did, jump *every damn fence* on a borrowed colt. *I do love the feeling of triumph of making the horse do what I want*, she wrote Paul. *Probably Freud would find there was something sinister in that.*

III

Persuasion

1.

ONE NIGHT IN JULY, BEFORE PAUL LEFT FOR SEATTLE, BEFORE HE announced to Jenny he was leaving, the two of them posed at La Rue for one of those photographers who wanders among tables at such places. She was wearing a satin dress with wide black-and-white stripes. The black stripes were black tooled velvet, the sleeves were short, and the neck closed with a string bow. Paul wore his summer uniform, khaki, stripes across his pocket for each of his three medals. They look relaxed and they are smiling; on the table is his right hand and her left—their other hands are out of sight. By the time the glossies arrived by mail at Jenny's apartment by mail, she and Paul were no longer an item. But the photograph ran in the *Herald Tribune*, and it seemed that everyone they knew saw it—friends, parents of friends, grandparents of friends. Further, everyone concluded that Paul and Jenny holding hands beneath the table, which caused a small scandal. In their still-Victorian, prewar world, such public displays of affection were considered barely appropriate, even for those about to marry.

Talk heated up. From New Zealand, David Devens wrote Margie, "What is all this I hear about Jenny and Paul Moore?" One friend remarked that he thought "they'd be blissful together if neither ever wanted a dull moment!" The news further blazed across the Atlantic to Harry Fowler in Sicily and Cord Meyer on Guadalcanal, both of whom wrote Jenny. Fowler didn't know they'd split: "from all reports you are so thick with P. Moore that something must come of it." And Cord had only just learned they were an item: "I had heard rumors of you + 'guess-hoo' appearing constantly together," he wrote Jenny, but since she hadn't written him of nuptials, he'd consider her still "the only single girl I know in the old country." Six people sent copies of the photo to Paul's prep school roommate Seth French, and even Jenny's Barnard advisor saw it: "Are you going to cease your fine work and get married?"

No, was the answer.

Her best friend Sylvia had just married Sandy Whitman. The ceremony was "simple," which during wartime meant only a hundred or so guests, only five bridesmaids in long matching dresses, of whom Jenny was one. Because J. P. Morgan was a great-great uncle, the *Boston Globe* proclaimed it the "wedding of the week." The item did not mention that the newlyweds would live with the bride's friend Jenny McKean until the groom received his Navy orders. *Our design for living is a scream,* Jenny wrote Paul. *Sandy calls me "Sis" and I call them Dad and Mom.* She also expressed horror at how quickly her fierce Sylvia had become "a domestic whizz." *Really it's fantastic the way she spoils him. I suppose it's easy to say that when you look at it objectively—all women do the same thing. Frankly I can't picture laying out anyone's clothes + damn near dressing them.*

She was taking six courses. The most exciting was Mexican history, a Columbia graduate seminar with a professor named Frank Tannenbaum; the class was racially mixed, which was completely new to her: *3 negroes, 2 negresses, 2 nuns, 3 priests, 6 Phd-ers, 7 Jews and me. I am flattered to be allowed in it—for the first time real independence—wonderful reading and thrilling men in that history, and you go at the speed you want.* Tannenbaum had been a "vivid youth" in his days as an anarchist—Emma Goldman described him then as coming "out of the ranks of starved and frozen humanity." Emma Goldman! Tannenbaum had been jailed for leading IWW marches of the unemployed on New York City churches, which responded with food and money until a Catholic priest complained to the police; Tannenbaum was arrested and sentenced to a year in prison. A Columbia professor of history bailed him out, and he graduated from the college in three years. *Did brilliantly, went to Mexico and became [President Lázaro] Cárdenas' brain trust of one, went up the Amazon with a native farther than any white man has gone etc. etc.*

"Who was the dark haired Communist girl who went to that weird New York College?" quipped a soldier she met one night with a Yale friend of Paul's. She was reveling in her studies, paying less attention to what "people" thought, and she loved to exaggerate about this in letters to Paul. I doubt that her hair, which she declared reached "her navel," was ever that long. She was putting her toe in the water, then withdrawing it: One afternoon, she got to Columbia early for Tannenbaum's class and talked to one of her classmates, *a black Puerto Rican gentleman.* His master's thesis was *on some aspect of Shakespeare*—and he invited her to see Paul Robeson in *Othello* (still the longest-running Shakespeare ever on Broadway). He was, she wrote Paul, *so bright and nice.* But there was no question of her actually going to the play with him, despite how cultivated he was with his *Spanish accent:* would be *just my luck* that some *Bostonian dowager* might be in town for the evening. Just a few years later, she would cringe at who she had been.

Though the model of Sylvia waiting on Sandy hand and foot horrified her, seeing the photo from La Rue had brought back her feeling for Paul, and I can feel the pulse of destiny: that certain postwar pileup of washing machines, dryers, casseroles, aprons, and *The Joy of Cooking*. So many of her friends were marrying, then abandoning college or jobs to follow their husbands, rent little houses on military bases, become immediately pregnant. The chatter of all the matrimonial congratulation is like a Greek chorus bent on preserving a way of life.

It was Paul who first raised the possibility of a joint future: "I don't know," he wrote, "but perhaps being apart is as good a way to find out as being together. I can't trust things I'm not sure of—can you?" Suddenly he might want to marry: "I'd like us to meet for 2 wks alone + find out for sure." When Jenny didn't respond, he tried again: "My car is on its way out—too bad I didn't think to have you stow away in it." When Jenny replied after two weeks of silence, she admitted it had been hard without him, but she'd recovered herself was not sure about starting up again. *I do miss you and think of you—Lets leave it at that—ok? Just comfy—ok?*

Paul wrote back that he was dating a redhead named Nona Stimson, whose family lived in what he described as a "rich house" in the Highlands, the Tuxedo Park of Seattle. They were seeing each other almost every weekend. Jenny reported that her friend Carol Warren's sister Camilla had married John Gardiner, USNR: *He got a sapphire in Australia, brought it back, popped the question, and they were married within 2 days.* Sandy Whitman's Navy deployment had been postponed, so Jenny's newlywed roommates were off to Florida and she was living alone again, as usual studying into the night. *Something is always wrong with me,* she wrote. Cramming for a midterm, she'd fainted in the bathroom, almost hitting her head on the sink, then she got a fever—*100°–104° for no reason* except exhaustion—*I am so done in, even after sleeping till 12, I can hardly see.* Her parents rushed to New York, even hired someone to take care of her. She'd caught something, it turned out. She was still sick in bed when she read devastating accounts of the bloody Marine invasion of the Gilbert Islands—the newspapers reported it was the most brutal fighting in the Pacific since Guadalcanal.

Paul's old division, the first Marines, had landed November 20 on Betio, a tiny island in the Tarawa Atoll and crucial to supply and refueling for fighting farther to the East. In the first four days, nearly 1,000 Marines were killed, and almost 5,000 Japanese soldiers. Arriving the morning after the invasion, Robert Sherrod of *Life* reported of the carnage, a land-scape thick with the suppurating bodies of the dead. Jenny wrote Paul in a panic: Had Cord been there? Or Quigg McVeigh? Her letter crossed his: "I would have sworn a year ago when I was cowed + frightened + still had nightmares that I'd never feel this way again," he wrote; "This may sound melodramatic, but I've made up my mind to go out there again if I ever can. You can't let the others do that stuff + stay home + have people make a fuss over you. The doctor here said he thought I'd be OK for fall duty. I just wanted to tell someone, but be discreet:—the family think I'm here in the States for the duration. PS, Sort of a silly letter."

How might one construe what he'd just written as *silly*? To himself he scribbled a few notes—"the fast hot throbbing drink of death" . . . "drinks in gulps of explosion."

That night he went to Bainbridge Island to have supper with his friends Ann and Charlie—and with Charlie he "downed" two bottles of rum in two hours. At dinner he felt just a "slight hum on + then WHAM, his head hit the table." He would remember only that Charlie put him in a taxi, and that he could barely navigate the ferry back to Seattle: "I couldn't come near walking straight." This would not have surprised his Yale friends, who remembered his epic drunks. But the graphic accounts of fighting on the Gilberts had an impact. He had never blacked out before, and it scared him: "Will have to be careful from now on—." Again letters crossed, so Jenny didn't know about his drunken night when she replied to him about returning to combat:

I was touched that you should send me your thoughts as they come. It felt almost as if you were here and I were holding hard onto your hand to help in the confusion. I know that whatever I say will make little differ-ence for "no one understands" and if anyone does it would surely not be a woman, it's a man's war etc. etc. But from what you have taught me, I think I can understand to a degree at least. I know how hard it must be to see that those you went through all of Guadalcanal with are now being put through something that is even worse than what you knew. But it is not your fault that you cannot fight now.

She was right—he was thinking of the "lads" who had died when he survived Guadalcanal, and he tried to explain:

Saving oneself from something does not work, especially if the something is dangerous + involves someone else doing it if you don't. . . . I well remember making the decision to run fully exposed into the face of heavy machine gun fire with complete expectation of being killed to see if a body of one of the other men was still alive—it wasn't, but that doesn't matter. . . . Anyhow, the bullets did spray around my feet, but God (?) or Fate kept them from me. Wouldn't I be of little faith not to respect that?

Jenny wrote back immediately:

I am not anywhere near enough of a person to even think of telling you what to do, and you will probably think I am trying to sound like a messenger from Yahweh, but I mean every word I say, irrespective of my own personal feelings.

She really does not want him to fight again:

You are too much for the world to lose. And as for myself I cannot think of America without your kind soul to write and hope to see. You will never know how much you have given me. Goodness knows I am not anywhere near enough of a person to think of telling you what to do, but I mean every word I say, irrespective of my personal feelings.

My love—dear Paul—
I'd like to see you soon. Jen

A different tone—acknowledgment of the closeness they'd had their long summer together, the talks about family that had so reassured her. That night she dreamed she and Paul were climbing on their stomachs up opposite sides of the golden dome of the State House in Boston. Later a fortune teller told her she had a lover whose first initial was *P*, whom she had "emotionally met" early in April and who had been wounded in the war and was now on the West Coast. In real life, in the library to get a book in Spanish by a man called Pabamó for her Mexican history course, she found herself in front of the drawer marked *MO–MY* looking up *Moore*. She had wanted to keep things merely "comfy," but some part of her disagreed.

2.

Two days before Christmas, Jenny got terrible news. Her riding teacher Pat Keough had died of a heart attack—her beloved mentor, the man who had led her to all those blue ribbons. *It seems to draw a too sharp, too final a line around childhood—a lot of wise things I remember from him—and my most happy memories are memories of riding.* She wrote Paul about the funeral, because she knew he would understand: *The flowers were wonderful all around the casket and he looked so sweet and happy, so much a proof of something after.* Everyone was crying. *And I was so touched because there was a picture of me on a horse winning a race on the wall nearby.*

The morning after the funeral, she woke up believing she'd spent the evening with Paul. But it had been another dream, his brother Bill's little girl Pammy in a green field wearing a sunsuit, and Paul had a wrapper on. *You kept wandering around tightening the belt for some reason and telling me you planned on silkrooming. That girl Francise was lying on the lawn, and to end it all, Plowright—the butler at Hollow Hill—had wings and flew out an upstairs window with the cocktails.* At a lunch when she returned to New York, friends from Madeira teased her about "the big Marine," and Francise from her dream quickly made mincemeat of her denials of interest. Gales of laughter. Enclosed in a letter from Paul came the letter she'd written him to Guadalcanal before he was wounded—*it still smells of the place,* he jotted; for a Christmas present, he sent a stuffed bear. *When I woke up there was his little head right on the pillow beside me,* Jenny wrote— *oh so sweet.*

In her grief about Pat Keough, need dissolved her caution. Soon she and Paul were writing regularly and planning to meet. How to manage it? Because they weren't engaged, she couldn't visit alone; but her brother Harry had been posted to Tacoma—she could visit him, and Margarett could come along as chaperone. The idea of Margarett worried Paul, but Jenny reassured him: *She is one of the most self-sufficient ladies I know. She craves spending hours sketching bell boys and that type of thing.* Jenny's only worry was her studies: *Will I be able to use the library?* She managed a note from her eye doctor to get excused from classes, and Papa gave permission. She insisted to Paul they keep the trip secret since, when things went badly, *the woman takes the brunt,* but she made the mistake of confiding in their friend Babs Denny, who lambasted her: "What on earth are you doing chasing Paul Moore out to Seattle?? He'll never marry you if you're so easy!"

Which made Paul furious: "Why shouldn't you come out here?" he wrote her. "This has nothing to do with MARRIAGE!"

Maybe not from his point of view.

But for her, yes, something to do with marriage—suddenly she really wanted him back, his love, that feeling of connection. At the very least she wanted to be sure about crossing him off on her mental list of prospects.

Her list was extensive—letters from her suitors turned up in a green silk document box, one of several jammed beneath a cabinet in my living room: a sheaf from Harry Fowler, several pages from Cord. And one from Julien McKee: I had a memory of his name, something about a hand—and there it was, late 1942: a pilot, his plane downed somewhere in the Pacific; he and his crew adrift in a rubber rescue boat twenty-seven hours before a British destroyer rescued them; two fingers blown off. He was writing from a hospital in Jacksonville, his mother taking dictation, his impaired signature and postscript: "I do wish you'd write to me. I think of you so very often—so lovely and so nice. I miss you like hell."

From Seattle, Paul wrote about the women he was seeing—Dixie and

Tupper, a "little blond secretary who is really trying to make me," Nona Stimson and later a dark-haired girl named Lois Stretton. Jenny replied in kind—in Boston with George Cheston, movie canceled because of a hurricane, trains not running; they spend a night at the Ritz, she in a second bed, wearing his spare pajamas.

But as Paul's letters and her replies multiply, other names recede. Her vivid verticals, his scrawling script, driven by renewed excitement, whip across the continent, pass in the air, drop into post office sorting bins and mailbags, their out-of-sync questions and answers causing little rifts. I think of certain 1940s movies, sheets of U.S. Marine stationery and college notebook paper swooping into view, swirling closed like a camera lens then open, whirling through possible dates for a reunion.

"I'm a little scared," Paul wrote, "but hell." He telephones. *I have just hung up,* Jenny writes, *and I can't help but be sweaty with frustration—your voice did sound strange and all the time I couldn't help thinking, is this the person I have been writing all this while?* "My fingers are crossed," he replies, "but I think there is a certain inevitability about it." *Listen Boyo,* she wrote back, *unless you write me a sizzling letter I am canceling all plans. You remind me of a hot water bottle that has cooled, or a drink found in the living room in the morning.* "The way you phrased your 'Listen Boyo' letter was so funny. I didn't take it as a blast—but in case it was, consider this a sizzler." They make a plan to talk when she's in Boston the following weekend, and after the call, he writes her quickly, " I liked the phone conversation, your original 'Hello' was good and exciting."

The montage fades, and she is again at lunch with girlfriends, behatted and smoking Chesterfields as the camera cuts to a vista of ocean, her "big Marine," my father at twenty-three, at a desk writing her a final previsit letter to New York. He is aware that she has become "a thing projected out of my own ego. . . . But you also are somebody who is above all NICE. And someone who can stand erect and face the slings and arrows with pride, self-confidence and surety of soul. Someone who is rugged but soft."

Rugged but soft, she reads.

She can't wait to see him, but how aware is she of his life on the base, how it is soaked with grief and sorrow, every relationship, it seems, distorted by the war. As he walked Ellie Cunningham home one night, she was in tears—her husband had just gone to the Pacific, and she couldn't push from her mind the newspaper photographs of the carnage in the Gilberts. Paul was thinking how much he wanted to talk to Jenny about how he can't think about "living or not living," just about going back to battle "with no thought but the accomplishment of a mission. Call it a high recklessness."

Jenny cabled final details: *Will arrive Friday nine p.m. unless I wire.*

This twenty-four-year-old boy, this twenty-year-old girl, these children who became my parents, believe, even desperately hope, that after ten days together in wartime they'll finally be sure, sure they should marry. They have different visions of marriage. In my father's case the bond between his parents was invisible—safety, the abundant comfort of four places to live, but never, he sensed, what he would call real love. In my mother's case, any erotic charge between her parents had long since gone sour and fractious. Paul will want a spiritual and physical intimacy he had never seen between his parents—communication with a woman less like his needy mother, more like the wise, thoughtful, and intellectually adventurous grandmother he adored. For Jenny, romance would bring safety, consistency, respect. Her father had always demonstrated that a man took care of things, was loving in a quiet way, did not express need. Her criticism of her mother was that she was not "a wife" to her father—Jenny will be a wife to her husband, and, despite how she derided Sylvia's attendance on Sandy, will take care of him.

They go out drinking with his Marine buddies, have their picture taken at a bar called the Town Ranch, one afternoon have ice cream after he shows her his office at the university, and one day board a steamer to Bremerton, Washington; on the next ferry, to Victoria in British Columbia, seagulls wheel so close Jenny can see their hungry glare. There were meals at the hotel and an afternoon when Nona's mother gave a cocktail party at the Stimsons' house right on the ocean. Six decades later Nona will remember Jenny: "Your mother was so glamorous. She was wearing a purple suit, in the Russian style."

After the marvelous first two days, Jenny was so carried away, she declared her love.

I can't believe she is doing this again!

Doesn't she know that Paul will react the same way he did eight months ago? I do not know exactly what she said, but in a letter describing the scene, she uses the same figure of speech as she had that summer: *I put my cards on the table*.

The next day, Paul got a cold and began to sulk.

"God, you're so in love with me," he said in the bar, and later, in her room, "I really hate you tonight." It seems he can't rein in the boy who always needs to protect himself from his mother and his equally hovering nanny. To make matters worse, he somehow lost his gas ration cards so they couldn't drive up into the Sierras to ski, and in town it rains. And rains. He won't stop sulking; even at lunch with her brother Harry, he distances himself. "Why don't you write me three letters a week," he said, "instead of six?"

The night he took her to a dinner party at his friends the Gunners on Bainbridge Island, he drank and drank. By the end of the evening he could barely walk or speak, and Jenny had to help him to the car. A "major drunk," he wrote her later, one of the occasions that prompted him to stop drinking, which he could never manage for long. He should cut back or stop altogether, Jenny kept saying.

When he couldn't quite walk to the car, she thought of Margarett falling asleep at the supper table, which made her take Paul's alcohol consumption more seriously than he did: *Haven't you almost had your fill of a good time?* Paul had an excuse: "I do have a full time job for which the Govt. is paying me $200 a month ($2887 in 2019 dollars) and it is fairly connected with the war effort," he snapped, and "I don't happen to get drunk every weekend." There was also, I think, a dimension Jenny did not consider: a gnawing ambivalence, despite his bravado, about returning to combat; a rising panic that he could, at least temporarily, drink away.

Is it presumptuous to say that my mother at twenty had less knowledge than I do of the man she so wanted to marry? Little sense of what might be going on in the moments he seemed distant or dazed? If only I could sit her down and talk to her as I would a student or a young friend, ask what she thought she was doing rekindling a relationship with someone so vulnerable, ask how her feelings for Paul Moore compared to those she'd had for others she dated, the young men who wrote her with such sweetness. Instead she tried to change Paul: Why couldn't he just say *in a nice voice* that he wanted *to nap or be quiet*—she would have left off *the pleasant chatter.* Why couldn't he just admit he felt guilty letting work go, anxious about the Marine colonel's visit in three weeks, the massive welcome parade he had to organize?

She was so disappointed, confused, and angry that she barely kissed Paul when they said goodbye. As the train pulled away, she could see that his smile was crooked, and as she continued to watch from the window, she could just make out that he was miming dangling something—"the keys to my heart," he wrote later. Sitting next to her on the train and airplane was a Marine called Peter whose eyes got crinkly when he smiled. She was trying to study her Mexican history but he kept interrupting her.

I HAVE A NEW LOVER she wrote Paul on a postcard, its comic illustration a vase breaking in the air; "I missed you so much dear," shouts the angry cartoon wife who has thrown it. The next postcard, a collage of American flags, she wrote and mailed during refueling in Minneapolis: *Peter (my new lover) is grander by the day.* She called Paul from Chicago: "Nice of you to come out + break up the monotony of winter," he snapped.

So the sweet letter that awaited her in New York was confusing:

"It was a good visit wasn't it," he wrote.

She didn't think so. It wasn't his *vacillating about the big step, that's beside the point, it's the business of one minute being utterly close and the next being disinterested in things we had been close about.* This kind of hurt was all too familiar; it was what her mother made her feel.

My father first told me the visit had been a disaster when I was twenty and confiding a romantic heartbreak of my own. "I lost my ration book," he said. "It rained every day. We were stuck in the hotel." His face was a twist of disappointment, as if recalling those days hit an all too familiar scar, as if their failed reunion contained the seed of every painful misunderstanding they had in twenty-eight years of marriage.

"I think you were extremely tolerant and I thank you for it," he wrote in his first apology. "Most would have told me to _____ off! We had a gay and pleasant, more than pleasant, time, but honestly Jen I think you are stupid to string along with me. . . . it will be a long time before I'll be worth anything to settle with." In the next letter, he proclaimed the visit a mistake, also "a mistake" to start writing her again, weak of him. He'd done so purely "to have someone to write to."

She replied: *It is inconceivable to me that someone, a Christian like you, would let something drag on because it was easy and pleasant to have someone in love with him. The whole business, letters + telephone calls, must be dropped completely.* She now understood something: *I am in a false position to myself, the hell with what people say or think, that is completely secondary. I must lead my life in as worthwhile a way as I can.*

3.

For the first time since she'd fallen for him, Jenny was free of Paul Moore, of any obligation to him as a future. It was March 1944, and she was about to celebrate her twenty-first birthday.

I must lead my life, she had written him. But despite her determination, she felt humiliated and lost.

After a breakup of my own in my early twenties, I went into therapy; but in 1943, when Jenny found herself without the possibility of marrying Paul Moore, psychotherapy would have been a source of shame— even her mother, clearly mentally ill for at least two decades, had never consulted a psychiatrist. My mother's historical moment was extreme, but even so, no one really worked through the impact on a young woman (let along a young man) of friends or lovers dead or disfigured in combat. I can't emphasize enough how the culture in which she grew up required silence about feeling.

I have come to understand that among my parents and their friends, becoming serious about the church and belief provided what psycho-therapy would for their children—support in freeing oneself from the almost Victorian way of life of their parents, the atmosphere that Jenny called *so prewar*, the intricate social architecture that had held the world of the rich more or less in place since the Civil War. Paul Moore was bucking robber baron ancestry, a family of entrepreneurial bank-ers, and an extremely monied childhood that made him feel guilty. For Jenny McKean as a young woman, the first line of rebellion was against her mother, for whom she had *no respect*, and a father who was loving but whose values and politics she increasingly did not share. For both my parents, the church provided an entrance to their inner lives and a humanist faith that would inspire progressive, even radical—though nonviolent—activism. *I am convinced that all of us, who are the so-called rebuilders, will do that thing, after the war, that appears the hardest*, is how Jenny put it a little later.

But now, in a final note to Paul, she declared what she called a "chop," not only in words but by enclosing a photograph of herself at a night-club with his Yale classmate Joe Walker. The blaze of white in the dense black of her hair was a birthday gardenia that had arrived from Paul the day after she turned twenty-one on March 12. By April she and Joe were *going steady*, he calling her "Muffin," she calling him "Bunny." Some-times writing from a bunk on a ship in the Pacific, he'd embellish the muf-fin with "melted butter" or transform it into a "nice crisp breakfast waffle with a thin coating of maple syrup," and at least once when Jenny wanted to tease him, "Bunny" became "a gross hare." He was tall and wiry with a subtle smile and a lot of charm. He encouraged her confidence, chided her for denying her "great brain" when she got straight A's, dubbed her a "child poet" when she described a fish as a "stream-lined pickerel in the metallic waters." He saw the sadness in her eyes and laughed at her eccen-tricities. He wanted to know why she wore sneakers to cocktail parties, and in a photograph of them pasted into the back of a scrapbook, her face has an open expression I hadn't seen before.

At Barnard she was finishing up the spring semester, taking European history, her International Studies honors seminar, and a second semester of religion, taught by Ursula Niebuhr, the Oxford-educated Anglican wife of the great Protestant theologian Reinhold Niebuhr. Jenny had realized that when wartime questions of morality were debated in terms of religion and belief, she felt ignorant, and that when Paul had discussed the church, she felt uneducated. He had warned her that religion classes could be dull, but he did not know the visionary Mrs. Niebuhr. She was the first of my mother's wise women.

Mrs. Niebuhr's bible class the previous fall had taken Jenny through the Old Testament prophets and the coming of Moses, and she had received an A. Now she was deep into the New Testament, coming to understand Christianity as a movement, making distinctions between the Gospels, the Epistles, and the Acts of the Apostles—learning about *the tremendous happenings of this new age,* and about St. Paul, who had introduced the idea that human beings exist *in Christ in the fellowship of the Holy Spirit.* In Christianity, she now understood, a life of active faith replaced the Jewish devotion to the ancient texts of the Torah—*entrance to Heaven,* she wrote, *was guided by an inward rule of love and self-sacrifice.* When she became a wife and mother, how she defined "love and self-sacrifice" would become a concrete and complicating question in her life.

It doesn't seem far-fetched to imagine that Mrs. Niebuhr's teaching inspired my mother to consider that Christianity might guide her; the surprise was that it brought relief from the rupture of her expectations in Seattle, a way to claim a voice and a new self in her struggle to release Paul Moore. *I never asked you about God,* she'd written him after their first breakup. She was studying the Bible to correct that *gap in her knowledge;* now she wanted to explore worship. First, she went to see the Episcopal chaplain at Columbia, a man named Stephen Bayne, whom I would know later as a handsome, prematurely white-haired bishop. But sometime in early April—possibly on Easter, which fell on April 9 that year—

she made her way to the Church of the Resurrection on East 74th Street, where Paul Moore's spiritual mentor was the rector. "Father Wadhams" was a figure from my childhood—perhaps already in his fifties then, with a deep voice and a British accent that made him seem closer than my young father could ever be to God. In Seattle, fighting off Jenny's emotional need, Paul had harshly suggested to her that Father Wadhams might "do you some good."

Now she remembered how Paul and their friend Quigg had praised him as an influence on their religious thinking. They thought of themselves as Catholic—not Roman but Anglo-Catholic or, on the spectrum of practice in the Episcopal Church, high church. Brocade vestments in colors corresponded to the seasons of the Christian year—purple for Advent and Lent, green for the summer season of the Trinity, red for the days of martyrs and saints, white for feast days. "Smells and bells" was the nickname of this intense form of devotion—daily communion, individual confession with a priest rather than only group confession, incense, and the liturgy often sung in Gregorian chant, all to achieve a more visceral relationship with Christ, especially the Christ of the Passion and Crucifixion. During the 1940s and 1950s, high church Episcopalianism was the mode of worship of many with progressive, even radical politics. And in the years after the war, young Episcopal clergy and laypeople like my parents were inspired to activism and work with the poor not only by the Anglican priests who worked on the London docks, but by the Roman Catholic French worker-priests.

Jenny began to go to the Church of the Resurrection every Sunday she was in New York. Sometimes she even spent a weekend in the city so that she could get to Communion mass both Saturday and Sunday, making some excuse to her parents, whom she had not yet told of this new part of her life. She went to see Father Wadhams and soon confided in him her friendship with Paul, also meeting with him privately to study the prayer book. She had been baptized as a child—christenings were a social ritual—but she was confirmed an Episcopalian, women and girls veiled, the bishop saying, before laying his hands on her head, "Defend O

Lord this thy child with thy heavenly grace, that she may continue thine forever; and daily increase in thy Holy Spirit."

Jenny soon made her first confession, the sacrament in which, by confiding one's wrongs to a priest, one is granted absolution, or forgiveness by God. None of this interested her boyfriend Joe Walker, so the night after her confession, she wrote Paul for the first time in two months: *I am breaking the silence.* Reading the letter, I identify a new tone; no longer do I sense her looking to Paul for what he cannot give her—the freedom to be herself. She reminded him he had once told her that some experiences *never seemed as real or wonderful until they were shared.* Now she understood what he meant *and because you in part are responsible I wanted to write you how happy I feel this morning. It was so wonderful. I practically flew the nine blocks home, I felt so pure. And then this morning early was first communion and afterwards, we all went down to the Parish Hall for breakfast.*

Father Wadhams told them that having breakfast together was a kind of communion, which she didn't understand at first, sitting down at a table of strangers—*a fine looking man with a Harvard twang,* a woman of fifty *who always talks as if she were half crying,* a Scottish woman who loves to travel and now *so help me is going to go to Rio,* a woman *who never stops talking about writing stories for* Life and who, when Father Wadhams asked what was essential for Communion, cried out, *"Oh Gordon, at Guadalcanal they used rifles to make the table."* Jenny knew Paul had been at that mass, so she blushed; Father Wadhams, of course, had also heard the story. *"Someone here knows a good deal about that,"* he said with a nod to her, and then they *all laughed and to me,* Jenny wrote, *it seemed like a clue to the happy tone of things. I now see why the Church as a community is so fine and necessary."*

Afterward, *practically running* down a Sunday-empty avenue on her way home, the sun as it is on a New York spring day—bright—the air clear and not very hot, she felt *wonderful,* had *a feeling of belonging, of being welcome, a sense of everyone there authentically happy.* This feeling was hers, I believe; but it was Paul Moore, alone in her life, who would recognize and affirm it. She understood more about him now, she wrote, and hoped, really hoped, that he would decide to *become holy,* meaning become an Episcopal priest.

4.

On leave and on the train to Santa Barbara to visit his sister Fanny, Paul had time to reflect. How terrible he'd been toward Jenny on her visit suddenly became very clear to him, and he could hardly bear it. The apologetic letter he wrote crossed hers about joining the church; when she got his letter, she wrote him that she was struck by its *humility and lack of self-confidence.* She too had been rethinking Seattle and had determined just what had been so wounding about his behavior. She'd had sympathy for how on edge he was about his job, but she *could not stand having what I tried to give flung harshly back in my face . . . I did not want to stand with my hat in my hand.* She was *sick and tired of going whole HOG for you every single solitary step of the way.* It had all made her feel *damn lonely & damn lousy.*

As for her new lover, hadn't he heard the gossip? *Maisie is convinced that I am about to marry Joe,* she wrote him, *because Joe came up to New York from Norfolk on his last leave to see me—this all adds up to frightful significance for the Dickermans.* So, go ahead, she taunted, *Why don't you have a business with Dixie!*

But Paul was not in a sarcastic frame of mind when he wrote back, fast, a serious amends.

He has learned "that one should be a *great* deal more careful with other people's feelings. So I don't want to have a business with Dixie. Your letter also made me very nostalgic and lonely—we did have a grand time, what?" He was not being "dramatic or sentimental"—how he'd behaved and what he said to her in Seattle was, for him, "water over the dam," and he hoped "we can date if I ever get East." On the other hand, he had, of course, heard who she was seeing, and "if Walker is the gentleman in question," he approves: "I think he is probably one of the best people who ever drew the breath of life." Joe Walker was in his eighties the only time I ever spoke with him, my mother dead thirty years, my father a few months. "Oh there's Joe Walker," my father's brother Bill said, pointing him out across a Florida golf club dining room.

I had seen him just once before, handsome and fit at my mother's funeral; now he was ninety, blinking at me through rheumy eyes. "You were a friend of my mother's," I said. "Yes," he said, "but your father, too." It seems that everyone always stayed friends, the tribe more significant than its individuals. This was before I read Joe's letters to my mother, which tell me that on their final night out, Jenny wore the black-and-white *vertical stripe dress* she wore the night she and Paul had broken up a year earlier. I wish I'd known the young man who wrote Jenny the most delicious love letters I found in the cartons. He was "sitting reading an old copy of the Communist Manifesto in Gaelic when the mail orderly staggered in and dropped eight letters from Jenny McKean on his desk. When his destroyer was not "trawling for Japanese in the Philippine Sea," he wrote her, he spent hours reading Arthur Koestler or imagining himself on a train from North Station to Prides, reading *Alice in Wonderland* aloud"—"I watch your ear and think about how angry I am that I have to go away. In Wonderland fashion, he writes the rest of the page upside down. On a mossy lakeshore, "It's just evening twilight and we're sort of vaguely casting for trout. There's no war, no trains to rush for, in fact no time. Then after a while, on looking up and seeing me watching the sky, you say, 'Bunny, what are you thinking about?' I answer, 'Heart, you see I can't decide whether you can do more for the world by trying to formulate something tangible and fair in the relationships of groups of people or whether ultimately more is gained when one person devotes himself to trying to develop faith or love of civilization or whatever you call it within individuals.' "

I like how Joe Walker looks, light brown hair, gazing at the camera, and I'm jealous that at that moment in her life my mother had the attention of someone who charmed and loved her, never mentioning, she wrote later, her liaison with Paul Moore, even though Joe knew Paul quite well and would have heard the gossip. Does Jenny feel any guilt at being back in touch with Paul while still receiving Joe Walker's declarations of "not inconsiderable love"? She doesn't seem to: While Paul was at pains to downplay his attentions to other women, Jenny was easy with him about how she felt about Joe: *Someday I'll tell you why it was so wonderful!*

In August, two months after D-Day, Jenny's twin brothers, now almost twenty, were at Army points of embarkation, and news had come that Harry would be posted to France on October 1; he'd fight in the Ardennes, in the Battle of the Bulge under General George Patton. To his disappointment, Shaw was kept out of combat by a hernia operation. On August 30, Jenny dreamed she and Paul had married and that she was pregnant with her own twins, and on the same day, Joe wrote her about the Normandy invasion, signing his letter "nary a wit less love than always." His ship was out from Pearl Harbor in war exercises. In her dream, Paul is in the Pacific. In a panic that he won't be home in time to name the babies, she lies awake *trying to decide whether to call them Phil + Pine (pronounced* Peen*)*—Joe was likely bound for the Philippines—or *Guadal + Canal. I never decided—when they were born they assumed the attributes of 2 year olds immediately—one had dark hair and blue eyes like me,* she wrote Paul, *and one had blond hair + blue eyes like you.*

Now I am reading the third binder of my parents' letters, and she's still writing six letters to his one.

"Saw some Marine officers just back from Saipan today," Paul wrote. "I don't like the sound of the recent operations." The battle for Saipan had ended in the early July suicides of the Japanese general and eight thousand civilians.

What did you mean about not liking the sound of the recent operations that the Saipan gentleman told you about? Jenny wrote.

"So many people got hurt," Paul replied.

In mid-July, the Marine division Paul had been part of at Guadalcanal led the invasion of Peleliu, one of the tiny Palau islands. The Americans were confident of a ten-day rout, but the Japanese waited, hidden in caves, until the Marines, finding no evident targets, moved inland. The air was humid, the land muddy, the temperature 115 degrees. Paul and his Guadalcanal buddy Beres figured the odds. "In 2 years overseas your chances of not coming back are 1 out of 3 damn near."

Monk and Hickox are on Peleliu, Jenny wrote; "Monk" was the nickname of Cord Meyer's twin brother, Quentin, who would win the Silver Star there. The battle at Peleliu took months, not days, and the Marines lost 1,200 men; of 11,000 invading Japanese, 87 survived. The Japanese general did not admit defeat until November, and by then the island no longer had strategic value.

Paul was thinking of applying for a transfer. Despite his success in Seattle and the pleasures of teaching, he was bored. He'd love to be sent to Quantico for brush-up training, and if he got the chance to fight, he'd like to command a battalion again. *I wouldn't presume to touch the touchy situation of your going over or not,* Jenny wrote. Her only concern was his health—*I would not think that jungles and rice and fatigue would keep your lungs under control*—his lung had been wounded at Guadalcanal.

"I'm young and healthy," Paul replied, "and therefore there's no reason on earth why I shouldn't be sent over again."

As he had before explained that for him not going "would be like saying a person who went to church for 3 hours on Good Friday shouldn't have to go on Easter." He had "tactfully" made himself available, he wrote Jenny—the Pacific War would end only with the defeat of Japan, and that would require an invasion, though no one knew when. His predicament was resolved when the Marines announced that the University of Washington operation would be shuttered; as of November 1, student-recruits would be sent to Parris Island and Quantico. Paul's own request for Quantico was granted a week later: "It's given me a new lease on life."

Jenny was back at Prides after "snap" summer courses in sociology and Spanish. *I am a lazy bitch,* she wrote Paul; *I have done nothing for two weeks but sit on my fanny in the sun, ride, play tennis, eat, sleep and not go to church—with that schedule I have no right to preach. . . . I feel as contented as a pussy cat.*

One night at the Myopia Hunt Club, where she'd won all those riding ribbons, she encountered Paul's father on the porch during cocktails—a droll enough scene to dramatize in a letter:

Hello, Mr. Moore. I haven't seen you for ages. she said.

"No," Mr. Moore answered (with fat nose twinkling), "it's been just about a year" (long pause then louder so whole porch could hear)—"I hear you" (pause) "went to" (terribly long pause) "Seattle."

Mrs. Moore was there as well: *My moustache*—Jenny enjoyed making fun of her dark facial hair—*turned 8 shades lighter when your mother kissed me!* He mustn't think his mother *an ass, or crazy. She used to be my great idol in the Vermont drugstore days.*

The reference was to the Vermont drugstore where my parents always said they trust met when they told their love story. What actually happened is misty—I don't know if it is memory or imagination that conjures the winter day, teenage girls dressed for skiing, snow on their boots, the cordial hello, my black-haired mother's dazzle of a smile breaking through her natural reserve.

"Where did you meet?" I would ask, childhood curiosity hungry.

"In a drugstore in Vermont," one of my parents would say.

Since it's my mother I see in red-and-black plaid wool, it must be my father who is speaking. Vermont when I was a child had no reality for me except its designation as "the most beautiful state." Later I learned that when Jenny was a little girl, the McKeans spent summers in Dorset, Vermont; but did they go there in the winter? And what were the Moores doing there? A ski weekend while Paul was at St. Paul's School? And where was the drugstore? As an adult, ever the researcher, I'd drive Vermont scrutinizing every refurbished general store, but no detail ever identified the real thing, a place where I might stand and take in the past. In a photo I have, Jenny wears a knitted hat against the cold, a piece of plaid visible, so it is that girl I'll place in the vanished drugstore, appearing out of nowhere, an apparition.

"Is that when you fell in love?" I asked my father once, feeling the snow, the smell of moist wool.

"Not really," he said, "but I never forgot her."

5.

I have been trying to get my parents married for months, trying to understand their courtship in the tangle of war, of the circumstances in which they live, and how the church comes into it. I have typed out the letters of the weeks that begin with her conversion, those of his that break their silence; much as a historian sifts through archives in search of the vectors of energy that finally converge in a peace treaty, I have read every page. But I find no dramatic moment; rather, I feel their correspondence become a courtship, subtly, like a change in barometric pressure that arrives before you're conscious of what it measures.

It is nice not hesitating to respect your trust completely and implicitly, Jenny wrote Paul on July 27, 1944. As one comes to the end of Jane Austen's novel and pieces of the story fall toward resolution, it comes clear that in the novelist's thinking, *persuasion* does not mean talking someone into something but rather the removal of obstacles, the resolution of dissension—in the world of course, but also in consciousness. When Anne Elliot's family rejected Captain Wentworth as a suitor for her, they were concerned with his lack of prospects and certain their daughter, though she had no dowry, could do better than a navy man.

The most consequential obstacle to Paul and Jenny's alliance resided in a matter one might call breeding—in the matter of her mother.

Paul Sr. and Fanny Moore of course "liked" Margarett McKean, even found her fascinating, but they were aware of certain facts. On one hand, the Sargent family harkened back to the very first ships of settlers to reach North America, and its members had distinguished themselves in the history of New England; on the other hand, one of Margarett's brothers had been a suicide, her older sister suffered some sort of depression, another brother was an eccentric Harvard instructor who wrote poems, and a third never married and lived with his mother. As my father was coming to love Jenny McKean, he did not concern himself with her inheritance; in fact, while he was aware of Margarett's shortcomings as a mother, he was fascinated in her as an artist, a wit, and not least, a Catholic convert.

Jenny became aware of the Moores' misgivings through Mabel Story, a rather gossipy friend who knew both families very well. She immediately wrote Paul: *Mabel told me that your mother always says that she doesn't want you to marry me because of Mama's career; i.e. lesbian reputation affairs, drink, etc.*

"I didn't mention anything to Mother and never have," Paul replied. "I don't talk to her of such things—she is too emotionally interested—"

It had never occurred to me that "like mother like daughter" would be an issue, Jenny replied. *Has your mother ever brought it up? It would be too bad if my future love affairs were ruined because of that. I suppose it's naiveté that makes me repeat that I never thought for a moment that would be an issue.*

"The reason you never thought that," Paul immediately replied, is that "your mother's mind doesn't function that way and a father's never would." Jenny could trust his discretion about Margarett: "It would be very disloyal to go into that with anyone, because you see, I am very fond of your mother for herself as well as for her being your mother." Further, "I sympathize with her troubles + do not censure them." He and Margarett often talked about matters of the soul, and he instinctually understood her art as an expression of a relationship to the unseen, her drinking and depression as protest against the constraints of her marriage and situation. How well my father understood art as communication I didn't take in until, as an old man in clericals, looming, white-haired, and in tears, he approached me after a poetry reading I gave two years before he died.

He loved his mother but accepted her limitations. Prejudice on her part was "perfectly possible . . . but she never risks saying anything I wouldn't approve, even though she is confused at my broad mindedness about anything un-Puritanical, being Protestant in her way of thought." Jenny should remember what he'd told her, that he'd never taken a girl out whom his mother hadn't found "something a little wrong with. . . . that old animal-mother instinct." Or putting it another way: "Victorianism—middle class morality . . . breeding theory. She has raised too many horses and dogs and cows."

On September 1, a Friday night, the telephone rang at Prides, and Jenny was called from the supper table. "Seattle," said the operator—

Paul's voice for the first time in seven months. He'd waited four minutes after the operator said "Salem"——"The beautiful difference was that your voice was not a memory," he wrote her right after the call; "And I love to hear you laugh."

He had been "useless" because he was "nervous and giggly." But maybe, he hoped, she'd liked the call anyway. "Gee I'd love to see you. It's been too damn long. I could kick myself for being nasty out here." It seemed his resistance had dissolved. "I want to see you more now than ever before——during last summer, or before you came out, or any time ever. Maybe I'm crazy, but I don't think so——oh derrrrrr."

Would she please send him a picture?

After the phone call Jenny tossed and turned *for hours——for the pure +simple reason that for the first time in my life, I really wanted someone in bed with me,* she wrote. He was having romantic fantasies, visualizing her on the North Shore. "There's a full moon caught in the branches——can you see it shining over the lake by the old ice house? Or are you coming along the shore, to catch it whitening over the swamp land and glistening on the harbor beyond?" He didn't hear from her, so he wrote asking if his candor had surprised her.

Her reply was harsh. *Of course I wasn't shocked by the post phone letter, It's high time you started slinging a little crap like that. Everyone else does.* She went on to tell him of a new crush, French, *brown eyed, blond, cunning*——whom she'd met on the ferry to Nantucket. If she was joking or if residual anger bled through her humor, Paul didn't get it. He had found his way back to her, and she'd blasted all his faith, had become, he wrote, "a completely different person, a rather cheap, snippy, selfish, superficial, son of a bitch." He had written her another romantic letter, he added, which he tore up. He waited for her reply; he would not write or call, he was too angry, suffering "the cold impersonal feeling that comes with anger——and the loneliness."

On the day he finally wrote back, Jenny had a date with Senny, at the Singing Beach Club let's say, where Senny had taken her when she was their very young governess and she and Margie were little. It was a wide beach on a small bay encircled with big rambling seashore houses where many of the families they knew summered, coming up from Boston town-houses on Commonwealth Avenue or Beacon Street, or sometimes, like the Moores, from New York. I first saw Singing Beach with Senny when I was six, when practically nothing had changed since my mother's child-hood. Fifty years later, when I stood there with a Bostonian in her eight-ies, she identified each house—renovated now and marking a new social order—by naming the family who'd lived there "before the war."

My mother and Senny sat at a small table beneath the awning on the terrace, each dressed in light summer colors. The club itself was clap-board, not terribly big, with no pretensions—something like a neighbor-hood café where everyone knows your name and the person who serves you, Boston Irish, knows what kind of sandwich you like, or if you want today's crab salad. Knows also what you drink on a hot day: gin and tonic, a beer, or maybe just iced tea, please, that came with lemon and a fresh sprig of mint grown right there, beneath and between the hydrangeas.

Jenny wants to know about her teacher John, Senny's brother, whom she hadn't seen since he'd been overseas in the Navy. He was back now, but "drinking heavily," Senny said. "There's one in every family," they agree, someone who won't stop drinking. It's so reassuring to be with Senny, the closest she has to a mother—someone she'd emulate, she thought, when she had children. Senny, now almost forty and teaching public school, was so comforting in her attention and lack of judgment that Jenny could be honest about Margarett, need offer only a familiar detail like an empty gin bottle in a riding boot and they'd both laugh. With Senny, Jenny can admit she hardly ever misses the family when she's away at Barnard: *I thought it so wrong I told God about it.* She's told Senny all about confession and confirmation. *I really wish that I loved Mama and then maybe I could help. I have no respect therefore I cannot love her.* I imag-ine Jenny leaning across the table as she says this—all of which she also wrote to Paul—looking into Senny's hazel eyes. *How can I be a Christian and feel about Mama the way I do?*

Of course Senny had heard "talk" about Jenny and Paul Moore, chiefly from the redoubtable and perfectly named Mabel Story, who was certain they'd soon be engaged, what with the visit to Seattle, the letters thick and fast, of which she'd heard from Fanny Moore and Shaw McKean, from Paul's sister Polly, even from Margarett. Jenny and Senny both laughed at what Mabel had said about Paul the last time Jenny saw her: "Dizzy—he's such a *catch*." Jenny found her attitude shocking—*I always feel like saying 'there's a slight item called L-O-V-E' involved.'* Mabel was ninety-two the last time I saw her and could barely speak, but her almost black eyes still had a conspiratorial flash, and her big mouth still turned up at either end in a Cheshire cat grin. How much Jenny then knew of the "catch" aspect of Paul Moore, I do not know. Paul's grandfather William H. "Judge" Moore and his brother Hobart had made fortunes in the Gilded Age. "Judge"—a nickname, not a profession—Moore left Chicago for New York in 1903, purchased an unfinished Stanford White house on East 54th Street and continued—with his brother—purchasing small companies to make larger ones like American Can and U.S. Steel; one of those companies. Nabisco, was comprised of small independent bakeries that survive in the names of its cookies—Lorna Doone, Oreo, and the like. When William H. Moore died in 1926, his estate was worth $2.5 billion in 2015 dollars and, with Republic Aviation, which started in 1939 and extended through the war, my father's father made millions by manufacturing airplanes. Mabel Story, then, was correct—Paul Moore was "such a catch."

6.

Right then Jenny wasn't concerned about Paul's money; she was appalled at herself for her "slinging crap" remark. She'd been trying to be *less sensitive*, she wrote Paul, trying out *hardboiledness* learned at her mother's knee, and not quite confident of him after her Seattle hurt. But now she felt deflated. She wrote her first apology on a long narrow card, like a poem:

I wish you were
home now. I really am

sorry . . . I'm not
trying to butter you
up. Please call up so
I can apologize again.
I wish we were to-
gether now, I mean it.

She was in Boston, staying in Grandma's rented house in Louisburg Square, when she decided that even though she was nervous, she would call him. On the back of the telephone book, she made notes about what to say. She even jotted what endearment to use.

When they heard each other's voices, everything was immediately all right.

"Funny," he wrote after the call, "that a lone sentence"—hers about slinging crap—"could toss out hours + days of talk + companionship."

I really have a heart though you may have wondered about its existence, Jenny replied. She couldn't get over hearing his voice forgive her. *And though I tried to apologize, what I really meant to put over was that although my charming remark didn't connote it, I hope to get many more letters like the one you wrote.* It was time to start with a clean slate. *They'd seen each other at their very worst.*

She was barely in the door in New York when the telephone rang. It was Cord, whom she hadn't seen since he was wounded. *We went out immediately and had 88 drinks at 21 from 330 till 7 when he had to dine with old maid aunt. He had the jitters, a kind of post-wound anxiety, which reminded me of you the night we all went to the Copa and everything started.* But, she reported, *He is still the same, so charming and so Cord, even with a black patch, no teeth on one side and the fuse of the grenade in his cheek and a bad neck scar, I thought he was beautiful.*

The martinis kept her awake most of the night drinking water, but in the morning she was up at Barnard arranging her schedule—Blake to Byron because it will be so *divinely relaxing*; her final International Relations seminar; Religion + Contemporary Social Issues *with my lovely Mrs. Niebuhr*; and a graduate history course, Europe 1914–1944.

A lover's schedule, she wrote Paul: she had no classes on Mondays.

He'd asked for a picture, and she sent two. He immediately removed his goddaughter and his dear friend Seth French from their frames and replaced both with her. Having her pictures on the bedside table was "naughty, naughty," he wrote, "like "going to bed together." When Lois Stretton arrived to pick him up for a dinner date, she made faces at them, but he distracted her by showing her photos of the house at Hollow Hill. "I must be out with a rich man," she said.

In New York that very night, Jenny wrote to ask if he'd entirely lost his faith in her.

"It's coming back," he quickly replied. "Let's bury our hatchets, pull in our cat-like nails, and not misunderstand anymore." The night she got that letter, she was pulled from sleep at 5 a.m. A call he'd put in before supper had finally come through. It was 2 a.m. in Seattle. His voice. All, finally, was forgiven.

No one had yet heard from Hickox or Cord Meyer's twin brother Quentin, and John LeBoutillier—another Yale classmate—a fighter pilot during the attack on the Marianas in July, was officially missing. Paul started packing for home, even though he wouldn't be leaving for a month. Almost every two or three days, he wrote Jenny: "I get a sort of a third hand remark, or a casual smile, or a call from a parent that seems to add up to the fact that the guys here, the Marines, have some use for me (I wouldn't write this to anyone but you.)." In New York, Cord, now convinced she and Paul were certain to marry, refused to take Jenny out, even for supper. *We're not even engaged!* she protested to Paul. Would he drop Cord a line giving permission?

Paul dreamed he got wounded in a banzai charge by a "Jap" grenade and booked himself

"on the bird for 1 Nov."

If he got to New York by November 2, a Thursday, he'd go straight to Hollow Hill and the family. Could she come out there on Saturday? If not, he'd come into town and they could take the train, spend Sunday and Monday, and maybe they'd go out there a couple of times during the week, and then a weekend house party with Cord, George Cheston, and maybe the Dennys?

"Wouldn't it be hideous if something happened," he wrote, "and I didn't get any leave?"

The final letter to Seattle I have of Jenny's is dated September 24; later ones are lost, but I have Paul's replies: continued plans for his return, the house party, the flight home. "Your letter was awful nice, Jen. Don't fight any feelings. I'd hate to admit how eager I am about getting to see you. Gee whiz, if we can't be as attractive to each other on the spot as we are in our letters, to hell with it!"

My father loved to tell the story of flying back, which sounded like a wartime song: Over Idaho, yes, I'll marry her. Over Minnesota, no. Over Illinois, yes. The plane landed in New York on November 2, and he immediately telephoned. They met at Fefe's Monte Carlo; and very late in the evening, he proposed, so drunk by then Jenny didn't believe him. She hadn't seen him in eight months. Would he call in the morning so she could be sure? That he did not do, so she was on pins and needles the entire day. He always said he forgot because the family had asked that he be with his sister Fanny at the New York apartment when she got the news of her husband Jock's death, but Fanny was in Santa Barbara and John Denison had died two years earlier, so my father misremembered.

He did remember he'd proposed, however, and in a happy daze, he took the train to Hollow Hill as my mother sat in class at Barnard, unable to concentrate. Back at the apartment she was sharing with her sister Margie, she waited by the telephone; an undertow of past disappointment was tugging, but Margie reassured her. Before supper at Hollow Hill, Paul got up his nerve to tell his father, trembling as he blurted out the news; Paul Sr. mentioned the mental illness in Jenny's family, but he didn't object to the match, and Fanny adored Jenny McKean—of course we'll have a house party on the weekend!

He finally did call Jenny. How could she have been so silly as to disbelieve him?

The house-party guests were not told the news, Paul and Jenny "feigned indifference," Babs Denny later commented. After the guests left, Paul telephoned Shaw McKean to ask for Jenny's hand, and they were able to celebrate with his parents.

Back in New York on Tuesday, Jenny wrote Joe Walker the difficult letter. She felt so *guilty*, she really hadn't meant to mislead him: she was a terrible person, he must find her *confusing*. His ship was prowling near the Philippine island of Leyte, so the letter would not reach him until he returned to Pearl Harbor three weeks later, on the day of her wedding. An engagement notice appeared in Boston and New York papers on Saturday, November 11, dateline November 10, the night Grandma Haughton gave them a dinner in Boston. In the photo that accompanied the announcement, Jenny's wearing a dark sweater, her Raven Red lipstick.

As all her friends had on marrying, she would withdraw from college— a letter to Barnard, special notes to Mrs. Del Rio, her Spanish teacher of two years, and to her religion teacher Ursula Neibuhr, inviting each to the wedding. On Saturday afternoon, she and Paul sat down with her parents at the Copley Plaza where they were living that winter and talked about the guest list; Papa was giving the reception at the Cosmopolitan Club.

For the Boston dinner, Paul sent Jenny a gold dress he'd bought her in New York, which arrived by Railway Express—in a large Bendel's box. She unpacked it, thrilled. She was staying at Louisburg Square with Grandma Haughton, who was busy ordering Jenny linens from Maison de Blanc, showing her alternative designs for her emblem of triumph, her monogram—Jenny would choose the design that compressed *JMcKM* into a diamond shape. Did Mrs. Haughton even see the gold dress before declaring her disapproval? She considered the gesture vulgar, New York money colliding with Boston prudence—buying a dress for your fiancée was too close to—? Jenny couldn't begin to imagine what! She had gone to college, voted for Roosevelt, was welcoming the progressive attitudes about race and politics she was learning at Barnard. Now she must stand her ground on glamor and sensuality, a front on which her mother had fought old Boston her entire adult life.

Her father intervened with his mother, and Jenny wore the dress. The triumphant engagement dinner was at the Somerset Club and the guests were both families and friends, whoever was in Boston. Wartime train disruptions kept many away, and wartime haste produced a mimeographed menu: canapés Muscovite, oysters, consommé Madriléne, smelts split and grilled, sliced cucumbers, Suprême of guinea chicken, string beans, and Delmonico potatoes. For dessert there was ice cream and cake, and late that night Paul returned to Quantico to be back at work Monday morning.

In the mail at her apartment, along with confirmation of her withdrawal from Barnard, a delicious letter from Paul awaited Jenny: "This is the first time ever on paper, I'm able to relax completely and tell you how I've missed you, how I love you and how I've missed you + loved you over the last 9 months, and so, my darling, we can pray that we always will wish to talk this way." Before she crashed to sleep, my mother wrote back: *Your wonderful letter was AMBROOOSIA after a hideous day in the pouring rain.*

I love her happiness in getting a letter from him in which *no one feels frustrated and there is nothing lacking.* Her innocent pleasure is so contagious, I let myself feel it. *I get more excited every day about being with you always, and I want you to promise not to feel at all that I'm lonely and unentertained in Quantico because being able to make you even half happy would make me completely so.* His grandmother's ring had been cleaned and resized; he'd so wanted to present it in person. "Oh darling, we've missed so much of the little fun things of getting married." In the end he sent it and she got him on the phone, exclaimed as he listened to her open it, put it on her own finger, a diamond so big it spent the Jersey City years in a safe deposit box. I never saw her wear more than a wedding band until we moved to Indianapolis.

At supper clubs and over lunch, the news of "Paul and Jenny" again contracted into one name was gossiped about and celebrated. The time between announcement and event—just a day over two weeks—was so short they improvised invitations: Telegrams were sent, telephone calls made, and Jenny, Margie and Papa, Margarett, and even Fanny Moore handwrote notes inviting friends and relatives. Some invitations were delivered in person, to friends they ran into on the street. "Paul and Jenny are getting married on Sunday and you *have* to come." Because Paul could not get special leave, he'd return the night before the wedding; no time for premarital counseling, so Father Wadhams wrote them each a letter. He would marry them at the Church of Resurrection on East 74th Street at noon on Sunday, the 26th of November.

My mother wore her grandmother Jenny Sargent's wedding dress, which she brought down from Boston. On Monday she had a first fitting at Bergdorf's—some of the lace reattached, the waist taken in a little. Léon, the tailor, suggested a new veil; the original, he insisted, was terribly out of date.

They would live together in Virginia while Paul was in Quantico. A friend of Fanny Moore's had found them a place in Fredericksburg: an outbuilding on the plantation that had belonged to George Washington's brother—"the uncle of our country," Jenny wrote Paul after he sent her the floor plan he'd penciled, along with his sketch of the tiny white clapboard house. After the ceremony, they'd fly to Washington. Mother Fan had arranged a driver to take them to a hotel in Fredericksburg for their wedding night; the back of a car is *much the best place to "twosy" in,* she told Jenny. *She's so cute, she kills me,* Jenny wrote Paul.

On Friday afternoon, Jenny had the final fitting of the wedding dress and saw the new veil for the first time. Léon, she decided, had been absolutely right.

Margarett would come to the wedding, but she was absent from the plans—*in terrible shape.* Shaw was the parent who sprang into action, *racing around* making arrangements; his penciled list Jenny captioned *Papa's efficiency:* "Flowers in church? Wedding cake? Jenny to choose. Music for reception. Automobiles—3 cars for 11 o'clock. Bride's table, roughly how many vases? Flowers on table? Awning at club?" Rain was predicted.

Jenny still had not heard from Joe Walker. Did she think about him? Did she have any idea that his reply, when it finally arrived, would be the very model of magnanimity? In fact, her apology lay unread in a bag of "9000 letters" to be delivered when his ship returned to shore on the day of her wedding.

The rehearsal dinner was Saturday night at the River Club, right on the water at East 52d Street. Paul arrived to tumultuous applause at about nine and at once took Jenny's hand for a dance—seven months later, at another rehearsal dinner in *the very same rooms,* that ecstatic night would come racing back when the groom took Jenny's hand and led her in a dance to the "Marine's Hymn."

Margie would be Jenny's only "attendant," as Jenny had been at her wedding three years earlier. Among Paul's ushers would be Cord Meyer with a black patch over one eye, George Denny, Seth French, and Shaw McKean—Harry was in Europe with General Patton. The best man was Paul's brother Bill, whose daughter Pam, Paul's goddaughter, would be the flower girl.

After the party, Paul and Jenny and Margie and George Thomson wandered out to a Beefburger and had martinis and late-night hamburgers with thick slices of onion; the girls got home at 2 a.m., "wasted" as one would now say. The weather had already turned cold. In the morning both sisters woke with terrible hangovers. Even gobbling last-minute parsley that Margie cadged from a Madison Avenue delicatessen didn't clear their breaths, which had the "smell of a monkey cage," as Margie put it.

Bergdorf's delivered the dress to a room at the Cosmopolitan Club on East 66th Street, where the guests would dance and dine in the ballroom after the ceremony: Margie and the Aldrich girls, Sylvia, and Paul's sister Polly gathered in a bedroom to dress the bride, whom the photographer caught in giggles, hands on her hips in a hula pose in her lace-trimmed satin underblouse and flared briefs. Anna de Schott, Margarett's New York maid when she was a young woman, made sure the bride was downstairs just in time; and in a black chauffeured car, Papa picked her up, and they drove the eight blocks. I see her father behind her as she steps out of the car onto East 74th Street. Her snowy veil, lilies and clematis bouquet in one hand, her hair glossy in the light; with white-gloved hands, she lifts her skirts from the damp pavement.

The nuptial mass took more than an hour—for years friends joked about the length and solemnity of the service, and Margie, though she always said the whole day was "just lovely," remembered that her hangover held on. "I could hardly lift my head," she said, "nor could your mother. There we were, thumping up and down on our knees." In the union of the young people he had counseled and was now pronouncing man and wife, Father Wadhams, a celibate, found the expression of a postwar ideal.

"I shall never forget what it was to turn about, look down on you two kneeling there," he wrote them later, "two persons, of a mind about things that matter, penitents, disciplined communicants, willing in the presence of 'this company' to witness to their faith in 'the means of grace and the hope of glory.' " Years later, when trouble arose in their marriage, my parents both spoke of Father Wadhams, how he had inspired them, how sad they were to have to tell him they had failed him.

But that was decades on. From the look of the wedding photographs, it seems bridal adrenalin quickly burned away Jenny's hangover. In the shot for the papers, my mother's smile is blinding. In the ballroom they sit at a table with Polly and Bill, Margie and Shaw, Papa and Bill's wife Mouse, others I see only from the back. At a table to one side, Margarett, dressed in black, sits with a group of her friends; Jenny did not want to risk disruption at the head table.

After an hour of dancing, the newlyweds cut the cake with Paul's Marine sword, fed each other a white-frosted square—there is a photograph. But in my favorite photograph of my just-married parents, taken after the service in back of the car, they are suddenly the grown-up magical royalty of my childhood: my mother, bridal lace and tulle crushed against the gray velvet interior; my father in his Marine cap and blues, his medal ribbons making a pattern on his pocket. Surely my mother is more radiant than any storybook princess, my father taller and more handsome than any prince. Will I be as beautiful a bride as my mother? I wondered, looking up at the picture again and again when I was a little girl? And would I find a husband as strong and brave as my father?

In my favorite photograph of my mother by herself, she'd been turning to a girlfriend, the smile on her face, a grin of utter dizzy mischief.

She finally got Joe Walker's letter. He dismissed her apology and guilt. Hadn't they worked hard to banish her constant insistence that she was "hideous"? He was paying homage to her insecurity right now, wishing it a fond farewell. She must know she had made the right choice. "Now, Muffin, I'm not going to pretend I didn't love you no little (ghastly English) but I think we both agreed that my interest in the third economic conference of the Baltic states would never exactly fascinate you and surely you can't forget that sort of hunted glassy stare of mine that used to appear when you mentioned the church. As you once so aptly stated 'Don't' you think there's just a little something missing?' " He was as courtly as could be, and she was reassured. They would see each other at weddings and funerals, the odd cocktail party, and their lives would reconnect almost thirty years later.

In a photograph taken as the newlyweds leave the church, so thick are the well-wishers that all you see clearly as they run for the car is a spray of thrown rice illuminated in a camera flash. "She looks so beautiful, so strong," said a friend to whom I showed the photographs. How young they are, I say now, and how clearly just married. On the plane they try to look dignified, but they keep their secret only until my father takes off his Marine cap, rice spills down the front of his dress blues, and everyone in the cabin breaks into applause.

IV

Size of a Coconut

1.

"TELL US ABOUT YOUR HONEYMOON," WE SAY—FOUR OR FIVE OF US
still little—and my father makes it a story: carrying "Mommy" up the
stairs in the small house, the two of them laughing, and he tosses her onto
the bed. And the bed "collapsed"! I hear the crack of the old spool bed,
see Jenny on the mattress on the floor, their laughter turned to hilarity.

There were other stories to tell about the little frame house *surrounded
by ploughed fields and red clay roads:* its history as a plantation slave quarters, its small rooms, the yard planted with raggedy evergreens patrolled

by a flock of guinea hens and seven cats they named for their friends' mothers—Mrs. Aldrich because her daughter Liberty came to visit, Mrs. Bradlee, Mrs. Seyburn, Mrs. Meyer because of Cord, Mrs. McVeigh because Quigg is there more than anyone. Composing these months, I see them on weekends, riding a bicycle built for two—they actually had one—and taking walks. I like a letter from Margarett wishing them well "on the move to the box planting & wizardry of Virginia landscape." The property has seen better days; if there are boxwoods, they are not pruned, and the house has the smell of November dampness, its few rooms heated only by a woodstove downstairs. It was an outbuilding on the plantation called Beauclair, which once belonged to George Washington's brother— I can hear her voice describe the house as "a little beat up."

When they'd left Beauclair and Paul was back in the Pacific on Guam and Jenny in Prides for the summer, she missed their *little F-burg* house, cleaning and cooking in the morning, waiting all afternoon until he came home—reading, writing thank-you notes for wedding presents, sorting letters and photographs, learning needlepoint, eventually beginning to stitch a large landscape of the house, the cats standing like sentries in the front yard. Her copy of *The Joy of Cooking* was already stained and worn when I was ten—it was how she learned to cook, she said. She didn't know how to clean either, expressed embarrassment to Sylvia that despite her idealism, her sense of not wanting the servants of a *prewar* life, she'd hired a maid named Miss Annie.

A taste for solitude is learned, and my mother was still a novice. She thought that marriage meant the end of loneliness, so when she felt anything but happy, she panicked that she'd end up like her mother, half the day in bed in a dark room. She called even an ordinary dip in mood *my depression*, and she'd developed remedies: a good sleep, diving into her studies, going out. But she wasn't in college now, and there was no night life in Fredericksburg. A contemporary woman might have considered staying in New York or going back to Barnard in January, but travel wasn't efficient, and that wasn't what anyone did; anyway, she and Paul had been apart enough. Married or not, she was learning, alone was alone, and she had no car. Did Miss Annie come every day? There must have been a telephone. *I want you to promise not to feel that I'm lonely and unentertained when you're at Quantico,* she'd written Paul, but sometimes when he got home she was angry with him; she'd try to hide it but from time to time she'd explode—out of nowhere, it seemed to him—apologizing the next day for being *so difficult.* As if a normal human feeling were proof that what she and Joe had dubbed her "hideousness" was a permanent condition. When she got that way, she'd think of how easily Joe teased her out of a bad mood. Had she rushed into marriage? *And then Paul came back East before going overseas, and I somehow felt I couldn't* not *marry him,* she would write thirty years later for me to find slipped between pages of unfinished memoir. Had she chosen the wrong man? Couldn't even think that way, she'd conclude, waiting for him to come home.

Waiting all day. What she was actually waiting for was the end of the war. An entire generation was, even as they made plans for a new world. Sometimes she forgot what she believed, *that all of us, who are the so-called rebuilders, will do that thing, after the war, that appears the hardest.* She understood what that meant, but she also recognized the contradictions Paul would face as a veteran going into the church—*sort of queer to try to stay ready psychologically to fight some more + try at the same time to prepare for the Church. Galahad*—the knight of King Arthur who found the Holy Grail—*must have been extraordinary.*

But wasn't it as time-honored for a woman to make a home for a husband at war as it was for a man to fight or become a priest? Perhaps, but it felt insufficient to a young woman as educated as Jenny was—a whole generation of "overeducated" women, Mary McCarthy bitterly remarked. As inadequate as my mother's lack of domestic skill made her feel, I'm sure she knew that burning the macaroni or undercooking a chicken was not a moral or spiritual failing. And anyway, she would finish college. But after that, what for her would be *that thing that appears hardest?* She had many ideas and none. She and Paul didn't need one salary, let alone two—she wanted to do something real, something to help the recovery after the war. What could she venture within the constraints of a married woman's life?

Some time toward the end of the war, photographs of women and children who were clearly European and under duress begin to appear in her scrapbooks among the wedding photographs, clippings, thank-you notes, and birth notices. There was a correspondence with a family in Austria. She sent clothes and chocolate, writing paper and tissue, socks and mittens, and asked, with Boston courtesy, what else they might need, how the little girl was, the little boy.

Their needs were so much simpler than those of her own family.

Within days of her wedding, perhaps even brought on by it, her mother fell into a paralyzing depression. This time Papa acted decisively, and early that December Margarett voluntarily entered Four Winds, a sanitarium in Katonah, New York. Jenny had once mentioned to Paul that the family was contemplating *the hospital idea* for Margarett, but never in her 1945 letters does she mention her mother's first hospitalization. Margarett had been at the wedding, nervous; I remember photographs, enameled fingernails against a white cheek, her dark lipstick. Four Winds offered shock treatment, and Margarett began a course immediately. They are "undoubtedly efficient, but extremely disagreeable," she wrote my grandfather after the first series. The headaches were brutal, but eventually the depression lifted. *She remembered nothing of the wedding!* my mother, outraged, told me when I was about twelve; then, suddenly aware of her lack of compassion, she summoned a mother's calm, explaining carefully that short-term memory loss can be a side effect of electroshock.

She had a letter from her brother Harry about the wedding: soon to be promoted to sergeant, he was still in London, with Patton's Third Army. Just twenty, he'd launched a grand social life—supper at the Fountain House with his father's cousin Pauline Fenno and her friend, "Lady Reading, Grand Dame Commander of the British Empire," whom he found "perfectly wonderful." And the girls who joined them! "After quick reconnaissance, I picked the one I wanted," he wrote; "Molly Mills, the daughter of Lord and Lady Millingdon." As for the wedding, at the exact moment Papa walked Jenny down the aisle, Harry was cleaning his colonel's latrine. Six weeks later the division embarked for the Ardennes, where Harry fought in the Battle of the Bulge and survived. It was the bloodiest engagement of the European war: 19,000 American lives, 47,000 wounded, 15,000 captured. After victory, Patton and his fighters pushed east to Vienna and beyond. Harry had heard rumors that the war in Europe might end in early November, but the unexpected strength of the Germans in the Ardennes erased that optimism—fighting might continue for eighteen months, even two years.

As the weeks in Fredericksburg passed, there were visitors. Jenny's friend Sylvia and her husband Sandy came over from Norfolk; Mother Fan stayed a few days and took Jenny antiquing; and Richard Wood spent a night. Paul had met him in Washington; his father was Lord Halifax, the former British prime minister and sometime supporter of appeasement. Richard had lost both legs when fighting in North Africa, where his older brother had been killed. Now Halifax was ambassador to Washington, and Richard was traveling from city to city, stopping at hospitals to encourage American wounded. He was a warm and charismatic man, as I remember him, the effect of his prosthetic legs giving his walk a kind of heroic excitement.

With Margie in New York, Harry in Europe, Margarett at Four Winds, and oil rationing in force, Prides was again closed for the winter. Jenny invited Papa and young Shaw down to Fredericksburg for Christmas and the first holiday meal she had ever cooked. Whether she made turkey with stuffing or roast beef with Yorkshire pudding, I don't know; but there were sweet potatoes, which suggests turkey. Paul gave her a porcelain cup with a forget-me-not pattern, which became her favorite thing. In January, on a few days leave, they visited Paul's parents in Palm Beach, and Paul—"shaking," he wrote his sister Fanny—had a conversation with his father about his future.

He was going to divinity school, he announced, sooner rather than later; and no, he would not first take a year in business. He was considering General Seminary in New York City, High Church like he was; it was located "downtown" in Chelsea, at the time a poor, mostly Puerto Rican neighborhood. And what after that? He'd had hints he might be a candidate for the headmastership of St. Paul's School; because of his work with young Marines in Seattle, he'd be ideal. *I wonder why I hate the idea so much?* Jenny wrote. She wanted him to do postgraduate work at Oxford, which meant she could study too.

In February Paul was transferred. They left Fredericksburg for New Rivers in South Carolina, where they lived for a month as Paul trained officers for the coming invasion of Japan. In early April his post was completed and they drove north, stopping in hotels along the way and spending a night at Hollow Hill. Before they left for San Francisco and Paul's leave, they had a few days in New York: *We'll be at 825*, I can hear my mother say—it was the nickname for the Moores' Fifth Avenue apartment. There was a drunken party starring their old friend Quigg McVeigh, supper with Cord and his fiancée, Mary Pinchot, who'd been two years ahead of Jenny at Vassar. Jenny and Paul, leaving in days for Paul's point of embarkation in California, would miss Cord and Mary's wedding three weeks later, the nuptials performed by Reinhold Niebuhr.

Cord's short story "Waves of Darkness," about losing his eye and his sight in battle—was published in the *Atlantic* (later collected the *O. Henry Memorial Award Prize Stories* of 1946) and widely read, and he'd been chosen one of two "American wounded" to attend the San Francisco conference that would form the United Nations. He passionately believed in creating new institutions to prevent war, while Paul argued for change by means of spiritual transformation within the individual, certain there was "no permanent value in building more and more economic, diplomatic, social and political cages for the lion or human beast—you can't tame a fighting lion." The task for Christians, he believed, was to "think & pray like hell so that God can someday enter the lion's heart."

Cord had given up on the church, even threatened to move to Russia, which Jenny and Paul thought a "ridiculous" idea. Such divergence in belief was not unique to these two war heroes and would surface again in disagreements they had in the 1960s about the war in Vietnam, but that night the spirit was agreement that change was crucial to the survival of the world and that everyone had a role. Such discussions would become increasingly fervent as the end of the war drew closer.

Jenny liked Mary—beautiful, blond, already a journalist—and was very happy that after all his suffering, wonderful and mysterious Cord had fallen in love. And she loved their evening together—the application of real ideas to their lives. Wherever they lived, she and Paul decided, they'd have a salon, evenings for conversation as interesting and consequential as that night. This was how she would keep herself alive; this was part of being with Paul. To be married, they both believed, was to make *something*. Even before they were engaged, Jenny had written him that for her *the wild, abandoning kind of love was dead; the right kind* she imagined, *must be more passive, secure and less doubting*. Paul replied that marriage was "a hell of a lot of hard work," and that a "blind way to happiness" was "not the stuff of which marriage is made."

Not mentioned that evening was that, along with their spirited love, something else was beginning, something they weren't yet telling anyone.

Jenny was pregnant.

"It was probably too early in our marriage," my father said decades later, "but we wanted a piece of me to survive if I didn't come back from Japan."

2.

It must have been morning when they got to California, because some time that first day, they had the energy to go shopping at Gump's, the legendary San Francisco department store, where Jenny chose *an ensemble*—maternity clothes? Yes, of course, they'd return for a fitting tomorrow afternoon.

She was almost three months pregnant, though not yet showing, and they had new intimate names for each other. She had been Jen, J, sometimes even Gladys, and he Ralphie or P or Paulo. Now they'd abandoned irony—were "Mummee" and "Daddee," the number of *e*'s when written a measure of the moment's heat. I find the names and the little drama they make of them unnerving, too much, like candy that's too sweet. Is the fierce sardonic girl losing her edge? I'm relieved when she flirts, calling her husband's underwear his "skivvies," noting his "heaven legs." And the Fairmont Hotel penthouse does accentuate the Hollywood of things. The 1945 Academy Award for Best Picture had just gone to the highest-grossing movie that year: *Going My Way*, a sunny musical about a Catholic parish, won out over *Gaslight* and *Double Indemnity*, movies that engaged the idea that women were weak or had the wrong kind of strength. Apparently the culture, or those who made movies, preferred the lighthearted, seeing Bing Crosby sing his way through the tale of a new priest succeeding an old pastor at a city church, suggesting the change in the air would be painless. Crosby also won best actor, and Ingrid Bergman took the prize for *Gaslight*, more than hinting that the woman who fought alongside Gary Cooper in *For Whom the Bell Tolls* could not survive emotionally if she was alone.

Jenny had never been to California. The war crowded San Francisco with sailors and soldiers, the city with its halogen sunshine and easy bustle made her feel free. She was thrilled with the prospect of the coming week when *Mummeee* and *Daddee* would be newlyweds again, forgetting the war to have a real honeymoon. Looking out at a dizzying view, she lolled in bed as Paul put on his uniform—just a quick trip across the bridge to Oakland to dump his duffel and receive orders, and he'd be back for lunch, the Gump's fitting, and shopping in Chinatown for his sister Fanny's little boys, whom they'd see in Santa Barbara in a few days. Jenny loved having her in-the-flesh husband next to her, the frisson of being lovers, married and together all day long. She hadn't yet had morning sickness, so the pregnancy was almost unreal.

But Paul never got back to the Fairmont. He had just minutes to call and tell her he was flying out that afternoon, barely time to get to a florist, where he burst into tears when there were no red carnations (her favorite)—which was why, he wrote her, there was just one red bloom in that bower of pink. When the bouquet arrived she wept, and thinking he might be aboard when she heard the roar, raced to the window and waved at a military plane flying over the hotel—*My daddy was naugh-tee and went a-way.* At Gumps' that afternoon, she was fitted for the new suit, and in Chinatown she bought the presents. That night she moved to his side of the bed and nuzzled his smell, which was still on the sheets. He'd left some things behind, she wrote him—*a pamphlet called "Solution of Map Problems"*—if he wanted it, she'd send it along, *with Shakespeare and the Bible.*

The next day, on her way to Santa Barbara, writing a letter kept him present—the train south was *frightfully chic. There's a maid to take care of ladies and babies and a suave announcer who pointed out spots in the scenic panorama. My seat is next to a lady who works in SF and she's coming to see her daughter who runs a movie theatre.* Stepping from the train in Santa Barbara, seeing no one familiar, she waved, and immediately Paul's older sister Fanny, whom she'd never met, *rushed up* with the boys—*tan and thin and chic.* Jenny stayed three weeks, helped with the little boys when her sister-in-law went to work for the Red Cross. *I am a little scared of Fanny at the moment,* she wrote the first day, *but I have to go through that phase, as you know.* Soon though, they're having a *wonderful time,* gossiping about Mother Fan, about Mouse and Bill, and Jenny telling stories about the wedding—*cutting the cake, throwing the bouquet.* There were weekend luncheons, afternoons by the pool, cocktail parties, and Jenny got a sore throat—it felt as if she'd *swallowed a razor blade.* The sudden death of President Roosevelt—*so dramatic it would have been more typical of Churchill*—slips into the narrative like a mere social detail. She'd give *a good deal,* she wrote, to overhear their fathers talk about it. In Boston, Papa cracked open a bottle of good champagne.

Doctor Mullholland who lived next door soon cured the sore throat. He *plays the piano like a dream,—and this weekend is having a houseguest called Ramona and they are going to entertain us with constant duets.* Jenny has quite a tan, she boasts, and at one party, *shook hands with Ronnie Colman, my dear*—the British silent star turned American leading man. Richard Wood came through on his tour and gave two speeches at the hospital where Fanny worked—*spoke extraordinarily*—and exhausted from the hours with the wounded, came back with them for the night. *We had many scotch & sodas—Fanny adored him.* Jenny was now off to Los Angeles—she'd spend Wednesday night with Paul's Uncle Leonard in Beverly Hills and leave for New York on Thursday.

In conversation she might have called Leonard a "fairy," though with respect; I don't remember my father's unreconstructed term; he adored his charming uncle and somehow understood that Leonard's friend Winsor French, a Cleveland society writer, was what we would now call his partner. Mother Fan had her own version of her half-brother's life: Len was unmarried because he'd never recovered from the girl he was "so in love with" who "so tragically" died. Leonard was a Broadway and film investor, and it was he, when Paul was at Yale, who glamorously took him and his friend Potter to the set of *The Philadelphia Story* and introduced them to Katharine Hepburn, Jimmy Stewart, and Cary Grant.

I was a tiny girl the only time I met my great-uncle. My father took me to his apartment, which I remember as having been on Park Avenue. At the door, a quiet man in a dark suit—Winsor?—directed us to a bright living room; on the sofa, Uncle Leonard, an old man with a lively, curious face. The walls were ablaze with Impressionist paintings—I remember a mist of intense greens, pinks, and azure—and I later saw them at the Cleveland Museum, to which he left his collection. Fifty years later, I would recognize his apartment when the actor Tab Hunter described it in his memoir. I wrote asking Hunter if I was right: "I remember Len Hanna very well," he replied in an e-mail; "he has stayed in my mind all these years."

Leonard inherited vast fortunes from both his Hanna father and from his mother, Coralie Walker Hanna, whom my great-grandfather married when his first wife, Mother Fan's mother, died in childbirth. Work in the family company, Hanna Mining, and an early investment in National Cash Register as it became IBM brought him untold riches, which he directed after the war to philanthropy, especially in Cleveland: the museum, Hanna House a medical center, and Karamu House, the first African American theater in the United States. In his will, leaving $8 million, he directed that the money be distributed only when the institution in question did not discriminate by race.

But that was years ahead; now, in April 1945, Leonard is just back from England. There, through the Red Cross, he had set up a hundred "clubs" for American GIs—Norwich; Manchester: "Got in a week ago tonight," he wrote the family, then reported whom he'd seen—the actors Kay Francis, Emlyn Williams, the stage designer Oliver Messel. Cecil Beaton was out of town, and Bea Lillie was busy doing a play—and, of course, Noel (Coward). The Manchester club, his first, was a great success: "Christ-

mas night had several hundred of the men for turkey and mince pie dinner and then had a dance with girls from the British Women's services for
partners. . . . I finally caught up with Coca Cola at the last minute, which
saved the day. I think they drank 1500 bottles over the weekend. The next
day was Boxing day and we had a party for eighty needy children."

Wearing *white slacks, a sky blue silk shirt, moccasins, blue linen jacket &
gold identification bracelet,* Leonard arrived to pick up his new niece in a
black Buick convertible with red leather seats, *His rented house in Beverly
Hills is fantastic!* Jenny wrote to Paul: *The living room has French furniture
& then suddenly one corner is all Dorothy Draper Hampshire House-ish. The
drinking room is copied from the Mocambo Bar, mirrored walls with a gold
tarnish motif. His bedroom has an 8 by 8 bed with bronze carved cherubs on the
headboard and shocking pink walls. The mail box is a bird house—the owner
is married to a Mexican and is now trying to get rid of him in Nevada.* In a
crystal vase on the breakfast table was a giant magnolia blossom sent by
"Judy"—Leonard's friend Judith Anderson, late the villainess Mrs. Dan-
vers of *Rebecca*; her recent film, an Agatha Christie British import called
And Then There Were None. Jenny was disappointed to miss "Cole"—
Porter—Leonard's Yale roommate, with whom, by WASP coincidence,
her father had shared lodging their one year at Harvard Law School.

Len was true to his promise to show Jenny all the chic Hollywood
places. They dined at Mike Romanoff's on Rodeo Drive in Beverly Hills.
Jenny, now almost three months pregnant, was still keeping it secret.
"Mike Romanoff" was a Lithuanian-born con man, who variously presented himself as a cousin of the late Czar Nicholas and a great-nephew
of Prime Minister Gladstone. Now he'd achieved respectability—thus "a
traitor to his former self," ribbed *Life* magazine in a photo spread. The
large, airy restaurant was *the* place for movie society during wartime, so
of course Len went there, as did everyone else: Jenny's adored favorite
Gregory Peck, Margarett's sometime Paris friend Elsa Maxwell, Cedric
Hardwicke, and Van Johnson, who had four movies from MGM that year
including *Thirty Seconds over Tokyo* and *The White Cliffs of Dover*. Near
the bar sat Monty Woolley—*The Man Who Came to Dinner*—at "his
own table" reported *LIFE*, where he ate, drank, and wrote every night.

Bright-green and yellow wallpaper—at lunch you might see Romanoff himself, seated on a banquette between his two bulldogs, Mr. Confucius and Socrates—he ate "cold cuts," the dogs "cold scraps."

As she swept in on Leonard's arm, who should Jenny see but her childhood friend CZ Cochrane (later Guest) on the arm of Robert Benchley, a generation her senior—*they're having a "do"* Jenny informed Paul: *she looked ghastly and white but the same old CZ*—Benchley would be dead in seven months. At Leonard's table gathered Nancy Wiman (sometime actress), *an ex-Aquacade and her husband who is an ex-Field Service, ex British 8th . . . he was lovely looking—called me Daahaahling*; and then, just at the moment Monty Woolley, very drunk, staggered over and sat down, Jenny fainted and had to be helped to the ladies room. *I thought it was marvelous fainting in Romanoff's,* she wrote Paul, *and everyone thought it was simply darling that I was pregnant.*

After supper, on to Mocambo, decor and music à la south of the border and the walls lined with glass cages of living cockatoos, macaws, seagulls, pigeons, and parrots. They were joined there by the blonde model-turned-actress of the moment, Cobina Wright Jr.—*very beautiful & surprisingly normal & 7 months along,* and her mother, notorious for pushing Cobina's career, *dropping names like mad,* on her arm *a young Swiss banker worth 5 million*—the banker asked Jenny if her husband was learning the hula ("oola") in the Pacific: *I said you had lessons from 9–11 every morning.*

The next evening at seven, she left for home on the Super Chief—41 hours to Chicago, then on to New York. At the long stop in Pasadena, *reclining in a roomette,* she began a letter to Paul. At lunch she had her first bout of morning sickness, only to be rescued by one Mrs. Tiffany, a *friend of your mother's,* who provided soda crackers and mints; when her stomach calmed, she ate *heavenly steak.* At breakfast the Swedish movie star Signe Hasso did everyone's numerology: she *said you were the perfect homemaker.* In Chicago, Sylvia and Sandy Whitman met her train and took her to the Buttery for lunch, then she was on the 4:30 for New York. By the way, she wrote Paul, Sylvia thought that definitely, *I had a bump,* and now, Jenny wrote, she'd decided they should tell everyone: *If Monty Woolley knows, why not, my dear!* But no one was to be told the name until the baby was born, which would happen, it was predicted, on October 25. Until she went to Prides for the summer, Jenny would stay at 825 during the week as she looked for an apartment. On the weekends she'd be at Hollow Hill.

3.

When I was a little girl, the family, or parts of it, often spent weekends at Hollow Hill, which is the name my grandparents gave to the hundred-acre farm in New Jersey where they had lived since being married in the enormous and comfortable house they had built. I thought of Hollow Hill and the apartment at 825 Fifth Avenue as luxurious extensions of home. I even think I believed everyone's grandparents lived in enormous houses, and that Hollow Hill was big and beautiful because of how wonderful and dear Gami was—"Gami" was what we children called my father's mother.

My father and his siblings had grown up there, and "the place" as it was often called, was his mother's life. She raised Guernsey cows for their milk and steer for their meat, chickens for eggs and eating, beehives for honey,. There was an herb garden, and an enormous vegetable garden. Ducks with colorful feathers and shiny green heads swam in a pond, and horses for riding and driving inhabited a stable. My cousin Pam rode the chestnut gelding, whose name was Jackson, every day it seemed to me—around Hollow Hill and on the riding paths that crisscrossed the countryside all by herself—and she and Gami seemed to be special friends. I wanted to ride all the time like her, but I came to the farm on the weekends, and I was always with my brothers and sisters and Gagy, who had taken care of all of us as babies and now often filled in for my mother.

I remember seeing Pam once, out the window of Gami's bedroom. She was dressed in riding clothes, on Jackson, a very green lawn and forest stretching off behind her. If I'd had the language, I might have said Pam was an Amazon—whatever she was, I wanted to be that too. When I expressed this to my mother, she let it be known that she and my father considered Gami's relationship with Pam suspect; that left to her own devices, Gami might love me too much. What did that mean? I slowly learned, no detail provided, that Aunt Mouse and Uncle Bill thought that Gami had somehow stolen Pam. It didn't seem so bad to me, but from then on it was hard not to be wary of Gami's attention. She wasn't allowed to give me special presents—the others would be jealous—and once when she gave me a big doll, she had to take it back.

If Aunt Mouse and Uncle Bill didn't want Pam at Hollow Hill all the time, why didn't they move farther away than where they lived, two miles down the road? (The logic of a child.) Pam was blond and so beautiful and barely spoke to me; it all enhanced the magic of her special status. Late in life, when she was in her seventies and I in my sixties, she came to New York from Wyoming where she lived and we went to see *Warhorse,* a play about a horse during World War I and the little boy who loved him. I learned that night that she had always been painfully shy and would have spoken to me back then if only she'd had the nerve.

My mother seemed so at ease at Hollow Hill and with Gami and Gramps that when I was little I thought daughters-in-law became automatic family, even biologically, an idea supported by the extraordinary fact that my parents shared a blood type—O negative. My mother also frequently confided that Gami had been "the only mother I ever had," this in spite of what she and my father communicated: my mother often said Gami was a *desperate, poor thing;* fifty years later one might call her mother-in-law's neediness "an issue with boundaries." When she arrived at Hollow Hill as a new daughter-in-law, my mother heard the stories—such as when Bill got home from the war after a year away from his wife Mouse, he'd barely changed out of his uniform when Gami and Gramps appeared uninvited for cocktails and stayed three hours.

Jenny arrived "home" to Hollow Hill in April 1945, fourteen weeks pregnant with me. She wanted to be a good daughter-in-law, a project she started with a letter she wrote the morning after her wedding. That letter, written to both of Paul's parents, seems to have been a pledge to become a loving wife; it does not survive, but Fanny Moore's reply found its way into one of my cartons:

Dearest Jenny,

Your letter came and ever since I have been trying to get a moment to answer it. You touched our hearts with your expression of love for Paul and your determination to make him happy, as I am sure you will. No one is perfect in this world, and many are righteous because of never having had temptation. These are not the finest people to my way of thinking. . . . I had a very unhappy childhood and was brought up frightfully strictly & suffered a lot; my mother died when I was born, my unhappiness has made me cherish my home and the happiness I have had in my home. I don't now bemoan my youth, because I was fun-loving and had fun on the side; but because of so much unhappiness I can take things without a whimper & can bear disappointment & hard knocks. . . . I am afraid I am intolerant of some of my friends who spend so much time seeking pleasure and killing time and will have accomplished so little. Paul has a purpose in life, and embodies all my dreams of what a man should be. I am sure he will crusade for a better world and you will help him . . . I have had so many happy hours, days and months with Paul; he is the best companion I have ever had. . . . Perfection doesn't exist, but love is almost everything. If you build on that, you will be secure. Hitch your wagon to a star, keep your banner high.

"Keep your banner high" seems exactly in the spirit of the formality and exuberance of the woman I knew as Gami. I didn't really know her as an adult; by the time I was in my twenties and ready to have real conversations with her, she was in her eighties, close to the stroke that left her without speech. But the Gami I adored when I was little was in her sixties, and I remember her best wearing a pink crinkly velvet bed jacket, in bed answering her mail, her secretary Miss Reilly taking notes. It was Miss

Reilly, always dressed in a handsome gray suit, who dispatched presents, checks to charities; bouquets of delphiniums and daisies and phlox from Hollow Hill's gardens and greenhouses to people on "the place," "at the hospital," or friends; vegetables from the garden and Guernsey milk and butter to those in need—a list that later came to include "young Paul" and his family in Jersey City.

I saw the serious part of Gami only in church; at home she loved to laugh, read aloud to us, drive us along bridle paths or around the place in a pony cart. Later when we were teenagers and doing "the twist," she disapproved only because it seemed so purposeless compared to the waltz: "The way you children dance, not touching, I just don't understand it!" She became positively gleeful when she told us how she knocked an admirer to the ground in the receiving line of a Cleveland wedding— he'd kissed her unbidden. By the time she was Gami, her hair was white, rinsed a tiny bit blue. In cool weather, she dressed in tweed suits with a blouse—she called a blouse a "waist." In hot weather, she wore flowered dresses to mid-calf and old-fashioned high heels, the kind that tied up. She wore "a scent" and expressed her love of the color and fragrance of lavender by extending its first syllable—laaaavender—and the furniture in her bedroom was lilac-patterned chintz. In art and decor, she had flexibility in taste; she loved antiques and also appreciated what was "modern," but neither at the expense of comfort.

She was always ready, it seemed, to take us for "a drive" in her black Buick convertible, which had red leather upholstery and, because she raised dalmatians, a chrome one on the hood. She'd whip along the narrow curved roads, taking us everywhere: to "the Dodge place," where there was later a poetry festival; or to visit my father's governess Jean Watson, who lived in a small house near the vegetable garden; or to "our new hospital," whose foundation had just been laid. I was less interested in the construction site of the Morristown Memorial Hospital (for which she and Gramps had "given the land") than in another of Gami's projects. The Tempe Wick House had been the home of a little girl during the American Revolution. She'd refused to give her horse when British soldiers ordered her to, galloped away and warned "our boys" that the "redcoats" were coming, and successfully hid the horse in her bedroom. "We" gave the spinning wheel, Gami said as we stood in the tiny house, furnished "as it was then."

The house at Hollow Hill was enormous but also filled with light and color. From its many windows there were pastoral vistas out of eighteenth-century British landscape painting. It was easy to make herself at home there, and Jenny did so, dining every evening with "Mother Fan" and her father-in-law, whose family nickname then was "Sudden" for reasons I have been unable to discover. With *Sudden,* who still went to his office "in town," she ventured into New York on the train and stayed at 825 for the days she'd search for an apartment, purchase things for the baby, see old friends. Otherwise she basked, still in early pregnancy, relishing Hollow Hill life, most of the time solo with her new in-laws, dining with them in the library where my grandfather, austere and quiet in contrast to Gami, read his newspapers and held court. *Goodness, this luxury is heaven,* she wrote Paul after a week.

4.

For the six months approaching my birth, my mother wrote my father at least once daily, numbering her letters—I appeared as "Honor" at least seventy-five times. It seems that after Jenny conceived, they first decided what to call a daughter, their only option for rebellious naming—a first son would have to be Paul Moore III. Once in a while though, my expectant mother imagined alternative masculine names. *I am getting more + more partial to the name Geoffrey—we will obviously call him Jeffy for short and won't that be spelled with a "J"? Are you still pining for Adam? The real thing I have against it is that it doesn't sound well with Moore.* On the other hand, she thought *Mark Moore* would be *heaven,* had a pang of jealousy when Mouse and Bill named their second son *Timothy*; "Michael" she thought *chic* but *overdone.* Eventually though, she acquiesced to patriarchy—a son must of course be Paul, though *it's going to be so complicated having 89 Pauls!*

Why Honor? The competitor in my mother, I think; she called it *perfectionism,* the trait that had made her a binge-studier and winner of horse show ribbons. Their daughter, she and Paul agreed, should have the most original, unexpected, most timely, most *divine* name of all. My mother had an aesthetic appreciation of a beautiful name, felicitous initials. When Alice, the daughter of Gagy, who took care of us as babies, married a man surnamed Vatne, my mother couldn't get over the married initials: "AWV," she kept repeating; "What a beautiful monogram!" What both parents told me when I asked was that they "liked the name." Each had known an Honor: my mother, Honor O'Rourke, one of two black-haired, blue-eyed sisters at Barnard; my father, Honora Hemingway, the daughter of the farmer-priest he worked for in Vermont summers before the war. And there was the war—wasn't "Honor" an appropriate name for the child intended to take the place of her father, become his relic should he "honor" his country by dying in the war's final invasion?

But if Paul Moore survived, I was not to be an only child. They tossed about numbers early, maybe unconsciously. If they didn't marry, Paul wrote Jenny in 1943, he'd send her *eight porringers,* one each for the children she'd have with someone else. If bad luck punished naming a child before birth, they'd have no daughters at all, just *nine sons.* Why eight or nine rather than five or six? Everyone was having children—this was "the baby boom": Jenny would have the most, win a blue ribbon for the largest brood. I keep hearing her say, as if her reason for wanting nine wasn't at all odd, "a baseball team, a small orchestra." Two of my sisters studied flute, my father learned to play the recorder, a brother later played jazz piano, two sisters play guitar and sing, one country and western—and I was encouraged, first with trumpet, then piano lessons.

Or did it have to do with love, its renewal manifest in a different form each time a child was born, as if their story were an unfolding myth?

It's something else entirely, if I think of her then—a young woman turned from study and writing to another task of authorship, the project of family, of correcting the one she was born into with her own celebra-tory brood. An eighth-grade friend remembered coming to our house in Indianapolis for the first time, stopping to say hello to my mother, who was crouched near the driveway planting tulip bulbs as several of the younger ones screeched past in a game of tag. "You have a lot of chil-dren," my friend said. My mother turned and looked up, smiling. "Aren't they marvelous?" What my friend didn't know was that we were meticu-lously planned and contraception employed from the beginning: *I might start one up spring of '47 and have it when Honor is about 2 and a month or so. I should like to have a good year with Daddy before feeling hid-hid again. Also I should like to finish college, start the piano, & do some work at school before being preg-preg again. I will have twins next winter if you want, though, darling.*

When she was deep in planning, her own family seemed far away. She often stayed one at 825 and had friends in for supper. The building had a restaurant and meals could be sent up, served in the dining room by "Alice," the housekeeper. Sometimes Gramps and Gami were there as well, and once when Gami was in town for a Metropolitan Museum board meeting, Margarett was in New York. *Both were calling me on different phones at the same time,* she wrote Paul, *so I just screamed.* Margarett's shock treatments hadn't made much difference, she didn't think: *I sort of expected she had changed but the fact that she is "well" makes her hectic—she just rubs me so the wrong way.* the same guilty questions: *I wonder if I'll ever not close down with her. How can I be a Christian and have nothing but loath-ing for everything about her except as a prima donna—brilliant, quick and beautiful in a drawing room.*

On the other hand, she was happy to report delight with her mother-in-law: *Your mother seems well and gives me 9 presents a day,* not all of them for the baby: a long coat from British Tweeds to be *used at the very end of Honor's career in October & then will be reconverted;* more recently a white silk evening dress with a black-velvet ribbon around the waist. Bill's wife Mouse, Edith McKnight of St. Paul, Minnesota—a funny, svelte, witty, and fashionable woman—was an expert at Hollow Hill and things

Moore, someone to roll eyes with when Mother Fan's clinging slipped into the outrageous, as it did one day when Jenny found four new letters to her from Paul, opened and sloppily resealed, obviously read by his mother.

Mouse was also a comrade in pregnancy; her insurrectionary mischief was contagious and her experience reassuring. She already had two children and was pregnant with a third. When Jenny complained of heartburn, Mouse said it meant the baby would have *lots of hair. Mouse and I are as one*, Jenny wrote Paul, *We have the BEST time.* Nothing was out of bounds. *Today we discussed circumcision. She is going to have her son circumcised so I can see it & I am going to leave mine without it done so she can see it. Seriously*, she wrote Paul, *do you want it done?*

It was Mouse Jenny called when the baby first moved inside her.

While I was at the dentist yesterday Honor kicked for the first time. (4 months and a few days old which is apparently quite soon for wiggling). I bounced off the chair 6 inches & then felt too silly to tell the dentist why. It feels like a bubble bursting near your naughty. I called Mouse to see if it was the sensation and not just something in my colon & she said it was Honor for sure. It's all too fascinating. I felt my tummy with my hand when it happened today & I could feel a little throb.

She was getting big all over; the Dickermans, she wrote, are *absolutely certain* it is a boy: *you know how violent they are about their prophecies.* But in spite of many having *decisively and emphatically pronounced that it will be a boy*, she wrote Paul, *I know it will be Honor.* They had still managed to keep the name secret—when Margie saw that Paul had scrawled "Honor" beneath his cartoon of a baby in a letter, Jenny swore her to silence.

The days looking for apartments were long and hot. It seemed that every place she saw was too big or just wrong, but in her second week of looking she found a two-bedroom with a maid's room; though *a bit grand*, it seemed possible. *I got sweaty* (nervous) *and asked Mouse if it would seem flashy.* Mouse said to relax, *that you would want me to have it nice.* The address was 149 East 73d Street, and sometime in early June, she signed the lease. *I am paralyzed at the first decision I have made all by myself—except marriage!* I called Mouse desperate for moral support *& feel better*, she immediately wrote Paul, *The apt. is heaven—3 bedrooms—hall with closets.* In a black and white snapshot Quigg took, she stands beneath its canopy triumphant and very pregnant. Recently I located the building: simple, brick, and seven stories, off a stretch of Lexington Avenue that still has small restaurants, shoemakers, and a cleaners advertising "alterations"— I could have been in a time warp—forest green canopy, art deco door.

She got to work right away, and everyone wanted to help. When Mother Fan took her furniture shopping, Jenny felt a throb of need beneath her generosity: *She has already written where everything is going all over the floor plan. I want to do it myself!* Her own mother, in a twist, was the opposite, even though she was famously expert at interiors: *We had a wonderful time about the apt. & furniture and pictures & she suggests nothing.* By the time Jenny left for Prides in early June, one truck had brought wedding presents and baby furniture from Hollow Hill, another boxes from Fredericksburg and furniture from the apartment she'd shared with Margie.

She was almost five months pregnant, but no matter: *three flights of stairs and again I was occupied till 5.* She had the baby room painted pink and the master bedroom gray. She decided not to repaint the living room, which had cream woodwork and cream wallpaper with a red-and-yellow design. *It sounds revolting but everyone has raved. The wallpaper isn't very good but I didn't see any point in changing it for a lot of dough for what might be just a year . . . Thank goodness all that is over, that I finally have most of our things in one place.* One place, the first decision made all by myself: She'd ventured independence earlier, going to Madeira and college, but this was the beginning of a life that would be free, she would make certain, of the burdens and anguish of her childhood—*I love so having a home I just can't tell you.*

Having this new life was such a wonder she began to tell its story, which she did in a traditionally female and domestic medium, the scrapbook. The pronoun was *we*, but it was she who arranged the pages—pasted, labeled, and captioned photos or souvenirs in her vertical hand, their shared jokes once in a while seeping through her formality. The story she conceived was not only of the family they were quite self-consciously making, but of the world their generation was rebuilding. She began what would become a twenty-five-year project with Paul's experience in the war, which was where she considered the story began; she herself might as well have come from nowhere, appearing for a courtship and marriage that, viewed on those pages, seem inevitable: no horses, no Prides, no Madeira or Vassar, little of Barnard.

In Fredericksburg, she'd sorted and boxed all his Marine memorabilia— letters from buddies, mimeographed sheaves of curricula, Paul's notes on what he and others taught, a lecture he gave about the battle at Guadalcanal, inspirational talks to recruits in Seattle. There were snapshots of antics on the transport ship the summer of 1942, newspaper accounts of Paul's heroism illustrated by earnest wartime graphics, accounts of his medal ceremonies, a Marine portrait, eight by ten and glossy. *I am up to May 1943 in your "solo" scrapbook,* Jenny wrote soon after she arrived at Prides, *about to launch into Seattle.* She didn't censor: there were images of Nona, of Lois, and of her visit to Seattle as well as photographs of recruits he coached rowing in unison across Union Bay and of the parade he organized the week after her visit, his Guadalcanal commanding officer, General Vandegrift, on the reviewing stand, waves of Marines in formation marching on the street below.

Wedding photos went into monogrammed scrapbooks they'd gotten for wedding presents, and some she'd purchased—*I got a dream red leather one in Santa B. with our initials on it.* Now, when they slipped enclosures into letters, they'd mark them "scrapbook material." I can hear each of my parents' voices say the phrase, and I still get a tiny shiver. I always understood the phrase meant something beyond the designation, that the thing on paper had a slant, delivered a piquant sense of moment or cultural incident, revelation or a bit of snark. While my father perfectly understood what "scrapbook material" was, I sensed that my mother had created the category, its tone and definition. *Keep the New River Pictures,* she wrote once. *I have a scrapbook set.* To the outsider, the scrapbooks contain what any scrapbook might: snapshots, flyers, matchbooks, letters, bits of hair in envelopes, posters, campaign buttons, postcards, mimeographed notices, birth and baptism announcements, Christmas cards. But at their best, in arrangement, timeline, and caption, the volumes create a narrative as well as express my mother's stringent sensibility, leavened and enhanced by the straightforward, even romantic photographs my father took—good black and white portraits of each child and pet; often poignant candids of friends, games, and every summer group on the porch year after year at the Adirondacks. There, ritually, he balanced his camera on a wicker surface, set the timer, and leaped around to take his place among us.

As she sequenced and glued, Jenny marveled that it had been just a year since she saw Joe Walker off at LaGuardia. So much had changed! She began the wedding scrapbook with two clips of the notorious *Tribune* photograph, with their hands under the table, taken the awful night before Paul had left for Seattle. No caption exposed the pain of those months. Why two copies? I first wondered. Then I saw the dates: July 1943, when they were socialite and marine; below it, November 1944, they are engaged. It was her revenge on the gossips so confident that their holding hands in advance of engagement boded ill. Only a few people knew the details of the year between the two dates—Sylvia, Connie who'd been there the night of that first breakup, and of course the utterly discreet Joe Walker.

The scrapbooks were a distinct and quasi-public creation, a wish: this was a family chronicle, not to be illuminated, complicated, or distorted by the intimate. Until I found and read the courtship letters in 2003 after my father's death, I would have told the story of my parents' courtship as a simple arc from the Vermont drugstore to the Church of the Resurrection. How much more dramatic the real story—a two-and-a-half-year courtship that began with three months of dating but actually took place through the mail—two thousand pages of correspondence broken only by her two-week visit to Seattle. Where the letters were stored all those years I do not know, but they ended up in cardboard boxes, meticulously preserved in their original envelopes. My mother was not careless with them, and neither was my father: *I'm beginning to think we should number our letters,* she wrote him from Prides that summer when she was first pregnant. *Heloise and Abelard have nothing on us.*

Hard to know where my mother's passion for organization began—was it when she hunkered down to her studies at Vassar? A response to the chaos of the house in which she grew up? It actually surprises me to see my mother, a newly pregnant twenty-two, abruptly turned effective domestic executive: deploying moving trucks, deciding what to do in advance as she'd be seven months along when she got back to New York in September. And then I remember her planning the activities and whereabouts of nine children—her sense of achieving of what seemed impossible, her modesty broken only when she surprised herself.

At the end of June, she noted she was five months pregnant and that soon *Daddy will have been away 3 months—it seems an eternity but the summer always goes fast and October 6 it will be six months.* She was staying with her father, alone in the house as Margarett had "taken a studio" in Rockport. The North Shore summer was underway with its beach picnics and suppers, nights of dance parties and board games. *Is it nawti to play backgammon for money for me whose husband is going to round-collar it?* she'd joke in a letter, and then, suddenly, she'd actually feel it, that she was pregnant and her husband a continent and half an ocean away. Even though Mouse kept telling her that pregnancy intensified any mood, she had trouble keeping loneliness at bay—*not that I'm not perfectly happy, but I get champing at the bit. I wish we had gotten married a year ago.* Living at Prides, she felt like a child again, her father gloomy, nightly awaiting Jenny and anyone she brought home, staying up with them to joke and drink and smoke. His loneliness seemed contagious: *I have felt so terribly alone for the last week I have gone almost crazy. This morning I wrote you a long desperate letter about it all. I got sort of neurotic about it + decided it was because I didn't love you and had rationalized myself into marrying you and all that—it's funny the devil gets in for his inning when aloneness weakens you—I do worry, darling, at times, that I rushed into it + made up my mind to marry you rather than not being able to.* Decades later she'd return to this line of thought, but for now she concluded it was *all part of the old perfectionism.* Have you ever *felt you didn't love your mummy?*

Sometimes she'd worry again about his drinking—*will you be good about drinking when you get home—I really don't love you then and I worry about you,* memory of her mother distant and blank or *blasted* always tugging at her. I remember my father, in his seventies and a decade into his second marriage, drunk at a literary party I'd invited him to: for the first time, I saw not the courtly, attentive father I was so proud of, but a stumbling old man, and there was nothing I could do to get him back. Jenny wasn't the only wife in her group of friends to worry when her husband drank too much. One wild night at the casino, she reported to Paul, Bobby Potter got so intoxicated that Zobby went home alone—*she was worse about Bobby high than I am about you. I was so relieved to know I ain't the only one.*

But she quickly pulls back: *What little thing drives you wild about me, besides the way I flop on a sofa and throw my head back?* Or, *Honor kicks now so you can see my tummy pop up in a little hump!*

5.

Margie had managed to be authentically present for Jenny's wedding, caught up in the excitement, but now, her husband deployed, she was living alone in the apartment where the sisters had lived together with little Jenny. It didn't help Margie's state of mind that her family—from whom she kept private details—belittled her reasons for wanting to divorce Wally Reed and that Jenny, with the self-righteousness of the newly married, thought her sister should stay married—after all, she had a four-year-old child. Margie's social adventures had shocked Jenny for quite some time: *She had an affair with an English navy guy last spring & summer,* she wrote Paul, *and now spends every weekend with some other jerk. Wally has written his father that they are "separated." It all makes you want to vomit.*

The two sisters had always been different. While Jenny found Prides and its *fretwork* confining, for Margie it was the source of everything to learn, a manifestation of the tenderness her mother had bestowed when she was her only child. You could say that Jenny drew from their mother a clear sense of how *not* to be a woman, while Margie navigated a more difficult terrain: how to be the woman her love for her mother promised— the person Margarett might have been, if only things had been different.

Margie had been the girlie girl of the sisters, and her warmth and beauty made her successful with men. "Sex appeal," my mother called it. Though Jenny was "flat-chested" (her phrase) and athletic, her sister had "a lovely figure" (also my mother's phrase) that Jenny envied. Margie was a rebel in matters of sex, and Jenny in going to college, but neither diverged from the proscribed path to marriage. Margie married charming and older Wally Reed "to get out of the house," she always told me, and had a daughter at twenty when she was "certainly too young to be a mother." But much of her life before her final happy marriage was a mystery to me until I read my parents' correspondence of the summer my mother was pregnant with me, the summer after Margie left her first marriage.

"To get out of the house." For Margie, life growing up at home was the life of a capable oldest child; on Senny's days off, she made sure the twins did not see the worst of their mother and explained to lunch guests when Margarett did not appear that their hostess was "not feeling well." All of this she described with tough irony. She was very early aware of her mother's unhappiness; but unlike Lewis Galantière, who advised Margarett early on to leave her marriage or at least get help, Margie—like her father—saw the problem as willfulness and alcoholism. Margarett's years in mental hospitals extended through my entire childhood, along with knowledge of my mother's fear of mental illness. But until I read my parents' letters from the 1940s, I had no idea Margie herself had entered Four Winds, only a week after Margarett left after her second stay.

Decades later, supported by some progress for women in divorce law, Margie might have found a rational way to change her situation. But living in the milieu of wartime New York, she took another kind of action, leaving her daughter to live with her parents with a nurse and vanishing with a lover the family would find wildly inappropriate—a man who, it turned out, had a reputation for preying on society girls. I'd known of Margie's two divorces; but I'd not heard of this never-named lover or this affair, complete with the lover stealing her money and pawning family jewelry, or that her father, desperate to protect her, eventually took matters into his own hands.

Jenny heard the rumors when she got back from California—a report from Zobby Potter's sister of seeing Margie at the Stork Club with *a man,* meaning a man she couldn't identify. Within a month there was worry, expressed more as concern for little Jenny than for Margie herself: *No one knows where she is!* In another month, by June, Papa was fully involved. *The reason I don't go on about Margie is that it upsets me,* Jenny wrote Paul. *It's so hard to write about and so tragic. . . . She apparently takes 7 or 8 aspirin a day and has waves of cheer and then violent depression. . . . It seems violent to make her go to* Four Winds, *but it is not safe for the baby to be with her or Rita* [the nanny] *and she ought to go somewhere she can get organized and be watched over.*

Since Paul's parents summered barely 20 minutes from Prides, Jenny was sure they would hear the news. She wrote Paul to tell *the Moores* that Margie was in Four Winds to recover from *nervous exhaustion.* But conclusions would be drawn; Margarett's condition was no secret, nor were the alcoholism and depression that riddled the families of both Jenny's parents. Given that legacy, I might read Margie and Jenny's rivalry as a battle against an undertow—Margie seeking relief in parties and men, Jenny staking a claim that she was made of stronger stuff, more like her great grandmother Pauline Agassiz, who was roused from depression by activism and good works.

Paul promised discretion, and Jenny tried to joke it all away: *your father and mother must think we're the most fantastic family—Mama batting thither & yon and now Margie. They probably think I'm next. Goodness I crave normalcy.*

I can hardly imagine the warm, stable, and generous aunt I knew as was once the desperate young woman Jenny describes—*she has given her diamond bracelet and a ring to that guy and she says she has lawyers working to get her out.* Their brother Shaw went to see her, but she confides nothing, *never tells the same story twice.* Jenny wrote her please to come home to Prides—*I'd love to spend a month with her,* she wrote Paul. Margie replied that she loved her but *didn't want any company. Obviously the guy is after her money . . . she has written out many checks to him.* In the end their father paid Margie's debts and put detectives on the lover's trail. *Papa is really shot and of course it has given Mama a big setback— and so it goes.*

Margie does come home to Prides after only a few weeks at Four Winds. *I spent the afternoon with her and tried to keep off all but ordinary conversational topics,* Jenny wrote Paul, *so we could start to have fun again and not feel so separate.* There was a momentary return to closeness—*we had a lovely time and I hated to leave. I think she feels unstable and desperate and her emotions are like fish nets. . . . Perhaps I can work a slow cure by never openly criticizing.* Of course there was little Jenny could do about her sister's collapse; Margie was envious. Her own trust income was not enough to support her, and her sister had married into a family that was wildly rich. *Perhaps,* she told their brother Shaw, *she could get Papa to split mine between her and the twins.* Jenny was appalled. *Have you ever?*

In fact that is exactly what did happen when Papa died twenty five years later, but I am getting ahead of the story.

6.

Paul was so earnest in making everything all right, writing Jenny— "It's your & my life, our life, and we can do a lot with it—we are strong enough together to take it."—that I am immediately reassured. Jenny should remember that in their new family, "Mummy and Daddy will always be there, calm and collected, unhurried & wise . . . laughing at the silly things Honor is doing, and wondering whether the curate will ever get married."

My father was writing Jenny a first letter from his new post on the Pacific island of Guam. He's relieved to be back on active duty, even though "duty" is a desk job at division headquarters and he hates working at a desk. He was reading Thomas Wolfe, *The Web and the Rock,* and writing arty, cringeworthy observations about the native population:

> A few dirty brown bodies in dirty gray clothes moved in and out of the piles supporting the roof. Old women and little boys with usual quizzical eyes half smiled and wiggled their big toes in the smoothness of the stamped earth. It seems rather strange to me always, to see the earthiness of the old and the young, their blending with the damp earth and hot dirtiness of the tropics.

Jenny is suddenly very down, and no one has explained the emotional roller coaster of pregnancy. *Before this week I have always been able to reason myself out of it, but today my despair has been overwhelming,* she wrote Paul. First she figures out that it's better to confide than *let it fester . . . I'm dying to be told it's normal . . . Actually I just feel old and wanting to be young.* She remembers the last weeks in New York, how good she felt organizing and moving into the apartment. Was she still down when she got his ebullient letter saying he left the hated desk job?

> Gee I'm happy. Just like a baby with a new rattle. I'm in a hovel, the area is ugly, muddy and hot—as compared to the cool, breezy beauty of Division Headquarters, I have to work every night & get up at 530 or 600 (as compared to 715). But I'm happier than I've been since I left [the States] by 100%—new responsibility & new experience it is damn interesting & you get out in the field and exercise.

In her next letter, Jenny has energy again—*I can't wait for next February when I can get my teeth into college. Idling is not for me.* Out of nowhere, she's had an idea: *I hope that we get a sad, poor parish where we will have many many people to help*. That night she sleeps 12 hours, *the first time in 2 months that I have slept more than 8 or 7 and it really made a difference*. Which makes her feel selfish: *How can I ever be as good to people as you are—you are so wonderful I'm afraid I will always be a worry to you rather than a support*. Paul replies that all she needs is "a little preoccupation, and your scales of gloom will clatter down." And having the baby will help. "Happiness is not a series of events. It's more a series of experiences . . . the same event can be a completely different experience for two people . . . Gee what pedantry, apologies."

She next writes from Maine, where she's visiting her friends the Aldrich sisters. While waiting for the ferry to Islesboro, she notes, *I wanted my bag carried. I stood with my feet wide apart and made a big effort to stick out Honor every time a kind gentleman came rushing by*. The Aldrichs' enormous house was on Dark Harbor, a tiny cove—all the sisters there, the one brother away in the war, various beaux arriving, departing. *We had steamed clams—bliss*. Charades and a game in which you extract as many words as you can from a longer one; from "prophetical," she produced 81 and won! *I was frightfully proud of HARLOT*, she writes Paul, but when she tries to sleep, *Honor kicks like a wild thing*, keeping her awake, bringing worry about Paul: *Of course I have you knee deep in blood with a knife in your teeth 99% of my waking hours. I can't wait for normalcy and peace and a real home*.

"Normalcy is gratifying, isn't it?" he wrote back. "You sounded more rested and quiet and less hectic in your last letter which makes me happy." The next day she gets three letters, one very long, Paul dreaming a summer day after the war:

Honor says, "Let's go for a picnic, Mummy!" So we make sandwiches of cold chicken and lettuce & juicy tomatoes (how I'd love one now). And I sneak off to the butcher for hamburgers and we bring some grape juice for Honor and beer for us & milk. And maybe fresh peaches. The wretched boat needs bailing and we have to lug the heavy sail-bag out of a sea-smelling closet. . . . But soon we are in the boat and the big whiteness of the sail leaps up from the

crumpled cocoon. . . . Gusts shiver it and yaw the boom. The last
fog has lifted, leaving sky-bright water, clean firs and bright flicks of
white houses.

In the actual sail Jenny took that day across the harbor with Lucy and
Harriet, *Honor kicked like mad the whole time.*

I wonder if it's time I allowed myself into the story, remembering how
safe I felt when my father taught me to sail on the lake in the Adirondacks, the two of us in the hand-built wooden sailboat he'd learned to
sail as a boy. I have no memory of being with my mother in a sailboat, so
I summon her now, conjuring a sail across an expanse of the Atlantic on
a summer day. That's as far as I get. It is not my mother I imagine safely
steering the little boat, but my father. And then comes another image: my
mother placing one hand on her pregnant belly as I saw her do so many
times, a certain proprietary happiness crossing her face. I have never been
six months pregnant, so I am free to imagine myself on that sailboat in
Maine, kicking like mad toward the heat of my mother's hand.

That evening was an ordinary summer night, until it was not. Home
from the sail, contented and sleepy at the end of a day on the ocean; house
guests, Mrs. Aldrich, and the sisters all gathered, listening through static
as the news comes: *Over the radio, the US bombing Japan with the bomb the
size of a coconut that releases atomic energy,* she writes Paul that night. *I
guess it's nice in a relative way that we learned how to do it first, but still I wish
it hadn't happened. I am sure we will destroy ourselves.*

I visualize Jenny in a guest room, bent over a small desk or writing in
bed, and I think of her seriousness. Her description—*the size of a coconut*—exposes her cast of mind: human vulnerability at the effect of a
larger force; then an impulse to resist two opposing inclinations, first an
earnest support of the war effort—*we*—and then a *wish* against its hor-
rific consequences: *I guess it's nice in a relative way that we learned how to do
it first, but still I wish it hadn't happened.* Her final phrase, *I am sure we will
destroy ourselves,* seems evidence her mind has taken her to a stark conclusion. And then I see her lie back, head on the pillow, and settle. When she

finds a comfortable position, I watch her place her hand on the taut skin of her belly.

The broadcast she likely heard was President Truman's announcement from the SS *Augusta*, on his way back from the Potsdam Conference, when he announced the dropping of "one bomb on the city of Hiroshima." No mention in that broadcast of the actual size of this "new and revolutionary increase in destruction," a uranium bomb, produced at the cost of $2 billion, that released the explosive power of twenty tons of TNT. It was called Little Boy; was shaped like a rocket, not a ball; weighed 9,500 pounds; measured 10 feet long and 28 inches wide; and killed 80,000 people, half of them instantly. Three days later, on August 9, a plutonium bomb known as the Fat Man for its shape—10 feet long, a diameter of 5 feet—was dropped on Nagasaki, exploding twice the TNT power of the Hiroshima blast. The losses—30,000—were far fewer because the city of Nagasaki is shielded by hills.

Despite the seriousness of the president's announcement, no one knew at first what the effect would be on the course of the war. After all, the Americans had been firebombing Japanese cities for weeks.

Jenny didn't hear from Paul for days. When she did, it confused her that in letters dated August 7 and 8, he did not mention Hiroshima, and on August 9 his only news was of the surprise arrival of Challinor: "It was most delightful. We talked of you (nothing clutchy). A little over 2 years ago, I was telling him in the silk room that I would never marry u!"

She left Maine on Thursday, the day of the Nagasaki bombing, and at home found everyone predicting the end of the war, *talking in terms of days*. But it was nearly a week before Emperor Hirohito delivered a radio address to his people, announcing his acceptance of terms of surrender. "Should we continue to fight, it would not only result in an ultimate collapse and obliteration of the Japanese nation, but also it would lead to the total extinction of human civilization."

Even after the announcement, Jenny remained wary—*a tiny germ of fear in the back of my mind with all those Jap troops still untouched & Hirohito still the symbol*. General MacArthur, who accepted the surrender, had made the decision to maintain the emperor in office in order to unify the Japanese people to stand with the peace and support the American occupation that followed. *Can you believe it?* Jenny wrote Paul on August 10; *The war is all but over.*

Finally, one could make plans! On the weekend she saw her old beau Harry Fowler, whom she'd last seen in December 1941, the night of the attack on Pearl Harbor. How much they had to catch up on was a measure of the length of the war. *He said he couldn't get over how much my looks had improved!!!* Not surprising considering that the debutante of nineteen to whom he had paid court was now a married woman in the flush of pregnancy. The night he arrived, they had supper with the family at Prides, and on Friday he took her to the Casino, then on to the Essex Club dance. All night, he entertained her with stories of the war in Greece, of Alexandria where he was stationed, fighting out of his window *with a gun in one hand and a cocktail shaker in the other. He had a girl there called Kiki!* "Alex" was a *very nawti town—a brothel for enlisted men and one for officers.* He wants me to find him a wife. *It was a frightfully gay evening for Mummy till one o'clock and I didn't get tired till at the very end. Honor must be exhausted as she played dead all day today.*

When victory was declared the following Wednesday, Jenny missed the broadcast. Having been *glued to the radio all day,* she was driving to supper with Paul's mother at his grandmother's house, Rockmarge. *Can you stand it?* she wrote him. It would be two weeks before the actual treaty was signed, on board the USS *Missouri* in Tokyo Bay.

The end of the war did not mean Jenny knew when Paul was getting home. One heard that General MacArthur didn't want the Marines for the occupation, but in days the 4th Division was commandeered. Papa and Gramps were pushing Jenny to write Paul to take advantage of the rating system—medals, rank, and other conditions translated to an advantageous position on a waiting list. She passed on the message, but Paul calmly explained that he wouldn't do that, which of course she had predicted. *To think of plans almost kills me!* She did not want to waste any time. It was as if someone put a nickel in to start the baby boom:

If you did get home before Xmas would you want to study for half a year and then go for a nice Mummy-Honor-Daddy summer & then seminary or what? I just can't believe this is something concrete & not just some wild futuristic dream. . . . I am sort of feeping out on England—I am getting so eager! Also the children—note the plural—would be a problem if we went there. When would you want another?

7.

As if life and human inevitability might be forestalled, and she might actually stage-manage the event: herself dewy-eyed with birth and *by some quirk of fortune you'd get home*, night after night she dreamed herself *coming out of anaesthetic & finding you bending over me.* Hard to hold onto that, as Paul might not leave Guam for weeks, not get back for the birth, for Thanksgiving, or even for their wedding anniversary November 26: *So if you came home for Christmas,* she wrote, *could we have our own? Honor would be too tiny to drag out to Hollow Hill. Mummy might be still feeble and, if nursing, couldn't go. Mummy could cook & we'd have to give Ernie time off & make her stay while we went to church.*

On Guam Paul and his battalion waited, idled, playing "foot-ball, & soft-ball + volley ball & grab ass to our heart's content. 4 beers per fellow." The mess was another matter; he ate with other company commanders: "How we are going to lay the geisha girls is all they talk of," he wrote Jenny. "Days will go by when it isn't so bad, but then bang! Right in the pit of the stomach and I get lonely, so damn lonely, and sick of the coarse masculinity & the illiterate talk."

Plans: She will leave Prides and fly to New York on September 9, so he can write to her at their apartment! *Dr. Parkhurst said I could go down then but that there was no reason to think Honor would be early.* As if I were outside in a vestibule, checking my watch. Early? She never had a baby early, always late, sometimes as long as two weeks.

She nudges Paul about his date of arrival, but it seems no less unpredictable than the baby's. *You said not to alter plans but then said you might get out "fairly early" in the game.* Day after day he writes that he doesn't know, can't know the date, so okay, he won't be back for the birth, and Sylvia will move in with her until he gets back. Increasing agitation and anxiety: it's only August and the baby's not due till October 25.

On Saturday, September 1, the Moores had the McKeans to a celebratory end-of-summer supper at Myopia (full name the Myopia Hunt Club), scene of all Jenny's blue-ribbon horse shows, the "clubhouse" vast and gray clapboard on a great lawn with beautiful old trees. It's the night the Japanese will sign formal documents of surrender, and a radio is set up in the capacious dining room—reassuring white tablecloths, small vases of summer flowers. Mother Fan would have seated the table, the two sets of parents and Jenny's friends—Sylvia, Sally Cole, and Ben Bradlee's wife Jibby; Ben was still in the Pacific.

Everything was fine until the broadcast—from the USS *Missouri* in the Bay of Tokyo—except on the porch, where Paul's sister *Polly, unfortunately among them, talked, giggled & told jokes* so loudly that one could barely hear the president: "The thoughts and hopes of all America,—indeed of all the civilized world—are centered tonight on the battleship *Missouri*" At that point from another part of the dining room, Cord Meyer's father, his son Quentin killed at Okinawa, strode out to the porch and asked if he might shut the doors against their jubilation—No, oh we're sorry, they said—of course they wanted to hear the broadcast.

"We think of those whom death in this war has hurt, taking from them fathers, sons, brothers and sisters whom they loved, No victory can bring back the faces they longed to see," Truman continued in his flat Midwestern accent. More laughter from the porch, and Mr. Meyer went out a second time, and again, *between giggles,* they insisted he leave the door open, tipsy, assenting youth—they wanted to listen. At the Moore table, uncommon emotion: *Your mother crying continually,* Jenny wrote Paul, *tears streaming down her face.*

I was frankly disappointed in Polly. Her husband Fred had served, was still in Europe. *Sylvia, Sally, Jibby and I were in a state.* When the broadcast ended, Papa stormed out in a rage. Back at Prides that night, it comes to Jenny that *this will probably be the last time I'll spend any length of time in this house. Strange to think of.* Such radical change ahead, not only the birth of a first child but the end of a way of life—"the end of an era" was how she would have put it later. She wants Paul to know how much she loves him, again apologizing for her recent moodiness, which she now considers *hideous* behavior. And then she makes a surprising admission: *It took me a long time to fall really & truly in love with you, but don't worry for a second ever again. I love you so much & I want so much to make you happy.*

A deluge of baby presents was arriving at Hollow Hill—a silver fork and spoon & two Disney animation cels of Bambi in the great forest from Mother Fan's sister, Auntie Claire in Santa Barbara. *I hope I don't get hectic moving into the apartment and start worrying you again.* Even if the worst happens and he's delayed till April, she'll start back at college in February and finish. She's *champing at the bit* to think again. *I am going to look into the "New School" courses; they have weird little 6 week numbers & maybe I could knock off a few points in January. There are so many things I want to do—a seminar on Plato, piano, sewing & having another baby & maybe social work school.*

Suddenly moving day arrives, and she flies from Boston to LaGuardia on September 9. *It was a heaven flight & the stewardess wouldn't let me carry the Reader's Digest, let alone my bag.* Mother Fan *met me which was so cute,* supper at the apartment, to bed early, and in the morning straight to work. *Curtains are up in Honor's room,* then downtown for tea with Father Wadhams—*the minute I came in the door he went rushing out & got some milk and ginger snaps!* He'll escort her, he says, to look at apartments near General Seminary—*I think he's sure Honor will arrive on the way down, but he's being brave.* She's ordered a bed seven feet long (Paul is six foot five), a double-width mattress, two custom-made single box springs that can *get into rectories in a minute.* That night, with her Vassar friend Ruthie Du Pont, she goes to see *The Glass Menagerie. It's absolutely extraordinary . . . Laurette Taylor as the ex-southern belle—whose husband deserted her—& who tries to marry off her crippled daughter Julie Haydon, whose whole life is her glass menagerie and worn out Victrola records. . . . & the gentleman caller who . . .*

kisses her forgetting himself. And then desperate at having hurt her has to tell her he has a "steady." So ghastly *and beautifully done & acted!*

If "Honor" is a boy, she's now thinking, they could nickname him "Pat"—and that day, as if to protest being misgendered, Honor *catches hold of my right rib and then does a double back flip and kicks my nawti so I have to fly to the toidee.* It's September 26, and Paul's anniversary gardenias arrive: *I finished your whole Guadal-Seattle scrapbook last night. It ends with the telegram saying the Links Club thinks it'd be grand to have you— rather killed myself over that being the last item.*

The baby's gymnastics are now often waking her, but despite sleep deprivation, she presses on and within a week has settled the apartment into a household. Prewar luxury eases her transition—she hires Rita Horn, an older Irish woman and *a marvelous cook* who indulges her by bringing her breakfast in bed. When Margie and Mother Fan came for lunch, she wrote Paul, *Rita whipped up a soufflé that practically leapt from the dish;* after lunch they went shopping and Mother Fan bought her a long black-velvet skirt. In that day's letter to Paul: *I decided this morning that I want at least 6 children—4 girls and 2 boys—but ask me a year from now how many I want!*

And then a citywide elevator strike—*the building next door has struck and they say this will be next. Apparently the Board of Health will run elevators for people who are above the 6th floor; we are the 11th.* On October 21, her parents arrive in New York and settle in; they will stay through the birth. Their presence, both at the same time, reassures even me; as if it's my own pregnancy, I've started to ask friends who are mothers about the final days before a birth. Carol couldn't imagine how the huge presence in her belly would ever get out; my sister Marian reveled in singlemindedness—there was nothing else she had to be responsible for. I wrack my brains to recall what my mother said: I remember the birth of my second brother, George—the first of us born by natural childbirth, how she said *Poppy was right there!* which I find especially poignant now, given how much Jenny wanted my father there for my birth, her first. And there's a story about Marian's—my mother's water broke at Hollow

Hill, and after barely a contraction, the baby started to crown, my mother holding her in as she was raced to the hospital; a champion at giving birth, ever the blue-ribbon athlete.

But in October 1945 she is a novice. She knows there will be anesthesia, and Sylvia and Mouse have warned her to expect ten days in the hospital—she quoted the cost to Paul, $300—then three weeks in bed at home. It would be three months, Sylvia said, before the body mended, the hormones settled, and she was herself again. She was nervous about Paul's whereabouts: *Where should I cable about Honor?* He'd check into it, he replied, but why not wire him directly and also through the Red Cross? She can't help her impatience—when will he be home? "Unhappily I can't choose how & when I'm to be discharged," he replied, and she wrote back asking that he please not arrive unannounced—she wanted Sylvia to have time to move out. In the next day's letter, she suggests that after his transport ship arrives in San Francisco, he stay with Fanny in Santa Barbara for a week or two; that way she can have the baby and recover undisturbed.

"Listen here," he blasted back, "I don't want any more of this stay in California talk. "Even if I didn't want like hell to see *you*, can you imagine how long you'd stay in California if your first child was sitting in New York & you'd never seen it?" Jenny calmed herself by addressing postcards for Sylvia to fill in when Paul or Honor arrived. *Is there anyone you want me to wire aside from our obvious mutual friends?* she wrote Paul. And the bassinet had arrived *all trimmed from the Women's Exchange. It is out of this world. It is pink under white frothy lacy stuff and the crook that goes over Honor's bed has a giant pink bow!* Father Wadhams has agreed to take her to the hospital, but he's very nervous. *He really slays me,* Jenny wrote Paul; *I leapt out of my chair to get butter knives and he shrieked and blanched. He is so convinced that I am going to have Honor anywhere but at the hospital!*

And then one day comes a date—my father's big crooked capitals on Marine Corps stationery pasted in the scrapbook, the date October 16. Not for his arrival home, but his departure for the transient center. No telling how long he'd wait there for a berth on a transport ship to San Francisco, but he was quite sure he'd be home by his birthday on November 15, or at the very latest November 26, "our anniversary."

8.

I'm lying on my back in a treatment room, wearing loose clothes. It's summer and this is one of those quiet, sunny rooms where alternative bodyworkers have their massage tables. A young man is working on my head and hips in a modality called craniosacral therapy, which banishes my most vicious headache or back pain. Writing this book has brought a kind of stealth tension; it can suddenly produce a spasm that wrenches me from writing, and that is what has happened. I can barely move without shooting pain. The therapist put his hands first on my feet, keeping them still for several minutes. Later he reaches his hands beneath my pelvis, and still later he stands behind me, my head in his hands. As is typical, I feel my cranial plates move, the pain slowly dissolving. Toward the end of the session, he again holds my feet. That is when I have a kind of physical hallucination, feeling myself, my body inside the anesthetized abdomen of my mother, myself alive and her body not alive: I did not return to the experience of my birth, only to the moment before, when I became aware that she could not feel me. All I know about my birth is that my mother had anesthesia and that I was born with my right eye smaller than my left, which I discovered the first time a craniosacral practitioner was able to even out the cranial affecting adjusting the size of my eyes. My father thought my asymmetry was charming; I wondered if I'd been stuck in the birth canal, pulled from my mother with forceps; but my mother had died before I could ask her these questions.

The exact time of my birth, according to the baby book Jenny kept, was 4:37 p.m. And it was not her husband, but her parents Margarett and Shaw, whom she recognized as she opened her eyes. It was one of the times she would say *Mama was marvelous*. So reassuring to have them there, and together: Mama as always "dressed" in chic hat and suit; Papa looking so formal, grandfatherly. Does he wear a golden tweed jacket like the ones I remember him in? Nan O'Sullivan, the hospital nurse, brought the baby in, swaddled in white, infant hair miraculously dark—so dark that in the baby book, Jenny wrote *black* under "color of hair." She was "exhausted and just emerging from anesthesia," Margarett reminded her later. Still in bed, she took the infant in her arms—gingerly, the nurse reassuring her. Exactly seven pounds is what I weighed at birth, and I was nineteen inches long.

Jenny had already asked Sylvia to be a godmother; she'll wait for Paul to decide about another godmother, a godfather—a child has two of her own sex, one of the other. Should they baptize her at Church of the Resurrection where they were married? The next day Mama and Papa visit again, this time with Gramps and Mother Fan; and of course, Father Wadhams came often,, and Sylvia every day. Jenny learns to give a bottle, formula—in accordance with the times, she does not nurse me, even though she had wanted to very much. A day after I was born, a letter arrived from Paul, dated two days earlier: "It is so wonderful that any child can have as tender and fine and sweet a Mother as you!"

As if I am a camera, I pull back to watch Jenny now, taking notepaper and pen and beginning a letter, this one about how Honor is asleep in the nursery bassinet next to her or that Nan O'Sullivan has taken her to the nursery—she'd been fussing. I imagine that my mother wrote my father how worn out she was but also how amazed, what it was like the first second their child was in existence—yes, it *is* a girl as she had known it would be; and yes, she *had* named her Honor, *Honor Moore*—how does he like the sound of that? She'd barely started writing when his cable arrived—*love and congratulations*.

But it was not until the day she left the hospital—Friday, November 9—that Paul's plane left San Diego. "My darling," he wrote Jenny just before the flight, "That was the nicest letter I ever got. I love you more than you'll ever know. Forever darling, Daddy." As I don't have that nice letter, I'll take this from one she wrote in September: *Oh darling, I wish you were here right now!*

I like this room at the beginning of my life, and so in my imagination I stay there happily moving like newborns do, tiny hands opening and closing, little jerky movements as I start to learn in my tiny body what a body feels like, my eyes still unseeing as once in a while I am lifted into the air, someone's long fingers around my little torso. There are many flowers as I picture it, bouquets from shops, and buckets of them from the greenhouses at Hollow Hill, bunches arranged by Mother Fan. It makes me a little sad that I don't have anything my mother wrote right after I was born. Was it lost deep in my father's Marine Corps duffle bag? A jacket or pants pocket?

On the eighth day after I was born, my mother returned to the apartment on 74th Street. There she received telegram after telegram from Paul about us flight delays, which were so egregious even for wartime that American Airlines later wrote him a letter of apology. He wired Jenny *when his plane was grounded twice in Texas*, and *Then finally he was home.* He arrived November 13, sixteen days after I was born.

What happened next?

When I come into the story, my mother suddenly becomes . . . Hmm, what? "No longer just herself?" "Suddenly a mother?" "A woman living with a husband and child?" My stomach churns from nerves—this is when Jenny's life "as a woman" diverges from that of the daughter just born, the only one of her six daughters who will not become a mother. For months now, reading my parents' letters has carried me, pressed forward the story; and now, without those letters, I feel at a loss. I do not have the freedom a novelist has—to imagine or find in lives she has imagined what *must* happen next. Instead, I know something of what *did* happen, which is that my parents quarreled over my crib the night my father finally returned from the war, the night they were no longer voices letters but flesh and blood, full of longing, nerves, fear, and expectation.

What did they fight about?

I am talking to a friend who has three children, a psychologist. I tell her

I think my mother was vulnerable, that the jolt in her hormones brought on by giving birth had made her feel vulnerable.

"Hormones have nothing to do with it," my friend says, chiding me for resorting to cliché.

"Well, doesn't one feel a bit vulnerable after having a child? Tired? Less in control?"

"Yes," she says, but insists that, in spite of hormones, "they must have fought *about* something."

Whoops! I thought I could weasel out of this—why had I used the word *quarrel* to describe what happened? It's a word I hardly ever use. I wanted to give the event both lightness and weight, I admit to myself, and also I like the sound of it—quarrel. But hadn't they fought *about* something?

Yes. They fought because she had endured it all alone, the pregnancy, the setting up of household, the birth. She hadn't intended to blow up, of course she hadn't. She was longing to see him. But when he strolled in two weeks late, she couldn't help it, even though a world war excused his tardiness. In letters to Paul late in her pregnancy, Jenny had confessed loneliness and dips in mood as if they were shortcomings; but, also, she had described how after a nap or meal she was herself again. The only time she'd ever gotten so angry was the night before he left for Seattle. They had long ago buried that hatchet, but neither had learned to make the distinction between having a feeling and expressing it, and so a belief remained that she was prone to overreact.

Which was what, in my father's view, happened in the baby room when he took his infant daughter in his arms for the first time. I remember him telling me the story years after her death: "Suddenly she was in a rage," he said. He was stunned, even frightened, so different was this woman weeping and shouting from the Jenny he had been imagining. He must have put the baby down, because he opened his arms to her, and she would not let him touch her.

In the decades since my father told me the story, my imagination has staged and restaged the little scene. The room small and dark, lit by one lamp. The two of them standing there. My mother in a fury, sobs heaving, unapproachable, and him afraid. What did they fight *about*? I ask myself again. Suddenly I understand that inadvertently, I have always taken my father's side, even as now I exonerate my mother by laying the blame on her hormones rather than trying to understand what she was angry about.

What happens when I place Jenny at the center of the story? Not the Jenny of my father's memory, not the mother of my own memory, but the Jenny I am coming to know now. She is sensitive, yes, but she is also intelligent, forceful, and capable, and she is moving this narrative forward. It's a truism that a shift in the dramaturgy of a memory is not possible, but I disagree. Not so easy though, as it requires going back into that room and looking at the little scene again, then editing, carefully editing the repeating loop until the events as I envisioned them in my father's account begin to fade, and the being of my young mother takes on life and feeling and speech.

She is twenty-two, her three-week-old infant asleep in the baby room. She is waiting to greet her husband, whom she last saw when his orders were changed and the Marines cut their three-week San Francisco holiday to less than twenty-four hours—it was all so tender then, the pink carnations with one red one, racing to the window to wave when she heard the plane pass over the hotel. She thought they could keep each other present in their imaginations, and for the most part they did: the numbered letters, her accounts of life at home, his dreams of Honor, their dreams of Honor, her arrangements for Honor—the bassinet with its pale pink flounces. Then the summer was over, and she was back in New York. She had almost expected him to be there waiting; oh, but the war, treaty signed but soldiers still posted. When the war was really over, everyone coming home, she waited for him to give her a date of return, which he did not, could not. She understood this, but her feelings did not. And then the baby is born, and he does not appear as she imagined he would right up to the last second, bent over her smiling as she comes out of anesthesia.

Now he is finally coming home and she is waiting for him, alone in the apartment. Perhaps she has a drink. She had told Ernie, the baby nurse, to go home. She has a cup of soup perhaps, or a sandwich. She's sitting there and she hears a knock—and, panic of her insides dropping, she opens the door to her tall husband with his duffle, saying "Jenny" the particular way he does. But somehow he doesn't look like himself.

Did he take her in his arms?

And then he wants to see the baby. It seems to her almost as if he wants to see the baby more than he wants to see her, though she wouldn't have admitted that. She takes his hand and leads him immediately into the baby room with the gray walls, the Disney Bambis on one wall, the crib that would embrace every single one of their nine children.

V

A Baby under One Arm, a Cabbage in the Other

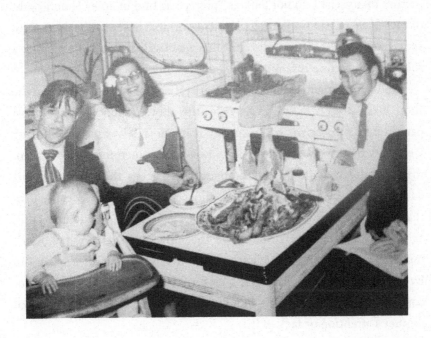

1.

A LITTLE GIRL IS LOOKING INTO HER MOTHER'S EYES. THE PHOTOGRAPH
was taken at the edge of a garden, under a pair of apple trees espaliered
into a leafy canopy. I am the little girl, and the mother is my mother.
We are poised on an outdoor chaise on the terrace at Hollow Hill. She is
stretched out on the chaise, which is painted white; I am scrunched in next
to her, and the cushioning is the pink that comes if you add some white to
tomato red. Beneath us is a planting of lily of the valley, their dark pointed
leaves; behind us, a shrub in flower rising against the dusky, pale red brick

of the house. My mother's right elbow is bent and her head rests in her open hand. You can't see her face, just her black hair, a little bit of the side of her face, and the leg of her glasses frame. But I could see her whole face then, from where I was, leaning onto her lap looking up into her eyes, smiling, my little girl teeth showing. When I first found this photograph, two or three years ago, I felt myself sharply take in breath. The hunger of the little girl's smile was a shock, and also her satisfaction: I have my mother to myself! I do not look as "pretty" as I do in other photographs of myself as a child, rather I look uncomfortable in the white dress with short puffed sleeves, uncomfortable in a way I still am when I walk into a room where no face is familiar.

I know my father is somewhere nearby, because he's just grabbed the shot. What does he think as he takes the photograph? That his eldest daughter, his firstborn, will someday frame it in silver on her bureau? Certainly he does not imagine it will become something called a scan, that his wife will die before the daughter reaches thirty, or that this daughter will be left alone in the wilderness of hunger so evident in that gaze into her mother's face. Nor does he imagine that hunger will, at times, almost entirely submerge the movements of his daughter's mind—curiosity, the investigation of different aspects of a question. Even these decades later, when I look at the photograph, that hunger comes—my childhood self's entangled wandering; the labyrinth of that mother's attention or lack of it.

Memory: Smile of the man with glasses in the grocery store at the corner of Ninth Avenue and 21st Street; he seems old, but I met him again in the 1970s and he remembered! I'm in a stroller pushed by Gagy, the Norwegian American woman hired to take care of me, who comes to take care of my siblings and me for the rest of my mother's life. I don't remember much more than jumbles of light and flashing color really, except for the Greek Orthodox church on the corner of 21st and Tenth Avenue: it seemed enormous and so beautiful, and I was shocked to discover as an adult that it was not the cathedral size I'd held in my imagination, but a tiny architectural gem built of brick. I do not, however, remember my first bedroom as any larger than it was; and after a visit to my mother's

1946 scrapbook, in which my father's black and whites of the apartment are neatly pasted, I am reassured that I correctly remember my white crib, the view of the seminary chapel out the one window.

But still, any time an errand takes me to the west of Chelsea, toward the High Line, I feel a surge of the excitement that comes when everything is new. Now, in my imagination, I leave the present to feel my mother as a young woman entering the new world she evoked in her 1968 memoir, *The People on Second Street*, which opens in Chelsea—*banana venders, Puerto Ricans, and Ninth Avenue drunks . . . whistles, insistent and triumphant, of ocean liners announcing departure.* Was it my imagination or could I actually see, through the breaks the cross streets make, the giant seagoing ships slowly moving north along the Hudson? *Ninth Avenue was thick with trucks, shops and shoppers. On every corner, there were groups of unemployed men. Sometimes, one of them would peel off from the little circle, sally jauntily into a dimly lit bar, emerge unsteadily a few hours later to rejoin his peers. On the stoops on side streets of the avenues were pathetic piles of furniture—a few chairs, a mattress or two—guarded by little bands of Puerto Ricans, virgins to the urban crush. You never knew whether they were waiting to move the furniture in or had just been evicted.*

Writing in the 1960s, my mother remembered her years in the guts of cities and the lives of poor black and brown people in America, years in Jersey City spent battling the caprices of landlords, brutal evictions, welcoming people made homeless into our house. I had a roommate in Jersey City for a while, Sammy Taylor, an African American teenager who slept on a cot near the window—he was at risk for tuberculosis, and the family apartment was damp; a woman we called Mrs. Early, burned out of her apartment, lived with us for a year; and once four children named Harley stayed for a week. Their names are all in the guest book, and pasted in the 1952 scrapbook is an account of Mrs. Harley and her ten children burned out of the coal bin they rented. The New Jersey *Afro-American* had broken the story, and the *Jersey Journal* ran it with a bright red headline: " 'Coal Bin" Family of 11 Refused Relief by City."

But Jenny, a new mother when they arrived in Chelsea on September 24, 1946, had no knowledge of such stories. The duplex on 21st Street expansively accommodated the three of us and seemed to call out for another child or two.

It was nervy to move away from *East Seventy-third Street, with its monogrammed pram covers, its fancy grocery-store windows filled with alternate rows of thick pink lamb chops and huge grapefruit wrapped in green leaves.* My father ignored advice from his father and earned praise from his mother, who was a devout churchgoer and had her own guilt about wealth. You can do anything you want, his father pleaded, just first take a "business year." Why? I asked his brother Bill, a banker: "So he'd know what he had." *The reactions of our own generation were less conventional,* my mother wrote; *laughter and real and embarrassed sympathy, and a suspicion that we just might not know what we were doing.* Twenty years later, she was chagrined—*we did it with a louder, more self-conscious noise than I care to remember.*

They had not entirely abandoned luxury; they'd had Christmas with the Moores in Palm Beach. I'm there in a photo, wearing bathing trunks and sunhat, scrutinizing what I find in the sand. Jenny, as pledged, returned to Barnard in February, leaving me in the care of Ernie. Paul, having decided to start General Seminary in Chelsea in the fall, took a semester of history with Jacques Barzun. That final semester, instead of returning to Romantic Poetry, Jenny took another class with Mrs. Niebuhr, along with Spanish and International Relations; her culminating straight A's got her elected to Phi Beta Kappa for academic excellence. In May, in cap and gown, she graduated—in a color snapshot, I am the baby on her hip. Her father was there, and Margarett, in Four Winds again, "knocked down the bars" to be present.

My mother was not the only woman to find seminary culture appalling when it came to women; she and the other eight student wives soon organized, making short work of the policy that barred women from lectures and events, even from most chapel services. The "close" as the campus was called, was pastoral with its lawns, trees, and paved walks, but not really set up for families. One couldn't marry while a seminarian; if you already had a wife, you had to reside with her off-campus. The atmosphere was ecclesiastical and righteous—when my parents skipped the reception for new students because they had tickets to *Carousel,* it caught the notice of the powers that be, and one morning, as they pushed me across the close in my carriage, they ran into the seminary dean. *He eyed us rather quizzically and said, "How interesting."*

My mother did not yet know she'd be chafing at the limitations of her role as a clergy wife for her entire adult life, but she had a visceral understanding that the church made it difficult for a woman both to do the right thing and to innovate: she wouldn't wear a hat and dispense tea every Sunday, but she'd make the odd exception and perform with grace, calibrating—*I have to go and "be lovely,"* she'd say. But how to contribute her brain, imagination, and energy to Paul's career? She'd watched the Niebuhrs—Reinhold, American and a Protestant whose work came out of the German evangelical tradition; and Ursula, her Barnard religion professor, who was British and Anglican (Episcopalian in the United States). Jenny wanted to work beside Paul in that kind of partnership.

Around the corner, next door to the seminary entrance on 20th Street, was a rundown old Episcopal church where C. Clement Moore, the author of "The Night Before Christmas" and no relation to my father, had been vicar. St. Peter's was stuck in the past, kept its doors locked except on Sundays when a dwindling white congregation wandered in for services. The only weekday activity was led by students from General who held religion classes for children from the neighborhood—not so well attended; why not add baseball, even basketball? With $150 from the seminary ($1,300 in 2018 dollars), my father mounted a full-time recreation program with seminarians as staff; in the meantime, Jenny teamed up with other seminary wives, one of them a trained teacher, to start a nursery school in seminary buildings for neighborhood families.

Soon, wanting to know more about the kids' families, she began visiting parents. *Those hours weren't easy. I learned of the chasm between us when I heard a mother say of me as I left her rat-infested flat, "She asks more questions than the relief worker."* It wasn't the first time Jenny's interest would be taken for meddling. But she was not someone to give up—instead she tried to learn more, was apt to go right up to the impossible thing and find a way through it, as she had as the ten-year-old turning a horse that resisted a jump. Soon the boundary between her life at home and the life of the children on the street became porous. A little boy had followed her home and quickly was doing so every day—*he climbed all over the furniture and onto the windowsills,* and *picked up and examined each article in our apartment with the infuriating innocence of the disturbed,* his hand slipping into hers *electric with need.* At first she considered what she was doing just *love:* in her book she calls the boy Frankie Butler—he became her first lesson in accepting what she couldn't change, her first bout with the limits of love.

What to do? She and Paul went to see Frankie's mother. *The smells of cheap wine and stale urine are commonplace to many college students of the sixties, but to us twenty years before, climbing the four flights to Mrs. Butler's door, they were shocking. A young white couple was standing with her in the small kitchen. "Meet Mr. and Mrs. Moore, the Christians," Mrs. Butler said. "This is Connie and Dick, the Communists."* This was a joke in 1968 when my mother wrote her book, but the encounter took place in the *Alger Hiss year,* and she and Paul had never met a Communist. They had no clue how to make *even a stab at putting Mrs. Butler at ease.* Just in time, Frankie tugged at Jenny's skirt, his mother thanked them for *being friends to her boy,* and they were back on the street. As they walked home, my mother thought of the contrast—Frankie's street life, her childhood afternoons at Singing Beach—*soft gatherings of air . . . sea water drying on my hair.*

My first sibling—Paul III, nicknamed Pip from *Great Expectations*— was born at the end of July 1947. They spent that summer at Hollow Hill, my father commuting 45 minutes for hands-on pastoral training at a New Jersey State mental hospital called Greystone. When they returned to 21st Street for his second year of seminary, Jenny wanted to do more for Frankie. She went to see the principal of his school, a big *Harry Golden hulk of a man;* after a few minutes about Frankie, he wanted to talk about his seventh- and eight-grade girls. Might Jenny do something with them?—*my girls aren't bad,* he kept saying, *but no one cares.*

They were mostly Italian, *living in overcrowded apartments with a mother at work,* my mother wrote, *too many brothers and sisters to care for, and nowhere to go.* The principal introduced her to Marlene, their leader, and

Jenny took her to the corner for a Coke: Would she and her friends like to start a girls' club? Of course they could meet at the Moores' apartment— their Catholic priest, Marlene said, would never allow them to do anything at a Protestant church. Yes, they could organize dances, or they could just talk. *"I'm not a whore like my mother thinks,"* Marlene said as they walked down 21st Street. *I made an inane statement to the effect that I knew she wasn't and turned the key in the front door. She waved from the corner.* On the day of the first meeting, Jenny was nervous. She was too rich, the apartment was too big and too fancy. Would the girls hate her for where and how she lived? *My panic began to wear off when they came giggling up the stairs ten strong in tight sweaters and tighter skirts. They shrieked with pleasure over the brick walls and rough beams of our top-floor living room and raced to the window to ogle the students visible in the seminary courtyard across the street. Occasionally they looked to me for comment but for the most part prattled on as if I wasn't there.* Soon they organized the first of many Saturday night dances in the seminary gym, and with the proceeds, bought pale blue satin jackets embroidered with their names as if they were a gang. *Sometimes they would tell me of their dreams of getting out of New York to a place where things must be different, but mostly they said they'd always be poor, that men were no good.*

The work at St. Peter's and, during Paul's third year at a downtown parish in Poughkeepsie, changed my parents in a way that must have seemed abrupt to their uptown friends, whom they still saw for martini evenings on days off. They were working with people different from themselves and were in constant conversation with seminary friends about the church's place in a postwar world. Paul and Jenny did not have to work to support themselves; they could afford to throw themselves into a life of service, away from the spiritual emptiness and lack of community in which they had grown up. Their passion was emotional as well as intellectual. They believed they were ready to change.

They were not alone: They had begun to hang out with two young priests who were seminary instructors. C. K. Myers, originally from upstate New York, taught church history. The initials masked a family name, Chauncie Kilmer, but he was called Kim unless Jenny teased him and drawled "Kilmer." Robert Pegram, from Maryland, taught Latin and Greek and was called Peegie though in her book, my mother was merciful and called him Bob. He had a game leg from polio that gave him a limp, and he was bald. With Kim and Peegie and a few others, Paul and Jenny talked about what the church might be. At St. Peter's they kept bumping up against frustrating limits. What would happen after they left and the dances and ball games were over? What would happen to the girls of the girls club, to Frankie Butler?

Jenny and Paul had now rejected a year of study in England, and the idea of a suburban parish was unimaginable. Kim and Peegie, for their part, wanted more than teaching at General where *black-gowned seminarians strolled to class with arms full of books.* Conversations among the *four of us* became consequential. Where and how in America could they do the kind of socially alive work that Anglican priests were doing with workers on the London docks and French priests incognito with workers in factories—the kind of work whose spirit an artist named Fritz Eichenberg rendered in a weekly paper called *The Catholic Worker?*

2.

I don't know where we hung *Christ in the Breadline* in Jersey City; but when I found it again in an Internet search for Fritz Eichenberg, I felt a wave of comfort and familiarity, and a renewed sense of its power. I might place it in the tradition of Käthe Kollwitz's war images, but that association is not what brings back the enduring force of the image, even in this secular age: a line of poor men, rendered almost entirely in black, and near the middle of a row of bent heads, Christ's head, his halo a bright white orb, its rays piercing the stark black. Here was the presence of the sacred, as if the men in their hunger knew who stood among them; I recognized the drunk, impoverished men who would sit in the entryway of our house, smelling of stale whiskey and filth, to whom nonetheless my mother served bowls of the hot soup she kept on the stove.

The theology that guided my parents' thinking had not come out of nowhere: *Some of us had heard of Dorothy Day, a Christian radical who ran a hostel for anyone who needed food or shelter, and edited* The Catholic Worker, *a monthly penny-sheet that embraced pacifism, anarchism, and voluntary poverty.* There were hostels, shelters that practiced a rule of community, farms that were organic and reflected an idea that working the land brought hope and that the earth needed devotion. The breadline woodcut was a version of a soup kitchen—feed the hungry—and the newspaper was a way to spread the word. In every issue Dorothy had a column called "On Pilgrimage" as it was usually an account of her travels to Catholic Worker hostels around the county. The first issue had offered the sheet at one penny, but the Irish protested the penny's association with the British currency that had so oppressed them, and so issue number two cost one cent.

Eventually the four of them invited Dorothy to address the student body, and one evening—it must have been the spring of 1947—a very tall older woman *came through the arched gate of the seminary, in ill-fitting, shabby clothes.* Jenny, twenty-four-years old and pregnant with my brother Pip, greeted her. The clothes were from the hostel's clothing room, Dorothy explained. She was a bit younger than Margarett, in her fifties, and wore her prematurely blazing-white hair in braids encircling her head. She had a sense of humor and a sense of irony; she was both principled and warm. Jenny *was stunned by her simplicity.*

I know I saw Dorothy Day at my mother's funeral, and I think I saw her in Indianapolis when I was twelve, but an earlier memory comes from Grace Church. Someone has knocked at the front door of the rectory, the entryway where the men ate my mother's soup. She comes into the house and I follow her, flat daylight of the living room, the street kept from view by my mother's homemade curtains; and out the back window, backyards vacant or sparsely gardened, white sheets and underwear fluttering on clotheslines. But I don't see Dorothy Day there: she's standing in the front hall at the bottom of the stairs—the braided white hair, the strong cheekbones, much taller than any older woman I'd ever seen— and not dressed like my white-haired grandmother Gami in a suit with a gold brooch watch.

Dorothy Day bends toward me as my mother says, "Honor, please shake hands with Miss Day"—did she say that? She must have. We were instructed to call Kim Father Myers; and Peegie, Father Pegram; and Bill Penfield who played the organ, Father Penfield. The tall woman doesn't speak like Gami either, and if she smiles, as she may well have because the atmosphere around her is of kindness, the smile breaks the angular solemnity of her face. I see her bending toward a little girl, toward me, her rangy body, her height, that face illuminated in the lunchtime light.

But that moment was years later, when Dorothy and my mother really knew each other, when Grace Church took busloads of Jersey City kids out to Catholic Worker farms on Staten Island or in Pennsylvania for the day—farms because the Catholic Worker cofounder, Peter Maurin had grown up a peasant farmer in France and believed that poor people from the city, homeless women and children, and men who had lost everything in the still-recent Depression would be rejuvenated by growing their own food, cooking, and caring for each other. His idea, Dorothy wrote, was to create a world in which "it was easier to be good."

Now Jenny is escorting Dorothy into the room at General Seminary where she will speak, and the older woman is asking the young woman to *pray for her,* because standing and speaking to people, though she does it often, makes her nervous. Her modesty was so striking that Jenny's own shyness and stiff politeness dissolved.

I had never met anyone like her, Jenny wrote in *The People on Second Street.*

It was my mother, not my father, who I remember as interested in how the actual lives of people, especially women, could change in a moment that later could seem to have been an encounter with the unseen. Jenny had felt something like it the day of her first confesssion—*I practically flew the nine blocks home, I felt so pure.* When I was little, she read me stories of women saints: St. Lucy born rich in Sicily, detained for giving her jewels to the poor, her eyes gouged out in torture, sometimes pictured holding a golden plate, on the plate; her eyes round and whole, an offering to God.

That night at the seminary, Dorothy Day *described her younger, Bohemian days,* my mother wrote—childhood in Brooklyn, Chicago, San

Francisco, then Chicago again; her father, a newspaperman and sports-writer, cruel, impatient with children, hater of Jews, Catholics, blacks, and radicals. Dorothy came to New York in 1916, having left the University of Illinois when her father joined the *Daily Telegraph*, and lived in a furnished room on the lower East side with a view of an air shaft. She wrote a series for the socialist daily *The Call* on how to live on $5 a day including rent: "I was surprised myself at how cheaply one person could live, once having given up the kind of standards set up by a family such as mine." No money for "recreation, books, clothes, doctors (there were the free clinics)," lunch from pushcarts or restaurants "with sawdust on the floor where one could get good bean soup and plenty of bread and butter for ten cents." Soon she was a beat reporter for *The Call*— "a reporter could listen to Trotsky one night at Cooper Union and the next day interview Mrs. Astor's butler." Noon to midnight, "We walked the picket lines. We investigated starvation and death in the slums." She interviewed Elizabeth Flynn, knew John Reed, met Leon Trotsky and Alexander Berkman—but not his lover, Emma Goldman, whose free love principles unnerved her. Did she mention the first time she was jailed? In Washington with the suffragist Jeanette Rankin to demonstrate for women's voting rights, she joined a women's hunger strike in prison to protest the treatment of suffragist activists. This was the first of Dorothy Day's many acts of civil disobedience—important to her not because it was successful, but because the experience brought her understanding of the cruelty of prison and tested her strength: "I was unable to face the darkness of that punishment cell," she wrote, "without crying out." She did not speak that night of the abortion of a first pregnancy and her guilt about it; rather *she told of her common-law marriage to an anarchist,* my mother wrote, *and of their child, whose birth had brought her such joy and thankfulness that hardly knowing why, she had joined the Roman Catholic Church, her conversion ending her relationship with the child's father.* After the talk, my mother remembered, Dorothy answered questions: *When a seminary student raised his hand and asked her how many people in her breadline were converted, she reddened, then quietly said that God cared about their empty stomachs and broken spirits, and not about their baptisms.*

As they left the seminary, Dorothy *thanked me for my prayers and said they had helped,* and later, at their apartment, she refused a drink, saying that she *couldn't bear the burdens of alcoholics and drink herself.* Could Jenny have predicted how much that evening would influence her life? It seems to me that Dorothy Day articulated a need my mother herself had—to bring about a personal change that would never be reversed, a way of thinking about others that had meaning beyond what she then understood. My mother and this daunting woman would visit and correspond for the rest of Jenny's life. Tamar, the daughter whose birth inspired Dorothy's conversion, would also have nine children; and for years Jenny sent them boxes of children's clothes, our hand-me-downs— "outgrown but not outworn," as Dorothy put it in the small tribute she wrote in the *Catholic Worker* after my mother died. She wanted readers be aware not only of the work my mother and father had done in Jersey City but also of "Jenny's "fine gifts as a writer," her book about Jersey City, and the closeness with this younger woman that had come about through a shared love of writing. Twenty years later, when Jenny wrote about life at the seminary, she marked that night and tried to put her sense of Dorothy Day into words: *She was a wind from another land— strong, warm, and a little frightening.* Yes, she was frightened but also, I believe, excited. Her three male colleagues had found inspiration in the work that priests who were men had done with the poor. Without knowing it, my mother had been looking for, and had found, a woman whose life could inspire her future.

3.

It was Kim, with his black hair, intent blue eyes, and impatience to put thought into action, who initiated the idea. Jenny and Paul were strolling the close one day, or at least that's the story, and Kim leaned out a gothic window: *"Why don't we four take a city parish, one of the dead ones?"* He'd already talked to Peegie, who was willing; instantly it seems, Jenny and

Paul agreed and *we four* set about writing a letter, and out it went, saying more or less that *two priests and a married seminarian to be graduated the following June would be ready to go to any downtown parish on one man's salary.* Paul had inherited more than enough money for himself and his new family, and Kim and Peegie would split the balance, both continuing to teach a course at the seminary.

Two priests and a married seminarian! It was clear to all of them that the mission included Jenny, but I hadn't known it was official—if that's the word—until I began writing about them; even in her own description of the letter, written twenty years after the fact, her existence was subsumed into *a married seminarian.* How was she to navigate these occasional erasures? In a first-grade questionnaire, I listed her profession as "cook," a story she told with resignation and only a little humor. But really, who was she to be, this educated, questing young woman? How, without a clerical collar, would she get people to look past her privilege, her motherhood of three (she was pregnant with her third child when they sent the letter), the assumption (which she shared) that she was the person tasked with running the household, overseeing cooking, cleaning, and childcare. She was involved in the decision to run an "open rectory," that the four of them and the three Moore children would live together, and that home would be an occasional hostel. Did anyone, including her, consider the work of brewing the coffee and making the soup for those who arrived at the door? Of fetching and unfolding sheets, making up cots for those who needed a bed for the night? On 21st Street, she still had uptown help: Gagy came whenever summoned to help cook, babysit and keep house, and probably there was also an Irish woman my mother may still have called a "maid."

I do not believe that my mother ever imagined what keeping an open rectory would require of her, nor do I believe that it occurred to her to articulate the patriarchal construction of her situation working among male clergy. She and other student wives had pressured their way into the all-male community at General Seminary, but even if the notion of women becoming priests had come up, I believe she would have dismissed it, might even have argued that only men should be priests, as when she declared in a Barnard paper that men alone should wear the military uniform.

"Did she ever think of becoming a nun?" a friend asked, trying to help me think this through. "Absolutely not," I snapped: How could my questioner not understand that my mother was not the convent type? Not for her the celibacy or flowing black robes or crispy white facewear even Episcopal nuns still wore in 1949. Imagining her future, Jenny might have thought about Dorothy, whom they continued to see, taking note I'm sure of how she managed to navigate the conservatism of the Roman Catholic Church and operate as a free agent: to the extent that Dorothy Day had a ministry, she had ordained herself to it.

To consider the question of priesthood and my mother would not have occurred to me had I not found in a scrapbook Union Seminary tuition receipts that have "Jenny Moore" enrolled there during Paul's final year at General. In letters just before they married, she'd pushed Paul toward the *liberal* uptown multidenominational seminary, but I had no idea that she herself had studied there. The courses she chose went to the heart of the matter: Systematic Theology and the Nature of Christian Worship. No matter that a woman couldn't be a priest; she would learn what she needed to work and think alongside her husband.

Courses in Systematic Theology are designed to lay out a coherent account of the doctrines of Christian faith and trace their development in light of the histories of philosophy, science, and ethics—such a class at Protestant Union would differ from the version taught at Anglican General. The community at Union, whose guiding spirit was the socially and politically conscious theologian Reinhold Niebuhr, was somewhat more open to women. There were female students and faculty even then; Paul had studied classics and English in college, and his intellect was born in the high church Anglican atmosphere of St. Paul's School, a theology he continued when he was at Yale at Christ Church in New Haven. At Barnard, Jenny studied anthropology, political history, and international relations, so it follows she'd find the emphasis at Union sympathetic and a return to the Barnard neighborhood, the locale of her intellectual awakening, reassuring.

The Nature of Christian Worship, her second course, was a multi-denominational history of the development of Christian worship from its beginnings. The curriculum included lectures, a monumentally long reading list from which one chose books to read and outline—books that Paul owned, she marked *P* on the lengthy mimeographed syllabus. There were ancient texts, histories of the various denominations, and classics like *The Varieties of Religious Experience* by William James and *The Dark Night of the Soul* by St. John of the Cross, which she had read with Father Wadhams: *The soul must climb the rungs of the mystical ladder to union with God: The understanding is "blinded" by faith, the memory is "emptied" by hope, and the affections and desires of the will are emptied of everything that is not God.* My mother's notes are painstaking, and she found some of the reading thrilling; with typical intensity, she read and outlined 1,241 pages.

The course also required visits to Manhattan places of worship. In her notebook are lists of Eastern Rite churches to choose from—Russian, Serbian, Ukrainian, and Romanian Orthodox—and notes on the Lutheran, Roman Catholic, Quaker, and Methodist Sunday services she attended, including descriptions of the churches: *There is a balcony at the back and around the church there are eight pictorial windows portraying the Last Supper, the Crucifixion and other scenes in The Life of our Lord. There was a polychrome dome over the altar*—this was the Lutheran church, Holy Trinity. She chose Madison Avenue Presbyterian Church, where she heard the great George Arthur Buttrick preach about the anger of Jesus: "And when he looked round about on them with anger, being grieved for the hardness of their hearts, he saith unto the man, Stretch forth thine hand." Mark 3:5 was the text—she found the sermon *a very definite, unsentimental statement on personal religion, a detailed analysis of anger and its motives . . . an attack on the sweet and gentle Jesus and a plea for honest self appraisal.*

She was becoming a knowledgeable Anglican laywoman, and the mid-twentieth century was a great moment for such figures: Ursula Niebuhr, her teacher; Evelyn Underhill, the pacifist activist whose history of Christian mysticism she read; Dorothy L. Sayers, the theologian who also wrote mysteries and was a friend of C. S. Lewis. At the end of the year,

Jenny could analyze and criticize any Christian service, which meant she might also have imaginative ideas about ways to make a liturgy engaging, part of life. *A sad, poor parish where we will have many many people to help,* she'd written Paul five years earlier. She might write the same words now; but their meaning had expanded, as had her dreams for her life.

4.

For weeks letters came, cheering their idealism. But no offers were extended until finally there arrived *unreserved encouragement* from Bishop Benjamin Washburn of the Diocese of Newark. Available was Grace Church (Van Vorst) in Jersey City, the parish established in 1853, the nineteenth-century church built on the farmland of a family called Van Vorst. There it still stood, though a grid of streets and rowhouses had long since replaced the pasture that once stretched out from the rectory.

We four, Jenny and Paul and Kim and Peegie, set off for Jersey City on July 1, 1949, *that kind of summer day that makes heels stick to the tar strips of sidewalks,* my mother wrote in *The People on Second Street.* They followed the moving truck, Paul turning left on Erie Street. *Looking out the window of our station wagon, we saw a Tootsie Roll factory, and smelled the cloying smell that lay heavy in the hot summer air. Near it stood a brown building with an ancient-looking sign, "The Home of Ken-L Ration Dogfoods." On the occasional small vacant lot at the edge of the highway, ball playing went on: boys appeared, then scooted into oblivion as if dispersed by the insistent horn blowing, truck drivers' oaths, and policemen's whistles.*

They turned onto Second Street and parked. The church, built of brownstone, had

a tower and a three-story rectory—*It looks like something out of Charles Addams!* My mother always said. When she fantasized the *sad poor parish,* she'd imagined the two of them in a kind of Dorothea Brooks idyll of good works. But four of them would be living here, seven if you count me, aged four; my brother Pip, aged two; and my sister Dee, who arrived on the earth six weeks after the move. Also brownstone, the rectory was set back, looked jammed into its space, church to the right as you faced it. When they arrived that first day there was a dying dog, gasping for breath; their first humanitarian act *to which we attached great significance* was to call the SPCA.

The house was not spacious and while it may once have been well appointed, it had not been loved for quite a while. The previous residents—a couple from something called "the Church Army," which organized laypeople for service—had closed off the basement and the top floor. Outdoors, any grass that had ever grown in the front yard was long gone, the earth packed firm. They would soon pave it with concrete, and as we grew up, we'd play handball and tag there with our friends from the neighborhood. It took a while to figure out that the basement was the only place for an office; the ground floor—living room, dining room, kitchen—would be shared, *in common*. Our family would inhabit the second floor with its three bedrooms and one bath, and Kim and Bob Pegram would each have a room on the third floor, sharing a tiny bathroom with no tub, its stand-up shower in a tin enclosure. They decided that Kim and Bob would have their breakfast in the parish hall, and the three clergy would have lunch together to discuss the work of the day. Supper would be communal. *Bob said it was a Moore household, that whether we ate in the dining room or not was my affair, Kim insisted we were in kitchen-table land and it was important that we break down this simple barrier and eat where we presumed lower Jersey City ate—in the kitchen. We agreed with Kim but without his passion. By fall the white enamel kitchen table was set with forks and spoons and plastic ware, the silver and wedding presents put away.*

The parish was not just *sad and poor*, they quickly learned, but also small, all white, and nearly dead—an opportunity for resurrection was how they thought about it. This was when they made the "open rectory" pledge: everyone should feel welcome, though when they made the decision, "everyone" was an abstraction. Kim got concrete right away, unlocking the wrought iron front gate, tossing padlock and key, and tearing down the "keep out" sign that taunted the carved inscription on the lych-gate: "Enter into these gates with thanksgiving." While *the symbol shattering was going on,* Paul was assembling the crib upstairs, and Jenny, *seven months pregnant,* was standing in the kitchen: *I was in that cast-a-glazed eye-at-the-world mood of late pregnancy, when internal focus suffuses any purposeful action with a female vagueness.*

Through the grime, my mother observed that the interior was *in its way beautiful* with cornices, high ceilings, and Victorian wall sconces. The kitchen, once the parlor, had high ceilings and on its wallpaper little soldiers marched in a forest of cone-shaped trees. The refrigerator, however, was *apartment-size,* meaning tiny; the sink *a suitable height for someone four feet tall,* and a *linoleum rug* protected the floor—you could see parquet at the edges. Bulked in the corner was a dark green safe that almost reached the ceiling; Sunday collections were deposited there, and various valuables—*Put it in the safe,* my mother would say, and I'd watch Father Myers or my father twirl the dial till the huge door fell heavily open.

Late that first afternoon, the sexton (church language for janitor) arrived to say hello and unlocked the church. My mother described the interior exactly as I remember it—*rays of sunlight mixed with the artificial light overhead streaking the pews. The color of the wood was like maple syrup.* They all knelt down and she gazed up at the heavy wooden beam across the chancel: carved and gilded there were these words: *Thou hast overcome the power of death.* How unlikely it was, she thought, that she found herself reading that particular inscription as she knelt here with a husband who *had almost died in the war.*

I love the tenderness in my mother's voice early in *The People on Second Street,* speaking with a part of herself I never knew, of a woman making an alien place a home, how she evoked the four of them walking the neighborhood that first night saying, "Good evening" to those they passed; and how people stared at the group, four clergy and one very pregnant woman. In their black clericals and crisp white collars, Paul and Kim and Peegie were indistinguishable from the celibate Catholic priests who served St. Mary's, the enormous Irish basilica across Erie Street, and Italian St. Boniface, across Second Street. Was she their mistress? The housekeeper?

In a photograph saved in the 1949 scrapbook they are at a bar somewhere, laughing, posing, raising their drinks. She's the only woman with a bunch of guys. What are they drinking to? What Jenny's raising is a can of beer, and Paul, too; but he's goofing, laughing, holding the beer so it pours into his open mouth. She's just raising the can, that amazing smile across her face, not a shred of self-consciousness. On her left is Kim holding a bottle of something, looking a little dazed. The three of them are standing behind what looks like a bar; Bob Pegram and a seminary classmate John Wing are in front of it, both leaning on the bar as if they are regular customers. She looks so happy and pretty in the center of that group of men, one of them her husband, the others great friends who are coming to seem like family. And they're all so young! She and Paul and John Wing in their twenties, Bob and Kim a little older. When I first looked at this photograph, I imagined them at Coney Island, off for the day from Grace Church, which is why the men were wearing coats and ties and not clericals. I didn't want to say at first that the guys were priests—I'm writing in a secular world, and what kind of woman hangs out with a gang of priests? When I was little, it didn't seem strange to me that my mother consorted with clergymen—my father, her husband, was a priest—but now I see there are people to whom it may seem strange. Looking again, I see they are not at a booth in Coney Island, but somewhere more like a restaurant: arched shelves, glasses, bottles painted on the wall behind them, like a painting by a sophisticated child or like a stage set. To the right of the photograph is a vase of chrysanthemums, white and spiky, the bouquet so enormous it reaches out of the frame. So frustrating a photograph: It's just surface, I can't just go into that place where they are, see their clothes brighten from black and white into color, hear Paul say "Oh, Jenny!" and hear her say "Oh, Paul!" or make one of her sly funny remarks. I can't just be in the feel of their bodies, the blood running through them, no sense of an ending.

Though I'm close to three times their ages now, I look at them as if I am a child, still admiring, still confident of their guidance. I always assumed that everyone my parents knew admired what they were doing at Grace Church; but looking at photographs, thinking about my mother and all those priests, about the cramped, shabby quarters of the rectory, I wonder. So many of their close friends were people who had rarely seen the inside of a kitchen, let alone considered eating at a white metal kitchen table, people who still lived the way my parents had until quite recently. Some of course made their own way into service. At Zobby Potter's funeral in 2017, I learned that she had spent a lifetime on the board of the Henry Street Settlement House, raising millions of dollars, and that her husband Bobby had always worked pro bono for social justice. And there was Tony Duke, who founded and for fifty years ran Boys Harbor, a camp for underprivileged children at his estate on the East End of Long Island. I was considering this question when I visited Wattie and Maisie Dickerman's daughter recently. What had Maisie really thought of my parents in Jersey City? (Wattie died young.) Her quiet, temperate voice immediately swerved to her mother's opinion: "It really pissed her off."

"Pissed her off?"

"She thought it was ridiculous, those two very rich people pretending to be poor." Laine's voice embodied her mother's irritation and judgment.

They were not pretending to be poor, I protested.

But their choice of Jersey City and their creation of a life there was radical for who they were. They didn't commute from a nicer house somewhere else, and they arrived on Second Street with no household help—a philosophical choice that was moderated as reality closed in. Reality began their second morning in the rectory, my mother standing in a roomful of unpacked boxes, relying that day on what she called *masculine support*. Paul had set up the crib, yes, but what was Peegie doing wandering among the boxes with a dust rag when the dirt upstairs was so appalling? When she complained things were *not yet nice*, Kim, the revolutionary, declared her standards *tiresome and bourgeois and plunged downstairs into the basement to contemplate where an office might fit*. For all they knew, the thigh-high piles of church records, newspapers, and offertory ledgers lay on packed earth. "We can put the clothes room down there, too," Kim proclaimed at supper; he'd reached the linoleum surface of the concrete basement floor. They had decided to emulate the Catholic Worker, which had clothes rooms where anyone could pick up a free jacket or dress. They'd canvas their Manhattan pals for cast-offs.

The first Sunday there were seven parishioners at mass, all expecting a prim morning prayer. They were also all white, female, and over sixty-five, with the exception of two bachelor sons and one spinster daughter. But word traveled fast and within weeks the streets were abuzz with talk of the new "fathers." Black and Puerto Rican people suddenly found themselves truly welcome, and the old guard either stayed or left, though none of those who left were spared a call from one of the team explaining the new enterprise and seeking help. The first of the old guard to visit was Mrs. Flynn. Kim noticed a white-haired woman sitting on one of the lych-gate benches and flew out to greet her, shouting to my mother for lemonade; it was a hot day. Jenny quickly complied, ice cream too; but the tray tumbled, lemonade and clotted ice cream drenching Mrs. Flynn, who kept saying that she'd needed to cool off anyway. She became a regular and an ally. Fierce and opinionated, I remember, and full of Grace Church history and gossip—the great Canon Bryan, whose ghost still haunted the rectory, how she'd left the Catholic church. In my mother's book I learned, to my shock, that when we got to Jersey City and for years afterward, this very elegant, very old lady began work at five a.m. as a cleaning woman at city hall: she'd been left a widow and penniless.

By the time I was capable of remembering, Sunday church was always so full there were two services. I think my father and Kim and Peegie spent a lot of time on the street, walking up to boys playing stickball, asking if they wanted to play real baseball, then meeting their parents and talking about their plans for Grace Church and how they saw it as a community center. My mother went "calling" too, taking me and Pip and Dee, the baby, with her; soon she was overseeing the women's groups at the church. A ladies auxiliary and altar guild were soon mixed race—the word we used was *integrated*. A friend of his gave Peegie a television, and they set it up in the parish hall and people came, since in 1949 not many people yet had TVs. The evening showings became a gathering place, rows of chairs filled with people who did and did not come to church on Sunday. Soon there were weekend dances. A community was beginning.

5.

My brother Pip, then four, had prayed and prayed for a brother—sister Dee was two—and now he ran from his room in floods of tears: "God lied! God lied!" They named her "Jenny Augustine," for my mother and the fourth-century bishop who, for his book *The City of God*, was their patron saint.

But when they actually saw their tiny daughter, the name seemed just wrong. She became Rosemary, the only one of us born in Jersey City, the only one of nine who's always lived in a city. She became the star of the kitchen, holding court from her high chair. *It was to the kitchen that people came*, my mother wrote. *It was there that the invisible reality of the action of the altar became for many a visible reality. It was here that George Grace, a Bowery "bum," asked for a match and said, "I really am the beggar but I feel at home." It was here that Diana, three months pregnant from an encounter in a tenement doorway, told me she was scared of what would happen on her wedding night. It was here that Jim, an unskilled laborer, when sympathy was offered for his dying wife, said, "but it is such a loving time." Seated at the kitchen table, a moneyless Negro, when asked why he would borrow for an expensive funeral for his wife, explained, "We don't do too well in this world so we've got to have a big send-off."* The kitchen was not solemn. My mother loved to laugh, and she made the place welcoming, her girlhood shyness having become a capacity to pull in any visitor who came for a meal, anyone who just stopped by—*cooking, people, listening*, she wrote decades later in a one-page summary of her life. And on the Victrola, *Oklahoma*, a 78 rpm of people laughing, or Danny Kaye as a whiney child saying, "Mommy, give me a drink of water, I'm thoisty!" In that kitchen, on the radio, I first heard the Platters sing "Smoke Gets in Your Eyes," my mother telling me it was "an old song." And there she played her records of Bach or Vivaldi—the two composers a discovery she marked as crucial in that one-page summary.

I want a sense of her alone in that kitchen, but of course she's rarely alone. And now someone is taking a picture that does seem to catch her in solitude, an ice-cream cone in her right hand, her left hand on her hip, a watch on that arm. She has on an Indian-print cotton dress with cap sleeves, drawstring at the neckline loosened so you see the shadow of a clavicle, the line of her jaw, her black hair against pale skin. She's wearing her red glasses, which are as I remember them, and she is looking up, as if "up" were some distance away, and she's forgotten the ice-cream cone. Her tall figure casts a shadow on the white kitchen cabinets behind her, and you can see way up top of them a cake plate with a white cover. At hip level is the kitchen counter painted some dark color, and on it, an electric mixer, a salt shaker, a bottle of something like Worcestershire sauce, and a dish rack slotted in, the lid of a saucepan drying.

In the rack, sweetie, she says to whatever grown-up is washing the dishes; no end of old friends come to check out the alien scene. After one bout with dish rag and Brillo, Tony Duke, tobacco heir, St. Paul's and Yale, had a dishwasher delivered—the apparatus not common in the mid-1950s—white, freestanding and plugged into the wall. But what was she *thinking* right then, looking up that way? Or has the photographer just caught her in that odd spaciness because he has a sense of humor? Look!—Jenny!—dreamy and studious in glasses, holding an ice-cream cone as if it will never melt.

Red spots one morning, and Doctor Mokowski comes; he has a black moustache and is bald and proclaims we have head lice. She calls the exterminator and Harry, a former elephant wrangler fired when Barnum and Bailey left, goes to the drugstore—to me he was an old man, so it was funny that he called her "Mommy." He's back with the stuff and one by one, we sit as she applies smelly oil and takes the strange two-sided comb to our hair, raking out the "lice," so tiny you hardly see them. That's one morning; and maybe every morning she does the laundry, but one day a rat jumps off the washing machine, *the tail whipping my legs as he raced by*. It was *the last straw* and she shrieked, racing upstairs.

"*You can't expect to be happy all the time,*" Paul said.

"*I'm not a two year old,*" she wept back, tears of fury. That crisis passed, as did others, though people always marveled at how she managed all that work, all those children.

It would take her years to gauge energy spent.

The *four of us* learned tolerance as tensions between them built and dissolved. My mother reflected on this in her book, conscious that anyone else trying to live in community would run up against differences: *Kim was extreme. Personal comfort meant little to him, and he always thought of concepts like Welcome and Succor in the most absolute terms.* Father Pegram, who was from the South, was mellow and easygoing, and *though he shared Kim's concerns, more conservative than Kim*—in temperament. *He wanted to help each individual,* she wrote, *in whose dignity he deeply believed, but he also wanted time to be alone;* he couldn't write his sermons without solitude. And there was also what she and even Paul called *the vagueness of bachelors. Kim and Bob couldn't understand why we needed plans (or at least so many of* them)—*Kim was the most lenient, Bob tended to be strict, and Paul and I stood somewhere in the middle.* After a while total agreement was less necessary—*each person simply acted as he felt he should in each situation. It was our way of reconciling individual differences, or at least of not confronting them head on, and usually it worked well enough.*

Once in a while, they needed a break. A group sojourn in the Moore place in the Adirondacks once a year, but also days off separately, staggered so there was always someone holding down the fort. Not a luxury, it turned out, but crucial to keeping everything going. *Kim had great endurance, but there were times when he would grow impenetrably silent, descend to the basement and sit in one of the damp rooms on the swivel chair that didn't work. There he would stay for perhaps an hour, arms at his sides, feet stretched out on another chair, with his black fedora pulled down over his face.* Peegie simply climbed the stairs to his room; she'd recognize his uneven step— his polio limp. Paul *had a slow, steady ascent to boiling. He would become more and more conscientious, the furrows on his forehead would deepen, the jaw would set firmly. The explosion was marked by a compulsion to straighten up his bureau. The only abnormal part of this operation was that it took at least fifteen minutes to complete.* . . . As for herself: *irritation when too many people asked me where someone else was or when the children and our new baby were kept awake by front yard departures and arrivals.* . . . *My temper would then wear itself out in a hyperactive attack on the white woodwork, where finger marks and industrial soot stubbornly remained, despite my scrubbing. We all*

were aware of the danger signs in each other, and there was much predicting
among us of impending emotional storms.

The photograph looks like a movie still: Kim's white shirt is open at the neck, and he's wearing a tweed jacket. His eyes are narrowed against the sun, as if he's just said something and is waiting for an answer; his black hair is fallen forward onto his forehead, one lock of it curly, his left hand reaching for the water that in the photograph looks nearly as black as his hair, nearly as black as Jenny's. They're all in the Adirondacks—time off to talk things through? The back of Bob Pegram's balding head is in the foreground, and Paul's behind him, outside the frame, both rowing and taking the picture, letting the boat glide a little. They look like something out of *A Place in the Sun*, thinking now of Montgomery Clift and Shelley Winters in the rowboat, of Elizabeth Taylor with her black hair.

One night at supper, a woman named Sarah Crocker from San Francisco was visiting. Everyone whispered that Montgomery Clift had wanted to marry her, my mother told me. Who was Montgomery Clift? A movie star, sweetie. Sarah Crocker with her blond hair, so different from my mother; she wore a flaring skirt, I noticed, a wide belt around her tiny waist. Why didn't she marry Montgomery Clift? He must be a special kind of movie star to get talked about at the supper table, since usually what got talked about was the inner city. I was learning to make conversation: from my mother, how to turn a phrase so that older people like Father Myers and Father Pegram and Sarah Crocker would laugh and pay attention; from my father a whole idea, like what the Holy Spirit was and how, when people could understand each other and you felt it, you could say the "holy spirit" was present. I fashioned opinions from what I heard. My mother was charming the whole table, a blinding light. My father, cool and tall. When he listened, there was quiet around him. When my mother said something, people marveled that anyone would see it that way. She could hit on an actual truth that came straight from feeling, while my father reasoned with his emotions, even about things that were not reasonable, like the "holy spirit." He might have the last word, but he was outside the important transactions, which were what happened in the heat of my mother.

Heat, yes; but rereading her book, I am carried by her calm, reasoned syntax: How an idea is described through a story she tells; how, as in every experiment, contradictions whittle at what was hoped for. How the rectory at Grace Church, which I remember as always open, was eventually locked after supper to keep things safe—there was occasional stealing; how children from the neighborhood, even our best friends, were allowed upstairs only if invited. I can feel my mother coming to terms in the cadences of her sentences: *Our youthful visitors had lost their awe of our house and reluctance to enter it. They came, they saw, and often they took.* Quarters and dimes disappeared from a bedroom bureau; from the kitchen table, Paul's huge bunch of keys to everything; and once, from the safe, left unlocked, an entire Sunday's collection. The thieves were both *Negro and white* and almost always kids we knew—familiar became the *pit-of-the stomach reaction when something was gone, the ordeal of accusing the culprits, the conflict we felt, since no matter what the accused had taken we had more, which obscured the simple fact that he was a thief, and the discomfort of feeling we'd been an easy mark.*

My own stomach knotted when one of the older boys—white, an acolyte on Sundays and everyday, an older boy we played with and admired—stole two typewriters from the office and went to jail for a while. My father's earnest explanation of the consequences—stealing means he broke the law—stayed with me: I had thought the police were always bad, not on our side. Frankie was our friend! He couldn't have done it on purpose! Oh, but he had, had admitted it when the police found the typewriters in a local pawn shop. "What is a pawn shop?" Oh, money. Always that gnawing reality.

They began to lock even the church before they turned in for the night. *We had found that our theories of a wide-open church and rectory needed limits.* When my mother used words like *limits,* I knew she hated what they described. She and the others struggled to withstand the contradictions, to think them through, to protect their ideal of community—we *spent many hours discussing its meaning for us and for the people who were gathering under the shelter of Grace Church. We also began to accept the fact that things couldn't be changed overnight, and in some cases, never.*

The church with its vaulted ceilings, its mahogany pulpit, was beautiful to them, but what did it say to *our new tenement friends?* Peegie put it this way—the church was *"the gift of the dead rich to the living poor."* Like Father Myers and my father, Father Pegram was trained *in the intricacies of theological dialectic, wore cassocks and cottas and brocade chasubles from the religious closets of other centuries and other lands,* and led *prayers in language like "propitiation," "made flesh" and "lamb of God."* But what, Jenny wondered, did this mean, really, to Ralphie Walker, his mother, or even to middle-class African American parishioners like Mrs. Cade, whose landlord raised her rent with impunity? Would any of them ever say what they really thought? These were the questions they talked through in two-day retreats in the Adirondacks or elsewhere, a practice they continued the eight years they stayed in Jersey City.

6.

To get to where we lived in Jersey City, you emerged at the Grove Street station of the Hudson Tube from beneath some sort of shelter. In the shadows there, a row of small shops, one of them the optometrist my mother took me to at the end of fifth grade. The doctor prescribed glasses—my entrance into the destiny my mother dodged by taking her glasses off when photographed, a practice I imitated. But it is sixty years later and the Hudson Tube is now the PATH and wearing glasses is chic. I have decided to go back to Grace Church for this book, to visit the parish; no matter how much has changed, standing in a place where the past took place helps me remember. Now the escalator ascends into the light, into a station, glassed-in and octagonal, that sits in the open air—no row of shops, no optometrist. Through my one-day-wear contact lenses, the new trains are sparkling, and one uses a card for fare. What cost two dimes then is almost three dollars now.

In a mist of spring almost-rain, I turn left on intuition and walk a few blocks, ask directions. I am given amiable reassurance that I am head-ing toward the corner of Erie and Second Street, only to deduce, when I pass the handsome gray granite city hall, that I am going in the wrong direction. I know this for sure because I know I have never seen the city hall before—I would have remembered. "City hall" was so demonized around the supper table that I formed an image of something sinister: "a machine" is what they called it, and I imagined actual grim machinery, manipulated by the corrupt, notorious, and racist Democratic political boss Frank Hague, even though he was no longer mayor. It was "city hall" that my parents and Kim and Peegie battled for "fair housing," open to all and affordable. A law passed in 1949, the year we got there, had allowed homeowners to divide the old brownstones and charge whatever rent they pleased and keep anyone out. These owners had lived in their houses for generations and, my mother wrote, *stayed in Jersey City, walked to church to sing the same hymns as their silken-gowned grandmothers, in emptier pews. They grew old behind shutters; or a modest sign above the doorbell advertised "Rooms for Rent"; or they sold their houses to be made into apartments.*

Fair housing—such a big subject at the table sixty years ago—is probably still a big subject, I am thinking as I walk. I have turned myself around, and with a growing sense of familiarity, walk along Newark Avenue. There is no more Wonder Store, the big emporium where I saw my foot bones green through an X-ray machine and where my mother took us for T-shirts and blue jeans, socks and underpants and sneakers. I remember her pushing a stroller with Rosie in it, Pip and Dee completing the entourage. She says yes when we ask for the most delicious thing on earth, lemon ice in a little pleated paper cup; the soundtrack is a woman (Patti Page) singing "How Much Is That Doggie in the Window?" We didn't get dresses and coats at the Wonder Store; they came mysteriously, purchased in New York by Gami or my mother and arriving by Railway Express. Dee and Rosie and I often wore identical dresses on Sundays and on what my mother called "special occasions."

Now I'm dressed in black with a bright scarf, and there are restaurants along the avenue, a deli that looks old, an electronics store where I buy an extra chip for my camera, a McDonald's—everything seems either garish or too small, even the brick and brownstone rowhouses that I remember as looming over Erie Street. And then, suddenly, there it is! Grace Church. I'd imagined seeing it from a distance, but it comes up fast, oddly small like everything else but still protected by the black wrought iron fence about five feet high; behind the fence at the corner is a large wooden cross, on it a bronze Christ. Unlike the church, the crucifix seems larger than it did when it was installed. All of us gathered for the dedication, performed outdoors: three vested priests and acolytes in cassocks and cottas, Kim Meyers saying in the blessing that the crucifix signified that what went on inside the church honored the suffering of Christ, and the suffering of all of humankind, no matter who you were.

The brownstone church is still pinkish, blackish, as it was in 2003, the year after my father's death when a few of my sisters and I returned for the naming of the block "Bishop Paul Moore Place." The front yard where we played handball seems tiny, a patchwork of concrete fixes that now serves as a parking lot, and the lych-gate with its hospitable benches, which Kim painted bright red, is completely gone—as if a raft of pageantry and memory had been simply lifted off into oblivion. I try to get my little-girl self back as I walk the path from the street to the front door, ring the bell in the entryway where my mother served the soup and coffee. There's the bench where the men sat. Laurie Wurm, the vicar, opens the door with a warm greeting—despite my feminism, it startles me that the priest here is a woman. No one lives in the rectory now, she tells me—it's for offices and parish activities—she and her wife live with their children half an hour away.

Alone for a few minutes while Laurie makes a phone call, I wander the house. Every room seems as it was. though the bathroom has been redone, a built-in tub in place of the old claw-footed one, a sink inserted in a vanity instead of what my mother described as *a marble washstand whose cracks were filled with old mortar and newer sediment.* My parents' bedroom—where I first remember their king-sized bed with its red-bordered headboard, photographs of us as infants arranged on the wall above it—was now a room for handcrafts, on the wall a poster: "I am the potter, you are the clay," a verse from Isaiah.

It was time to go downstairs. Laurie has invited some of the women my age from the "old families" who first came to Grace Church "when your father was here in the 1950s." Walker, Skipper, Williams, I'd written her—all of them African American, the girls with whom I jumped rope double Dutch or played jacks. These women had spent their entire lives in Jersey City—as nurses, teachers, professionals. I wanted to know what they'd made of my mother, of the three young white priests suddenly appearing in their lives when their parents were young, the world so different, we children only vaguely conscious of the significance our parents attached to our after-school games, black and white, playing together.

First Doris Walker and Mary Aiken arrived, and after a shy silence we started to talk. "I don't remember much about your mother. She was in the kitchen or with the kids," Doris said. She was one of the red-haired sisters of Ralphie Walker, my brother Pip's best friend—and when I was seven, my first boyfriend, our first too-wet kiss occurring just feet away from where we now sit. Doris's redheaded sisters, Irma and Audrey, were closer to my age; Irma and I once had a screaming, hair-pulling fistfight while lining up as angels for a nativity pageant—who goes first? I remember that my father separated us. Doris and Mary and I were settling into slow conversation when Gerry Williams slid into one of the chairs. She and her sister Shirley were two of the older girls I worshipped—vivacious and fashionable in tight skirts. Shirley had died, Gerry said. I remembered her so well, alternating with Joanna Smith, who was white, as leading lady in plays that Freddie Bradlee, an actor from New York, directed—he was Ben and Connie's elder brother. For instance, the girls portrayed the Barbara Bel Geddes character in a one-act version of *Rear Window*.

I hadn't really known Gerry, but I'd known her brother Noel (pronounced No-well), whom I pictured as having become a distinguished citizen in a three-piece suit; he had died as well. As we talk, I realize how close a community we were—Gerry's memories were like those of a cousin. "You were quite—well," she said, "not easy," and we all laughed. Were they talking about the terrible fights my mother and I started to have when I got to be seven or eight? "What do you mean?" I asked.

"Just running all over, talking back, not quiet." More laughter. I had thought myself invisible.

Gerry was a storyteller, and she soon got going. All the girls had crushes on all the priests—hoots of giggles, recognition—especially Father Myers, who was both handsome and single. The fathers were effective with the police. Any street fight, of which there were many, ended when "the fathers" showed up; the authority of a man in a black suit and round collar was so potent to the mostly Catholic policemen that they just "backed off." I should be sure to take that in—if *anything* happened, you went to Grace. That is, if anything bad happened to your son, you called, and the fathers would go down to the police station and the cops would let him go.

"Your parents and the fathers were the first white people we ever knew," Gerry continued. "I mean, to talk to." It was important for me to know this, to hold on to what had really happened, to understand how unusual it had been. I had known that my parents hadn't

known black people until they worked at St. Peter's in Chelsea, but I didn't know what Gerry had just told me—how rare mixing races had been.

Now I was asking again about my mother.

They remembered her wearing black glasses, while I remember her in red glasses; her long, shiny black hair and how she was always rushing in and out, working so hard, and that she had "opinions"— she was a woman who said what she thought.

"She was a trooper," Gerry Williams said.

They also remembered Gagy coming once a week to take care of us, that she was afraid of black people "at the beginning"—I knew that, even as a little girl—but "she changed," ended up at the kitchen table talking to whoever turned up—they remembered her with Mrs. Williams, Shirley and Gerry's mother.

They called my father Poppy like we did, remembered how funny it was, him so tall, all the kids following him in a giggling throng. An extraordinary time, their memories are telling me. Grace Church was a place to play and hang out, either in the front yard or in the parish hall. Jersey City was a different place than it became later: "We all walked everywhere then, it felt safe."

They repeated this: that never before "your mother and the fathers" had any of them seen "white people goin' up in them nigger houses." Write that down, Gerry said. I remember coming home and asking, "Where's Poppy?"

"Out calling," my mother would say.

"And we had never gone anywhere," Gerry continued.

"Right," said the others.

"They took us to Broadway, to a play called *The Ponder Heart*" (an adaptation of a Eudora Welty story about a mentally disabled son of a rich white Southern family) and to a restaurant where they had spaghetti— "We'd never had spaghetti. And they took us to the movies, one of them *Edge of the City* with Sidney Poitier and John Cassavetes." (Martin Ritt's first film, about a friendship between a black and a white dock worker); some of their fathers had worked on the docks.

There were trips to the ballet in New York and to Birdland "for jazz."

"They took us to the park! To Riverside Park in Manhattan. We had never been to a park!"

"And to a farm!" (a Catholic Worker farm, where once they arrived unannounced; my mother apologized in a note to Dorothy Day, who of course didn't mind).

"Leaving the city," Gerry Williams said. "I loved that. We had never left the city. I don't think I ever would have thought to leave the city if it hadn't been for your family. Seeing trees," she said, "and grass!" And there was summer camp, swimming, and field day. "We felt safe," someone said again; "welcome and special."

And Joanna Smith, who was white, went out with Theophilus Brown, who was black, and of course she too had a crush on Father Myers. "On Saturday nights, there were dances. Dances in the parish hall! There was no place else where we could dance!" Black and white, they all danced. "Even with the fathers."

On Sunday night in the parish hall, there were discussion groups, Gerry now said; about "the world and about the city." And they remembered Friday night TV. "It was a new life," she said more than once.

I had never before talked to the people we had known there, so this conversation renewed my sense of Jersey City as an ideal, even while it had also made differences clearer—"race and class," one would say now. I said to my father once that I'd loved the years in Jersey City more than any other part of my childhood. "But you said you had no friends; you were so happy when we left!" I don't doubt his memory, but what remains are glimpses of what can happen among people, and an enduring belief in that possibility.

Laurie, the vicar, was now driving me through the city. "Mrs. Skipper doesn't go out any more, she was saying, and she insisted you come over. She has stories." I didn't really remember Mrs. Skipper, only all her daughters. "Stories about your mother," Laurie says; "and they've invited you to lunch." The Skippers, it turned out, had lived across the street and down the block on Second Street—a family of four girls and one boy named James. Susan Skipper and I were in the same Sunday school class, and I remembered that Geneva, the oldest, had died young, in the 1970s. Joyce, the second oldest, answered the door, her daughters and grand-daughters crowded behind her. The Skippers own the house, and Mr. and Mrs. Skipper live on the second floor, which functions as a kind of round-the-clock care facility—Joyce had a career as a nurse.

We sat down in the living room, in a circle—Laurie and I, the Skipper sisters including Stella, who walked me to school. I remember that Joyce was best at double Dutch, or was that Susan? And that Susan and Joyce looked alike, but now Susan wears glasses and is much taller than Joyce. "Would you like some cake?" someone asks, and then, suddenly with what feels like a flourish, one of Joyce's daughters wheels in her grand-mother, Catherine Skipper, who is ninety-five years old—the matriarch. No matter that she's bedridden, she is a woman of enormous power, wiry, with gray hair and warm, light golden brown, very youthful skin. She starts right in.

When they first moved to Second Street, Catherine had watched white boys play and break windows; "I was always looking out the window," she said, and then one Sunday, she saw people, even colored people, dressed up and saw "they go to that church down there," and her husband said to her, "they even wear suits." So she dressed up her kids. "I only had three then, but I couldn't dress them. Salvation, here I come! She went to the Salvation Army, the thrift stores, and told the kids the clothes were from Best and Lord and Taylor, and so the family joined "Grace."

"She'd come over here, your mother, a baby under one arm, a cabbage in the other—those cabbages were as big as a child—they must have been from the farm." She meant Hollow Hill; Gami had "supplies" delivered twice a week.

"The first day she came, I remember it. I was washing clothes in the tub when the doorbell rang and it was Mrs. Moore calling." There was a huge pile of laundry by the tub—"Your mother was . . . horrified."

"Are you going to wash all of them by hand?"

"Yes yes I am but he helps"—her husband, who worked at the steel mill.

She'd come north at six years old, the year "things began to go bad in 1915." Her family was from Orangeburg, South Carolina." Her father had been a sergeant in World War I, the 369th, he had fought in France, returned home, and become a longshoreman in Jersey City. When Catherine was little, she sold sandwiches out of a knapsack on the docks—five cents, ten cents—and she'd come home with a fistful of money. Her father never found out. As a teenager, she sang in places—"Am I Blue," which Ethel Waters first sang in the movie *On With the Show* in 1929.

"The second time your mother came, she said, Mrs. Skipper, how would you like to have a washing machine? I have a friend who's giving one away. Do you want it?" (Was a friend really giving one away?) Two days later, two men arrived with it and set it up. "I was so excited I washed all day long!"

"We were close," Mrs. Skipper said. "She was a little older than me. One day she was wearing red shoes, and I complimented her, and she said, 'Monticello Avenue. Ten dollars.' "

And so they went shopping, out to the shoe store on Monticello Avenue. " 'My friend wants a pair,' your mother said, pointing out the shoes to the white saleslady. And I tried them on and they fit and then your mother said, 'those, and those, too.' She paid for them. She bought me three pairs of shoes! 'Make sure you bring her back again,' said the saleslady.' " Catherine Skipper chortled at the memory, sitting full height, majestic in her wheelchair.

"She was so down to earth, your mother. That black hair and blue eyes. She would come to the apartment, and we'd sit by the window and talk, about the church, and what could be done, done for people. And about money. She wanted to understand how I took care of seven children on my husband's salary."

One night they went out together to a movie—"It was packed!"— Catherine remembered it as *Your Cheatin' Heart*, about Hank Williams, but that was not made until 1964, and this was ten years earlier. Maybe it was the Doris Day movie made that year with *cheatin'* in the title. It was a girls' night out—one of them black, one of them white, in a city where white people, as Gerry Williams had said, did not "go up in them nigger houses." After the movie, they had a drink. Catherine sat them down first at the bar, but Jenny said, "No, we're going to sit at a table," so they sat down at a table and talked. And talked so long, they missed the 99 bus home, and had to wait another hour, so they "walked around" and "we were solicited!"

They got home at 1 a.m. "I walked your mother home and dropped her at the door, then turned and ran," just as she heard my father say, "Jenny, where were you!?"

"But I figured," she said, "he's a priest, he's not going to beat her." When her friend Mary Drayton heard she'd taken "Mrs. Moore" to a bar, she said, "You shouldna done that. You never should have taken her to that bar," and I said back at her, "We wanted to hang out, and so we did."

One night at a parish hall dance, Catherine and Angie Williams were chaperoning and decided to have a dance contest, and Catherine "got up and danced the Charleston, "which I learned from my father and mother," she said. "I danced fast at the front of the stage, snapping my fingers," and soon Angie was dancing too, and then your mother joined us! 'Oh Mrs. Skipper," she said, "I didn't know you could dance!"

7.

Did I think going to school would leave a space that would be filled by another baby? "I worried about you," Pam Morton, a friend of my mother's said just a month ago; "You were replaced so many times." Her remark was echoed by a friend of my mother's when I stayed with her for the Women's March in 2017—even that recently, I shut out the suggestion: "I never thought of it that way." I have, of course, thought about it "that way" as an adult, associating it with a feeling I still get, brain turning blank, thought to static: "You have trouble with transitions," a therapist told me when I was in my thirties. As she elaborated, I began to understand what she meant. I could remember the feeling of pulling myself together to start again after a sibling was born, coming to know him or her, only to be given, again, the good news: "I'm pregnant!" my mother's dark blue eyes bright with pleasure.

Public School #37 was five blocks away, and Catherine Skipper's daughter Stella, a year older, was commandeered to walk me to school. I had turned five in October, too late for September, so I started in January—I remember the lavender gingham smocked dress I wore the first day, and also my brown oxfords. I soon complained to my mother, but she wouldn't buy me a frothy pastel-colored nylon dress, and my patent leathers were "for church and special occasions, sweetie." I didn't know any of these white girls who had last names like Suzicki. Where were my Negro friends? Most of them went to a different school, a closer school with no plumbing where the teachers were not as good: public school was a matter of principle for my parents, but only a "good" public school. But PS 37 was mostly white. Didn't that defeat the purpose?

I liked Miss Hart, the teacher, but I was way ahead, already reading, so I was always bored. A mnemonic device is all I remember learning: "Bow to the right, curtsy to the left." In the fall a raft of new classmates joined the class, and then in January I was promoted to first grade. I didn't like Miss Kelleher, the teacher. I don't remember why, only that once when she was herding us up the stairs, I called her a word I'd just learned and knew was bad, just as an experiment. I was facing the glazed amber brick of the staircase wall, and on purpose whispered loud enough for her to hear: "Bitch." What would she do to me? "What did you say?" she said, fiercely. I denied it or didn't answer, my face getting hot. I don't remember a punishment, but in the scrapbook there are plenty of notes in my (evolving) handwriting apologizing for being "fresh."

I did not understand that even for my daunting mother, things could be too much—"I'm busy, sweetie," she would say. Or maybe the baby would be crying. Once, in my big room with bunches of cherries on the wallpaper, she was in front of the wardrobe, maybe bending to put something away and then standing up again. Maybe I asked one question too many—*irritation when too many people*. It was so quick: Slap! And a sudden sharp burn across my face. In memory, she hits so hard I almost fall over.

"I'm writing the part about the first time my mother hits me," I say to my friend the novelist. We meet for tea sometimes to talk about our work, and she is at the sink, filling the kettle. "She hit me," I repeat, and my friend, who is the mother of three, turns quickly, startled.

"What were you fighting about?"

"I really can't remember."

"She had too many children," she says, and turns back to the kettle.

When another friend tells me how distant her mother was, I say, "Have you thought about what she was going through?" I saw my mother cook, change diapers, organize the little ones, do the laundry, get supper on the table; but as a child, I had no way of understanding physical exhaustion, the intellectual and spiritual effort, the physical toll of pregnancy, the actual work it took to keep renewing the mission of Grace Church.

When I try to pinpoint the year my mother slapped me that first time, I calculate that she was coming to terms with having four children under six—the pressure of the parish, only one day off a week when they went to New York. Gagy came to take care of us on their day off; otherwise, an occasional babysitter, a housecleaner twice a week. I was overwhelmed, too—starting school, oldest of four children, perhaps another on the way. "It only happened three times," I explain to a therapist about the slap, knowing that what matters is what changed. Abruptly, fear became one of the emotions I had about my mother, just as fear was an emotion she had about her mother. That shift was the first engagement in what I later called in a poem "the war with my mother"—I duck and swerve like a guerilla fighter, trying to love her at the same time.

"Why did she have so many children?" My novelist friend is pushing me.

I have experimented with various interpretations: that motherhood was an arena in which to excel as a competitor was like doing an arabesque on a moving bicycle, winning the Diana Cup; earning a Phi Beta Kappa key; winning marriage to the man she fought for; doing work she believed in against the expectations of her background; making the ideal family she had not grown up in. Did my mother even remember what Margie often told me, that Margarett had wanted nine children? But Margarett's frame of reference was Victorian: Her mother, born in 1851, had herself been one of nine. My mother's reproductive era was the 1950s baby boom; she was pregnant fully half the seventeen years between my birth in late 1945 and when I went to college in 1963—a total of 108 months or nine years, half the 216 months (or eighteen years) between the beginning of her pregnancy with me and the birth of my youngest sister, Patience.

Now I'm looking at a photo of her; she's wearing a white blouse and holds a diaper between the newly able-to-stand baby's legs; she's just about to pin the diaper closed. Her white blouse is sleeveless and ruffled, and she looks French or something with her hair knotted on top of her head. I can't get over how pretty she looks, her Indian-print skirt almost to the ground, black espadrilles, their ties crisscrossed around her ankles. The baby is Rosie, still almost bald, and it's field day at Ebbets Field—a Grace Church summer ritual. Everyone is there, kids from the church and some of the summer staff, college students, both black and white, who worked at the church during July and August—earnest, funny young men and fierce, smart young women who were my idols.

But I can't stop looking at that picture of my mother with Rosie, who still looks like a girl.

Suddenly it's difficult to use the name *Jenny* as I write about her, even though I want to, believing that calling her by her name keeps her separate, mine and only mine, woman rather than mother, and it's the woman whose life I'm tracking.

I mustn't separate her being a mother from her life as a woman. She loved being a mother and she loved being pregnant and she loved giving birth. She's already spent five-and-a-half years pregnant—Rosemary was born two weeks before she turned twenty-eight—and I have watched her get big and small again, big and small. Thinking about this is hard because it's not at all that I don't love my siblings: I join my mother in marveling at a sibling's particular trait; for instance, my second brother George's long, dark eyelashes that earned him the nickname "Gorgeous George." But I'd also get a little sad that my lashes were short. Or were they? As the babies get older and talk, I come to know and love them, even Pip, who at just about that time had started to rabbit-punch me and "indian burn" my arm. I can't help the draggy jealous feeling, though; each time someone new arrived to call her Mommy, she was further away from me.

I remember we made coffee cake in Jersey city—and artificial flowers, my mother wrote me when I was deep into my twenties. *There are so many times in life when you really don't know what you're doing!*

The year was 1971, eighteen months before she got sick, two years before she died, and she's reassessing her life. I do remember the flowers, the velvety material the petals were made of, but it's because making artificial flowers was so out of character for Jenny. I'm thinking now that I envied those who called her Jenny, as if the name called up someone different from the woman I called Mommy and later, Mom. The Jenny people got the person who talked to you intently, homing into the heart of the point you'd made. She was the woman I didn't have, so it's uncomfortable to call her Jenny at this point in writing this book, since I'm now a character. I'll see how it goes, call her my mother—still dignified—and Jenny if it works.

As for "Mommy," I watched her and, as I observed her, my young female mind was turning against becoming a Mommy myself—a turn made viscerally before I could dream of alternatives. At the same time, my sister Dee's mind was growing in another direction: "I always wanted to be a mother," she said to me once with her second son, an infant then, in the crook of her arm—she became a psychologist as well, and a writer.

Wanted to be a mother? I was truly startled by the idea. I had never *wanted* to be a mother—I didn't exactly *not want* a child, but having one was never a desire. If I had a doll, she was a stand-in for me, not for future offspring. Even as an oldest sister, I didn't want to play mother and hold the current baby, feeling a panic I couldn't identify when I touched a baby's skin.

Why not pleasure? Because, after a while, it seemed to me that my mother would always have another child, and that if I had even one, I wouldn't be able to stop—like Edmund in *The Lion, the Witch and the Wardrobe,* whom the White Witch cursed with a craving for Turkish delight, which caused him to betray his true self and everyone he loved and valued.

In front of me is a photograph of myself with Santa Claus—Rosie must have been a baby, because I look about six. It's in black and white, and I'm wearing a tweed coat and a scarf, and my dark wispy bangs stick out from beneath a pointed dark hat that was navy blue—one of many woolen things knitted for us by Jean Watson, who had been my father's nurse and who still lived at Hollow Hill in her own little house. I'm looking up at Santa, who looks like he really is Santa. What shall I ask him for? Certainly not what I most needed and wanted, the attention and embrace of my mother.

8.

I don't remember thinking, only taking the shiny scissors from her sewing table and cutting little squares out of every fabric I could find until I had twenty or twenty-five of them. I cut squares from the sheets on my parents' bed, the clothes hanging in their dark closet, my mother's dresses and blouses. I cut my father's black shirts but not his clerical vests or black suits. I cut tablecloths folded in a drawer, my mother's underwear, curtains, and towels. No one saw what I was doing. Did I cut from my own clothes? I took all the little squares to school and pasted them onto a chart, and with the help of my teacher labeled each one: cotton, wool, silk, percale. It was an assignment, to bring in samples of textiles, and I was in second grade. When my mother went to parents' night, the teacher complimented her on the variety of textiles Honor had brought in, more than any other child; that was how my mother learned why little square holes had suddenly appeared in everything: *The teacher gave her an A+ and said that she was "immensely resourceful." I agreed wholeheartedly and went into a rage which recurred each time I found a textile with a small square removed.*

It did not occur to me that my mother's dresses, the curtains, and my father's shirts would forever after have little square holes in them, that in fact I'd ruined everything I cut. I thought the material would grow back and the squares heal over like a scrape on my knee or a cut on my finger. How else was I to complete the assignment? When the teacher explained what a textile was—what at home we called material—I thought I should do just what I did. My mother didn't have bits of material lying around and because it was clear that she couldn't stop what she was doing to advise me, I didn't ask her for help—better to make my way alone. She was busy with Rosie and with everyone who came to the kitchen and the girls' club, Peegie and Kim and Poppy and the men coming to the door. It wasn't hard to believe that no one noticed me or anything I did. I wasn't punished, and the story became one my mother told about this oldest daughter of hers, for whom, she later wrote, the life at Grace Church was the *least natural*—true, I think now, except for the laughter and talk and the endless stream of new grown-ups at supper.

An astrologer looks at our charts, side by side: "You drove her crazy," the woman says.

We would never know, my mother wrote about "Honor" in her book, *where her intensity, her devouring of books, her playacting, her adult air all came from. She would plunge into the box of dress-up clothes we kept upstairs and, costumed in ragged finery, promenade with her doll and carriage up and down the side walk, dodging trash cans . . . wondering, we always felt when watching her, why the world around her didn't join her parade.* I don't remember that; more, I remember Hollow Hill where I adventured in the woods. I chose one of the dalmatians from the kennel, all their names starting with *D* because they were descended from a patriarch named Dipper, who had liver-colored spots. I was almost sure I could get Digger to talk to me like the animals did in Narnia, so close were we when I was nine, trying to make a solitary life in the forest as an alternative to the house in Jersey City and the gang of friends Pip always seemed to have. I didn't know that lonely was what I was feeling—how could I be lonely? There were so many of us now. George, Pip's prayed-for brother, arrived when I was nine and a half.

My mother was right that I went to extremes, that I wanted attention. Draw, paint, write, read, learn. I ran for it, threw balls against walls for it, jumped rope for it, galloped sidewalks for it, and got A's for it. Don't play with matches. Your grandfather burned his hand playing with matches. I see myself fingering matches. I see myself walk into a room at home or at Hollow Hill when she came there with us. She looked so beautiful when she got dressed up and stayed in one place. At home, she was always moving and not to be interrupted. Like a train, she stopped only for a short time at stations and elsewhere only when a derailment or power outage caused delay.

Or she was tired.

She is sleeping. I watch her. "I'm taking a nap sweetie," she says, turning her face to the pillow. Why was she so tired? It's tempting to find an answer that suggests an existential predicament, but in rereading her book, I realize I had no idea how much work she did. *I'm half-dead*, was what she said when she was tired. Not only physically, but intellectually.

As the years went on, awareness of what they'd fought for deepened, then paled in the face of events that brought up new realizations of difference—not only racial difference, but class difference, what it meant to lose a job, live what is now called paycheck to paycheck. There was the black Baptist minister who invited them to his church to celebrate what Grace Church was doing for his black parishioners and their children. He had little time for the rescuing and hospitality that took up the days of my mother and the three priests; he worked full-time in an upholstery factory: *"I got the Lord's work on Sunday"*—chuckle—*"but you do the Lord's work for my people the other six days."*

Grace Church was changing. At TV evenings and dances and coffee hours, parishioners of both races relaxed together. They even worked together on church projects, and kids of both races played together in the front yard, had basketball games in the parish hall. But, my mother wrote, *beyond those walls, they ignored each other. . . . on the street you were black or you were white, and you chose your friends accordingly.* Sometimes, she admitted, she and the others found themselves treating black people differently than white people, *overcompensating with excuses for any fault, and we had a nagging fear that no matter what we did, we'd feel guilty. About the Negro poor, we said to ourselves, however privately, "It's partly our fault"; about the white poor it was, "I wonder why they didn't make it."* Writing in the twenty-first century, when the terms of the struggle for equality have twisted and reconstituted themselves so that we live in another era of mistrust and betrayal, I find my mother's attempts to understand still fresh: *The Negroes did not show any obvious desire to be left alone, or open hostility to us, or even ambivalence—it was more a reserve, or an inability to catch the white glance.*

Or was it an unwillingness? The difference turned up most vividly in intimate circumstances, at the kitchen table or when she went calling. A black mother might speak of difficulties with her landlord while a white woman's complaints more often took the form of *intimate, emotional revelations.* The black people who came to Grace Church, many recently from the South, *rarely exposed their real grievances. Perhaps they didn't trust us enough; perhaps they had no hope that anything could change for them, and only the slimmest of hopes and dreams for their children.*

But *the four of them* kept faith with their ideal. If the *"we" who lived in the Victorian rectory and the "they," our tenement friends,* all became *"we" at my kitchen table and at God's altar,* then the parish must belong to all who worshiped there. The liturgy—the rituals of a service, the prayers chosen—must reflect that, they decided; and they began to make small changes that would surge through the entire Episcopal church in the coming decades. Prayers once said only by priests would now be shared, and they would change the format of the sermon so the congregation could ask questions. Gradually, my mother and the priests moved out of leadership of church activities, passing positions to parishioners—for instance, asking a black parishioner to join the all-white women's choir. That small adjustment was successful; and soon, of their own accord, the white altar guild invited some of *the new people* to join. Sunday school became more serious, starting in church with my father, who had a gift for the dramatic, acting out New Testament stories with the children, just like he made up bedtime stories for us.

At Grace Church, they *broke bread together;* now they would mimeograph together. The scrapbook is rich with fliers about the women's group, the girls club, the dances and baseball games. Writing a decade later, my mother is aware that those gestures had been only a fragile beginning. In Jersey City she had seen for the first time the cruelty of inequality among people she knew well, but she still had faith that equality could be achieved. By 1968 she understood that both the terms of that struggle and her role within it had changed. *Perhaps,* she wrote in the wake of the riots after the murder of Martin Luther King, *theirs is the last Negro generation to take the imbalance lying down.*

9.

I was eight when my parents sent me to have my education assessed at the Brearley School in New York. I wasn't told; as far as I knew, I was having an overnight with the Potters' daughters. I was complaining though I don't remember that, and my mother had noticed the teaching at PS 37 was mostly by rote and memorization. Of Brearley, I recall only that the gym was enormous and that I borrowed a bright blue gym suit and danced around with Poo Potter and her friends, all of whom were so nice, asking my name and where I lived. Apparently I excelled, which reassured my parents about sending us to public school, a choice that many of their old friends questioned. I stayed on at mostly white PS 37, but in September 1955, my brother Pip and I started at St. Luke's, a racially integrated, progressive Episcopal school on Hudson Street in downtown Manhattan.

My brother remembers being scared on the train, but I loved it—mornings, a couple from Grace Church who worked in Manhattan either drove us through the Holland Tunnel or escorted us on the Hudson Tube, as PATH was then called. Afternoons we returned by ourselves, and sometimes I brought one of my new friends home to spend a Friday night. Jill was the daughter of a theatrical publicist; Temma had long blond braids, was the daughter of two painters whom she called by their first names, and her mother was Icelandic. Shai, who had changed her name from Debbie, was already a dancer, the daughter of a divorced teacher who was also a children's book writer. Their worlds were utterly new to me. At St. Luke's there was chapel every morning, and even the kids who were Jewish attended; on overnights at their houses, I had my first Chanukah and my first Passover. Shai's mother lived with another woman, who was a famous black folk singer, and there was no father anywhere. Once when Temma spent the night with me, we sang hymns over the mic of the sound truck to advertise a "mission" at Grace Church. In English class, I was writing a novel about a girl adopted into a family during frontier days. Interestingly, it was the father who hit her and the mother who comforted her; the teacher read it aloud to the class.

I don't find my mother in these memories of St. Luke's, and it was my father I told about what I was learning in the weekly classes that led to confirmation. When the white-haired bishop placed his hands heavily on my head, I felt myself viscerally change; now I knew more about what my parents believed, and I could ask deeper questions at the supper table. When the day of confirmation came, my mother was at Hollow Hill awaiting her sixth child. I was a little sad she wouldn't see me in the white dotted swiss dress we'd bought, the see-through veil. My godmothers—my father's sister Polly and my mother's friend Sylvia—made the day festive. One gave me a red leather bible, the other a red leather prayer book with my name and the date in gold. My father arrived from the hospital just in time for his service. A new little sister, Marian, had arrived. My mother didn't get to St. Luke's the following week, either—my fifth-grade class had written a play called *Do the Scales of Egypt Balance?* and I was playing the pharaoh's daughter. Uncle Shaw's wife Linda brought me a tin of dried grasshoppers—they'd been to Egypt on their honeymoon; grass-hoppers were a delicacy there.

We had a dog now, a Scottish terrier named Smitty, and some weekends we went to the house my parents had bought in Connecticut—a warren of tiny rooms in Kent, a town where they'd taken a hike when they were first married. My mother now had a parrot named Cuppy. Had she bought it or had my father given it to her for her birthday? Her mother had a parrot, a macaw named Jack; he was still alive then, most of his feathers gone, and given to erupting with my grandmother's name, screeching Margarett over and over again. Since my mother associated the house where she grew up with sadness and fear, I didn't understand even then why she wanted a parrot. Perhaps Cuppy would not be ill-spoken and frightening like Jack, but buoyant and funny like my mother, bursting out laughing, saying something that made everyone else laugh too. She had an instruction book on the training of parrots and was painstakingly teaching Cuppy to talk; by that Sunday, let's say, he was meant to have learned "Hello"—the next word, my father's name. My mother loved the idea of the parrot shouting "Paul! Paul! Paul!" when most people we knew called him Poppy or Father Moore. Maybe I'm making that up, but that would have been her sense of humor.

My mother had long ago thrown over writing for having children and organizing the household, but I imagine she had thoughts and dreams she didn't put into words or sentences, didn't broach even in the long letters she wrote to one or two close friends—of overwork or anger, of doubt, of the attractions even the most faithful wife can feel when meeting a com-pelling man. Let's say she intended to teach Cuppy little speeches to pres-ent for her—in code, of course—as if he were an imaginary friend, or a clown in Shakespeare, someone who really knew her. Even though her name was firmly Jenny Moore, I thought of "Mommy" as different from the rest of us, as speaking for the odd, mysterious part of us, the part who did unexpected things, like play a laughing record, buy a parrot, or con-tinually introduce phrases into the family lexicon: *You are on the ragged edge. You have crossed the line. Life is too short.*

She was in the kitchen baking cookies or cleaning up after lunch, and

Cuppy was outdoors in his cage on the bumpy early spring lawn. We had watched him while we ate our hot dogs on the porch but left him there when we went upstairs for our naps, all quiet until my mother was shouting and then crying, which hardly ever happened. I jumped up from my nap and rushed into the kitchen and then outside. The cage was empty, and she was inconsolable. Soon we were all there. Had a fox eaten him? Or had he just flown away? She didn't really recover very fast, and for the rest of the weekend we looked for him in the forest with such intensity I thought that surely he would soon reappear, high in the trees behind the house, up the hill beyond the brook.

I am tempted by many things in this story: that Cuppy will speak things about my mother that she will not; that Cuppy was my mother seeking freedom from a life that was a cage—not her whole life, but her life in Kent, which was, as she put it, "too much work"; not a particularly grim cage, but a cage nonetheless, one she has chosen but that keeps her, if not confined, in restraints. Decades later, when I ended up living in the house in Kent, I'd once in a while look for a green bird in the trees, and because my mother had died, imagine her dressed in green, flying up into those trees still, looking down, laughing and shouting all our names.

It was that summer, after I finished fifth grade, that my father had an illness called cumulative fatigue. He took all summer off, and we went to Kent for two whole months. Poppy needed a rest, we were told. Much later, I learned that Jersey City had become too much for him, that my mother thought of him as fragile: from the war, what we might now call PTSD. It seems he was burned out, could no longer deal with being on call twenty-four hours a day. Despite the cumulative fatigue, he didn't seem sick to us; it was fun to have more time with him. I remember long, golden walks alone with him, or with Dee and Pip, and even Rosie; of flying kites in the field across the road. I remember swimming every day, driving down to a "spot," as he called it, on the Housatonic River where a dirt road ended and the ruins of an old bridge made a natural partial dam. It was a special occasion when Mommy came, leaving Marian, whom we called Babby, with a babysitter. That summer we drove across the New York line to see the movie of *Moby Dick*, which we had to see because my father had once "harpooned" a whale; and *The King and I*, a perfect movie for a girl like me, just starting to think about falling in love. That same summer, we all put on our yellow terry cloth bathrobes—including Marian, the baby—and sat on the edge of the front porch. My father, wearing one too, balanced the camera, set the timer, and ran back around to pose with us. Our family was a perfect size, I thought; everything in balance.

Pip and I returned to St. Luke's in the fall. The school had a new building, and I had a teacher I loved. I read the most books in the class, and I remember the teacher gave us "brainteasers"—long math problems to do in our heads—and that once I came in first, beating the two smartest boys in the class. Now in sixth grade, I settled in. In art class, Temma and I were painting a huge mural of a farm with a barn and all the animals; and in shop class, I made and carefully painted for baby Marian a wooden duck on wheels. My favorite school clothes were a black turtleneck and black tights—fashionable, though the word *beatnik* would not be coined for another two years.

At home I had a new bedroom—*Away from it all,* my mother said. Ledlie Laughlin, still a seminarian when he arrived to replace Father Pegram, had the big sunny room at the end of the hall. It was Ledlie who explained Communism to me—big *C* bad, small *c* a way for people to live together, everyone having the same amount of money. The big *C* now meant dictatorship, he said—the "right" had their version of it, called fascism. This all seemed very far away until one dark, rainy afternoon: My friends and I were walking down the path from the new building at St. Luke's to the street, and I saw the headline about the Russians invading Hungary—tanks in smudgy black and white photos. "It's World War III," I announced. I was certain that any skirmish would lead to another worldwide war.

There had been talk at the supper table about the Hungarians fighting for their freedom, excitement that they had peacefully "taken back" their government. Now the Russians had sent tanks, and in Budapest, the Hungarian capital, people were being killed. I knew about World War II because of my father, and boys from Grace Church had joined up for the Korean War. I had to get home. Poppy would know what was going on. Would the war get here? My mother was in the kitchen: "Where's Poppy?" It was he who knew about war. "Doing evensong," she said. I rushed to the church. The psalm for that day, November 4, was number 37: "The ungodly have drawn out the sword, and bent their bow," my father read, and the tiny congregation answered, "to cast down the poor and needy, and to slay such as be upright in their ways." Magic, I always thought when everything came together: "Their sword shall go through their own heart," the psalm continued, and we answered, "and their bow shall be broken."

My mother still corresponded with the German and English families to whom she'd sent packages during the war; now Hungarian refugees were coming here; the World Council of Churches was helping, and Grace Church was sponsoring a couple and a single man. At supper, I'd heard about the people escaping to Vienna and waiting there, the man who wept on the plane when given an orange, such a great luxury. My father drove with Dee, Pip, and me to a place called Camp Kilmer to meet the refugees. The woman had honey-blond hair held back with a kerchief, and they came toward us, she grasping her husband's arm, behind her another man. I recall a long, barn-like space, sparse electric light and people standing in line.

Helen Horvath was very pregnant, and her husband Igyula was slender with big dark eyes, thin brown hair, and sallow skin; he wore a suit, maybe gray or brown. The second man, Istvan, was silent and red-faced but beautifully featured and handsome, wore working clothes—maybe a sweater, and a long coat. He was silent because he spoke only Hungarian; he relied on the Horvaths, who knew German and could talk with a German translator there. In the car they were quiet. What was it like, I wondered—secret police, a massacre in a city square, escape across the border in the dark. An article I'd read had said 2,500 Hungarians and 700 Soviet troops had been killed, and more than 200,000 Hungarians had fled across the border. According to Istvan, the third refugee, those captured were imprisoned in a place resembling a Nazi death camp and slaughtered, their remains burned in a crematorium. A *Jersey Journal* clipping in my mother's scrapbook bore this headline: "HUNGARIANS

HERE BARE CREMATORY HORROR." Because I had seen *The Diary of Anne Frank* on Broadway, I knew about concentration camps, but I had no idea what a crematorium was.

My mother was at the door when we got home from Camp Kilmer; that night, and nights after, Istvan and the Horvaths sat with us at supper. The church rented housing for them, and soon the men had jobs, and Helen Horvath had her baby—her first child had died of starvation in Hungary. What would happen to the people they left behind? The people locked up in all these countries would keep wanting to get out, I concluded, and the Russians would keep sending soldiers to keep them in.

I was eleven years old now, Father Myers had left for a parish on the Lower East Side, and a young priest named Jim Morton had joined the staff with his wife Pam. "The Moores" with six children were now eight people, so the Mortons couldn't live with us. Bishop Washburn steered funds to Grace Church, and a brownstone down the street was bought and renovated. In a service held on its stoop, it was christened St. Christopher's House, for the patron saint of travel. The Mortons lived on the third floor, and the fourth floor was reconfigured as a small convent with a tiny chapel where three nuns from the Episcopal Order of St. John the Baptist now resided. They taught Sunday School and confirmation classes, helped with calling on parishioners and people in need. All year the nuns collected dolls and toys and refurbished them for a Christmas fair where nothing cost more than a quarter—"If things were free, they were considered worthless." When I first heard this story in 2014, a particular nun came quickly into focus, her wide face and wire-rimmed glasses. Yes, the fair had been the idea of Sister Eleanor Lucy; she washed the dolls, repainted their faces, and made them tiny new clothes.

One evening, toward the end of that spring, Dee and Pip and I were called into my old bedroom with the cherry wallpaper for an announcement. Had Gami or Gagy died? Had Frankie Wyman been thrown into jail again? The actual news was inconceivable. We were leaving Jersey City and moving to a place called Indianapolis, where Poppy would be "dean" of a cathedral. I was so happy at St. Luke's, and what about Hollow Hill? Temma and our painting projects? What about the house in

Kent and Ralphie Walker and the Skippers? I couldn't believe this! God had "called" him, Poppy explained. Yes, he would be doing the same kind of work, though we wouldn't live next door to the church. What finally made me a little excited was that he would have a new title, "Very Reverend." He would wear a purple vest instead of a black one, and a purple cassock, and we would have a house that was big enough. Five bedrooms, my mother said, and six bathrooms!

Just as I'd believed that the square holes I'd cut in the clothes would heal over, I assumed the rectory would forever stretch to fit us, even with a new baby coming in July. But our departure was all planned. Mommy would stay behind with Dee and the little ones and fly on when she recovered from the birth. Poppy and Pip and I would drive ahead in the station wagon and meet the moving vans in Indianapolis. I think I tried very hard to be grown up, act like the oldest, but the feeling of each loss hit me. What about Christy at Hollow Hill and my riding lessons? I was just learning to jump!

I have no memory of what it was like to say goodbye to Temma, Shai, and Jill; no memory of saying goodbye to the Skippers or the Walkers or Williamses, or to anyone. The church organized a huge farewell service, and the parish gave a testimonial dinner at a hotel downtown and presented my parents with an engraved silver pitcher. My mother pasted the accompanying proclamation into the scrapbook, along with a formal photograph—all the priests and vestry—evidence of the robust parish we were leaving behind. I don't remember the service, and the children weren't invited to the dinner. Also blank in my mind is the place where I might have imagined my new school or the Midwestern city where I would become, again, a stranger.

VI

An Institution

1.

JUST ONE LAST LINE BEFORE THE BIG DAY—BECAUSE I HAVE THIS SUBTERRA-nean feeling that once I leave the state of New Jersey things will never be quite the same. My mother is writing the first of many letters to Pam Morton, who was taking her place at 268 Second Street. *I loved our walk to the subway & remembering the rectory dirty & dark, with kids playing ball in the yard, James & Sonny making caustic comments at the lychgate, just the perfect way to leave.*

She'd come over from Hollow Hill for a good-bye supper, five weeks after number seven was born—Daniel Sargent Moore, named for her uncle, Margarett's brother. Fifteen years earlier, my father had been welcomed home, wounded from Guadalcanal, and eleven years earlier, my mother had graduated from Barnard, in cap and gown with her first baby—me—on her hip. It had been just eight years since she'd moved with Paul and three children to Jersey City, to live among the poor.

"I thought you might like to have these," Pam Morton said. She was in her seventies, and we were having tea; we were again living a block apart as we had on Second Street, this time on Riverside Drive in Manhattan. She handed me a blue folder, out of which slipped a sheaf of letters in my mother's handwriting—the move to Indianapolis, life there, and after. It's 1957 when they begin, the year of Sputnik, the year of school desegregation in Little Rock, the second year of Dwight D. Eisenhower's second term as president. The first is a letter from the Adirondacks, then the one about that last night in Jersey City: *The last person I saw, (downstairs in the subway), was the huge fat man who used to fix the fire extinguishers. He used to genuflect in church, & Peegie used to have to help him to his feet!* In two days, with Gagy, the four littles, and the baby, she'd fly from LaGuardia to Weir Cook Airport in Indianapolis. My father my brother Paul and I were already on our way west.

A wide-open world; our apple green, wood-trimmed station wagon filled, but only with essentials. In a few days, at the "deanery" on Washington Boulevard in Indianapolis, we would greet two moving vans—one from Jersey City, the other with things from Hollow Hill and storage. My mother and Gagy and the rest of the family would arrive a day or two later; we three were the pioneers. My brother Pip dropped his nickname and became Paul—my mother couldn't resist a nickname, though, and sometimes called him Paulie. I had never been west of Philadelphia—but I had read every single book by Laura Ingalls Wilder—after New Jersey came Pennsylvania. Indianapolis, Pop was telling us, was the largest American city on a non-navigable river; and a famous car race was held there, the Indianapolis 500. After the Pennsylvania Turnpike came the Ohio Turnpike—did every state have a turnpike? Could we have driven all the way to California on turnpikes? Why *pike* and why *turn* since the

road seemed straight? I counted broken lines. What I knew about Ohio
was that Gami had been born there, and also Uncle Leonard, who had
died two years before. We stopped to spend a night in Dayton, Ohio, with
the parents of my father's best Yale friend George Mead, who had been
killed at Guadalcanal, and for whom my second brother was named—
a big white house, a swimming pool. I remember crossing the state line
into Indiana. No more Howard Johnsons; just, it seemed, little towns
always named for someplace else—Paris, Indiana—and every farm stand
seemed to have more string beans than I'd ever seen in one place. The land
was so flat. Even as we crossed the city limits, Indianapolis didn't seem
like a city—cornfields, then fields of soybeans, then small wooden houses
with porches.

But our destination on Washington Boulevard was enormous, rising
three full stories from a big lawn, neighbors on either side though you
couldn't see them through the trees. The house was Tudor, I learned—
another Indiana imitation of something else. I didn't think I'd ever been
anywhere as hot and humid. We sprang out of the car and into the house,
and since the fact of more than Jersey City's one-and-a-half bathrooms
had been a promised wonder, I ran through the first floor and up and
downstairs counting—we'd been told there were six. *They called tonight
from 3665 Wash. Blvd & sounded on the crest of the wave. Pip allowed as how
it was the nearest thing to Gami's house he'd ever seen.* How could she forget
he was now Paul? *Honor said she found another bathroom, making the grand
total seven.*

The grand total of children was also seven.

I marveled as boxes and barrels were hoisted from the van and
unpacked: the familiar high chair and crib, along with many things I'd
never seen—a Victorian settee and chairs with black watch plaid upholstery that had belonged to Mark Hanna's sister, Gami's Aunt Lily; Great
Granny Moore's huge blue and cream Chinese dining room rug; and two
big easy chairs that had been in retirement since 21st Street, along with
wedding present porcelain plates and crystal. I hadn't known we had such
pretty things. My mother and father grumbled that a good number of their
wedding presents had gone missing from the Hollow Hill attic—Gami's

ambivalence about their Jersey City life enacted in sudden gifts of very nice goblets and tumblers to Bill and Mouse.

But everything was coming together—the inherited furniture some-how worked with Paul's *coup*—my mother wrote Pam—hanging the *Catholic Worker* Fritz Eichenberg woodcuts in their red frames just above the walnut wainscoting in the living room—divine! And the red-framed photos of the weddings of friends, once grouped above the bathtub in Jersey City? A grand procession on the way up the stairs, a space left for whoever married next.

There were even enough bedrooms—mine divided by a chintz curtain my mother later made from the room where Dee and Rosie shared Great-Granny's double bed. *We are producing new age groups all over the place,* my mother wrote Pam, exuberant. Rosie, George, Marian, and the new baby would become the "middles"; when two more girls were born, they would become the "teenies," but that didn't happen for a few years. *Honor says it's more like an institution around here than anything else, and I suspect she's right.* Oh, and there were the "blonds" and the "browns"; the blonds—Paul, Rosemary, and Marian—whose hair remained blond for years, not vanishing fast like my bright curls but turning dark slowly, blond return-ing in glints in the summer. The blonds were my father's team, his light brown hair considered blond. The browns—Adelia and George and me—all had dark-brown hair, though none as dark as our raven-haired mother, who was the leader of the browns. Because of the blackness of her hair, I believed she contained the essence of who we were as browns—usually wonks like her in school and a little artistic; the blonds, except for Rosie, a bohemian outlier who possessed an idiosyncratic version of my mother's wit, were athletic and sunshine-handsome like Paul. Orchestra! my mother said. Baseball team! I was still trying to figure it out.

My mother wrote Pam my latest remark on the subject: *Poppy and you have made the family a little church, so that's why Poppy can call the church a family.* I was cogitating, seeking balance.

The church was no longer next door, and Poppy drove to work like other people's fathers, except for three days a week when he left at seven a.m. to "take the eight o'clock"—there was communion every weekday. He now had a real office and secretary. With its renovated pale wood interior and parish hall, Christ Church seemed awfully sleek for my father's work and small for a cathedral. Built of Indiana limestone, creamy and golden, it nestled on a corner at the north side of Monument Circle, the roundabout that marked the center of the city. The street circumnavigated the baroque Soldiers and Sailors Monument, designed by the Berlin architect Bruno Schmitz and dedicated in 1902. From the center rose a 286-foot obelisk of Indiana limestone whose trim was both gaudy and extraordinary—two bracelets of bronze palm frond unfurled at intervals; at the top stood a bronze Lady Victory sculpture; around the base, limestone soldiers and sailors represented the Civil War and the War of 1812.

Of course, my father worked Sundays. There were services at 8, 9:15, and 11—*an exhausting schedule*—but he took Mondays and half of Saturday off. My mother was always pushing for more time, since he was gone most nights for meetings—so different from Jersey City, where the parish hall was a leap out the door. But he did not leave till after supper—he'd be with us by 5:30. Then the entire family knelt at the near end of the living room, in front of a mahogany drop-leaf table-turned-altar where candles stood in brass candlesticks and a silver Russian Orthodox crucifix gleamed on the wall above. Even though we weren't in church, my father was the priest, reading the prayer that changed each day (called the collect; emphasis on the first syllable), leading us in the daily psalm, giving the blessing. It was here we prayed for the dead and the sick—you could volunteer an "intercession"—"God bless Great Granny's soul; God bless Uncle Leonard's soul; help Gramps get better." For closing we'd sing "Now the Day is Over" or "Abide with Me," each of us holding a hymnal, kneeling. By quarter of six, the little ones were at supper in the kitchen. The older ones ate grown-up supper later and joined Mommy and Poppy for cocktails in the living room: "Would you like a ginger ale, sweetie?" They had Dubonnet or sherry, my father bourbon if the day had been particularly hard—"I need a drink!"—each of them always lit up a cigarette. She smoked Chesterfields, and he had switched from Camels to L&Ms. I remember conversations about the news of the day, gossip of family or friends, the sound of the little ones coming from the kitchen as twilight thickened outside the tall living-room windows.

Despite the August heat, my mother, six weeks after giving birth, raced up and down stairs placing things and chasing children, making curtains at the sewing machine she'd quickly set up in the master bedroom. I'd hear her breathless but laughing on the phone to the East coast, saying *I'm half dead!* She loved the big kitchen—a countertop stove, two wall ovens, the two refrigerators—*shelves that swing out so you don't knock over things when you take something out.* There was a built-in breakfast nook, and the high-ceilinged, carpeted dining room dominated by the many-leaved mahogany dining room table from Prides, had a chandelier. For now the parents and older ones ate in the dining room, but that summer in an antique shop they'd bought a German beer table with eight chairs for "the porch" off the kitchen, a loggia-like room with French doors, and we'd soon abandon the formality of the dining room except for holidays, dinner parties, and subzero winter days.

The Indianapolis heat had a throbbing emptiness, and it was still close and humid the day after Labor Day, when Paul and Dee and I walked to PS 66 for the first time—Mom must have been with us. We took 37th Street east and then turned north and east again—later there would be shortcuts. PS 66 seemed huge, coming into view on the north side of 38th Street, a wide thoroughfare that stretched west to the speedway where the 500 was held, and east past the TeePee drive-in (an actual plaster teepee on its roof!) toward the white suburbs. We couldn't cross until the traffic boy signaled; his name was Bob Jackson—I last saw him in New York in the early 1970s, blond curls to his shoulders, high as a kite on pot and praising San Francisco, but here he was stolid and shy, white band diagonal across his chest, his smile and greeting slow and quiet.

In my seventh-grade class, everyone was white. The girls wore either pleated or "straight" skirts (which I had never seen before). They wore "bobby" socks (which I had also never seen) or white woolen socks like those Poppy wore for tennis in the summer. Footwear was mainly brown-and-white "saddle shoes," also new to me, or "penny" loafers, which Poppy sometimes wore when he didn't wear clericals. What I wore that first day must have been totally wrong for this alien land where the ground was so flat. I met a girl named Marie, nicknamed Putzi—"little doll" in German, she explained—who would later go to Radcliffe with me. A quiet girl called Sue Harker became my first Indianapolis friend. It seemed at first that there were no black kids at all in the school until once, at recess when I saw a Negro boy wearing a striped shirt, sprinting across the playground. I was looking out the window with a classmate I thought I might be friends with, and then she said, "I can't believe it, a nigger at 66."

I said nothing at all, just stood there, that word cutting through me so fast I could barely breathe. I'd thought nobody I'd know would ever actually use it. So lonely, suddenly I wanted to cry. Did I tell anyone? I was too ashamed. My mother wrote Pam that Paul missed Ralphie Walker so much, he wept and prayed that his friend might come live with us: *But I guess he couldn't live on Washington Boulevard,* he'd said—the street we lived on was all white. *The Southern-ness pops up over and over,* my mother wrote Pam. *We are still at sea as to exactly . . . what we are meant to do, but we remain confident we are meant to be here.* I didn't understand the context then, that the black population of Indianapolis, firmly below 34th Street, was moving north; that neighborhoods were, in a prevailing white view, "falling" one by one—a kind of domino effect.

Though my mother was finding the cathedral congregation full of *stone age Republicans* and *surprisingly cold,* she also found that there were *many individuals & couples leading lives of non-conformity . . . in many ways, and of sacrifice (not necessarily financial) of risking reputation;* in the adult Sunday discussion group, *one man even stood up and said he was sure the group would eventually become 30–40% Negro & should we discuss it.* Who had brought my father here? Engineered this break in tradition at a church at the center of a state where the Ku Klux Klan had been revived forty-five years earlier? His name was Eli Lilly, and he was the senior warden of the Christ Church vestry, whose immense fortune had come from the drug company his father had inherited and built—the company that had introduced insulin.

Mr. Lilly was a nonconformist. By 1957, the year we arrived, he was president of the Lilly Endowment, the foundation he formed with his father and brother Josiah in 1937 with an initial gift of $249,000. With subsequent gifts, the endowment, in 1998, was the wealthiest in the world: totaled assets $15.4 billion. Mr. Lilly was an inquiring Christian, both fiscally conservative and philanthropically generous: he believed the church had responsibility not only to those who commuted from the North Side, but to the working poor who lived all week in the decaying neighborhoods nearby. Some were black people, brought north by the Great Migration, who settled in Indianapolis rather than continuing on to Chicago; others were poor whites from Appalachia. Between 1950 and 1960, the black population of Indianapolis increased 55 percent, the white population by only 23 percent. Eli Lilly, in partnership with John Craine (now bishop after being dean at Christ Church), who recruited my father and gave him a mandate to open the parish to the community. There would be two other priests, but the arrangement would be hierarchical; reporting to my father, a canon and a more junior priest, called a curate. There would be no official role for my mother.

Until my father met with the Sunday ushers soon after we got there, the parish was all white; "Negroes" who turned up for services at Christ Church were firmly directed to St. Philip's—a nearby Episcopal parish, all black and named for the apostle who in legend had converted the first African, an Ethiopian eunuch. Of course my father found this unacceptable and subtly put out the word among leaders of the African American community that those rules had changed—we discussed it at the dinner table. Soon a few black families began quietly to "integrate" the congregation; soon after that, my father baptized a black child during a Sunday service. Soon after the baptism, my father was invited to address a vestry day of prayer at the church retreat center in the hills of Brown County. Since Mr. Lilly was away, the junior warden was first to speak after the opening prayer: There had never been Negroes at Christ Church, and there would be none at Christ Church now. My father, by his own account trembling with fury, explained quietly that he was "terribly sorry," but inclusion of all people was central to his faith and theology; surely they had known when they hired him about his work in Jersey City and that he was a member of the NAACP.

"What is the NAACP?" one vestryman apparently asked; the gathering ended in an impasse, and my father left, certain he'd lose his job. The very same men had been so welcoming when they arrived! *These people are more reserved than they appear,* my mother observed to Pam. After returning from his travels the following week, Mr. Lilly made his way to my father's office. He'd heard about the meeting, of course, but he fully supported my father's vision. Not only that, he would endow a new inner-city ministry to the tune of a million dollars—$8,500,000 in 2017 currency—provided the parish remained in its downtown location.

Uptown on Washington Boulevard, there was *never a dull moment,* as my mother would have put it. *Yes, we have bedbugs!* she wrote Pam. *We almost wired you. I quickly got an exterminator who said "Lady, if the eggs get in the wall-to-wall, you're sunk!"*

Of course it was that very day the Lillys came to call for the first time, Mr. Lilly driving *the fawn-colored Rolls.* My mother didn't refuse when Ruth Lilly asked for a tour before tea; her guest didn't say a word when they stood at the door of the master bedroom—the seven-foot mattress was out to be refurbished, the armchairs and Granny Moore's chaise longue to be fumigated. As for Mr. Lilly, he invited the family to swim at their pool anytime—we called it the Lilly pond. *He restores one's faith in big business,* my mother wrote Pam—*one of the few really humble people I've ever met. Paul saw him on the way to our welcoming reception (next door to the church at a club—parish hall too small) on his hands & knees helping a little boy find a dime. When dime was finally retrieved, they proceeded into the club!*

2.

I move further into the front hall, staircase on my right, the brown carpet—closets in front of me to the left and the right where the "hi-fi" is.

I remember *La Bohème* playing, the Jussi Björling, Victoria de los Angeles, Thomas Beecham recording (1957), which I now listen to on wireless earphones. And *My Fair Lady*, to which my parents had taken me in New York, just me and Mommy and Poppy before we moved, my toothy grin in the restaurant photograph—I so wanted to look like Julie Andrews, her tiny waist. Or *Carousel*—*I saw it during the war,* my mother would say, humming her favorite, "You're a queer one, Julie Jordan," using *queer* in the old-fashioned way, perfectly describing herself; the LP always sticking on the line, "carry me cross—carry me cross—carry me cross." And Ella Fitzgerald singing "Don't Fence Me In": "I want to ride to the ridge where the West commences / gaze at the moon till I lose my senses." At twelve I felt fenced in, but of course it was my mother who actually was— clergy wife, champion mother of seven children under eleven.

Danny, the baby, is asleep, and Babby (as we called Marian) is at nursery school, and so Jenny is alone, gathers dirty clothes from every room, tosses them into a basket, then drops them all down the laundry chute. *The glories of a laundry chute!* Such a contrast to the washer and dryer in the basement in Jersey City, endless ringing of the doorbell. She could feel it now, all falling away—interruptions, the needs of others so pressing, her own children also tugging, pulling her from what she believed she was meant to do *for others.* She hadn't counted on how each new child added another personality, how much more work it was to cook for the seven we were now, wash so many more clothes, again change diapers, make plans for this many—not to mention how, as each of us got older, the family dynamic changed and changed again. Even though she still felt guilty for leaving, she realized now that Grace Church had been *a terrible strain for a long time.* I would not have known this had I not read her letters to Pam; I had seen a mother who popped right back to herself, boasted after every birth, conquered each spate of packing and unpacking for summer vacation. I didn't understand why suddenly, in this very big house where she had more time and space, there was not someone to help just once in a while; instead we had two cleaners and a cook named Mrs. Pendleton, who was black and wore a white uniform.

What on earth were they doing? Weren't we supposed to do here what we had done in Jersey City? Were we leaving all that behind? Why? Was it because Poppy was a dean and the house was fancy and we were therefore more like Gami, who had several servants—not black of course, but Scottish and Irish? (I realize now, their race was a choice.) Or was it that my parents were not actually who I thought they were? And the food was different—I remember creamed succotash and creamed chicken, lamb chops a little too well done, everything so tame on the plate. *I hated giving up cooking,* my mother wrote Pam, *but it seemed necessary to give up one big area of work.*

"Moore family residence, maid speaking," was how Mrs. Pendleton answered the phone; my mother, overhearing, nearly choked, explained immediately that Mrs. Pendleton should please feel free just to say hello or her name. My mother was not used to help who so overtly considered themselves servants. It occurs to me now that Mrs. Pendleton might have wanted to conceal her own identity. She was *a minister's wife,* my mother wrote Pam; they had *that in common* and as they worked side by side, they talked *freely on the subject.* They also talked about race: *She is quite amazed that we really feel the way we do and has about 1000 Langston Hughes-type stories.* (Like the short stories she read us from his book *The Ways of the White Folks,* which always made her voice break and me cry.) Nonetheless, here she was, Jenny Moore, with wall-to-wall carpeting and a cook who couldn't seem to stop answering the phone *maid speaking.* And not only that: when she drove along Washington Boulevard at the end of the day, she was forced to take in what it looked like she was part of, what she *was* part of—all the maids in their uniforms standing *on clipped green lawns* waiting for the "loop bus," an institution of the black community that every day circled the white neighborhoods to take the women home.

When she next wrote Pam she had just hired a *person for Sundays so I don't have to take the baby to church—such luxury,* and someone once a week for *heavy cleaning.* She expressed her uneasiness about the help she now needed—the usual guilt about the privilege not only of being able to afford it but of never having to think of money. There was, it seemed, no escape from the contradictions. A woman at the coffee hour after my father's installation as dean took her aside: *I hope you have a servant. Col-*

ored help is so cheap here. She had mumbled a reply, my mother wrote Pam; but she did need the help—the house was *really wonderful*, but it was also, as her predecessor had remarked, *a woman killer*.

Six years later, Betty Friedan, in *The Feminine Mystique*, would provide a framework for my mother's conundrum; twenty years after that, Arlie Hochschild in *The Second Shift* would argue that mothers who worked outside the home essentially held two jobs. Grace Church with its open rectory had given meaning to my mother's second shift; but the Indianapolis cathedral expected little beyond centerpieces for the annual parish supper, a dinner party now and then—women's work. *There are a good many new young things who have this theory (I'm told) that there is a gimmick to being a "clergy wife" & that they are lonely souls who can demand nothing of their husbands besides doing the Lord's work 7 days a week. It drives me wild.* She gamely tried to join in and wrote Pam hints she picked up for entertaining—*There is a good punch "for 50 people" in* The Joy of Cooking *which can be used with endless substitutions unless you're going to do coffee, or lime sherbet floating in ginger ale.* She missed really knowing parishioners. Jersey City had brought *strain*, but with the strain had come meaning, not to mention constant activity. As did a brand-new baby, the excitement of unpacking after a move. What would she do in this new place after all the curtains were made and hung?

We are in church, and my mind is taken up by the bass line of the organ; and then, as if from nowhere, ushers come forward, each taking his place at the end of a pew. For some reason I am at the eleven o'clock, sitting with Mom and Dee and Rosie, all of us wearing hats—not as ornament, but because a woman wore a hat when "in the presence of the Lord." My brother Paul is in the boys choir, which sang Bach and Monteverdi or finely harmonized Gregorian chant. The liturgy and music are building toward the consecration, the elevation when the priest raises the host— the large circular wafer of unleavened bread that represents the body of Christ. I am carried away by the prayer, which I have heard almost every Sunday since I can remember, the organ and choir and the incense; I will go up to the altar for Communion, as will my mother. She is praying too, her head bent. I assume this is easy for her, that she does not start thinking of other things like I do: right now, of the boy in the choir on whom I have a crush, whose older brother is my friend Susan's boyfriend—her father is the bishop, my father's boss.

None of us is moving, and then an usher reaches our row, and my mother and I rise and walk slowly to the altar rail to "receive"—first the wafer on the tongue, "The Body of Our Lord Jesus Christ," and then the sweet wine. *"The Blood of Our Lord Jesus Christ which was shed for thee."* This is what is said, though I know that unlike the Roman Catholics, we do not believe the body or blood actual—rather, a metaphor or reminder. We're standing now, and my mother is ahead of me walking back to our pew. I am feeling flushed and conspicuous as I slide past Dee and Rosie and kneel; now the hymn starts, the one I always consider my mother's favorite, whose language I do not consider until I am much older and try-ing to figure everything out. "Let all mortal flesh keep silence, / and with fear and trembling stand." We all sing the melody, which is in a minor key. My mother's voice is quavering, not the voice I'm used to, and the soprano voices of the boys choir soar in a descant composed by Ralph Vaughan Williams. "Ponder nothing earthly minded / For with blessing in His hand, / Christ our Lord to earth descendeth / our full homage to demand."

I am thinking of my mother at the time: as mortal flesh, as a woman alive and moving through her life. She was thirty-five, hardly finished with the flesh by means of which, by then, she had conceived and given birth to seven children. But in the hymn she considered her favorite, the flesh does not ask or reach, nor consider the flesh of another. Because my mother was precise about language, I must conclude that when she sang this hymn, she was asking her desire to be silent. To keep silent.

In that silence I think about what my mother meant by the word *Chris-tian*. I could not have imagined that one day I would have to make clear what that word meant to my mother. In half a century, even my own first association with the word *Christian* will be to the terms "born again" and "fundamentalist"—strands of Christianity I would come to read as reactionary, confining, intolerant, and small, even compensation for fear. For the family and community in which I grew up, *Christian* referred to people who were linking their faith to politically progressive movements; Episcopalians and other Protestants, like Martin Luther King and later William Sloane Coffin; and Roman Catholics, like Ivan Illyich, the Berrigan brothers, Thomas Merton, and of course Dorothy Day.

For my mother, the means to intimacy was belief. She wanted always to integrate what being a Christian meant into the life she lived, our family life. I'm thinking of the Catholic Worker idea, to create a life in which it was "easier to be good," but also easier to be happy with others. There was a tradition we practiced all through Jersey City and into Indianapolis; it was called Christ Kindl, which meant "Christ Child." On the first Sunday of Advent, the season when Christians await the birth of Jesus, we celebrated with a dinner, lighting the first of four purple candles in a wreath of evergreen that remained at the center of the table until Christmas. That first Sunday night, with quiet excitement, we would open the first door of the Advent calendar and then pass around a bowl of folded scraps of paper on which names were written; you'd choose one name, the person in the household was because your Christ Kindl, a secret until Christmas Eve. Each day you'd leave a note or a small gift on the person's pillow, might even do a favor and *not* leave notice—like folding their laundry or making their bed. I still remember the mother and child on linen that Ledlie Laughlin gave me one year in Jersey City. In an Indianapolis scrapbook I found this, my mother's penciled handwriting barely disguised: *Rest awhile I'll do it! Write me a note and leave it on your bed—put in it what you wish you didn't have to do. Put on the envelope this symbol—* and there's a small picture of a fish, the secret sign of the early Christians. Who was her Christ Kindl that year? I still don't know.

A Christian friend would be able to take this ritual delicately, seriously. By Christian, my mother meant a friend who would be present, perhaps encourage her to have faith that she would make her way in this new place, whatever the difficulty. A *Christian,* as my mother meant it then, was a person who thought of others, who wanted the world to change for the greater good of everyone, who insisted to herself that her faith be radical, as in going to the root of things, and who wanted to live by that truth—but also a person who would get the joke, like Pam, who understood her delight when she described persuading the Christ Church women's auxiliary to try a *snack bar* like they'd had in Jersey City. A great idea, they all agreed, much better than *a turkey dinner*!

After a month or so in Indianapolis, she found a few *crucial* things had gone missing in the move—Paul's typewriter, his winter coat, her sewing box. Would Pam look for them, and send them if found? *I promise never to mention it again.* Losing things has *stirred my bottom waters,* she wrote, scratching Pam's husband Jim from the salutation—*too female!*—and then pouring her heart out:

> *I have had a real dark night of the soul, from which I trust I am now emerging. I became terrified that I was or would become somewhat nuts, and couldn't seem to get any perspective.* Every single *characteristic, achievement, act, experience, relationship of the past few years was suddenly reviewed in a very black shadow—with only bad motives apparent etc. I had always thought I was aware of the pitfalls (for the soul) of Jersey, but it became obvious that I was only aware of them in the most superficial manner. As I looked back on it, I was guilty of the worst kind of pride in so many areas. I suppose anyone could have told me, had I sat down and listened.*

The first time I read my mother's letters to Pam Morton a decade ago, I somehow missed this entire episode—I'd discover it when reading a letter my mother wrote to Dorothy Day after Dorothy visited them in Indianapolis. Her daughter, Tamar, was in a postpartum depression. *Tell her,* my mother wrote Dorothy, that *I had one for two months.* I was surprised to read my mother making such an open declaration about her emotional life, though it was like her to share what others might make use of. She had expected the move to Indianapolis to bring immediate relief—I was so looking forward to putting all *my porch-set, telephone-answering, door-answering energy, into spoiling Paul and the children,* she wrote Pam—not to mention distance from Gami and Margarett, who was now in a sanitarium called Baldpate.

Where was that redoubtable Jenny Moore energy? The children—

all seven were at their most demanding. Insecurity and guilt hovered. *I'm sorry to inflict this on you,* she wrote Pam, *but must share it with Christian friends*—Pam would not judge, would reassure her that a recognizable self would soon return.

But it took two months. A downward spiral settled in, and though she understood that postpartum depression and moving could be a *lethal combination*, nothing had prepared her for this, how afraid she became. She thought of her mother's diagnosis, manic depression; two of her siblings—Margie and Harry—had been hospitalized at one time or another. *Mental hospitals are terrifying and I'm a bit panicked,* she wrote Pam that fall. But more frequently, what she wrote on the subject was cool, like this: *My mother is better. She's finally agreed to have shock treatments.*

Did this *dark night of the soul* mean that she too would need shock treatments? Even though I've had no children and therefore no opportunity for postpartum depression, my mother's response feels extreme.

In my thirties, when I felt down, I'd be at therapy or on the telephone—someone would remind me that the condition was not permanent—much later I would take medication. My father knew about Jenny's "depression," but he always seemed to pathologize these phases of hers rather than identify with them. Wasn't his "cumulative fatigue," whose symptoms certainly resembled hers, some version of depression? Wasn't her depression some version of deep, accumulated fatigue? I don't know how many small things helped turn the tide, but she wrote Pam about one of them: *When Paul was away and I was beginning to feel desperate, with bank tellers enticing children with lollipops when I cashed a check, music in the supermarkets & Negro maids on every clipped lawn on Wash. Blvd., a young man walked in & said, "I've come to meet the fabulous Jenny Moore."*

She was thrilled for a week. She also gave some credit to prayer, which seemed to shift self-hatred into self-love. *Once I realized that God was kind and would only show me these things briefly and then let me pass on, and once I realized that I was under a terrible strain for a long time which of course added to it, I felt somewhat more able to cope. Back to the children!* In the letter to Pam, which was twenty pages long, she then moved on to me:

Honor seems fine. I went on a campaign to let her emote her ill feelings (which were endless) the first few weeks. It was very rough, but seems much better now. She resented the years in Jersey City & its accompanying friendlessness, hecticness etc. far more than I was aware—and she felt guilty about it. Rather hard for a mother to take, but I urged her to say all the nasty things she could & it really worked I think.

I do not remember resenting Jersey City or being drawn out about my feelings. I recall only my mother's temper, which returned despite her efforts to control it—her hand pushing at my bangs, *get your hair out of your face!* Ridicule when I wanted a padded bra like the other girls I saw change for gym class: *What God has forgotten, fill in with cotton!* I fought back: through furious tears, nose all runny, the color red, and sweat—a frenzy. Attempts to retrieve additional detail return the familiar but scary blank: "I got holy hell for my messy room," I wrote in a diary—I couldn't seem to put clothes away, ever. "Mom and I had a fight. I plead the fifth." And down a black hole it goes. When she wrote about her *campaign* to have me *emote*, was she talking about our fights?

Nothing like a move to make one aware of what one has done or has not done, as a mother, Christian, etc., she wrote Pam. But if she apologized to me, I do not remember it.

To escape overhearing us, my brother Paul bolted out to start the car, no matter how cold the Sunday morning. Decades later, my father repeatedly apologized, repeatedly offering the excuse that his "shrink" had cautioned him not to intervene: "mothers and daughters."

Do the screaming and tears drown out quieter memories? I remember her shouts of my name resounding up the staircase. By now I'm sleeping on the third floor. *Honor it's quarter of seven, Honor it's 7:30, Honor? Do you want to go Doctor Browning on Thursday or on Friday?* It's an alarm, an emergency.

I was dreaming, of colors and of my father, or again of the squirrel with red and green lights for eyes and a tail that spins and whirs. He is unapproachable and terrifying. He has appeared on the dirt road at the foot of the hill near the vegetable garden at Hollow Hill, and Gami is standing at the open door of her car waiting for me to come to her. *Honor!* comes my mother's shout again, and something bangs or slams.

I don't ask why I have to go to the doctor. When I get there, he gives me a cream for something called acne. I don't know what acne is, and no one explains; it is as if I'm supposed to know. There are sweet times in Indianapolis. She wrote me about them years later, of making pumpkin and apple pie together, but all I remember is making artificial flowers in Jersey City, the soft feel of the yellow and pink petals.

Our fights knot and condense into something impenetrable whose fumes will lick through my life as inability to ask for help, a terror of being wrong, recurring headaches. "How did you get so hurt in life?" asked a lover when I was in my twenties; I didn't want to tell him about the fights. Offered by therapists, astrologer, friends who are mothers: she must have known, perhaps unconsciously, that I could take care of myself, leaving her free to care for the others, including herself. I don't believe that is the whole story. Continual criticism, shouting, the occasional slap may support a little girl's alienation but not her freedom, and the emotional violence of our later fights did not function as encouragement—there was something in me she was fighting off. My sister Marian, ten years younger, had so many tantrums when she was four years old, they took her to a psychologist, who suggested they pay more attention to her, which they did. I was sent to a creepy man in a Monument Circle office who gave me a Rorschach test: I was "managerial." Given the same test later at school, I gave different answers and the result was different—I was "artistic."

I might have responded to a simple conversation with an outside adult. What I got was the curate Father Roundtree at confession, telling me I had "a brilliant mind." Did I believe him? I was twelve and at a school where I was memorizing state capitals. What I had probably confessed was fighting with my mother, maybe stealing money from her purse. It's long over now, of course, and though scars remain—small tender places that smart at a friend or sibling's slight—I feel forgiveness. My sister Rosie, at ten, is standing at our parents' bedroom door in Indianapolis; our mother is looking out the window. She turns when Rosie speaks: Why are you so mean to Honor? And Rosie sees that she is in tears.

I would never have imagined she was hurt too: a dozen years later, my fights would find their way into one of my first poems:

I have a war with my mother.
She is on her side, I am on mine.
It is longer than
the longest war in history,
longer than a hundred years.

3.

She works her way through all of us, like ordering at a Chinese restaurant: Paul has best friends who are twins, Georgie has fun unrolling toilet paper, and Rosie cries at least twice a week about missing Jersey City. Dee is *so popular* and her best friends, also twins, live around the corner. In the letters to Pam, she dramatizes. At a parents' meeting, *Dee's teacher was scolding three mothers when I arrived & when I said who I was she smiled benignly, "Adelia* [Dee's actual name] *is the celestial star on the horizon of the 3d grade & reflects the home she comes from," & turning to the three tragic Hoosier types whose children she'd been berating, "This is the wife of the new Dean at Monument Circle."*

When you are experimenting, you make adjustments. By the time Danny was one, my mother wanted her kitchen back, didn't want such a "fancy" house. Mrs. Pendleton, the cook, departed, and Mrs. Lee, who'd come in a day or two a week to clean, now came every weekday. She did not wear a white uniform, and we quickly came to call her "Leesy," the name that Danny, with whom she had a special bond, had given her—he was now walking.

Sometimes Leesy made lunch for us; but my mother, cooking now with relish, was in charge. She'd bought a freezer, which was put in the basement; she ordered hamburger patties and hot dogs in bulk along with their respective rolls, set the two wall ovens to broil as we sat crowded into the Formica-tabled, leatherette-upholstered breakfast nook. Her lunch masterpiece was something she called a cheese dream, which it definitely was. Not American cheese, but sharp orange cheddar and open-faced. I loved to jump up and peek through the oven window and watch—six bright-orange-topped Pepperidge Farm slices jammed onto a cookie sheet—gradually come to the perfect bubbling temperature: too soon and some of the cheese would still be hard; too late and it would be brown and too crisp. Was adding paprika my idea or my mother's? At dinner parties she concocted veal this or chicken that, or offered roast beef or steak. The dish I most loved was not meat or even her macaroni and cheese, but her extraordinary crème brulée, which she never made for family supper and certainly never for lunch. The layer of broiled brown sugar was more a lid than a glaze, so I could lift it and spoon the *crème* from underneath, tasting everything my mother kept from me. Her Thanksgiving and Christmas meals were always a dare: make the turkey *divine*, pecans in the stuffing, for instance, stuffing between skin and meat; or, she'd experiment and cook a goose. Roast beef with Yorkshire pudding—the memory of Sunday lunch at her grandmother's must have been her guide.

Once for a weeknight supper, she made rabbit—would anyone notice it wasn't chicken? Spaghetti with her own meat sauce; salad with her own slightly too vinegary vinaigrette in which I remember the dots of pepper, the iceberg lettuce, in summer and fall the luscious Indiana tomatoes. When we children were on our own for supper, I'd assert my own cuisine, making creamed spinach as Gagy had taught me—chop the spinach fine, sauté a little onion in butter, make a béchamel. To avoid failing, I tried to excel in a uniquely individual way, to make something that my mother couldn't or wouldn't. Like her, I'd search *The Joy of Cooking*—ah, there it is. The chocolate, the flour, the egg. If you can't get buttermilk, sour the milk with vinegar. I followed the recipe very carefully, watching the clots form in the milk. I learned that like all sweet things, a devil's food cake, to satisfy ultimate longing, needed something sour at its heart. The frosting had to be like sweet dark butter (in the sense that peanut butter is butter) that shifted in consistency when it got cool enough to spread but never melted. I would plan in the morning and then cook all afternoon on a Saturday, though I don't remember what aside from spinach the rest of the supper was. Most important was that when I stood there offering the cake, they all paid attention. This was how I maintained my right to the privilege of being the oldest—giving something while simultaneously showing off.

My mother's great pleasure was any recipe from the *New York Times*, where Craig Claiborne, the first male food critic at a major American paper, was offering the American housewife culinary innovations—I'm going to brine the turkey, she might say, or stuff it with oysters! We subscribed to the *Times*, even though it came a day late. I do not remember recipes from the *Indianapolis Star* or *News*; my parents considered those papers, as my mother put it, "hopeless—to the right of Attila the Hun," the Huns being the Eugene Pulliam family, later represented in U.S. politics by Vice President Dan Quayle (1988–92).

The dinner parties soon began. Guests sat at the large table from Prides, with its gleaming mahogany and three centerpieces that were presents from Margarett—white Italian ceramic with fake green grapes overflowing. But there was an edge; while my mother of course understood that the dean's wife should entertain, a dinner party that was merely obligatory was certain to be a bore. How to describe what she did when compiling an invitation list? Assemble temperaments and interests based on who would spark with whom, but also add a person or two who might otherwise be alone: a woman from the Philippines who had been a nurse at the hospital in Indianapolis; Ruth Cook, a divorcee who dressed like a movie star in red lipstick and a green satin dress, and her tall son Walt, in his twenties, always in a gray suit. Other priests and their wives might come—they were friends as well as colleagues—and new Indianapolis friends, Alan and Betty Nolan, whom they had met though the Woollens. Evans Woollen was the architect whom I would interview all those years later at the MoMA lunch; his wife Nancy was dark-haired, wore horn-rimmed spectacles. Who to invite for Thanksgiving when Aunt Margie came for the long weekend—*it was a burden having her stay so long, but she seemed to become part of things*—and who when Dorothy Day made the trip to speak at the Cathedral and at the Marian Fathers monastery?

The group of friends, it seemed to me, assembled quickly. My parents had friends before I did: one day the only people they saw were from the cathedral, and the next they were surrounded by a tight group of like-minded liberal Democrats—lawyers and an architect, a professor at Butler University, a businessman who was a Yale classmate transplanted from the East, and their smart wives—couples also in their thirties with children more or less the ages of my sisters and brothers. In no time the three or four families were celebrating Memorial Day or the Fourth of July together, hot dogs and hamburgers grilled on the terrace out back; games of prisoners' base, softball, or croquet on the big lawn. To me these holidays were strange and new; in Jersey City we celebrated church holidays like St. Stephen's Day, the day after Christmas, named for the saint who was martyred, or Maundy Thursday, which marked the Last Supper. Now we celebrated like everyone else. It was a relief.

The Nolans became my parents' best friends. Betty was petite with long honey-blond hair she wore in a bun; she was relaxed and warm, spoke slowly but with a sly wit. Alan had a dark-brown crew cut; he was proudly of Irish extraction, one of two lawyer sons of Jeanette Covert Nolan, a prolific Indiana writer of historical novels for children. When we grew up, my sisters and I agreed that Mr. Nolan was the handsomest man among my parents' Indianapolis friends, and we all had crushes on him. The Nolans were Catholic liberals, and Alan, who practiced labor law in a big firm on Monument Circle, was an amateur Civil War historian who wrote books that later included an important revisionist biography of Robert E. Lee. When we met them, the Nolans had two sons and two daughters, the youngest barely out of diapers.

As couples, the Moores and the Nolans had do-si-do crushes; there were jokes even then about Pop and Betty, and a decade after Mom's death, Alan told me that "if things had been different, I would have made a life with your mother." By then Betty had died, suddenly of an aneurism, and Alan's new wife, with dark hair like my mother, sat with us as he confessed his old dream. Famously, the four of them took a trip to New Orleans—*great fun* except that my father ate a bad oyster—*the worst he'd felt since the war.*

These friends were the beginning of my mother's great happiness in Indianapolis—everything in balance, marriage, children, the church. No one from those years has forgotten her. Decades later, at a cocktail party on a lawn by the sea, a woman I do not recognize steps into a conversation I'm having: "One of my mother's favorite people was this woman's mother!" That summer at my fiftieth college reunion, I'd seen again a Radcliffe classmate whom I remembered knew my mother. "Oh yes," she said. "I lived with your family for two months." Another recollection from Indianapolis: a friend, over to study Latin, arrived early and came upon my mother in the living room with a cigarette in one hand and, in the bend of the opposite arm, a nursing baby locked onto her bare breast. "This was Indianapolis," my friend exclaimed. "I had never seen anything like it! She was so . . . so devil may care, so *relaxed*."

And a story Evans Woollen told that day at the Museum of Modern Art: My mother had gathered a group of women and their kids, the mothers to "yak" as the children played. "Jenny was wearing pedal pushers and *big* sunglasses with huge pink harlequin rhinestoned frames," his wife Nancy had reported. "We laughed and laughed and complimented her, and then she removed the glasses, took a pause, and said, 'Of course, I could ruin Paul's career.' " When we left Indianapolis, Evans presented her with a calligraphed certificate: "Merit Award to Jenny Moore, for her conspicuous contribution to dereliction in Indiana."

4.

We've already had spinach, lettuce, radishes & scallions and peas! I get such a kick out of it. My herbs are frightfully cosmopolitan, and I have just planted gourds for the fall, and corn for when we get back in August. I have not faced who's to take care of the garden in our absence nor who will keep the Sia-

mese cat. (Poo Chai, which means 'little boy cat" in Thai; he lived to be twenty-two). That's my mother, updating Pam, and I am alone in the living room, bent close in to the bookshelves on either side of the fireplace. Records: Vivaldi was being recorded comprehensively for the first time since his revival in the 1920s, and my mother had subscribed—a new LP arrived each month. Encased in shiny white with orange and black trim, the recordings were lined up where I was always searching for something to read, a book that was not a children's book. I remember *Other Voices, Other Rooms*, by Truman Capote—the author looked like a teenager and the photo, of him lying down, was scary; *An American Dilemma* by Gunnar Myrdal, big and thick but it looks boring, even though I know it's by a man who was Swedish—so he had a clearer view of the American race situation, my mother said. Not on the shelf were the books that arrived once a month, complete with return envelope, from the Society Library in New York.

I was twelve. My mother reported it to Pam: *Honor became a woman.* I didn't understand why I had blood in my underpants, so certain was I that I would "start late" like my mother who did not "fall off the roof" until she was sixteen—*forever etched on my inner eye of motherhood,* my mother wrote, *is the picture of her sitting on the toilet waving her underdrawers, shrieking "Mommy, Mommy"! I was so glad I was right there.* Yes, she was there, explaining the difference between a tampon and a pad, and by the next day she'd bought me a "belt" and "sanitary napkins." My brother Paul, she wrote Pam, thought I was *faking* when my new accomplishment was announced at supper. It was excruciating that she told everyone. And then, almost immediately, I was being accused of being "fat," though none of the pictures show me as even overweight. Was it that I ate fast, finished the first helping, then raced for a second helping in the noisy din of supper? The size of my "bottom" disturbed my mother, and she associated it with my appetite, for which I was now being ridiculed. I loved what the others did not, like spinach and artichokes and asparagus, any food that seemed "sophisticated," anything that would set me apart. Food was everything I couldn't get enough of—attention, privacy, allowance.

To make sure my weight was normal, my mother sent me to the

doctor—why not a gynecologist instead, someone to explain the painful buttons I didn't realize were my new breasts? This doctor dispatched me to a big house, turned medical office, where I lay in a quiet gray room for "a basal metabolism test"—drank something disgusting and sweet, then laid there for hours without even a book. My engine was a little slow, so I was prescribed a small beige pill that looked pressed from powdered bones, along with an orange one, Dexedrine, to make me eat less, get thin. And so the diets began; but I soon realized, when I got thinner and she still criticized me, that it was somehow hopeless.

We now have supper at the German beer table on the porch, and I am a freshman in high school. Since September there has been a chart of assignments above the kitchen sink—clear the table, rinse, load the dishwasher. Did my sister Dee paint it? I hated to clear the table, but I really hated doing the dishes. My mother was pregnant again. *Honor suspected for weeks because she kept finding maternity patterns on the sewing machine—and is just waiting for me to let her tell her friends; so gratifying that she's pleased!* Soon everybody knew. *We told the little ones last night & Georgie hopes "it will come out when I'm asleep!"* In the afternoon liberal paper, the *Indianapolis Times*, the columnist Irving Leibowitz joked that the dean of the Episcopal cathedral had a strange way of taking advantage of his membership in Planned Parenthood, given that his wife Jenny was expecting number eight. I had gotten a little dizzy when my mother confided she was pregnant again, but I had no language for what I felt: "What about me?" would have made me sound selfish. But it turned out that what was complicated for me was a thrill to my wonderful new friends Peggy and Laurie Kohn—they couldn't wait to come over to see my mother pregnant. They were identical twins with long golden red hair, big blue eyes; Peggy wanted to be an artist, Laurie was a serious pianist, and they were always talking about Izler Solomon, the conductor of the Indianapolis Symphony who lived across the street from them with his glamorous wife, Betty. Now all they wanted to do was touch my mother's stomach: "Feel," she always said, and they would, and then we would all go off into what my mother called *gales of laughter.*

No sooner was Susanna born than my father received an invitation to teach a course at an international conference at Canterbury Cathedral in England. They'd asked him to teach about the church and the corporation, but he'd suggested "The Church and the City." A trip to Europe! Just the older ones—Dee and Paul and me. Paris! London! Finally, a glamorous trip! To get away from it all, I was doing my packing on the porch. The 1960 Democratic convention had started on July 11, and we were leaving for Europe on the 14th. We must have rented a television— we didn't own one, on principle—because I remember the jiggly, blurry, black and white images; my mother watching Adlai Stevenson's speech, his last-ditch effort to get the nomination a third time. My father had told us that "during the war," Jack Kennedy had come to a dinner party at Gramps and Gami's house in Palm Beach. We left the day before JFK's nomination was final.

Dee was ten, Paul was twelve, and I was fourteen, and now we really were the older ones—in her sixties, my sister Rosie mock-complained about being left out of that trip: "I was furious." Paul needed a male pal, it had been concluded, and so Colin, my father's sister Fanny's son by her second marriage, came along—a mistake, my brother Paul still says, but he nicknamed Colin "Stanley," and he made us all laugh. "Five Moores and a mental case," Paul declared when asked by the purser on the boat to describe our party.

Neither of my parents had been to Europe since the 1930s, and the closest I'd been to a world city was Washington, D.C., where we'd gone for a weekend the year before. My father's two-week teaching job in England was the excuse, but a trip when two or three of us hit our teens became a tradition, a version of trips both my parents took when they were that age. Paris! London! I decided to keep a diary: "Horrible—although beautiful on departure from Indpls," I wrote in the first entry. "We left Weir Cook Airport at 10:35 EST and had a perfectly lovely flight to Laguardia. From Laguardia we took a taxi to Idlewild." I always preferred the original name for Kennedy airport—a trip could be both idle and wild!

My mother kept a diary too: *Idlewild for a couple of hours before leaving for Montreal—Idlewild full of Puerto Ricans. Felt at home again.*

"We sailed at 11:30," I wrote, "and it was a lot of fun. The name of the ship was the *Saxonia*, a British ship of the Cunard Line, and I learned that a ship is a little city." The tugs pushed and tugged to get us out onto the river and we finally started moving along at about 12:00," I wrote. I had never been on a ship, never even seen movies with shipboard scenes, so everything was new—bingo, betting on horses, the captain's table; table tennis, deck tennis, and daily quizzes overseen by the ship interpreter, who was Maltese and spoke seven languages. I began to learn what British meant—there was tea whenever you wanted it. Dee and I roomed together, and so did Colin and Paul.

When we left the St. Lawrence Seaway and entered the Atlantic, there were icebergs: "One looked like a battleship and another like a house. Also, there was a whale, a baby one. I didn't see it, but one of Dee's friends did! One of the icebergs was 145 feet tall, 125 feet long and 1-1/4 miles from the boat." On the first day, my mother sat in the sun and read; on the second she slept till noon. *Deck chairs are throbbing with humanity mostly rather shabby British types—a few numbers that could be out of "A Green Gage Summer" but very few Evelyn Waugh characters.* My father and I played shuffleboard—"Poppy beat me, but not too badly."

Two nuns sat with us at supper, and I made friends with a gang of girls from Toronto and Montreal. One of them actually knew a movie star named Franchot Tone. The girl's name was Caroline but she had changed it to Kim; she was the first Europeanized girl I had ever met— she smoked Gauloises cigarettes and taught me to "bat" my eyelashes. We flirted with the stewards and gave them fantasy names—"Pedro, Pancho, Chico, Napoleon (real name Gary—a doll!), and Bones." Soon they were waving kisses whenever we saw them, and I was "madly in love (just kidding)" with Pedro. Before supper, every day at 4:15, there was a movie: a Western with Julie London and Robert Mitchum; *Up in Arms*, with Danny Kaye and Dinah Shore: "just at the credits, the boat started rocking and we had to start getting used to an ocean voyage."

It was Sunday, and they'd overslept; my father almost missed celebrating the Communion service—*Church of England Prayer book; "Queen + Dwight"—finally unraveling,* taking *naps all the time,* my mother wrote. The diary is a thorough record, but I find no interior life. *Tried to teach kids*

Bridge. Bingo + Pop won. Dancing, "Top Hat" + waltzing until 11:30. One
night at supper, she wrote, they met some Republicans from Ohio, and
my father talked to a Ugandan diplomat. Another night, a chemistry student named David from North Carolina sat with us. We'd talked at home
about the Negro and white college students protesting at lunch counters
in the South—the *sit-in strikes* had started in February in Greensboro,
just an hour from where David lived. He hadn't joined them, but he knew
about the organization called the Student Nonviolent Coordinating Committee (SNCC), and that black and white young people were "sitting in"
at thirty-one cities all over the South. In April a civil rights act had passed
Congress, making it a federal crime to obstruct federal court orders or
cross state lines after committing bombing or arson; it also allowed federal courts to appoint referees to register voters.

The last day before landing, I decided to actually write in my diary
instead of just jotting: "The lovely sea or the angry sea, the lovely sunny
or wet and dangerous decks and the seagulls against the blue of the English Channel with land in the distance." We disembarked at Le Havre,
waving to our new friends who'd stay aboard till Southampton. We
picked up our car and were soon at American Express, my father making hotel reservations. He showed the boys how to read the map, and my
mother took Dee and me to something called a *patisserie* and bought us
each a *croissant*, an amazing glorious pastry not then ubiquitous in the
United States—she must have taught us to pronounce it: first syllable
"qua" and then "sant"—sounds like *song* without the *g* and said through
your nose.

Stopped to see some beautiful churches, old pews, and fascinating pulpits,
wrote my mother.

"Everywhere there were thatched roofs and miles of fields with hay-
stacks and men with hand plows," I wrote.

For lunch we stopped in a town called Lille—*a beat-up café.* "You just
ask for dejeuner and take what you get!"

Sardines and bread and butter, wine "instead of milk," and our first
pommes frites; Dee made the trip's first memorable observation, which
appears in both my mother's diary and mine: "French french fries are

much better than American french fries!" We were on our way to Rouen, "the place where Joan of Arc was burned to death by people who thought she was a witch."

"The most fascinating city I've ever seen," my mother said, and I wrote it down. "Acres of tiny narrow streets and motor bikes and tiny cars going in 'touts directions.' "

There were bullet marks from World War II on the walls of the cathedral. *Very battle torn*, my mother wrote, and at the art museum, Poppy asked, "Ou est Jeanne D'Arc?" in what I characterized as a "Hoosier-French accent"—"Boy was that embarrassing!" Swans glided in the moat outside the museum, and a "cute" French guard helped us on our tour. "En francais." I understood some from my special class in French, "but Mommy did most of the translation."

For supper we stumbled upon a restaurant called Auberge Couronne. which had opened, the menu said, in 1345. "We just kept thinking that knights on the crusades must have stopped and eaten here." In my diary, the clatter of incident, then what I am seeing: "Houses painted bright colors, tree roses and hollyhocks, and at times we'd pass through rows of trees that curled over and closed at the top like a gothic cathedral." Because my mother adored St. Thèrese of Lisieux, we stopped at the house where she had grown up—*terribly exciting*, wrote my mother—*all rooms w. original family furniture save for her room which is ghastly*—plaster saints, candles—we saw the confessional, the very *grille* Therese had looked through. Off again in the little Peugeot, rain and the ocean against the seawall at St. Malo, and walking the firm, wet sand to Mont St. Michel, a magic place that became an island at high tide.

I could feel my life changing, everything in another language, the air and every color deeper, it seemed. We drove the Loire Valley and one day bought bread and cheese and rented bicycles to ride to a winery. All of us got so tipsy we swerved on the way home, all laughing. Once, by chance, we arrived in time for a *son et lumiere* at Amboise and sat on folding chairs outside the chateau, hearing narration in French over loudspeakers: "the lights were kind of like people," I wrote, "and played across the walls the whole time"—war, shadows and the clang of dueling swords—*pranc-*

ing horses, my mother wrote—French kings, the Medicis, the first Italian architects in France, a visit from Michelangelo.

On the way to Paris, we stopped at Chartres, where, for me, the blue of the stained glass became the blue against which all blues must be assessed. In Paris there was a hotel mix-up, so we kids were in one hotel, Mom and Pop in another. Gami met us, and we all had supper on a boat on the Seine with my mother's brother Uncle Harry, who was *aghast* when he learned where we were staying—it was a *red-light district.* "Our hotel looks chic in the lobby, but our room is like Dick Whittington's garret although there are no rats," I wrote. Harry, newly living in Paris and working at a brokerage, was, my mother wrote, *fascinating about French society and wealth; boar hunt, stag hunt, shoots, shaking hands, royalty wedding etc.* One night they dined with at his apartment with Harry his fashionable friends— *Hairdos are fantastic. Francois Malle + Comte de Ganay both kissed my hand. Paul said I looked as if I'd eaten a lemon.*

One night Harry took them *out to 930 dinner + fantastic show at Lido—* a nightclub, my mother told us, where the dancers wore no underwear. I imagined crinolines, the naked legs of cancan dancers, and jazz band music—nowhere near what my mother wrote in her diary but didn't tell us: *Bosoms, Japanese girl on bike was marvelous, juggler with pigeons fantastic—twin German chorus girls—and a beautiful man with seals, swimming pool appears out of nowhere—skating rink on dance floor—aerial acrobatics on roof above.*

I was tired of being left out of grown-up activities, even though I loved Fontainebleau where we went, just the kids, with Gami. My mother had promised me a Paris dress, but the one we bought *after a few teary efforts . . . a white eyelet dress with red ribbons—very pretty*—felt not at all grown-up, more like something a little girl would wear than the glamorous woman I had imagined Paris would turn me into. Writing postcards home, I lied about the dress, boasting to my friends as if it were from Dior. Our last night, we celebrated my brother Paul's thirteenth birthday at the restaurant on top of the Eiffel Tower, elevator rising as you see more and more of the lit-up city. I had my first champagne, and we stayed up to catch the night train to London.

Everything more fun than I thought it would be, my mother wrote that night.

We've been in Canterbury, in a part of England called Kent, for a few days, and my father is already teaching. It's *cloudy and almost rainy,* my mother wrote one day, cold even in August. We explored inside the ancient cathedral the first day we were there—layers of Saxon history, Norman remnants, great fires, additions and rebuildings; the original structure, built in 590, was destroyed by fire in 1067, a year after the Norman conquest, the *fascinating verger* explained; I am learning history right where it happened! He tells us about Archbishop Thomas à Becket's murder on December 29, 1170, and we act it out on the exact site of the attack by four knights loyal to Henry Plantagenet, the very place where the pool of his blood sank into the stone. Chaucer wrote his *Canterbury Tales* about pilgrimages to this shrine, and now my father was actually to preach here! I don't get him back standing in the pulpit, only entering the cathedral grounds—patches of lawn hallucinatory green, pale blossoms vivid in the moist air, the stones deepening in color as we are borne along in a crowd of worshippers, a river of them.

What I am transcribing takes place on August 15, 1960, and I am fourteen. But, as I transcribe, 2009 intrudes—I have come to a castle in Italy, an artists' colony, to begin this book. Because my mother and I both kept diaries that summer and both journals survive, I decide to transcribe. How will our accounts compare? I am doing hers first, and we are in Northumberland. The long hike she's describing is a walk I remember, but I do not appear in her account, nor do the others—my father, my brother, my sister, my cousin. She writes as if she were alone. We are climbing a hill, and I am sweating and scratching bites and getting a headache. Everyone else is moving faster than I am, and I am wearing ugly, cheap pants my mother chose for me in the last town because we had lost a suitcase, the suitcase with my clothes in it. I have a furious tantrum.

After the second day of transcribing, the familiar sickness begins in my head. When I have a headache like this, I inhabit utter emptiness, as if there were such a thing as imagination not lit by color or sound. It comes, intense and debilitating, mapping the interior of my cranium, a throb along a curve of bone, needle prick of shock and intense ache marking the distance from behind the brow down into the neck, into the shoulder. If I can separate from it, I imagine I will be freed, will see color again, feel aspiration, the world. But the sickness does not easily release me; while I am in its custody, not only do I mourn imagination and thought, I must account for their absence, and in that accounting, those faculties seem forever limited by the physical space of the skull—and the skull is lined with pain.

In the two days before the sickness came, I transcribed my mother's entire diary of that trip—thirty pages. My name appears in it, but there is no record of interaction, and I do not find the mother I want, the mother I began this book to find. This headache sickness, I have been taught to believe, is old anger returning, not at the mother my imagination makes, whom I would idealistically place here, at a desk beside me, but the woman keeping a diary of a trip to Europe with her family in 1960, thirty-seven years old, self-involved, in a panic to record every church, every person met, the details of every priest and Nigerian or Portuguese clergy wife she meets during the two weeks my father lectures at Canterbury. How do I write about her?

Why am I still so angry?

That question is what makes me sick. I am still angry at her absence, the lack of her that made me cry on that walk those decades ago. It is raining. I lie in the dark castle room for thirty-six hours; the other artists here must think I'm one of those people at artists' colonies who always complains, but I am not a complainer. I tell them I am a little sick; they offer remedies. Outside the wind blows like a huge breath, and rain-filled clouds move not at all, and that stasis sinks into the bones of my head. On the morning of the first day, in the corridor outside my room, I encounter a woman from Ethiopia named Alem; she asks in Italian if I am all right. I say yes, but I am lying. On the morning of the second day, in the kitchen of the castle, a woman artist from China gives me a box of black healing tea; and on the third day, after hours of drinking the tea, of sweating in the wide bed, of closing the shutters against the world, the sickness begins to recede, along with the dampness in my bones, along with the rain and the wind.

The fourth morning, believing I have accomplished nothing but wishing to take inventory, I turn on the computer and search the document of my mother's diary for my name. It appears eight times in thirty single-spaced pages. I turn on the spellchecker and make my way through the transcription, correcting it. I still have a headache. "You felt annihilated," the therapist says. "I've seen it in you before." We discuss that walk and my long-ago tantrum. I have called him from Italy because on waking from the dark cold of the castle, I still felt hopeless.

Took picnic after breakfast. I have found her entry about that walk. *Took long walk along brook, tried to cross, terrifying slippery places but I had a stick. Ate in grassy glade, walked on, finally crossed on bridge and walked over fields. Had to cross again & forded river. Munched wheat in fields, crossed through fields of heifers and steers. Terribly pretty & exhausting.* When I reach that passage, I remember that I am recording in italics whatever my mother writes: *Tried to cross terrifying slippery places . . . ate in a grassy glade . . . finally crossed on bridge and walked over fields. Had to cross again + forded river.* If I turn what she's written into a metaphor, what does it mean? Obvious I know, but I'll give it a try. In forty-five days of diary, only in that entry do words like *terrifying* and *slippery* occur; but surely they overstate the demands of crossing a brook. What was she afraid of? Was her terror why we fought? Unimaginable to a daughter without children is that her terror had nothing to do with me, that she is concerned about her own fear, the life of her own mind and psyche. Was I afraid of losing her? Neither speculation would have occurred to me on that trip; I was too young, fourteen going on fifteen.

Soon after, in the north of Yorkshire, we have tea in a little hotel in Goathland. Sometime later, on a cold day at the beach in Brighton, my mother took movies—I am short-haired and awkward in a madras bathing suit. When we reach London the lost suitcase is returned, and I have my clothes, and memory of those weeks: the Brontës' house, the post office where they sent off their novels; cathedrals and castles, overnight

with a bishop and his family who live in a palace—my parents sleep in
the bedroom where Henry VIII and Catherine of Aragon once slept. A
week later we visit the Tower of London, where Henry's subsequent wife,
Ann Boleyn, put her head on a stone for the executioner. In Yorkshire, a
picnic with Richard Wood, now Sir Richard, with his wife and daughters,
looking down a meadow at the ruins of an abbey. I like how he reappears
in their lives, grown-up and still walking on the wooden legs, still the
son of Lord Halifax, who inspired those Americans wounded at the end
of the war.

I have not returned to those cathedrals, Canterbury, Ely, York Min-
ster; or my favorite, Durham, with its massive Norman arches and
columns—the columns have zigzag and spiral patterns; something about
the ghost of St. Cuthbert, who died in 687. The last day in London, we
go to a store called the Scottish House and buy Stewart tartans for the
whole family—kilts for the girls, vests for Pop and the boys. The night
before we are to fly home on two different flights, one parent in each,
British censorship keeps us kids out of a movie called *The Entertainer*
with Laurence Olivier as a music hall comic hitting the skids, but allows
us to see *The Apartment*, Billy Wilder's film in which Jack Lemmon and
Shirley Maclaine have an extramarital affair—only now do I find the
prohibition strange.

There is a small black and white photo of me that my father took on
that trip—he was quite serious about his yearly portraits of each of us.
In this one I am sitting on a stone bench that emerges from a stone wall,
in front of a window. Light from the window illuminates one side of my
face, and the near side is in shadow; both hands hold my straw purse
which is shaped like a small treasure chest. I am wearing a dark skirt
and a white cardigan, buttoned, and my bare legs are stretched out in
front of me; a hat that's just white feathers cups the back of my head.
I'm struck by how calm my face is. I don't know what the girl is thinking or dreaming—I realize I can't remember, so she's separate from me.
The antic diarist has become a young woman capable of stillness and
contemplation.

6.

Peggy Kohn and I had procured white plastic boater hats that made us "Kennedy Girls"; an oval photo of his face was pasted on the top. The campaign was in full swing and, hard as it was to believe, the Democratic nominee was an idol even in conservative Indianapolis! Kennedy Girls screamed in packs for him, a prelude to Beatles crowds a few years later. Had Peggy and I gone to the airport and then hitched a ride to the Claypool Hotel? Somehow we knew he was staying there, the building big and old-fashioned, a block or so off the Circle. Peggy had that golden red hair, and it was she, I am sure, who giggled as we flew past bellboys, climbed the back stairs, and for what seemed the longest time, stood in a back hallway waiting. A group of men were there, smiling at us. I could barely speak, and Peggy was just smiling and I would laugh, both of us would giggle; then we'd be quiet and official, like the guards, as we asked again, are you sure he'll come this way? We were determined to get our hats signed—I to add to my growing autograph collection, my latest acquisition a letter from Marguerite Henry, the author of *Misty of Chincoteague*.

Just then came a sound, or just a feeling, and Secret Service men, and there he was—it was a shock to the senses to see him in color—casual, a gray suit and tie, relaxed, that smile! It all took place in less than a minute. I am trying to imagine what we looked like, almost sixteen, so proud of ourselves for getting here, wearing our red white and blue, but really little girls still. We thrust our hats forward, he smiled and said in that accent, thank you very much, or hello how are you, or what are your names? and scrawled in ballpoint. We were beside ourselves, just the two of us, relieved and kind of hot with excitement, a friendly Secret Service agent now gently nudging us toward the elevator as the glorious candidate moved quickly down the hallway and out of sight.

The Kennedy campaign was the first to be a family affair. My little brothers and sisters picketed the house across the street where the John Birch Society had been founded just two years before: *Kennedy, Kennedy, he's our man/ Nixon belongs in the garbage can.* I had a Nixon autograph, but I was sure it was machine-written, and also I judged his handwriting too smooth for a president's. My mother had let go of her disappointment that Adlai Stevenson was not again the Democratic candidate and was thrilled about JFK; to Pam, who was skeptical even after Kennedy was elected, she wrote a defense:

I think he is going to bring people to Washington who are just in another category—world view & otherwise, than the General Motors set & I think this will have incalculable effects. Also I subscribe completely to the position that basically the Democratic Party is more compassionate in its concern for human beings—not to the position that there is no difference between the parties. I think Kennedy is terribly smart politically, not without positions on issues (as was his opponent).

By *positions on issues*, of course she meant chiefly race—and she was correct. In October before Kennedy was even elected, he'd called the judge in charge when Martin Luther King was sentenced to four months in state prison for violating probation on a traffic charge, and King was released. *Let me just add,* my mother continued, *that had you lived as near the Bible Belt as we do, you'd have gotten passionate about him—if only on the religious issue* (JFK was Roman Catholic, and Indiana was violently anti-Catholic). *The behavior of the local Protestants (not Episc) was beyond the pale.*

At Shortridge High School, I was deep in producing the fall musical—*The Pajama Game*, whose plot revolved around a strike by sewing workers in a factory. "Where will we get the sewing machines?" Miss Copeland, our music teacher, asked in her soigné voice. I had an idea, and soon found myself standing on the stage at assembly, calling for everyone's empty Quaker oatmeal cartons, which soon overwhelmed the shop room on the second floor. *I wish you could see her in the throes of converting, or having others convert, 65 oatmeal cartons into sewing machines,* my mother wrote Pam—two large cartons and one small, glued together to make each machine, spray-painted rusty red; I thanked everyone in "Stage Page," my weekly column in the *Shortridge Daily Echo* (Monday through

Friday, set in linotype by union workers at the school): "Seven and a half cents doesn't mean a hell of a lot, / seven and a half cents doesn't mean a thing," sang the chorus—the audience filled Caleb Mills Hall, which seated 1200. The hall was named for the founder of public school education in Indiana; the quote above the proscenium was his: "A disciplined mind and a cultivated heart are the elements of power."

Shortridge, named for the first Indiana school superintendent, opened in 1864 as the first high school in the city—a clapboard Wild West–looking building at the center of town, when Monument Circle was a dirt road. By the time I enrolled, Shortridge was ranked high among the forty top high schools in the nation: recent students had won national *Atlantic Monthly* writing competitions; Henrietta Parker, a veteran of the Manhattan Project, was teaching a mode of chemistry based on atomic bonding; and English teachers emphasized that Kurt Vonnegut, whose fiction was included in the anthology we read, was an Indianapolis native and an alumnus. Extracurricular activities—aside from sports, music, and debate—included a radio station and the Junior Vaudeville, a yearly show of four separate acts written and performed by students; at least once, the show had attracted a Hollywood agent. The school offered Latin, Greek, French, Spanish, and German; mathematics to advanced calculus; physics, chemistry, and advanced chemistry and physics; and biology and advanced biology taught by Dr. R. Ruth Richards—women scientists did not yet get university appointments. RRR, as she signed herself in red ink, knew how to stimulate her students' competitive spirit. In the spring she had us identifying birds (100 and you got an A) and watercoloring flowers and plants on index cards (100 for an A). In the fall (100 each for an A) we were mounting insects and preserving leaves (iron each leaf between pieces of wax paper).

I had been inspired by my father to take Latin. I never knew that my mother had also learned Latin and Greek as a child, I heard nothing of her essay about being a young Spartan boy. I loved even the elementary first term: the verb tense endings, which we learned by reciting in chorus—bo, bis, bit, bimus, bitis, bunt; what a case was, each with an identifying ending—nominative, genitive; and the virtuoso ablative absolute that could marry a noun and a participle. The inspired teacher was Josephine Bliss—in her forties, I would say, with a robust complexion, very white teeth, and glossy short dark hair. She and her husband were dairy farmers way out on the East side; their farm was called Windswept. Once she had enthralled with Latin, she began to seduce with the promise of a Greek class if enough of us were good enough. *Honor is fast turning into a Latin champ & is trying out for the school (freshman) championship with her eye on the gold medal (state).* I got only honorable mention, but I was allowed into the Greek class nonetheless, a dozen of us gathering for the double-credit intensive that met at 8:15 a.m. five days a week. Mrs. Bliss had us breathless to translate each march Xenophon took leading his satraps—she'd tell us about the next conquest or river crossing with a sparkle in her eyes. I reveled in the odd shapes of the letters, in learning how to pronounce a diphthong. I thought I'd be terrified by approaching an alien alphabet; but because of that, the thrill was even greater than in Latin, when words fell into order producing sentences that revealed how grammar made meaning.

The current high school was housed in a massive brick three-story square with an interior courtyard. The building was erected in the mid-1930s and designed to accommodate 1,500 students; by the time I was a freshman in 1959, there were 2,400 of us. From its founding before the Civil War until the revived KKK pushed through segregation laws in 1927, Shortridge was racially integrated. Eli Lilly's moderation on race might be traced to his having been in the Shortridge class of 1903. Segregation remained law until 1947; all black students went to Crispus Attucks High School, lodged further downtown in a previous Shortridge building. Since only black teachers were allowed to teach there, its academic faculty was famously excellent, comprised of Negro recipients of PhDs blocked from college teaching. Its remarkable music faculty was drawn from the jazz world of Indianapolis—its 1960s visionary was the great drummer Willis Kirk.

Mixed-race education was reinstated ten years before we came to Indianapolis. What I didn't know then, and what research tells me now, is that the racial attitudes that shocked me were carried forward from a time when three out of every four white men in Indiana were Klan members;

the Klan had been revived in Indiana in 1913. When I was at Shortridge, the black neighborhood uptown of Monument Circle was spreading north. By 1967 "the percentage"—that is, of black students—had grown to 27.5; white flight was in full force as white families moved north and east to the districts of Broad Ripple, which was exclusively white, and to North Central in suburban Washington township, where Negro students were fewer than one in ten. By the time I graduated from Shortridge, Negro students made up 60 percent of the student body. In 1968, after the assassination of Martin Luther King, a peaceful protest led to violence; and in 1981, a movement to make Shortridge magnet academic high school failed and the school closed. Alan Nolan's youngest son, Jack, born in 1964, gave the school's final commencement address.

I would not have imagined that outcome, so idealistic was I about Shortridge despite the evidence of race division that faced me every day. Negro students sat on one side of the cafeteria at lunch, and I joined my white friends on the other side, my urge to be popular greater than my social conscience. It was not until the end of my sophomore year that John Allerdice, the rising junior class president, gathered a group of both black and white classmates at his parents' house just blocks from ours; there we began, carefully, to talk about our experience of race at the school. John's election was an affirmation that the new attitudes of the 1960s were reaching into our lives—popular, a straight-A student, blond and hilarious, he had taken a stand, replying to a question at a Human Rights Club panel in Caleb Mills Hall: "If I fell in love with a Negro woman, I would marry her." This was the summer of the Freedom Riders—blacks and whites riding buses together across the South in defiance of segregation laws. As word spread about John's leadership, about the radical fact of students of both races talking to each other, a cross was burned in his family's front yard; his mother was fired from her job as an associate teacher at Mrs. Gates Dancing School, where all of us who were white were initiated into the complexities of the fox-trot, the waltz, wallflowers, and white gloves.

My mother was pregnant with number nine. Finally, I thought. Aside from being out of the house whenever I could, I was navigating the size of the family. At my insistence, we'd applied to host the AFS student my junior year. *Honor in her letter to the Dean of Girls, said we have a big house, the student would even have her own bureau!* Of course I didn't read the letter to Pam, in which my mother confided her grand scheme to top off the family: *We have felt for some time that we have reinforced the old family life since 1957 & hope now that things like the exchange student will bring back again the old abandon and wonder that outsiders can contribute to a family.* She and my father planned, she continued, *to adopt a refugee baby at some point in the next few years—probably after my last fling at childbirth (only one more, I promise!) This has been a thing with me for years (the refugees) & something that I want to get involved in more & more.* My mother annually signed up for Save the Children pen pals for each of us, and the Europeans she'd helped during the war still occasionally visited; but learning that my wanting a temporary exchange student dovetailed with a grand plan of hers delivered a shock. No wonder Pam Morton even now expresses her concern for my teenage self! *What I really mean is that one can get too content with not sharing with others.* Ah, she does still think of Jersey City! They never adopted a refugee baby; but in 1963, a friend who was headmaster of a school in Colorado wrote that a Somali exchange student from Kenya needed a family to visit on school vacations. Abdillahi Haji joined the family that September. For now, though, I looked forward to the arrival of Sri from Indonesia. Gazing upon the beautiful girl in the photograph we'd received, I didn't consider my siblings: she would be my very own sister. My mother made plans to turn *the house topsy-turvy— move Dee & Rosie to the 3d floor to the hitherto sacred guest room, leaving one free bed in Paul's study . . . the 3 boys in 2 adjoining rooms & Marian and Susanna next to me.*

In August we found out that a diplomatic conflict between the United States and Indonesia had prevented Sri from getting the necessary papers. For a week or so I nursed disappointment, and then suddenly a host family dropped out in another part of Indiana, and we were looking at a photograph of Elly Engelkes of the Netherlands. *I wish you could have seen Honor and I meeting her at the bus (2 hours late) accompanied by a reporter and photographer from the school paper. She is very relaxed, somewhat sturdy and a lovely sense of humor & fits right in. She is now at a football game in Fort Wayne! She speaks excellent English and is very fluent in French and German, plays the violin and wants to be a doctor for UNICEF.*

Elly and I were very different. I was playing the anguished popularity game, yearning for acceptance into social clubs and student-directing plays at school—there were seven productions a year. Elly was interested in the plays and the A Capella choir that I was in and that once a year performed with the Indianapolis Symphony. She was not interested in the Girls Ensemble, which I'd finally been invited to join—fifteen girls who performed standards at Lions Club and Junior League lunches, dressed in identical plaid sheath dresses and black suede high heels. It never would have occurred to me to confide in Elly that I was late for a biology field trip because I'd sneaked out at midnight to drink whiskey and neck under a bridge with someone else's boyfriend. She took advantage of Shortridge in ways that were alien to me; she played violin in the school orchestra and joined the photography club. I had dreamed of our visitor becoming my special friend in the family; it hadn't occurred to me that, unimpeded by the sibling rivalry of which I was unconscious, she would become a much more attentive older sister than I was. That year, the Christmas card photograph was of everyone in our kilts and vests from London; Elly fit right in, wearing a plaid skirt of her own.

And she was with us for the birth of number nine. I know I was at home, but I don't remember if Elly was. My father came bursting through the front door on May 2, 1962, exhausted from his delivery room vigil: "You have a new little sister, named Patience." That spring, I applied to become an AFS exchange student myself—for the following summer.

7.

There is a clipping in the scrapbook, in Urdu text, with a photo of five 16-year-old girls, including me, stepping off a small plane. The air was hot, like an oven was hot, and also humid, and the sun was very bright. I didn't know how to describe the light and the penetrating, alien heat. We were AFS summer exchange students come by ship and plane across half the world, the ship docking in Rotterdam where I spent a day with Elly. And now, with four other girls, I had arrived in a city called Lahore, the ancient capital of the Punjab province in Pakistan. In a seminar on the ship, we had learned that partition had divided the Indian subcontinent into two countries; and that Pakistan, divided into West and East—all of India between—was "an Islamic state," a phrase then without twenty-first-century associations. I had no way of realizing how my summer in Lahore would illuminate my thinking, first about the position of women and much later about how people actually lived in a part of the world that came starkly into public consciousness forty years later, after 9/11.

I was to live for six weeks with the family of Chaudhry Abdul Karim, a wealthy, secular Muslim; his middle daughter, Nighat, would be my "sister" as Elly had been, in Indianapolis. Her elder sister Khawar was married and lived in Karachi, and her younger sister Noreen was still a mischievous eight-year-old. Nighat was a tall, reserved, and solemnly beautiful girl who dressed in *shalwar kameez*—a pair of loose white trousers, a tunic of patterned or colored fabric, and a scarf, called a *dupatta*, that she would pull up to cover her head when we were out shopping or sightseeing, and pull forward to obscure all of her face except her eyes when we walked past the men who stared and hissed wherever we were in the city. Noreen dressed like my little sisters, a dress above her knees, Mary Jane shoes. Khawar wore saris, as did Mrs. Karim, whom I was invited to call by the intimate "Biji." She was tall and handsome, her skin quite pale, and I think she had green eyes. Her family was from the north, she told me, therefore she was Pathan—a tribe said to be descended in part from the Greeks who invaded with Alexander the Great; this was the tribe that would be called Pashtun in the wars that began half a century later.

Abbaji (Abdul), Nighat's father, seemed not as tall as Biji, though my letters say they were the same height. He looked like my idea of a fierce man of the desert, and the name *Karim* has an Arab origin. He had a strong nose, graying hair pulled back from his forehead, and he dressed most often in Western clothes—a pair of slacks and a short-sleeved shirt.

He was kind, soft-spoken, and distinguished. Every day at lunch and every evening, the entire family sat down at the dining room table to eat. Biji asked me quiet, witty questions, and she and Abbaji answered mine—about religion and politics, the social segregation of the sexes, arranged marriages—one cousin, I would learn, had two wives. I had the impression that the Karims abided by custom but were becoming more Western; Nighat's marriage might be arranged, but her happiness would be taken into account. She was mostly quiet until Khawar came for a visit and made us all laugh with her imitations in American and British accents of Western snobbery. In my letters, having inherited my mother's role as chronicler, I described a typical meal: *chapati*, flat bread prepared by the cook on the wood stove in a tiny kitchen that looked more like an outdoor shed, and lamb, goat, or chicken curry—chickens were bought live and slaughtered. We also often had vegetable curry, with raita and chutney and also rice, sometimes prepared as *pulau*. I'd never been to an Indian restaurant; the only curry I'd have in Indianapolis, I'd cook myself the following year. Though there were forks and knives, I was courteously encouraged to eat the Pakistani way: with my fingers, delicately scooping curry and rice with a swatch of *chapati*. Once Biji announced a surprise: the cook had made pork curry just for me, she said, pointing to a bowl; when I began to thank her, everyone cracked up: no Muslim, even the cook, was ever allowed to touch pork.

We were waited on—"hand and foot," I wrote home, by "servants," and the house was kept perpetually clean by sweepers, who were "traditionally Christian," which fascinated me. They had very dark skin and moved gracefully in a squatting position across the highly polished floors. A cow in the backyard produced all the milk; at first I thought the milk made me gag because it was boiled to sterilize it, then I learned it was because the cow was actually a water buffalo. Biji was concerned about my calcium level and tried hard to get me to drink it. If dessert wasn't *firni*—coconut custard with slivers of pistachio and a tiny fragment of actual silver film on the surface—it was mangoes, which I had never heard of, much less eaten. I especially adored mangoes, until one made me so sick I didn't eat another for forty years.

One morning we woke to rain—a day for a picnic! A picnic in the rain? It was monsoon season, the only time of year it was cool enough to spend time outdoors, which I thought hilarious. We'd bought special breads in the old city, where women wore black *chador*. "I can't get used to the turbaned men sleeping by the side of the road," I wrote home— I'd never seen a homeless person on the street, not even in Jersey City. One day early in my stay, Abbaji, Nighat, and I went to see the Bad-shahi Mosque. I was stunned at its beauty, the three huge white marble domes. "The size of a cathedral," it was built in 1678 of pink sandstone inlaid with white marble—of course, I'd never seen a mosque. Abbaji spoke of the emperor who'd built it, and how it had been reclaimed after Independence—the British had used it as a garrison! This didn't surprise me, as I had already seen the famous Lahore Fort, its inlaid jewels "tragi-cally looted by the British."

Biji was one of three sisters who lived in adjacent houses, and a gang of cousins were our constant company. Nasir was the handsome oldest son of the sister who lived next door; Ruchsanna and Qaiser, the children of the sister who lived across the street. Nasir's father was a senator and flew once a week the nine hundred miles to Dakha, the capital of East Pakistan (Bangladesh as of 1971), where the legislature met. The president of Paki-stan was Ayub Khan, a Pathan who was also an Army colonel. I would learn after I got home that Ayub was a dictator, that Pakistan wasn't really what I called "a free country," especially for women, even though there was a representative government.

One day Nighat and Biji took me to the Provincial Assembly. In the street outside were crowds of women: women of all ages in saris, *shalwar kameez*, and many wearing the all-enveloping *chador*. They were dem-onstrating "to repeal the family laws and let women have their rights," I wrote home. Arranged marriages horrified me despite Biji and Nighat's explanations; now I found that even though women had the right to vote, many could not leave their homes. "How can a country advance when the women are kept behind?" I wrote in outraged innocence. "Virgin-ity is the key to marriage," I continued; "love is even discouraged by some families after marriage by separating the couple for long periods of time. The only obligation of marriage is having offspring. Pakistan is an Islamic state founded on religion and in this religion there is an iron band around the women." The year was 1962. American women seemed entirely free in comparison.

One evening a family friend, a politician named Quayyum Khan, came to supper; he was staying with Auntie's family across the street. He was very tall and bald and wore all white; he seemed powerful and had an aura of generosity—"a handsome version of Khrushchev if that's possible," I wrote home, and "really nice." He was in delicate health—a heart condition—and in Lahore to protest Ayub's martial law and support the movement in favor of the freedom to form new political parties. After supper, he went out to give a speech in the streets; he returned afterward, "to get his medicine (for an ailing heart) and for some coffee because he had a feeling he was going to be arrested." At 3:30 a.m. Nighat and I, who slept on beds on the roof, were awakened—the CAD (secret police) were "all over this house and there were about ten cars." I looked down from the roof—the image is still clear in my mind these decades later—the police escorting Quayyum, his tall white-garbed figure vivid in the darkness as he bent to get into a police car.

I could hardly believe what I was seeing. "I really admire a man with this kind of courage;" I wrote home. "He was forewarned that the government was looking for reasons to arrest him—he is very popular." Later Khawar told us that Quayyum had said that "if Ayub kept arresting people, there would be a revolution." A revolution like the one that produced the country I was part of, I thought. "This kind of thing makes me feel so lucky to be an American because I'm sure all of us would have life imprisonment if our government worked that way." Innocence but also patriotism—"I was thinking about the civil rights movement: "It's almost unbelievable to me, that one can't speak out against the government." I would later learn that Quayyum had been a rival of Khan's ever since the partition and that their division was more complicated than my teenaged idealism could reckon.

If only I could speak Punjabi or Urdu! The cousins wanted me to stay longer—they were sure I'd soon understand everything; but for the time being, I had to be content with Nasir's flirty translations that set even solemn Nighat laughing. She and I were always laughing, it seemed. Social life was segregated by sex, and the AFS girls were much in demand. At a sequence of tea parties we taught the twist, a global sensation since the Kennedys had danced it—on a tiny Victrola, the eponymous Chubby Checker record: "Round and round and up and down we go"—all of us twisting, older women in saris and younger ones including us in *shalwar kameez*. We got invitations from Americans, too, but the only Americans we really wanted to meet were the Peace Corps volunteers. To girls like us, they had the status, by association with JFK, of movie stars—the first wave of volunteers had been there six months.

We met two of them. Janet Hannaman, a psychiatric nurse in her twenties from Kansas, greeted us in *shalwar kameez*. She introduced us first to a patient who had been an editor of books, who lived in a small, clean room with a desk and reading and writing materials. Next she led us out into the courtyard, where there were contiguous dirt-floored cages—in them not zoo animals, but patients. Is this where my grandmother Margarett would have been confined had she been a rebellious Pakistani rather than a rich American? When Janet got there, the editor lived in one of the cages naked—all the patients had been naked. First she clothed and fed them; now she wanted indoor space for all of them. The second volunteer we met was Jim McCoy, a former U.S. Marine who'd spent six months building a bridge in one village and was now building a school in another. We toured the village, then sat with him around a table, four girls and one very handsome man with whom we were madly flirting—a man from the village walked by, and he and Jim began to speak Urdu, then both laughed, Jim translating: he'd said Jim had been "very intelligent" to marry the limit of four wives! One invitation was formal, and with my family, I went to a reception for the president of the Philippines—"he said that even though he had been told that Lahore was very hot and that it was indeed hot, he thought the weather only made the Punjab hospitality hotter! He had especially chosen Pakistan for his first state visit (cheers) since the two countries had so much in common—they should work together for less dependence on the Western powers (cheers). The Philippines was mostly Christian, he said, but there was a sizable Moslem population (cheers) and they were treated with absolute equality." I pulled my pink silk *dupatta* close. I was not used to even mild anti-Americanism; part of me saw the logic of what he was saying, but part of me was frightened. I knew so little of the world

In Lahore, I bought a sari for my mother—a deep oriole orange with bright silver embroidery at the borders of the silk that were frothy and then like syrup. At the end of our stay, traveling with Pakistani AFS returnees in a Volkswagen van, we drove up the Swat Valley, into Landi Kotal, at the border of Afghanistan. On our way, we spent one night in Rawalpindi and were invited to a tea dance at an army outpost—we thought it hilarious when one of the soldiers dancing with one of us said, "I've never danced with a girl before." Forty years later the Swat Distract would become a war zone in the search for Osama Bin Laden. I remember a tall turbaned Pathan with bright blue eyes, carrying a Kalashnikov rifle; a little girl in a turquoise dress with kohl around her eyes; and at the top of a hill, from behind a fortress wall, women gazing down at the white American girls, who were free and laughing. On our final night we wandered the glittering night market at Landi Kotal, where I bought red and blue glass bangles, and a fur hat for my father. All these images returned to me in a poem sixty years later: *"glass bangles of every color and fur hats, fumes / of incense, and also a marketplace for guns."*

8.

I came home with new friends and new knowledge. In Greek class, I reported the on 36 hours I'd spent in Athens on our way eastward to Pakistan, how the white stones of the Parthenon burned beneath my sandals, supper and a first taste of retsina at a rooftop restaurant in the Plaka, the night view of the Parthenon all lit up. I could also boast I'd been to Egypt—our Qantas jet with its flirtatious Australian stewards stopped for an hour for refueling and, for a dollar, I bought a bracelet of "cheap turquoise scarabs."

We were beginning to read Homer, a yellow textbook, verse instead of prose; Mrs. Bliss was explaining iams and trochees and dactyls and something called a formulaic epithet. She had been teaching us about figures of speech, and this was one particular to Homer, a set of words that characterized something—the most famous, she said, was about the Aegean, which always appeared as the "wine dark sea." Louis Kelley, the one black student in the class, was on the football team, and we decided to celebrate him with a float in the homecoming parade. I remember the idea forming in my imagination—a chariot! My classmates and I built it in our Washington Boulevard driveway: we constructed a frame of two-by-fours to fit over the roof of our secondhand, bright aqua Volkswagen beetle, two beams extending to the front to support the horses, all of it covered with corrugated cardboard. Recently Martha, also in the class, told me Mrs. Bliss gave us a homework-free week. Did Peggy Kohn, our artist, come up with the design? We spray-painted the chariot itself white, added a pattern of orange and gold flames, painted spoked wheels; the horses were enormous and painted black with orange harnesses. Who built the complicated wood frame? Where did we get all that corrugated cardboard?

Face-timing, my sister Marian is saying, "I remember a float." Yes, our Greek class made a float. "I remember dark red." Yes, we spray-painted the trim rust-red. "It was so big!" Her eyes are sparkling, fifty-two years drop away, and she is at the edge of the driveway, just seven years old, watching. "Yes, I watched you. It was HUGE. I couldn't believe it, but I remember it as clearly as if it was yesterday!" And now my memory comes clear—it's dusk, and we have to finish so that tomorrow we'll have time to wrap the cardboard around the frame and staple it, then lift and lower our chariot onto the Volkswagen. Marian—still called Babby— was voraciously watching, lurking at the edges; the next day, the rest of the family stood with her waving at us, all in white sheets for togas, as we ventured forward. Martha, Putzi, and Christine are in a white convertible leading us, and I am driving the VW down Washington Boulevard, Tom Ehrich next to me, toward the parade gathering point where four of us will climb onto the roof of the car, now become a chariot. I can barely see out the window. It's in black and white in Mom's scrapbook, but in my imagination, I remove all the obstacles, and we are all in the gold and white and orange chariot, moving forward into our lives. College would start the following fall. I had applied to Radcliffe—would I get in? I had a boyfriend named Frank who was a class below me, and that summer we listened to the Beach Boys "Surfin' USA" in his parents' driveway, necking in the car.

I have just come in from school, run up to my parents' bedroom and stand at the door. My mother is at her small secretary desk: Thirty-nine years old, she is sitting in an upright chair and writing letters. Across the large room is her bureau, on it a book by St. Thérèse of Lisieux; a tube of Raven Red, the lipstick she always wore, by Revlon; Je Reviens, the blue perfume by Worth, the bottle not blue but the liquid itself. On her bedside table are *The Prime of Miss Jean Brodie*, or another novel by Muriel Spark, and *Notes of a Native Son*, by James Baldwin, or another fierce book about civil rights. And on the bed is her purse.

When I think of Jenny's life in 1962, and what she hadn't done that she wanted to do, I come back to that memory of her, unusual because it is quiet. She's bent over the small desk writing letters. If collected, the letters would form a lively narrative of a woman of her generation—what she was reading, what she was thinking about, who she was voting for and why, what each child was doing that day, and news to friends about friends, or about her children. Or she is writing a thank-you note and looking up at me and saying, "Have you written Aunt Linda to thank her for your birthday present?" which would make it late fall, when I have just turned seventeen and driven a chariot in the homecoming parade.

Or, perhaps, she is not writing letters but in a notebook. Once in a while she would "write" and declare to me that she wanted to write; or I might have heard her say she wanted to be a social worker. I did not know then what a social worker actually did, but we always had family friends who were social workers, serious unmarried women who came to supper, especially in Jersey City. She had even started to go to school for social work, had taken a course at the Indiana University downtown extension. She wanted to learn to do something with people, something like what she and my father had done in Jersey City, something she did then with no school for it at all.

When my mother said she wanted to be a writer, she seemed tentative, unsure of herself, and when she said she wanted to be a social worker, she seemed resigned to something, as if she were saying, "Well, maybe I'll just be a social worker." I had not then read the poem about the moon that she wrote when she was twelve or the stories she wrote in college. I didn't know they existed; she never told me that she had actually written, only that there had been an English teacher at Vassar she liked, and that his name was Mr. Brooks. A vague cloud of confusion drifted in my mind whenever my mother talked about doing something else; always, she had continued having children, becoming more of a mother, and then there's the letter about adopting *a refugee child* to make ten of us.

But now the *something* was finished, and there was time for the *else*, time for my mother to split that epithet of ambition. She had achieved her goal, to have nine children—enough for a baseball team or a small orchestra. It didn't occur to me that she might be frightened of doing something other than what she had been doing ever since I was born—when she was twenty-two. When I think of her as a mother, "Mommy," I don't think of her as thwarted, and the woman everyone else called Jenny was powerful—a champion, ebullient, enthusiastic, and imaginative. Pam Morton says that my mother lay awake at night considering which of the younger children might like to take a pottery class, which flute lessons, which join a theater group or work in a bookstore. "For me," said Marian, who—at sixty—is again taking riding lessons, "it was flute, pottery and horseback riding."

But becoming the woman who stayed awake at night figuring out what each child might do is only one layer of the life my mother had already lived. Now, her nine having been born, she was at the brink of emphasizing, bringing to life some other layer of herself. Maybe if I stand there long enough, hovering as she writes a letter or writes in her notebook, she'll really talk to me, the way she talks to her friends on the phone; maybe when I go to college, she'll write me the kind of letters she wrote Pam Morton. When she talked to me as if I were an adult, which she started doing when I got back from Pakistan, applied to colleges, and got into Radcliffe, I would feel myself become taller and begin to consider, for instance, which would be better for this extraordinary mother of mine— to become a social worker? Or a writer?

What shifted her attention sufficiently away from all of us, away from her marriage? What pushed her finally to engage the surge of power I always sensed in her, that came toward me as anger, that I felt in her as she strode forth pregnant, nursed an infant bare-breasted in the living room, or planted the vegetable garden on Washington Boulevard? It's the spring of 1963, two weeks before I am accepted at Radcliffe, and she opens the *New York Times Book Review*. I am picturing the bedroom in Indianapolis, her reading about a book that was reviewed on April 7 after being published on February 19, during a newspaper strike. *The Feminine Mystique* was written by a journalist named Betty Friedan, and my mother told me that reading it was *a bolt from the blue*.

> Millions of American women stand victim of "the feminine mystique," a philosophy that has convinced them that their only commitment is the fulfillment of a femininity found in "sexual passivity, male domination and nurturing maternal love." They are dangerous in that, unable to find their real selves, they feed emotionally on their children—thus crippling them—and are unable to satisfy their husbands because they cannot enjoy sex for sex's sake. They try to relieve their feelings of depression and emptiness by seeking "strained glamor." They have won the battle for suffrage but little else. This is the damning indictment leveled by Betty Friedan in her highly readable, provocative book.

I can't remember if my mother herself told me that *The Feminine Mystique* had changed her life, or if it was her brother Shaw's wife Linda, who in her eighties clearly remembered the telephone call from Indianapolis, Jenny not even saying hello before delivering urgent news: there's a book you *must* read. I told a friend this story the other day, and she said, "Oh my mother read the book too, and it had the same effect on her. She became a social worker." My mother did not choose to become a social worker, she chose to become a writer. I don't know when she first sat down with her pen and yellow pad to begin. Was she interrupted by having to dispatch her eldest child off to college? Or by the news on September 17 that my father had been elected suffragan bishop of Washington, D.C., to begin an inner-city initiative in the capital where John Kennedy, a man of their generation, sat as president? The archconservative *Indianapolis News* took note of our departure in an editorial: "Dean Moore's . . . dynamic leadership in race relations could not find a better stage for demonstration than there." My mother set herself to packing up the enormous house and the belongings of eleven family members, as notes and letters arrived testifying to what she had meant to people there. "Thank you so much for allowing us to enter your family," the widowed Ruth Cooke wrote. "All of you have been so wonderful to Walt and me and erased the feeling of being so alone."

It's not until the following summer in the Adirondacks, the summer after the assassination of President Kennedy, the summer after our January move to Washington, that I find news in a letter to Pam that she is making progress on something she calls *the book*.

VII

First-Person Singular

1.

THE HOUSE AT 3400 NEWARK STREET NW WAS THE FIRST YEAR-ROUND
dwelling my mother had a hand in configuring, the first purchased by
the church just for us. "The needs of the Moores are but few," wrote the
search chair: "ten bedrooms, three guestrooms, four playrooms / A den,
and eight acres will do." Brick with white columns at the door, large but
not grand—my mother's excitement is palpable in her letters to me—a
bamboo forest at the foot of the backyard, and beyond that the neighborhood playground. A sunroom with windows on three sides would become

a kitchen big enough to accommodate not only the family, but anyone who dropped by. Black and white squares of linoleum tile on the floor, she decided, and, rare then, a restaurant stove: *six burners*!

It was the fall of 1963: President Kennedy's *Ich bin Ein Berliner* speech, the first lady speaking French with Prime Minister Charles de Gaulle, a concert at the White House by Pablo Casals, the promise of action on a civil rights bill. On their first house-hunting trip, my parents had a few minutes with the president in the Oval Office—"Where are the children?" he asked, knowing there were nine—and of course he remembered a dinner party during the war at "your family's beautiful house in Palm Beach." My mother wore a new dress—a sapphire suede sheath: "You are terrific," the president said to her, and to my father he acknowledged his new job—to connect the Episcopal church with the poor people of Washington. I'm sure they both imagined future meetings, even invitations to White House dinners: Kennedy was of their world, their generation.

In the scrapbook, a White House note confirming the meeting; on the next page, "PRESIDENT DEAD" a tsunami of assassination clippings, headlines pasted double-wide across pages: Jackie Kennedy's tear-stained face, newsprint yellowed and crisp. I was in a Harvard biology lab when the professor appeared at the door and announced the president had been shot—that he was dead, not yet certain. A day after the funeral, my mother and my sister Dee, arriving in D.C. for a scheduled look at schools, saw Adlai Stevenson getting out of a cab at the airport, and U Thant, Secretary General of the UN, walking to catch a plane.

The house—with seven bedrooms—was in a neighborhood of big houses called Cleveland Park, within walking distance of the National Cathedral where my father had his office and of a very good public grammar school. My parents had explored living in a racially integrated part of town, but were told that schools in those neighborhoods were *totally inadequate*. In 1969, when they were leaving the city, my mother wrote a piece for the *Washington Post* magazine in which she recalls that choice: *We feel a twinge of guilt that we do not visit the schools and find out for ourselves. We capitulate.*

We moved to Washington in January. The consecration was in the

National Cathedral, and a planeload of Indianapolis friends wore buttons that Alan Nolan had commissioned—"Hoosiers for Moore"—my father would be doing great things. Absent in my mother's letters to me at Radcliffe is the homesick misery of the months spent in a rented house while Newark Street was being renovated—hard enough to leave behind friends and schools anytime, harder still halfway through a school year. Newspaper accounts of the consecration made the usual references to my father's war heroism. They especially irritated him since he'd just published his first book, called *The Church Reclaims the City*, an account and guide to downtown ministry inspired by the work at Grace Church. My mother had contributed a chapter—"The Clergyman's Family in the Inner City"—and the book's publication brought her a moment of attention and a twinge of envy from my father, who would later regret he hadn't written more anecdote and less theory. At the Shoreham Hotel lunch after the consecration, the new bishop's wife was graceful, even self-deprecating—her Indianapolis friends knew that her modesty was a public shyness not character. If she became a "cautious, sherry-serving bishop's lady," one friend wrote, he'd "haunt her till eternity."

The role of clergy wives was a hot issue, at least in the church. In England, one Brenda Wolfe, the twenty-seven-year-old wife of an Anglican Welsh vicar, published an irreverent and searing piece that caused a sensation. The controversy made the front page of *New York Times*, and the Washington Episcopal magazine asked my mother to respond. Without revealing any of her own ambivalence, she chided Mrs. Wolfe: *She says she wants to lead a life that satisfies "my conscience, my family and myself" . . . resents that she is . . . expected to turn up at church and every other connected social affair, whatever her domestic circumstances may be.* Her self-centeredness keeps her from sympathizing with her husband's female parishioners—*might they not share her resentment at the woman's lot?* Instead of complaining, my mother wrote, a clergy wife *must figure out what she thinks God wants her to do, not what Mrs. Jones would consider proper.*

A few years later, my mother might have written with more nuance and without condescension, but she was working out her own new situation. How would being a bishop's wife in the nation's capital differ from being

married to a cathedral dean in a mere state capital? As for the God reference, becoming a dean was a promotion, but being consecrated bishop
had sacred force. When five bishops laid their hands on her husband's
head, he was brought into the apostolic succession, which Christ had initiated by consecrating St. Peter in the very same ritual. *Mystique* was the
word my mother came up with to characterize my father's new status. But
in what *mystique* did a wife participate? A clergy wife, she'd written, *must
figure out what God wants her to do.* Would God keep Jenny Moore from
becoming "a sherry-serving bishop's lady"?

In July in the Adirondacks, she began writing the book by hand, my
sister Dee typing the first pages. Back in D.C. in early August, they moved
into 3400 Newark Street—*some furniture too big for the house—so put it in
storage—wild when they walk in and ask you where it goes. Everything in real
chaos:* for the first time, she was keeping a diary at home. Once school
began, she swiftly organized her life to have mornings child-free, dropping five-year-old Susanna at kindergarten and three-year-old Patience
at an establishment called the National Children's Research Center, a
nursery school two blocks from home. Their neighbors the Dudmans
were out at work all day, their two daughters at school; she could write in
their guest room. For the first time in almost twenty years, she had time
alone, and for the first time since abandoning fiction at Barnard, she was
undertaking a narrative—not the improvisation of scrapbook or letter,
but an actual book.

From her drafts it seems she barely hesitated. In that vertical hand, she
covered page after page of a yellow legal pad—she used a Pentel, a new
kind of felt-tip pen she adored. Did her seeming ease carry over from
writing letters or was it beginner's luck?

I'm envious. I'm nine days into three weeks at a writers' residency
where I'm working on this book, and I'm finding myself inarticulate on
the page and frustrated. That afternoon, I have a cup of tea with another
writer. She is working "very well," she tells me. This is her first book and
her first residency, her first time free of her full-time job and two teenage
children: "I can't believe how deep I'm able to go," she tells me. What
innocence! As it was for my mother in the Dudmans' guest room, her

solitude itself is a victory. In letters and her diary, my mother didn't reveal much: *I am working on the book,* she wrote to me. Where's her advice? I am, as usual, trying to wrest conversation from what my mother left behind. I remember the striking phrase in her Europe diary—*Tried to cross terrifying slippery places.* I'll take the liberty of turning it into a question I might ask: What made it so *terrifying* for you to cross into the *slippery places* of self-revelation? My mother isn't here to answer.

Some months later, I took a day to sort again through the photocopied legal-sized pages of her miscellaneous writing. I'd been over and over them for years; but now, suddenly, there appeared at the top of a page a sentence I'd never read: *I was almost always "we" and now I'm "I."* The page had no date, but I'll assume the issue of *I* first came up when she began writing her book. Using the first-person singular is a decision of language, but also a decision about who occupies the center of a story. My mother would dedicate *The People on Second Street* to her children, naming and characterizing each of us; but her first words were *to Paul, who has led a life worth writing about.* Even when I read the phrase in 1968 without consciousness of feminism, it made me cringe. Hadn't she led an individual life? Now I decided to look again at the book itself.

For my husband Paul and myself, it was moving day, she wrote. But she soon settled into a first-person plural that does not distinguish her from my father and Kim Myers and Bob Pegram: *we were on our way to downtown Jersey City and the Episcopal rectory we would all share.* My mother's *I* first turns up in jokes about her gender—who is the pregnant woman walking the streets with three young priests? To their new Jersey City neighbors, the black suits and round white collars rendered the three men indistinguishable from celibate Roman Catholic priests. Who then was the young, very pregnant woman? Their shared mistress? A housekeeper?

Since Episcopal priests marry, she might also be a wife. But who is she really? Just a few pages later, when I am about to conclude that Jenny's *I,* who is describing the kitchen wallpaper, will never let on anything about her inner life, I again find this, which I now read in a different way: *I was in that cast-a-glazed-eye-at-the-world mood of late pregnancy, when internal focus suffuses any purposeful action with a female vagueness.* She's just weeks from the birth of her fourth child, my sister Rosemary, in a Jersey City hospital. Suddenly, I have it. Pregnant, she is emphatically herself, an *I*.

And she's revealed something else—that during years of childbearing, pregnancy had given her a habit of *internal focus* that engaged and preoccupied her. The feeling was physical, as physical as riding horses in childhood, performing arabesques on a moving bicycle, or studying to the point of exhaustion at Barnard. Whatever else it became, the process of writing a book would also bring internal focus, like the preoccupation she loved and relied on while being pregnant. She'd missed that feeling. I'll say that her imagination recognized the metaphor and grabbed for it. When my father earnestly suggested that for her, inspiration was *a matter of being impregnated*, she didn't protest. She wants Jersey City back, so she remembers and conjures it, and you feel her characters quicken. Harry comes alive on the page, the Polish sea captain next door, and Catherine Skipper, Ralphie Walker, the kids; and Kim Myers again rips the Keep Out sign from the wrought iron fence and paints the lych-gate red.

Pregnancy had been a realm of privacy, which writing now returned to her: *I'm working hard on the book*, she wrote in her diary. I remember something my sister Marian, mother of three, said about our mother during those years: "I think of her as being distracted." Not the jittery distraction of nerves, I'm thinking, but a gazing-off-into-the-middle-distance distraction, the suffusion of simultaneous realities into the very individual life of a daydreaming writer.

2.

Mom! Mom! And George has lost his sneakers and Danny wants to be hugged and Susanna wants to show off her pet snake, and Patience is crying, and Rosie is off somewhere and Marian is late coming home from pottery class. Let's go to hear Peter, Paul and Mary! she announced to no one in particular. They are playing in Georgetown. Who's at the playground? She goes out on the back porch—how she loves this climate! It's never too cold—and rings the bell for supper. Is Dee upstairs studying? Is my brother Paul out playing tennis? Maybe my father is on his way home from the cathedral or maybe he is away—many speaking engagements these days. And she has to call Charles E. Johnson Jr.—the carpenter—to fix a broken window: "Mom, don't scream!!" Georgie had written on a torn piece of paper she pastes in the scrapbook the following summer: "I was playing 'ball-netto' in the front hall and broke a pane of glass in the front door." I'm living for the first time at a distance from the family spectacle—the news arriving in the letters she wrote me at least once a week, now in the intermittent diary she kept, the scrapbooks, bursts of recollection from siblings.

Her diary: *Went to Georgetown. Wildly successful time with decorator. Did living rooms and dining room. Made blackberry pie.* And then a dinner among Washington luminaries at the home of Cyrus Vance, a Yale trustee with my father: Of one couple—*she's really an aggressive ass— Bartletts very nice. All columnists are such gossips they'll tell you anything.* She's learned that Jackie Kennedy no longer spoke to Ben Bradlee because of an article he'd written about his friendship with JFK in *Newsweek— Jackie needs no one especially women—wanted Virginia place + then decided she liked Camp David—JFK felt he was going to be assassinated—used to joke about who would stand in front of the bullet if killer approached.* And my parents gave their own dinner parties: *Tonight the Bradlees are coming for a late dinner—*he'll become managing editor of the *Washington Post* in 1965, executive editor in 1968—now he's still editor of *Newsweek.* She and my father feel *very comfortable and very fond of them.* Friends from the past were becoming part of a circle of new friends, the easy, joking kind like the Nolans and Woollens had been in Indianapolis. And interesting new people were always turning up. The poet Reed Whittemore arrived to take up residence at the Library of Congress (later this position would be called Poet Laureate) with his wife Helen and three children. *I am going to have to revise my idea of how poets live—they have a pet rat (desert type) called Templeton and a skeleton in the front hall with a flower in its mouth & a hat on.* It was almost November when she could write me *I am finally no longer homesick,* and about then that she wrote Pam their new life was a *utopian existence*. Doubles tennis with my brother *Paul and Cord Meyer in the shadow of the Cathedral with all the beautiful foliage in the background. We miss you very much,* she wrote me. *I love you, Mommy.*

As I got older, my mother often suggested I was grown-up enough to call her Jenny, but I couldn't. In *Mommy* or *Mom* was her tenderness, and all these decades later, the word revives her vulnerability and mine and the moment in my first year of college when our relationship began to change. Though I wanted to be an independent college girl, I needed her, and she knew that: *Always remember,* she wrote more than once, *we love you very much*—the parental we. I think of the early Washington years as a time when my mother and I were in balance. There were no more taunts that I was overweight, ridicule of my attempts to talk about ideas, or fights about my hair. I was no longer the only child who had left home, and the family language had expanded to include the outside world. In this new phase, my mother understood and sympathized with my discomfort: *You have been a very good sport about Washington and I know it is hard to be more unfamiliar with it than the rest of us.*

That November 26, my parents celebrated their twentieth wedding anniversary with a dinner party. She always did her own cooking, and the children and their current regular babysitter did the serving. The last guests left at 2 a.m., a measure of the evening's success. A week later, the movie of *My Fair Lady* opened; my father was out of town, so my mother took Cord Meyer. *Sat next to Audrey Hepburn and Mel Ferrer, and one row away from HHH,* she wrote in her diary. The vice president was *so charming. RFK very thin. Audrey loved that everyone laughed at "the blooming arse" line even though they knew it was coming. Eunice and Sargent (Shriver) nearby. Audrey lovely but not beautiful. Great evening for a hick.* On February 11, having written away for tickets, she took Paul, Adelia, and Rosemary to the Beatles' first U.S. concert in Baltimore—the audience was the soon legendary mob of eight thousand, mostly screaming teenage girls.

And she was making her way with women friends. Two of the Aldrich sisters lived in Washington—Liberty, married to my mother's wartime crush Tommy Redmond; and her sister Lucy, who had a garden shop in Georgetown. McGeorge Bundy's wife Mary, whom she'd known at

Madeira, took her to a reception the Robert Kennedys gave at Hickory Hill: *Jackie—surprisingly tall—more shabby than I'd imagined—lavender thong shoes, hot pink old cotton slacks, black short sleeved jersey—straight hair—pink kerchief almost always smiling.* Later she met Polly Kraft, a painter and the wife of Joe Kraft the columnist; and, through friends in New York, Ric Haynes—African American and working the Africa desk at the State Department. Diary: *African parrot who says Lady Bird, Shit, and Freedom Now,* she wrote about dinner there; *all African art—Benin bronze, modern Tunisian water pot for lamp—African fur rugs. He was about to leave for Leopoldville* ... Mrs. Haynes taught high school art and was a native of D.C. who went to Washington schools she didn't realize were segregated *until she wrote for history class that anyone could be president— Negro teacher caught her up on it.* Once in a while my mother was reminded that having diverse friends was still unusual in Washington, as when a priest's wife solemnly warned that there was *ignorance of where the suffragan Episcopal bishop fits in on the city's political and social ladder ... "It's a very low rung—you're way down along with low judiciary."*

The following fall my sister Dee chose not Wilson High School where students from her junior high typically went, but Western, which was racially integrated: "Do you know what you're doing?" asked the guidance counselor: "i.e. because integrated," Dee (now Adelia) remembered, "which of course was why I wanted to go." By the spring, she had started an organization—Pupils United for Superior High Schools (PUSH)—to improve teaching at her own school; soon there were chapters across the city: "Dee on TV," my mother wrote Pam. When I'm home for semester break, I find, in my mother's diary, she and I stood with members of the Freedom Democratic Party in front of the Capitol—*George Lincoln Rockwell, the neo Nazi drove by in open Lincoln with corncob pipe. The cops really hate him + all jumped on their motorcycles and chased him.*

Later that spring back in Cambridge, I sat on the big lawn in the Radcliffe Quadrangle, listening to Kathie Amatniek, an upperclassman, a senior I'd often sat with at supper in the dorm. She had joined SNCC, she said, and would be registering voters that summer in Mississippi. My father had gone to the March on Washington the summer before, but the fear of violence had been so great he'd taken along just one of us—my brother Paul, who was sixteen. Decades later, Paul looked back on that day: "I identified with this crowd of peaceful, active everyday people. I wanted my life to be a credit to them." Just weeks after the march, a church in Birmingham, Alabama, had been bombed and four little girls killed. In July the Civil Rights Act passed—now discrimination in public places and employment was a federal crime. That fall, my father spent several weeks in Mississippi where a group of clergy from the National Council of churches continued the voter registration campaign after the student organizers went back to college. That spring, in a speech in Boston, Martin Luther King quoted the abolitionist Theodore Parker's line: "The arc of the moral universe is long, but it bends toward justice." When Dr. King won the Nobel Peace Prize in October, it seemed to me that despite the continuing violence, his image spoke an inalienable truth.

A month later, when three civil rights volunteers in Mississippi went missing in the night (later discovered to have been murdered by a gang of white men), I thought of my friend Kathie and remembered that night talking on the Radcliffe lawn. If I'd been older, would I have gone south with her? My father joined the effort in the fall. I thought what I was doing seemed frivolous—spending a second summer at an Episcopal camp in the Catskills for mostly black children from Harlem and Brooklyn. I slept in the cabin with them, put on *The Music Man* with them, and helped teach them to swim. I considered it high praise when a group of the girls applauded my mastery of dances they'd taught me—the down and dirty butt-wiggling "dog" and something even more outrageous you did to a song called "Louie Louie."

3.

Witty, a bully, unpredictable—warmth one minute, rage the next. He reminded me of my mother's temper when we fought. "He's jealous of you," friends said. How could that be possible? After all, he was the one who was directing *The Threepenny Opera*—his hunched back, near-sighted eyes, his alcoholism were simply the wages of genius in the light of which I was quite ordinary. I was his assistant director, and my first serious boyfriend was the producer. I was trying not to be ordinary. That fall I bought a bright yellow-and-black plaid coat—*I can't wait to see the coat!* my mother wrote in a letter.

In her diary, she noted a telephone call from a close friend, *telling us of Selma*—the march in which hundreds of demonstrators were clubbed and beaten by the police; of a second march turning back in fear of still more casualties. And that night, during the party my parents were giv-ing for Andy Jacobs, the new liberal representative from Indianapolis, news came that a white Unitarian minister had been beaten to death, and plans were underway for a larger march in Selma two weeks later. In the scrapbook I find a flier: "DC CITIZENS FOR FEDERAL PROTEC-TION IN ALABAMA urge you to WALK FOR FREEDOM." My father joined a demonstration at the Justice Department, and every day that week, there was picketing at the White House from 7 a.m. till mid-night and a prayer vigil from midnight to 7 a.m. Another leaflet: "Send telegrams to President Johnson, urging Federal action in Alabama, urge friends & fellow citizens to participate at the White House whenever and for however long they can"—and "to bring food." My father was one of twenty civil rights activists who went to see Vice President Humphrey. Apparently, my mother wrote in her diary, what he said *really hit home*: he warned that if the president did not send protection, this *might be the splitting apart forever of dialogue between Civil Rights and Government.* On her birthday, March 12, my mother was part of a group that met busloads of demonstrators from Ohio; she herself *arranged lunch for 100 of them at the Treasury Building—you never know what you'll be doing!* At Radcliffe, a telegram came from "Dee and Mommie": "*TRY TO COME DOWN ON SUNDAY. BIG RALLY ABOUT SELMA.*" I didn't go home—too much going on at *Threepenny* rehearsals, too much studying to do.

There was no room on the D.C. bus once my father decided to go to Selma, and by the time another bus was added, he'd decided to stay in Washington. A point man was needed in D.C. to organize keeping pressure on the president, who still had not provided National Guard protection. Demonstrations in Washington were growing in size. Friends from Indianapolis were starting to turn up in Washington to support protection of the marchers; by Sunday, they would occupy every empty bed in the house on Newark Street. *We got a telephone threat, and the FBI turned up to investigate*, my mother wrote, and suppers were interrupted by phone calls from Vice President Humphrey's office. My father's group of activist clergy pushed for a meeting with the president; no, they would not agree to a meeting unless representatives of civil rights groups, in addition to religious leaders, were included. Thousands were now traveling to Selma. Finally the president agreed to a meeting—scheduled for thirty minutes the meeting stretched to three hours; the President, my mother wrote, *talked for seventy minutes straight! Poppy has notes* (that were later lost). On Sunday, the 14th, my mother took Paul and Dee and Rosie and George to the rally in Lincoln Park, along with Dorothy Gill, the new everyday babysitter.

"I just tore up my notes," my father always said about speaking right after Fannie Lou Hamer. Meaning that it was necessary to speak from the heart. A photograph of him *with picket signs & the White House in the background*, giving that speech, was scheduled for the cover of *Newsweek* and then bumped when the Russians walked in space. Ben Bradlee wrote the magazine's article, which reported on the significant participation of white clergy in the Selma struggle.

But always, no matter what happened the night before, my mother returned to her book. She was discovering that writing a memoir was not so much trying to get back what had happened as to make sense of it. She could not shake the guilt—they could leave; their Jersey City friends could not. Did their Washington demonstrating and their few black friends in any way compensate for what they had left behind all those years ago? Instead of going to the National Cathedral, they'd joined St. Stephen's, a parish in D.C. somewhat like the church in Jersey City. The priest was a man they'd known since seminary; he'd worked on the lower East Side, was building an activist, racially integrated parish in an economically depressed part of the city—a 15-minute drive away through

Rock Creek Park. That choice meant something in the present, but she was writing about the past. How was she to write about their mission to the poor in Jersey City without *beating readers over the head?*

At first she tried combining: a *neo-baronial parish hall, carpets in the halls* and a well-dressed *cousin of Paul's* sympathizing that Jersey City wasn't a place *where the children can have friends.* But they *HAVE* friends, she has herself protest. *Yet I was also aware,* she wrote, *that those who had understood what I had said, who had looked briefly over the rim of the world I had described, would forget it all before they drove back into their pebbled driveways.* Was that too harsh? She decided to integrate some of these contradictions into the narrative; contradiction was part of the story.

> *Often, surrounded by polished antiques in suburban living rooms, I felt that I talked too long and in too much detail about the people on second street. While I was talking I could imagine Dennis beckoning me from the window to come up and meet his mother that first time, and his eagerness as he introduced me and the children—"Mama, this is the Moores." I told funny stories about Harry. . . . How could I go on to say, so that my audience would take me seriously, that the rectory was Harry's only home in the world after the circus had moved on without him? . . . Sometimes a member of the audience, honestly sympathetic, would tell me she was a contributor to Planned Parenthood and inquire if I had any statistics on unmarried mothers in our area. I used to answer that I wasn't good at figures, that it was hard to talk about statistics when they involved teen-age girls who had grown up around our house.*

Rereading, I can feel her gauging how much to say, what to leave out. Her sentences dramatize what she said when giving those talks but also convey what she felt writing the book. Would readers mistrust her *identification with people in the slums?* And what about the stories she told to make people laugh? Truth was, she felt cheap telling funny stories *at the expense of people who were suffering.* Audiences always thanked her, but she left those talks full of conflicting feelings. *As I rumbled home on the*

Lackawanna line, I would try to sort out my reactions to those well-meaning people—inchoate, angry and confused then as now. Often when she got off the bus home from the station, she'd run into Harry as she passed his rooming house on Grove Street. *"Hey, Mommy,"* he'd shriek, *"did you give 'em hell at the whatcha-call-it-meeting?"*

By early 1966, two years after the move to Washington, she confided to me in a letter how *hard* it was *to have perspective about something you have been involved in,* that *recreating is a somewhat different affair than fiction.* In the fall she wrote that she had an agent, and after a few turndowns, the book was sold to William Morrow, who published Margaret Mead, Erle Stanley Gardner, *plus Leroi Jones(!).* The company's president, it turned out, was a school friend of her brother Shaw's, and there was a celebratory lunch in New York with him and her thirty-three-year-old editor *(his first book at this job).* She wrote Pam: *Imagine a two hour lunch which is supposed to be devoted to you!* Now she was revising—*I have lots of new ideas.*

Was it her editor who suggested she examine her complicated feelings on the page? They worked closely, and Bill McPherson easily entered her life. He was the person to whom she sent the pages revised as they had worked out in weekly phone calls, and sometimes he called just to encourage her. Go back to the beginning, Bill advised—the reader needs to know *where you come from.* After trying to do so by recounting a WASP wedding in Short Hills, she began with *that Monday in late June, 1949,* when they left one world and emerged from the Holland Tunnel into a new life.

But she was hog-tied about an ending. It had been a decade since they left Grace Church, and now, at the end of 1967, the optimism of the early Civil Rights movement seemed in ruins: race riots had raged for days in Newark and Detroit, and President Johnson had dispatched 4,700 Army paratroopers to assist the National Guard. She understood that poverty as well as race was an issue, and she was wary of rhetoric that claimed substantive improvement in the lives of the American poor—she had been in their houses. There might be more jobs, more amenities like telephones and better plumbing, she wrote, *but the hard unavoidable fact remains that the people on Second Street live outside that world that becomes more afflu-*

ent at every turn. *They are still politically powerless, groggy from television's half-truths, patronized by handouts from a grossly inefficient welfare system. We had changed none of that,* she wrote, but we had become part of the community—*we weren't there to work the block then leave after two years. . . . Primarily, and leaving aside psychological motives from our own backgrounds—we lived on Second Street because we believed in God and the unique worth of every person.*

We believed in God—which I take to mean a belief in some power beyond individual human effort. *The unique worth of every person* is a phrase more typical of my mother, but while she may have crystallized her thinking, she still did not have an ending for the story her book told. *The People on Second Street* recounted and reflected on a time in the past, but what they had learned in Jersey City continued to resonate. How do you write an ending to something that is still changing your life?

As so often happens to writers, her need summoned a chance event.

No one was home—my father was at the cathedral, the children out playing—when there came a knock on the door. Though he was now a grown man, not the little boy she'd known in Jersey City, she remembered him clearly—*from Christmases, from hot summers, from scrawled letters (Dear Friends, I like this Fresh Air Camp).* He was a regular in kitchen table conversations *about being black,* and she remembered seeing him shining shoes outside the Hudson Tube station. *We talked the whole long afternoon.* He was still in Jersey City, though he had gone to college for two years; now, twenty-seven, married, and the father of two, he was holding down two jobs. *We talked of all the friends we both remembered, of their lives, the poverty, the rats, the housing, of his father's drinking, of how it had felt to be a Negro over the years since we had known each other so well.*

Was it a question she asked that prompted what came next?

Before you came we had very little hope, he was suddenly saying. *You started a chain of things. There was camp and different experiences like that, and when there was nothing else to do we could just go to Grace Church and hang around. You were the first white people we didn't hate. There was love and care for a long time.*

He hesitated before getting up to leave. *I must have looked startled,*

*because he touched my arm as we sat on the sofa and went on to explain.
"You're too hard on yourself. You mean you didn't know people remember the
love? Anyone could tell you. Even the guys who don't give a damn about God
will admit that when you pin them down."*

She had her ending, but she must have known how quickly such a
moment passes, because she closed the book with a date: *Washington,
D.C., 1967.* She didn't know that time itself was changing. For more than
twenty years, she had marked its passage within the life of her family;
now she was beginning to see the end of that phase: *The children are all
well but growing too fast,* she wrote Pam. *I can hardly bear it that Patience
will be five in May. Rosie is in love which has been traumatic for her mother
but serene for her. Paul is doing very well at Yale, loved an art course with
Vincent Scully—he is on the Yale Daily News" & writing editorials. Honor
is in her first play—a French bedroom farce and is thrilled to be at last on
stage.* Rosie would graduate from junior high, Dee from high school, and
I from college, all on the same day—June 14. *We are trying to sift out the
actual hours of events,* she wrote Pam, *but you may have to fly on as a mother
figure.* In fact, both parents came to my graduation in the Radcliffe Yard;
but our lunch after was rushed, my father left his camera at the restaurant, and there are no photographs. I wore an ecru lace minidress, the
same dress I would wear later that week when, as its first female president,
I presented an honorary membership in the Harvard Dramatic Club to
Alfred Hitchcock.

I see my mother's bare arm, twilight in the living room of 3400 Newark Street. What will it be like for her to step out, extend herself into the
public, not only as a bishop's wife and a mother but as an author? She had
always been shy, which still surprises me, because she always seemed so
utterly confident, funny, and at ease. But I identify with being shy, a sensation of fear when I first walk into a room of people. Like me, my mother
covered the shyness with social grace—that combination of modesty and
self-deprecation, in her case born of defending her privacy as refuge in
the unpredictable house where she grew up.

Finishing the book was the beginning of the end of my mother's shyness. In that light the dedication—*For Paul, who has led a life worth writing*

about—strikes me as elegiac, an acknowledgment, even an announcement, of the end of something. In speaking about her book, a part of herself that had always been private would come into the public; she would first encounter her surprising new voice in the McCarthy presidential campaign that began in a few months. In a journal entry some years later, she marked finishing the book as a turning point: *huge emotional investment, deep satisfaction, in writing, beginning of discovery of new self*—own *life*—*creaking and wrenching to old structure.*

4.

In early 1967, what my mother called *the old structure* was holding, steadied by a separation of categories not only in government—the Justice Department pursued civil rights while the Defense Department fought a war in Southeast Asia—but also in movements for change: a civil rights movement over here, the antiwar movement over there. Analogous separations also held in place unquestioned prewar class divisions as well as ideas of marriage and family: marriage here, love there; aspiration here, limitation on women's lives there; a husband's ambition here, a woman's desire and ambition over there. The cost of these divisions would soon be understood to fuel "contradictions" that were intolerable.

For my mother and many Americans, the terrain of moral thinking significantly changed. People who were engaged in separate movements began to speak of one movement and to find in the breaking down of prior separations a need for wholeness—*not making the public and the private different* is how my mother would put it later. I mark the beginning of this change with Martin Luther King's speech at Riverside Church in Manhattan on April 4, 1967. King had agreed to speak at a peace march in New York City on April 15. Until early that year, he had kept his feelings about the war private; but he was haunted by a twenty-four-page spread in *Ramparts* magazine of Vietnamese children with "stump limbs, shrapnel scars, and faces melted by napalm" and moved by the young black men who asked, "What about Vietnam?" when he sought to calm the 1967 Detroit race riot—so he had changed his mind. At the April 15 march, King would be allotted only 5 minutes—but to communicate this sea change in his thinking, he wanted to speak at length. A new group called Clergy and Laymen Concerned about Vietnam invited him to do so on April 4.

Four thousand came to Riverside Church to hear him. He could no longer tolerate, he said, "the cruel irony of Negro and white boys on TV screens as they kill and die together for a nation that has been unable to seat them together in the same schools," or watch them "in brutal solidarity burning the huts of a poor village" when "they could hardly live on the same block in Chicago." The speech was long, reasoned, and raw; King spoke with sympathy not only for U.S. soldiers but also for the Vietnamese dead. The four thousand in Riverside Church rose in several standing ovations that evening; and when he finished speaking, there was a sustained torrent of applause. The vehement attacks on the speech that began the next morning seem now almost unbelievable in their hostility. King had been "irresponsible," had made a strategic error. How could he speak with such sympathy about the enemy? How could he jeopardize his dialogue with "the greatest civil rights president in history?" Civil rights allies, liberal activists, and editorials in the *Washington Post* and the *New York Times* and almost every other American newspaper joined in protest, resulting in what his biographer, Taylor Branch, called a most "devastating ostracism" from the national dialogue. How could they not understand? "More than once he broke down in tears," the biographer wrote.

I remember sitting on a sofa in Washington arguing with my father, who took the position that the speech had been a strategic error. I knew that many had come to identify with King's desire for moral wholeness: If he did not break this silence, he had said, "I could never again raise my voice against the violence of the oppressed in the ghettos without having first spoken clearly to the greatest purveyor of violence in the world today: my own country." Though my mother would present her desire for that wholeness as new for her, it was not; inspired by Dorothy Day as a young woman, she had never departed from a desire for that kind of unity. My father, on the other hand, was used to navigating differences between movements and the power structure to reach a consensus: change would come as it was possible. My mother felt those methods too often failed the powerless—he was *selling out to power*, she would say. Like other powerful men of his generation, my father in those early years of struggle held the line between loyalty to the power he had been born to and his more progressive ideas about social justice. By breaking stride with *the old structure*, Martin Luther King abdicated his membership as the token black man in the corridors of liberal power and set himself on a new, more radical course.

Like thousands of others, my mother responded to King's Riverside Church speech. She organized a group of friends to join the coalition of student, peace, and civil rights groups that surged to New York City on April 15 for a march on the UN from Central Park; it was called the Spring Mobilization to End the War. That trip prompted the first of a series of features she published that year in the *Washington Post*, where her neighbor and friend Helen Dudman was women's page editor. The media had tarred the likely marchers as violent and out of control. My mother found the people on the train something else entirely.

The train ride was like a highly organized picnic, she wrote. *Marshals with raggedy-edge strips of yellow cloth tied to an arm for identification, one to a car, gave instructions about rules for arrival and return.* Quietly, she noted overheard conversation—*I haven't seen you since Selma.* There were civil rights activists she knew, and also *scattered through the crowded aisles with their very special expression of flat-heeled middle class zeal were smiling hardworking members of the Women's Strike for Peace* and a few of those later called hippies—*A girl explained a tiny silver circle pasted on her forehead: it's psychedelic, it's the groovy thing to do."* But it didn't seem to be, Jenny wrote, *because I only saw one other similar brow.*

I imagine my mother with her notebook, leaving her traveling companions to move through the train: *The conversation, most of it around a club car counter, went like this: "If this were disorganized, the newspapers would say it was a trainload of hippy kids—if it seems to be efficiently done, they'll describe it as part of a vast apparatus against the war effort." "I don't*

*like the fact that we're to meet in The Sheep Meadow in Central park; that
sheep connotation is bad."*

The demonstration was enormous—150,000 strong, the size a surprise
even to the organizers. Due both to King's speech and growing casualties, it was a huge increase over the 15,000 at the 1965 SDS march in
Washington. In eighteen months, the war dead had increased from 2,000
to 11,000 Americans; by June 1966, 280,000 Vietnamese fighters and
civilians had been killed. When my mother and her group got to the park,
the last of two hundred young men were burning their draft cards. It was
too crowded to get close, and the temperature had dropped to 30 degrees.
*Everyone was cold, conversational and very patient. The park area, from 72d
Street, as far as the eye could see to 59th Street, seemed full of people.*

The destination of the march was United Nations Plaza, where King,
Stokeley Carmichael, Benjamin Spock, and others would speak. When
the first marchers reached the UN, there were hundreds still in Central
Park—the organizers had underestimated.

*The trouble is, said someone, "there are no songs to sing like 'We Shall
Overcome.'"* That of course, would soon change. Peter, Paul, and Mary's
1962 song "Where Have All the Flowers Gone" would become a peace
movement anthem, as would Bob Dylan's "The Times They Are a-
Changin' " in 1964.

*It was 4 p.m. before we were on Central Park South. It grew colder and the
pauses for traffic lights seemed longer and longer. We marched behind a huge
wagon loaded with a terribly pale group of people huddled in blankets and coats
on benches and camp chairs.* Hanging out windows as they passed the Plaza
Hotel, *long-haired girls in party dresses looking like the cover of a Vogue for
Children, and, apparently at a party on the second floor, held up paper napkins
on which they had drawn peace symbols with black magic markers. On Madison Avenue going South the march quickened. A soldier with a pinched boyish
face called us Communists.*

When they finally got to UN Plaza, the crowd was so thick one could
not see the building, and the speeches were over. They would hear King
over the radio in a taxi on the way to LaGuardia—and my mother made a

note of something her friend said: *What no one understands, is that there is a mystique that pervades things like this. Somehow you feel the re-establishment of human dignity.* She'd end the piece with a very Jenny Moore move—a reminder that even as occasions like the march brought hope, the world one returned to remained as it had been: *The 6 pm shuttle plane was filled with businessmen reading the evening papers. The stewardess came by and said the fare was $15. "It's not a peak hour," she added.*

My mother wrote several more pieces for the *Post* before *The People on Second Street* was published the following year. They were usually profiles of extraordinary women of faith acting outside the established church, among them her old friend Dorothy Day, a black Planned Parenthood advocate named Ophelia Egypt, and the community activist Bishop Marie Reed, whose grandmother—*as white as you are*—was a slave. Reed had started her first parish in the basement of her home: *Sometimes I have a red hot sermon all ready, but on the way to the rostrum I get a different feel. Or God sends me a message, and I have to change the whole thing.* In a letter to Pam, my mother wrote of her excitement: *Bylines are heady stuff.* But in these subjects, she found a vein of journalism through which she would discover a world of belief and action that lay outside even the most liberal awareness.

5.

She had first met Senator Eugene McCarthy at a party the week of Johnson's inauguration in January 1964. The color's still rich in the panoramic magazine photograph of the Inaugural Ball, stretched across two pages of the scrapbook, and you can just make out my parents. Afterward, there was a party at Scotty (Fitzgerald) Lanahan's—*Washington Post* society columnist, daughter of Scott and Zelda. A year later in her column, Lanahan would name my father one of Washington's "sexiest men." Now my mother moved through the party: Cord Meyer was there, and Ben Bradlee took her around and introduced her to the people she didn't know—Adlai Stevenson, Eugene McCarthy, Lillian Hellman. *Really everyone you've ever heard of,* my starstruck mother wrote in her diary.

A year later the McCarthys became neighbors. Their children were the same ages as my brothers and sisters, and my parents had come to know them. They had a lot in common—McCarthy had famously nominated Adlai Stevenson at the Democratic convention in 1960, had campaigned in the Senate for the 1964 Civil Rights Bill, and was a poet; Abigail was a friend of Dorothy Day and had been a professor of English literature. My mother and Abigail became immediate friends; later and for years, she and "Gene" played tennis Monday mornings.

My mother's involvement in his presidential campaign began by chance on Thanksgiving afternoon, 1967, when the McCarthys came to our annual neighborhood party—always preceded by a family baseball game. *I believe the Dudmans arrived first,* she reported in the campaign oral history. "Mr. Dudman," as we children called him, was the longtime Washington correspondent of the *St. Louis Post-Dispatch*: *When Senator McCarthy came in, he was not only surrounded by college students, he was quickly approached if not attacked by Dick Dudman,* who had his familiar *story look—like a squirrel with a nut in his cheek.*

A challenge to a popular sitting president was at first unthinkable—Johnson had won election with 61 percent of the vote, a landslide. But in the context of the growing antiwar movement—in 1966, not quite half of Democrats had opposed the war; and now, a year later, 67 percent were in opposition—Congressman Allard Lowenstein had founded a "Dump Johnson" movement and was approaching possible challengers. When Robert Kennedy announced he would not run, McCarthy rumors started. That Thanksgiving night, right there in my parents' living room, the senator answered Dick Dudman's question in the positive: Yes, he would run; he'd announce in a few days.

By the time my mother affixed the date, December 1967, to the final edits of her book, the senator had made a formal announcement. Like Martin Luther King, he was appalled by the carnage in Vietnam and saw the war as pulling resources from both the president's signature poverty program and constructive foreign aid. And the toll on human life was unacceptable: more than 90,000 Americans wounded, more than 15,000 dead; and, in addition to massive military casualties, hundreds of thousands of Vietnamese civilians had been killed. In January, Mrs. McCarthy invited my mother along on her first campaign visit to New Hampshire, and the last weekend of January, accompanied by a gang of their kids, the two friends flew to New Hampshire. Abigail was meeting her oldest daughter Mary, arriving from Radcliffe; the two would visit possible campaign volunteers, and Jenny would wrangle the children on the ski slopes. No sooner had they arrived than news came that the North Vietnamese had surprised the United States, launching attacks on several South Vietnamese cities. In the weeks of fighting, which came to be called the Tet Offensive, 1,700 Americans and 100,000 South Vietnamese were killed, but most shocking was the enemy's brief occupation of the U.S. embassy in Saigon. As a result of the Tet Offensive, President Johnson approached Congress for 207,000 additional troops, but only 20,000 were authorized—the war was becoming a political liability.

My brother Paul, who cut his long hair to be "clean for Gene," and my sister Adelia were among the unprecedented thousands of college students who took weekends to go door to door for McCarthy during the primaries. They stayed on as his message evolved beyond pure opposition to the war to the idea that the political system must be returned to the people: "The President must not speak of 'my country' but of 'our country,'" the senator said. McCarthy stunned the country by winning 42 percent of the New Hampshire primary vote to LBJ's 44 percent, and on March 16 Robert Kennedy entered the campaign. My brother Paul was in Wisconsin, among 18,000 who on March 25 jammed a coliseum in Madison: "I felt the spirit of the campaign as never before," McCarthy wrote of that night. On March 31, in a shocking and contradictory announcement, President Johnson declared that because he wanted to guide the war to its end, he would not run for another term.

Gene McCarthy is the only person I've ever known remotely well that remains a marvelously gentle & admirable, humorous enigma, my mother wrote Pam. *I think he'd be an exasperatingly magnificent President.* "Exasperating" and "diffident" were frequent epithets used to deride a candidate whom many came to consider clueless. I remember my mother on the telephone: *We gave a party for him, specifically for the civil rights community, and after promising to do so, he didn't even mention race!* But she stayed with the campaign, certain that despite occasional stubbornness about what he would actually say, he shared her vision. My brother Paul, on the other hand, left his position in the McCarthy campaign to work for Robert Kennedy, who he thought could actually win. "I was 21 and the draft was important to me," he recently reminded me.

In the flush of the New Hampshire win, my mother traveled to Indiana with Mrs. McCarthy to campaign for the primary. There she made connections between the campaign and her cadre of Hoosier Democrats; she was about to return for another week when Martin Luther King was murdered in Memphis. In the devastation that followed, Robert Kennedy made an extraordinary speech in Indianapolis about unity: "What we need in the United States is not division; what we need in the United States is not hatred; what we need in the United States is not violence or lawlessness; but love and wisdom, and compassion toward one another, and a feeling of justice toward those who still suffer within our country, whether they be white or they be black." That night the energy of the primary campaign shifted decisively to him.

In Washington, as in many other cities, grief at King's murder turned to rage and people took to the streets. My parents drove quickly to our family church, St. Stephen's, which was located *only yards from the scene of the fire and the looting,* my mother wrote; its vicar Father

Wendt was an old friend. Her account was published in the Episcopal magazine.

Father Wendt was having dinner with his wife and two younger children in the rectory on Eighteenth Street, minutes from the church when the news of King's murder was announced. He went immedi-

ately to the church where his thirteen-year-old-daughter Betsy was participating in the rehearsal of a play with a group known as the Back Alley Players.

Other inner-city clergy, a few neighbors and parishioners gathered. After quick group planning they announced on TV and radio that the church would remain open for an all-night vigil. One idea followed another: the news media were notified again. It was 10:30 p.m.; looting and burning had started a block from the church.

Never had the two cities of Washington D.C.——West and East of Rock Creek Park——seemed so far apart; never had their destinies seemed intermingled. For those white people West of the park the assassination neither changed their landscape nor filled their spring air with sirens and the sound of breaking glass. It merely overloaded telephone wires, "Did you hear?"

Father Wendt announced a special night service. As the huge church filled, *a white priest was in the pulpit reading "Letter from a Birmingham Jail":* "We have waited 340 years for our constitutional and God-given rights." King's words rang in the cavernous church. *Had it always seemed so prophetic?* my mother wrote; was it right, she wondered, for *a white man to be reading the letter of a black man who, hours before, had died by a white man's bullet?* The service began, and the congregation joined in singing "Come by Here, My Lord," and "Blowing in the Wind."

The celebrant's words were interrupted by a siren: "You shall love the Lord your God with all your heart, and with all your mind, and with all your strength . . . You shall love your neighbor as yourself." Martin Luther King had obeyed; we knew that. None of the words in the service, "sacrifice" or "perpetual memorial of his precious death," seemed as remote as they had on so many Sundays. Sirens screamed.

There were shouts from the back of the church.

Why aren't we on Fourteenth Street where it's burning? That's where King would be." "You go to Fourteenth Street and 'do your thing,'" Father Wendt said. *"We're doing our thing here."*

The service continued, and then it seemed to my mother that the street got quieter.

Imperceptibly, then louder and louder, and you knew it wouldn't stop, everyone was singing, "We shall overcome someday."

I flew home for spring break; on Sunday, Palm Sunday, which celebrates the arrival of Jesus into Jerusalem, riding a donkey, a palm as a scepter, my mother drove the entire family to St. Stephen's for church. Within me was memory of Jersey City, knowledge returning from childhood—of sacrifice for a greater community, of the sacred in the presence of suffering and death. After Communion the congregation marched out onto the street, moving solemnly through the ruins of burned and looted stores, some glass still broken in the gutters; my father was in cope and miter, Father Wendt, other clergy, acolytes, the cross bearers—some white, some black—were all in vestments. I remember the sun, the heat, a smell of ash, unearthly quiet. There were balloons "with slogans on them," my sister Marian remembered; it was the day she first heard the phrase "right on"—"from you," she said. I remember my fear and the hope I felt, which as I was beginning to learn had always before seemed so separate from politics. "In Christ There Is No East or West," we sang, and "We Shall Overcome." Now, again, it seemed possible that all of us, every human being, might come together in renewal and resurrection; it is a belief that remains the most precious legacy of my childhood.

In her article, my mother suggested that conversations at St. Stephen's in the wake of King's murder offered *answers* to painful questions that lay in the charged space between black people and white people. But she also knew that however clear those answers might seem, *they are ambiguous.* The lack of ambiguity in her language strikes me, the stark clarity of her acceptance of that division. That knowledge, permanent, flowed beneath her sense of the fragility of connection, her tenderness toward the poor, her appreciation of the humor of contradiction: "You go out on 14th Street and do your thing. We'll do ours."

In six months *The People On Second Street* would be published. How would her book, its look back at Grace Church in the 1950s, with its tone of optimism about the power of community make its way in the cruelty of this moment? There were signs the book would have worldly success. She would learn shortly that *Life* magazine had assigned Kim Myers, their colleague in Jersey City, to write a review. A *Life* photographer, William Albert, Allard, had already accompanied her on a visit to Jersey City and taken photographs of the family in Washington, including a few of us at before-supper prayers.

6.

The presidential primaries had new urgency. My mother was lining up babysitters for a week there, a week here, and flying to California where an intense contest between McCarthy and Kennedy was being played out. She gave speeches for McCarthy all over the state; and, she told an oral history interviewer, often served as *ashtray emptier*—I hear slight irony in the phrase. Sometimes, instead of speaking, she accompanied Mrs. McCarthy to requisite brunches and teas. Once when the senator thanked her, she asked how on earth she made a difference. He replied that she did things no one else could—not the ashtrays, but how she greeted and spoke to those who turned up to help.

Now it was the evening of June 4 in Los Angeles, Robert Kennedy had won the primary, and on TV, in the campaign suite in the Beverly Hilton, with *two other people whose names I don't recall*, she was watching as *Frank McGee of NBC was droning on: I remember sitting in an armchair*, she told the oral historian; the room had been filled

and people had gone off to the other rooms or other parties or some-
where. Senator and Mrs. McCarthy and Mary McGrory and Blair
Clark . . . were in the bedroom, composing (as I understood later)
telegrams of congratulations to Senator Kennedy for his victory.

Kennedy had certainly won, McGee was saying, even though Los Angeles county returns had not yet been counted—right then *the door to the*
bedroom opened, and Mrs. McCarthy, with her hand over her mouth, turned
and said, *"Senator Kennedy—Bobby—Bobby has been shot."* A CBS
reporter appeared and confirmed the report, and we *switched channels and*
immediately got that mad, horrible scene that everybody recalls—of Senator
Kennedy surrounded by people and people screaming. . . . And then Senator
McCarthy came in and said that he felt that we shouldn't all be sitting around
in his suite—people had flooded in and it was loud, very loud. And he felt that
this was not appropriate. So most of us left.

It was 11 p.m. in the East. I was on the road, driving fast with a friend
to New York from the Berkshires, loud music, gossip about the theatre
where we worked, when there was an interruption—we were expecting
news of an RFK victory, but the word was *assassination*, and we pulled off
the road. Emergency, Ambassador Hotel—but hadn't President Kennedy
already been murdered? And Martin Luther King? We could not believe
what we were hearing.

I don't think I knew my mother was in Los Angeles.

She left the hotel for the airport with Mrs. McCarthy and the four
McCarthy children, the Secret Service leading them out through the hotel
kitchen: *It seemed the maddest possible way to get out*—through a kitchen—
after *what you had been seeing on television. . . .* On her commercial flight
were Mrs. McCarthy and the children—the senator was on another
plane—in the aisles members of the Kennedy staff, even senior advisors
like Ted Sorenson, were in tears. On landing in D.C., the Secret Service
rushed them home; it was dark, and they were led circuitously through
backyards to the McCarthy house. When my mother got to our house, she
woke the children to tell them what had happened.

She came to visit me in the Berkshires a few weeks later. Oddly, I don't remember her talking about Kennedy's assassination. Had we learned to go on with the present, creating a small compartment for each inevitable disaster? She wrote Pam that she saw one of the plays I worked on but didn't name it—*A Cry of Players* by William Gibson, with Anne Bancroft and Frank Langella. I had a grown-up job I'd gotten before the producer, Lyn Austin—realized I was the daughter of her Vassar friend Jenny McKean. The three of us had late supper after the play, and mostly I watched as they talked—the mother of nine and bishop's wife, and a career woman—trying to find common ground. Weeks before, Lyn had explained to me that while she wasn't married, she did have "a person." I knew the word *lesbian*, but I had never associated it with a happy life partnership. I would not learn until after my mother's death—in a conversation with her friend Sylvia—that Margarett had a lesbian relationship with my grandfather's cousin, Florence Shaw, that endured for "about twenty years." The closest my mother and I came to discussing her mother's bisexuality was a passing mention of Margarett's "lesbian friends," and we never talked about what Lyn made clear that night about her relationship with Leora Dana, an actress who had been my mother's Barnard classmate and would six years later portray my mother in my play *Mourning Pictures.*

I felt so proud, my mother wrote Pam of my summer—*heady, rubbing shoulders with Wm. Gibson, Arthur Penn, Elaine May, etc.* Did she not know what I had actually achieved? That as chief of publicity for the theater, I had managed to get several Theater section front-page photos in the Sunday *New York Times*? That I sat in on rehearsals, actually got to know the people my mother mentioned; Gibson, the author of *The Miracle Worker;* Penn, the director of the then controversial film *Bonnie and Clyde*; and Elaine May, writer, actress and comedy partner of Mike Nichols, whom I'd seen one night standing at the back of the theater, quietly watching his former collaborator. Lyn thought I was a marvel, and I reveled in her praise. I was working very hard. I'd learned the lineaments of press release composition from the great Broadway press agent, Harvey Sabinson—"start with who where when what how." From corralling my siblings, I'd discovered how to make it fun for teenage apprentices to stuff a hundred press releases, folding them so the lede hit your eye when you opened the envelope. *They were all so enthusiastic about her,* my mother wrote. *It made me very proud.* She added that I was *rooming in an El of a lovely frame house with two equally purposeful driven females, & one hung-up boy*—by *hung up,* she meant that he barely spoke and hadn't said hello to her. He hardly spoke to me either, even during the abrupt sex we had in my single bed whenever he turned up in the middle of the night.

The year 1968 was when my mother and I started to keep secrets from each other. Important events in my life—like having sex with the hung-up boy—were occurring in a part of me that I would not share with my mother. I did not know she too had a new private life, which she shared hardly at all, let alone with her daughter about to turn twenty-three. Four years later, she would share one very delicate fact, startling me with a confidence I could have done without: "I didn't have an orgasm until I was forty." I would learn decades later, reading their notes and diaries, that she and my father at some point agreed to "see other people" and that each of them had extramarital loves. I was able to confirm this when I came across that piece of paper I'd never read, the fragment in which she surrendered *we* for *I. Long relationship with man,* she wrote—*immense complications; his need for me totally different from my need for him.* The man she fell in love with was a man within the Harvard and Yale circles she knew; he was divorced and worldly; he knew the literary landscape and the political one, and he was often around the McCarthy campaign.

If my mother had lived longer, perhaps we would both have looked back on those years as women; but she did not, and the man who was her lover died in his seventies. Once in the early 1990s, I had lunch with him—I was going to ask him about my mother, but his wife was with him, and I could not. He was not married at the time of his love affair with my mother, so why couldn't I? "You were skittish," my friend the novelist said, "about morality." I suppose I was. Years later, after the man died, the wife described my mother as his "very close friend"—code, I was certain, for lover—but I didn't press her; we were standing with others at his funeral. Now, writing this book, I want to understand what I know, so I'll try imagining. Let's say that occasionally they sat together on a cam-

paign flight and talked about the old days—his ex-wife was a relative of
Wattie Dickerman's, etc., etc. WASP entanglements . . .

And those conversations led to talk about the primaries, about books,
including her book that was about to be published.

Had she and my father already decided to "see other people"?—painful conversation, letters, sadness, but new freedom. I remember my own
almost-marriage of several years, the realization that we were not sexu-
ally compatible and how, when I met a man I was powerfully attracted to,
nothing else mattered; I simply gave in. Was it that way for my mother?
The excitement of a woman in her forties, falling into attraction: when did
they become lovers? I imagine them at dinner together in New York—at
last quiet and alone. Or Washington. Or did it not start until August in
Chicago, during the Democratic convention?

The letters she destroyed at the end of her life—how many of them
were from him? I met him only once more, aside from at her funeral
where we didn't really talk—both of us, like everyone else, shaken with
grief: It was after a poetry reading where I had introduced Alice Walker
and Michael Harper. He was tall, I remember, and smelled of tobacco—
we air-kissed hello, but I was unbearably shy, knowing my mother, now
dead, had loved him. He was awkward too, and solemn, complimenting
me on a poem of mine he'd seen in a magazine.

So I put this together: He became involved with my mother after falling
in love with the woman he later married, a woman from Eastern Europe;
he was moving heaven and earth to get her into this country. He and my
mother were "together" for a year or two, then broke up. Why? Because
of the complexity, the pure size of my mother's life? Because of his love for
and commitment to the other woman? Then in January 1969, my mother
almost died in the automobile accident, and they were together again, on
and off. What of her mysterious phrases, *his need for me totally different
from my need for him—broken & mended many times—great resurgence after
my accident*—was that when she confided to a friend she planned to leave
my father for him? Later, when the woman from Eastern Europe was free
to come to this country, *the final break-off.* I had lunch with my mother the
day she was to meet this woman, her former lover's wife, for the first time.

"It's very important," she said, as if I knew the entire story, knew that she had loved this man, that they had been important lovers.

"Every married woman I saw during that period was having an affair," a psychologist told me about working in the late 1960s and early 1970s. The era's reputation for sexual freedom was real, extended even to my parents' generation—disorienting to think of, as I and my contemporaries claimed authorship of that revolution. In 1968 my parents' marriage was still my ideal; I was not aware of the fault lines long evident to both of them. Apparently, my brother Paul was: "The marriage," he said recently, "was over by 1968." These decades later, older by twenty years than my mother was then, I remember the urgency of sexual discovery. Awkward as it was to have her announce to me her first orgasm, implying what my father later confirmed, that they were never "a sexual fit," I was relieved by their disclosures—each of them had accepted the limitations of their marriage and moved on to live a sexual life. For my mother, that rediscovered sheet told me her exploration began in Jersey City with an *intense sexual affair with poet/self-styled mystic/priest,* and continued in Indianapolis with an *emotional attachment to a man, but always controlled.*

The power of a sexual love for a woman in her forties: He is the first man who breaks you from your past, you are in a revolution, you believe your life depends on him. He is the only person who sees your new self. Because he has not known you before, he sees only the self you have created, the *I.* But my mother also saw a larger picture, and she was beginning to acknowledge it: *What I guess I'm summing up is a switch—turn-about, change—from public morality style, rules, way of life, to a personal, hewn-out private one that, in a way, was always there, battling to be heard.* It took years before I was able to consider my mother's erotic life in terms of her female existence. In 1978, in an essay, the poet Audre Lorde articulated the erotic as a source of power for women: "The erotic is a resource within each of us that lies in a deeply spiritual plane," she wrote, "firmly rooted in the power of our unexpressed or unrecognized feeling. . . . For women this has meant the suppression of the erotic as a considered source of power and information within our lives."

At first my mother never even considered leaving my father; they were partners, and they loved each other. But as each of them pursued new work, things began to change. My father took a year off from being a bishop to do hands-on community organizing in Washington, her book was about to be published, and she was writing features for the *Washington Post*. "We were growing apart," my father wrote decades later. For my mother, a paradigm shift was underway: *I feel differently about marriage— or rather I've allowed myself to feel what I always thought—Impossible, outrageous! Two people in such a compulsory relationship, so you deal with it in as kind a way as possible.*

7.

She left the Adirondacks for Chicago on Saturday, August 24, the day of my sister Adelia's nineteenth birthday. Never before had she missed a family celebration—*life does change,* she wrote Pam. When the convention started on Thursday, McCarthy's candidacy was still in play. Though given the power of the established Johnson Democrats, his being nominated was close to impossible; the hope was that Vice President Humphrey would fail to gain a majority on the first ballot, resulting in an "open convention" that would allow a debate on the morality and viability of war on the convention floor. Awakened by the primary campaign and outraged by the assassinations of King and Kennedy, thousands of my contemporaries converged on Chicago for marches, protests, and concerts in opposition to the war and injustice. Mayor Daley was exploiting fears of violence and training police to use new riot gear—five thousand members of the National Guard were deployed nearby. *I hope Chicago doesn't blow,* my mother wrote Pam Saturday on her flight. She wouldn't have known when she arrived that marchers, including some McCarthy delegates, had already been jailed.

Abigail McCarthy had spent a week with our family in the Adirondacks, but my mother hadn't seen most of her campaign comrades since the night of Kennedy's assassination in Los Angeles. Gathered in the

Hilton suite with the candidate were Blair Clark, the campaign chair, and twenty-nine-year-old press secretary Seymour Hersch—who, as a reporter, would break the news of the My Lai Massacre the following year. Others soon arrived, among them the columnist Mary McGrory, who would later become my mother's friend, and the poet Robert Lowell. Proudly exaggerating what I was doing, my mother told Lowell that she had a daughter who wrote poems, to which the poet, ever courtly, replied: "Would I have read her?"

My mother was taking notes for an account of the convention that would run on the front page of the *Catholic Worker*. My brother Paul, now in Chicago, had been *racing all over the country for McGovern*—he'd started as an intern in the South Dakota senator's office and was now one of two "youth coordinators." George McGovern had just officially entered the nomination race, picking up many Kennedy delegates. My mother felt herself a Capulet to my brother's Montague, she joked to Pam. "Everyone was taking sides," Paul said. But the consequential division was between the antiwar position that McCarthy and McGovern shared and that held by supporters of LBJ's policies, which were now held by Humphrey. "It was like a deep freeze," my mother's friend Gil Harrison, publisher of the antiwar *New Republic*, remarked of his reception at a Hyde Park cocktail party given by an establishment Democrat.

The first victory for the antiwar Democrats was the rescheduling of debate on the peace plank; it would take place on Wednesday afternoon rather than late Tuesday night. Composed by antiwar Democratic senators, the plank called for a quick withdrawal of U.S. troops, an immediate end to bombing, and a postwar Vietnam government that included not only North and South Vietnam but also the Viet Cong. Demonstrations began in Grant Park, across from the Hilton, on Tuesday night. On her way out to supper on Wednesday, my mother saw people in the lobby *sniffling and holding handkerchiefs*—this was something new: *I remember running upstairs and saying, There's tear gas in the lobby*. Later, she and Gil Harrison went into the park, as they would every night until the end of the convention. *Twice, I was reminded that I had no business with that crowd, that I was a mother*, she told the McCarthy campaign oral historian. For others the demonstrators might be *hippies and yippies, programmed from the outside, agitators, anarchists,* but she had been working with young people all spring, and her own son, my brother Paul, was moving between the park and McGovern headquarters. Watching television in the Berkshires, I could make out the demonstrators' chant—"The whole world is watching, the whole world is watching"—I saw police beating demonstrators, and National Guardsmen packed into military trucks so massive my brother remembered them as tanks. I didn't know, as the newscast jumped to Grant Park, that both my brother and my mother were there, she "wearing high heels and the whole thing," Paul confirmed decades later, "and Mr. Harrison in a coat and tie." *We would be stopped every ten feet or so by a friendly pat on the arm,* my mother told the oral historian, *and people would say, "I'm sure you haven't had tear gas before, and we'd say "No" and they would give us wet handkerchiefs and tell us what to do and not to rub our eyes—we moved around for about two hours, and never had the feeling we weren't wanted, in fact we were thanked over and over again for being there.*

Her emphasis on peace was important, as it countered Mayor Daley's accusations of violence.

Back at the hotel Thursday night, my mother went immediately to bed—she and my brother were flying out early the next morning. The campaign bedrooms were on the twenty-third floor, hers without a view of the park. She slept fitfully, a rhythmic noise that was probably a train weaving into a dream so vivid that she kept waking *thinking there were troops or crowds running.* And then she heard a girl screaming, threw on some clothes, and ran out into the hall in her bare feet—*You've got to take care of her, she's out of her head—you don't know what's been happening on the fifteenth floor,* and then she saw Gene McCarthy with four or five people—*the senator took the time to tell me what had been going on on the fifteenth floor*—the police, claiming beer cans had been thrown from the window of McCarthy headquarters, raided the office suite and assaulted campaign workers.

I did not go to the fifteenth floor, because I felt it was a place for doctors and press and not onlookers. But she saw the kids, bloody and wounded; the room where they planned strategies for peace had become a temporary emergency room. What she saw there, she wrote, was, for her, *the crowning blow.*

How was she to make sense of this? "*The ones who were clubbed, the ones who sang and marched*" were not so different from "*the ones who cut their hair and played politics,*" my brother said on the plane. *I've yet to talk to anyone who is really bitter,* my mother told the oral historian and quoted a Grant Park protestor: "*We lost, but I am not discouraged. I'm very hopeful.*"

King's Riverside Church speech had broken down the division between the civil rights movement, which had inspired so much of my mother's thinking and politics, and the struggle to end the war in Vietnam. She had joined the insurgent presidential campaign that emerged from the terrible injustice and violence of that war, its urgency intensified by the murders of the two leaders who had fused the causes for social justice and for peace. She had seen black children beaten, and now she had seen white children beaten. *I think what happened to my older children,* she told the oral historian, *and to my younger children in a different fashion—was that we really began to think during the winter and spring and summer of '68, that the public and the private lives of people like ourselves who had become involved, could be, in a sense, one. It's a very kind of feeling reaction, but it is the whole business of honesty—honesty and integrity and involvement and caring and not making the public and private different.*

In Chicago she had experienced the feelings of powerlessness that were a condition of life for the black and brown and poor people she had known in Chelsea, Jersey City, and Indianapolis, and whom she now knew in Washington. Like others in the struggles she had been part of, she was now living the interplay between two realities that just a year later came to be called the personal and the political—*I certainly feel,* she said to the oral historian, *(though it's difficult to articulate) that I am a different person.*

Barely three weeks later, the "different person" was pictured in *LIFE,* an issue with the Beatles on the cover. She is beaming, standing before the lych-gate amid a crowd of children from Grace Church. Her joy at being back on Second Street was accompanied by an entirely new feeling— that of having what one has written merge with the place one had written about. She'd barely had time to consider what had happened in Chicago, but the experience fed the interviews she gave all over the country: in a bookstore on the North Shore, near where she grew up, and in Chicago, Indianapolis, and California. What did she feel when copies of the book, with its handsome apple green cover, its impressionistic renderings of people on a street, arrived? I remember the first sight of my own first hardcover, the fragrance of newness when I first cracked it open, the peculiarity of such intense emotion reduced to pages between those covers.

Her brother Shaw and his wife Linda gave my mother a book party at their apartment on Gramercy Park. I remember her, shy and gracious. By then she had been on the *Today* show on September 16 and received a considered and rapturous review in the *Washington Star* by Mary McGrory; reviews equally full of praise were to come from the psychiatrist and writer Robert Coles in the *New Republic*, William MacKaye in the *Washington Post*, and in newspapers all over the country—New York, Chicago, Denver, Cleveland, Chattanooga, San Francisco. The book would sell 25,000 copies. There must have been a celebration in Washington, and she certainly went to Indianapolis. Kim Meyers in *LIFE* talked about his fear of reading the book: given his own time in Jersey City and his friendship with the writer, he was at first so nervous reading that he "hated its words," but said that he read the book "cover to cover and my amazement grew." He was not alone in initial suspicion. "All the ingredients for literary disaster are there," wrote Mary McGrory, "a privileged, highly educated, ex-debutante, went to the slums of Jersey City with her husband and two other Episcopal priests, to minister to the poor. She could have been patronizing, facetious or sentimental about what she saw. But she avoided all the traps, and her book is a triumph of enlightened, warm-hearted astringency." McGrory, an astringent writer herself, also praised the writing: "shatteringly matter-of-fact and resonant at the same time."—"Mrs. Moore took every day what God sent, railing against the human condition, but never against the human nature that surged into the kitchen, the recreation hall and to a lesser extent the church: the rejected, the hungry, the drunks, the whores, the fools, the exploiters of poverty, the has-beens."—depicting them as "hilarious and pitiful without ever demeaning them." She "never fails to point out the chasm between the realities of Second Street life" and the "hollow and rather grand theo-ries" that brought her there. The psychiatrist Robert Coles, writing in the *New Republic*, considers that "Jenny Moore's triumph in Jersey City and in writing this book has to do with forgiveness—of herself." He means of her origins as white and well-off. He and Mary McGrory and William MacKaye in the *Washington Post* all single out the end of the book, quot-ing the Jersey City visitor who surprised the author by saying, "You are too hard on yourself. . . . You mean you didn't know people remembered the love? Anyone could tell you, Even the guys who don't give a damn about God will admit that when you pin them down."

It seemed to me my dazzling mother was everywhere at once that fall. *Adored speaking in connection with book,* she wrote—*TV, radio, speeches, etc.* In the weeks and months following publication, she gave so many speeches in so many cities that my father, asked about his wife's new prominence, declared to a journalist he was beginning to feel like "the Duke of Edinburgh if not Prince Albert." She had found a new way of life. Everyone was certain *The People on Second Street* would be the first of many books by Jenny Moore.

8.

I was beginning to scrawl at poems though my attention was not on writ-ing but on life, on love life in particular. *Don't come home pregnant,* my mother had said and kept saying in my head while offering no help with birth control, which did not become legal for unmarried women until 1972. It had not been easy for me to get a diaphragm when my first boy-friend and I decided to have sex the summer of 1965. Vivid in my con-sciousness were the girls who got pregnant at Shortridge: their sudden absence from classes, rumors of a secret wedding, the rental of a small house with or without a new husband on the far north side. There were sympathetic gynecologists in New York, fewer in Boston. The first I con-sulted was in Manhattan, his name passed to me by my boyfriend via his ex-girlfriend—I remember clearly the doctor's sentence refusing me: "Sex before marriage is not in your worldview." The next, located through my cousin's wife, prescribed the diaphragm I inserted for my first sex— awkward, stumbling, any sense of romance overcome by the cold spermicidal cream, its chemical smell, the feel of the rubber circlet within me.

I did not talk to my parents about it until after the fact. At lunch in Boston, my father said he thought that it was "probably not a good idea" to "have intercourse" before marriage—"Your mother and I did not." But he said he would not consider my doing so a sin. *Don't come home pregnant*, my mother repeated. I remember that recurring sentence as clearly as I remember the first time I saw her nude body: "Come talk while I have a bath, sweetie." It was in Indianapolis, and I was sixteen. We were always a little shy when we were by ourselves—such a rare occurrence, and her nakedness made me self-conscious. It was late afternoon and the water was greenish-blue. I remember the desultory sound of a splash at the lift of the wet washcloth to a shoulder or breast, and I remember noting that I was looking at a body that had submitted to the births of nine children.

Now it was 1968. Perhaps I would become a career woman, I mused. I'd triumphed in my first paying job at the theater—perhaps I could forgo children altogether. But even the woman I'd admired most at the theater that summer was a mother, albeit of only one daughter. Elaine May was the author and star of the first play of the season, and though I was intimidated by her fame and abrupt manner, I found her brilliant and fascinating. I mentioned to her that I was at Yale, and she said she knew someone there; he taught playwriting. I know him a little, I said. When I went back to school in September, I sought him out. Soon I was falling for his dizzying language and the eccentric, musical hesitations in his speech. His name was Arnold Weinstein ("stein," he explained; "rhymes with 'fine' "). He was shiny and sinuous, glamorous and quicksilver funny, and whenever I saw him, I stared. I told him I had met Elaine May: "Oh," he said, "Elaine." I had his attention. I tried to ask him questions, but he answered like a professor or dodged them with a clever reply, often in rhyme. He knew Latin and Greek, and so we talked about Catullus and Virgil, who suddenly came to life as poets when he quoted them, riffing, experimenting with a translated phrase, explaining how one chose this word over that.

Downstairs at the drama school, there was a low-ceilinged theater called the Ex. In that room I first beheld the Living Theatre; the dean introduced its artistic directors, Julian Beck and Judith Malina, and their company, a diverse collection of actors from all over the world. They lived, they told us, communally, everyone doing everything from acting to cooking, from keeping track of props to erecting the complicated sets. That 1968 afternoon they seemed horizontal and languid, their hungry bodies adorned in the ragged blacks of true art—just to see them was a shock. The dean, on the other hand, was dressed as always in a tweed jacket and tie. I remember that Judith Malina—pale-faced, kohl-eyed—and the actors answered our questions with talk of a society without money. I began to feel weighed down by my shoes, by the gold hoops that dangled from my pierced ears, and certainly by my purse. If money was unnecessary, why was I even wearing a purse?

Julian Beck, who looked like an angel or a prophet, spoke more softly than his wife, but his message was no less radical—anarchic, utopian, a solution to every anxiety. If his vision could be realized, I mused, all the contradictions exploding on the streets would resolve into a calmly ecstatic peace. But further contradictions soon presented themselves; the more the dean insisted on man's need for civilization the more the members of the Living Theatre, so beautiful in their raw but not terribly clean physicality, retorted that humankind was innately good, turned evil by civilization. To me and my friends, our much-admired dean suddenly seemed surprisingly behind the times, and though I didn't think I would run off with the Living Theatre, they had given me an inspiring and utterly new way of looking at the world.

What comes back of their *Antigone* is Judith Malina's otherworldly voice, its force all the more startling since it came from such a tiny body. By the time I saw the second play, *Mysteries and Smaller Pieces*, the drama school had begun to tilt from its axis, and a new giddiness distracted us as we struggled to focus in class. The third offering was *Frankenstein*, Mary Shelley as a parable of the human fall from innocence brought on by the cruelties of civilization. Julian Beck's astonishing scaffolding entirely appropriated the bare stage, now stripped of its red velvet curtain. Some of my classmates in acting and directing began to dress differently, to kohl their eyes, to be seen intensely conversing with the beautiful visitors. The scent of marijuana was everywhere.

Both Arnold Weinstein and the dean had known the Becks for years, but their new work and radical politics split the two friends—Arnold, probably stoned; and the dean, working to keep the peace as more students, eyes ablaze, dogged the steps of the pied pipers. It was rumored that the final play, *Paradise Now*, would involve nudity, even of audience members, so I took myself to Macy's and bought new underwear. I cooked dinner for two friends—a tuna casserole from *The Joy of Cooking*—and then we walked solemnly to the theater. The troupe entered from the rear of the house that night, Julian Beck and others slithering from armrest to armrest across audience seats declaiming, "I cannot travel without a passport."

As a theater administration student, I often tore tickets—now it was all too clear what tickets were surrogates for. "I cannot smoke marijuana," someone shouted. "I cannot take off my clothes." I and many of the audience ended up on the stage, and at the end of the play the Becks led many—but not me—in stripping to nudity or underwear and running out onto the street shouting, "Paradise now!" Ten people—including Julian, dressed in a loincloth, Judith, garbed in the female equivalent— were arrested for indecent exposure and jailed. The dean bailed them out at dawn.

What stays with me still is their language, stripped down to pure utterance, even to silence. I had an inarticulate sense something had broken open within me that would permit my future, and I wanted to talk to someone about it. Maybe that was how Arnold and I ended up having a drink. The dazzle of his brown eyes falls across my vision now, and I am right there, wanting to touch his gray cashmere turtleneck, his prematurely silver hair rising in wiry curls from his forehead. I was thinking of his narrow hips, imagining him sweeping me up into his gothic turreted apartment and ravishing me. No one had ever ravished me, but he was old enough to: four years younger than my mother, eight years younger than my father. He was nothing like my father. He was not married, had no children, and he did not have "a job." He lived the life of an artist, on an adjunct's salary, supplemented by royalty checks. Once, after he got one of those checks, I overheard him dictate a telegram to his agent: "Thank you, you lovely bank you."

But now, with him finally right there, I could not speak. I wanted to flirt, but instead I smiled and looked down at my hands. He thought I was sad and asked me what was wrong. I was only sad that I was mute, but I did not have language to tell him that, nor could I tell him I was trying to write poems or what I felt about the Living Theatre. Instead, I said I wasn't sure what to do with my life. Just then the waitress arrived, and Arnold, gesturing toward me, asked her how someone so young and beautiful could be sad. "She should be happy, don't you think?" I didn't think I was beautiful, so I couldn't believe in anything he said; but the waitress said, "Yes." That spring in a directing class, I staged a romantic park bench scene from a play of Arnold's called *The Red Eye of Love*. He loved what I did with it, he said, but he had so many ideas about how I might improve it that by the time he finished talking I thought he didn't like it at all.

One night he had a party, students in his apartment, all of us drinking, listening to music, maybe smoking dope, deep in conversation about the tension between politics and art. "All power to the imagination," the students in Paris had scrawled on walls the spring before. "The Whole world is watching," the demonstrators shouted in Chicago. As everyone was leaving, I helped in the kitchen, purposely cleaning up so thoroughly that I was still there after all the others had gone. I spent the night with Arnold in his bed, fucking as we called it, until we fell asleep. The next day he asked if we were "an item"—"Yes!"—and thereafter when he was in New Haven I spent nights with him in his narrow bed, newly freed by the birth control pills my new gynecologist had given me.

I was discreet, not because there was any bar to faculty-student romance, but because I wasn't sure of him. Sometimes he didn't call, and sometimes he skipped a week at the drama school. Incommunicado in

New York. I'd often come home to my apartment drunk and fall to bed without brushing my teeth, certainly without poking a birth control pill out of the plastic circular dispenser. One day that winter, in the common room at the school, a classmate, an actor, asked if he could photograph me nude. I thought of beauty, of the nudes painted by the French and Italians, and I thought of the photographs I'd seen of naked women by Edward Weston.

The classmate arrived at my apartment with lights and camera. It was pouring rain, which I remember because there were floor-to-ceiling windows in the living room, and as he set up his lights, I listened to the rain make a banging sound against the glass. In an art class I once took, the model had put on a nice robe when she took a break; now I wore a Japanese kimono my mother had given me. We drank Scotch, and he asked me to lie down, indicating I should do so, nude. I took off the kimono and lay down. I did not feel elegant, as I imagined a model would feel; I was just me, my own body, very white and awkward on the black fur rug on the white linoleum tile floor. He lifted his camera and I thought of his girlfriend, how nice she was. Click-click-click: Shooting, he was closer, and then he put down his camera and unzipped his corduroys. I was pulling away but my body was not—it was so fast. He was in me, and then I pushed to get him off me. I waited to cry until he left, and I told no one.

A few weeks before, I had given a younger friend money for an abortion and driven her to New Jersey for the operation. Having inherited what I called "my own money" at twenty-one, I could easily afford the gift. We had been instructed not to arrive before ten at night, so it was very dark when we got there. The doctor's office was in the back of his house on a suburban street. I took my friend, inside then waited in the car until she staggered out. I gave no thought at all to what she had lost in her abortion; I thought of what she had gained and what she had avoided. This was before *Roe v. Wade* made abortion legal, before national debate complicated such choices. All the white middle-class girls I knew well in 1969 were on the pill and fucking with abandon: pregnancy was the draft, abortion the female version of 4F, the draft category our male friends wanted that kept them from going to Vietnam.

My friend lived in the South; what would her parents say? She was sure that if she went home, she'd have to have the baby. I remember what she looked like in the car light, color drained from her face, her long platinum blond hair suddenly lank, like string. For the next few days, she kept vomiting. There was some question about whether the abortion had worked—it had cost $600 ($4,200 in 2018 dollars) andwas a saline injection, not a D&C. She said her stomach hurt more than anything; in the hospital they gave her a D&C, and soon she was back at school.

Yet I was careless with the pill; I was taking the kind whose hormone the intensity varied based on the menstrual cycle, so it was riskier to skip a day. And I did skip days. Even before I actually knew I was pregnant, I thought I must be. I was in a good mood, suddenly—I remembered that about my mother pregnant, and I remember the smoothness of my skin and hair, a creamy white shirt I wore, silk with long sleeves, a strand of Mexican embroidery around my waist. When I was alone, I would touch my belly with both hands as I had seen my mother do when she was pregnant, but I didn't want to have a baby. I wanted to work at the theater in the Berkshires again, rent a house for the summer commune that drama school friends and I were planning—two of us planned to write, four others had a rock band. And I had started to move on. When Arnold wasn't in New Haven, I flirted with a handsome set designer, a student and closer to my age; but even though I thought he was someone I could marry and even though he flirted back, he never called me.

When I missed one period, I paid no attention—I was working props for a production of *Coriolanus*. My mother didn't let on to me that she was worried, but I have this in my imagination: We are sitting in the living room of my grandmother's apartment; the deep blue carpet and there's a view of the seal pond in Central Park Zoo. My mother is asking me serious questions. I imagine my heart beating with shame as I try to explain what I've done, but also my relief as she listens and I listen and we find a way out. In reality, having no idea I was pregnant but concerned that her daughter was involved with a man so much older, my mother wrote to a professor of mine, a drama critic, and invited him to meet her in that very room above Fifth Avenue.

I see her crossing her legs, lighting a cigarette, making smart conversation about his work. Because she knows that he is Jewish but a Catholic convert, she asks him about Dorothy Day or Ivan Illyich, the radical Catholic priest who worked in Mexico. They had martinis, I think he said, and she asked him about Arnold Weinstein, who, he assured her, was well thought of. When the professor told me the story a few months later, I was furious. It seemed to me that my mother had been more interested in him and his radical Catholicism than she was worried about me, and that, like a character out of Edith Wharton, she was investigating my lover's qualifications: Was he talented enough for her daughter? What were his (not financial and social, but creative and intellectual) prospects?

If she'd invited me to the apartment and asked me directly about Arnold, I might have caved in and said that, despite being "in love with" him, I couldn't imagine marrying him, at least not yet. I wanted to write, and what I dreamed of was a husband who was nice and earnestly funny like Poppy and a wedding like she had, my parents had, celebrating true love among their friends. Would I have told her how my body felt when Arnold and I made love, entirely charged with desire? Or admitted that for several weeks Arnold had been withdrawing, how jumpy his brown eyes were from the vitamin and speed concoction he shot up? How his voice, to which I gave ultimate authority, was often pitched to a shout as I washed dishes and he criticized me for being a rich white girl whose destiny was irrelevant compared to that of anyone poor or black.

That mother-and-daughter encounter never took place. Instead, I was confiding in a psychiatrist about "Arnold"—I was no longer feeling radiant and beautiful, but bovine and sluggish. When I missed a second period, I went to a gynecologist and asked for a "rabbit test"—that was what my mother did to find out she was pregnant. When the test was positive, I called the older psychiatrist who had referred me to my young therapist. I told him I was pregnant and then burst into tears. My mother had somehow gotten me his name—was it that I wanted him to tell her without my asking him to? I didn't want to go through what my friend had. I'd heard of something called a therapeutic abortion—an abortion that was legal because it was performed for the health of the mother. Could I have one of those? I was sure I couldn't care for a child. I could tell the psychiatrist was listening carefully. I had come, I said, to him because I didn't think the young psychiatrist he'd sent me to would approve of my getting an abortion, because he was Catholic. The doctor paused, then said that he would talk to him, but that I had to ask him myself to approve the procedure. It scared me to do that, but I did it. With hardly any affect in his voice, my psychiatrist said that such a decision would have nothing to do with his religion; he wrote me a letter prescribing a therapeutic abortion. Since I could pay for it myself, I didn't have to tell my parents.

I went alone to the hospital. Prescription notwithstanding, the look on the gynecologist's face was nervous, even judgmental as he pulled on his gloves and told me what would happen. I knew I was not the only young woman of my generation to have an abortion, but I was alone in the operating room that morning, alone with a doctor, a nurse, and an anesthesiologist. The nurse took my hand. How I wish it had been my mother's hand, I was thinking as I went under. "Further along than we thought," the doctor said when I woke up. "There are flowers for you," he said, irritated. "I told you not to tell anyone."

I must have taken a taxi home from the hospital. I called the friends who had sent the flowers, the only people in whom I had confided, and they came over with soup. I thought I could feel the scraping where the doctor's instrument had been, and I wondered if he had hurt my insides to teach me a lesson. When Arnold came up from New York, he called. "How are you, baby?" he said, and because by now his desire was so infrequent, I was thrilled. I put on my Marimekko dress; it was the color of bubble gum, with big white circles. Of course, I hadn't told Arnold I was pregnant because I was confused. Of course I was "in love" with Arnold, but I might have been pregnant by the photographer.

There was another problem—the doctor had said I couldn't have "intercourse" for three weeks. How was I going to resist Arnold, as he came toward me, and how was I going to keep from making love? When he opened the apartment door smiling, I felt strong and independent. Soon we were in bed, and I told him a partial truth, that I had an infection and that the gynecologist had told me I couldn't fuck for three weeks. My insides burned like a scrape you get on your knee after falling on cement. After hours of near sex, we fell asleep. In the morning I had a fever, and while Arnold was still sleeping, I called the gynecologist. I didn't tell him I was at my boyfriend's apartment, because I was sure the fever I had was somehow from almost-fucking. After asking me a few brusque questions, he prescribed an antibiotic.

When Arnold woke up, he went to the drugstore for me. When he got back, he was so comforting that I told him the truth, that I'd had an abortion. I did not tell him that I had any doubt he was the father. Suddenly any concern he felt for my fever and infection, the tenderness with which he'd kissed me when he woke up, turned to rage, and he began to shout. "How could you do such a thing to your body?" And then later, "I would have married you!" When he said that, it was as if he had slapped me. Marry me only because I was pregnant? That wasn't good enough, is what I was thinking—if I had stayed pregnant, would he have spent the rest of his life with me? I realized I'd never thought so. I was exhausted and weeping. I was still crying when Arnold turned away, put on a jacket, slammed the door, and left me there. When he didn't come back by dark, I gathered my things and walked the three blocks to my apartment.

The doorman's name was Whitey, and he said nothing but hello as he opened the door. I was throbbing all over, so I was sure he knew everything, about my pregnancy, about the abortion and that he'd start yelling at me just as Arnold had. My friends Jon and Bob had already quit the drama school, and now I had decided I would. Before turning up for my summer job in the Berkshires, I flew to Chicago to visit Arnold. "Everything has changed, baby," he said on the phone. He had been fired from Yale—"I was too radical," he said—and now, in Chicago, he and his friend Paul Sills had started a theatre company called The Body Politic. Experimenting with the non-hierarchical, they wrote plays cooperatively, providing lines to be divided among the actors through a process of improvisation. The night I got there, Arnold didn't come home till dawn: "Rehearsal went late."

When I thought to go to Paul's wife Carol for solace, I did not know that a movement was beginning that would have helped me find a new way through all the confusion inside me, a way to assert my own first-person singular. In New York, Valerie Solanas, the same "crazy" woman who had almost killed Arnold's friend "Andy" Warhol, had written a feminist screed called the *SCUM Manifesto*, and a group had been founded called Redstockings (a takeoff on bluestockings). Right there in Chicago, radical women had formed an underground group called Jane to do, for many women, what I had done for my friend in New Haven and what money and a sympathetic psychiatrist had done for me. "Need an abortion? Call Jane," and a phone number, read scraps of paper posted and passed from woman to woman. Until *Roe v. Wade* passed the Supreme Court and legalized abortion in 1973, Jane secretly helped thousands of women find and pay for safe abortions with sympathetic doctors; eventually its members learned to perform safe abortions themselves.

I was looking for freedom. I wanted to go to New York and write—or I wanted to stay in Chicago and live with Arnold and write. (Did I think he'd suddenly stop criticizing my writing?) "Well," Carol Sills said, pushing a stroller; "Just get knocked up; then he'll marry you!" Well, I wasn't going to do that, I thought to myself, not telling her about my abortion. I asked Arnold if I could stay in Chicago; he refused me, addressing me with his most undercutting nickname for me, "I'll come visit you, Pussy."

I have a faint memory of telling both my parents about my abortion when we still lived in Washington, but I can't get back a conversation. I know that the one time my mother was advised to terminate a pregnancy, when she was pregnant with Marian, she refused—she was certain the complications would recede, and they did. In 1969, choice was not yet the complex issue it would become in the next fifty years. I did not tell my mother at the time because I was ashamed that I didn't know who the father was, and I knew, despite my broken heart, that I didn't want to marry Arnold. Or anyone, then. Thinking back on it now, I feel certain that she would have helped me make a decision, find a safe abortion. I understand now that I never wanted children and that my mother always wanted children and adored having them.

I was an artful dodger growing up in my mother's ideal, not a team player at *baseball*, or in the *small orchestra*, somehow always more physically awkward and too restless to play any instrument other than my own voice—I loved to sing. I found ways to spend time away from the house, never allowing any discontent to surface; it took decades even to admit to myself that I was a jealous sibling. Rethinking my childhood and its consequences for this book, I've had the shocking thought that if I were writing a tragedy in the manner of *King Lear,* I might think of my abortion as an act of revenge against my mother for having so many children. In my forties I made a friend, a successful film director who by choice had just one child; more than once she expressed her admiration and love for me by raising an idea that I found dizzying and utterly alien: "If I had been your mother," she would say, "I would never have had another child."

After the abortion, I did quit the drama school. After my final summer at the theater in the Berkshires, I decided to move to New York. Someone had told me about a place called the Chelsea Hotel, which had suites with kitchens; I called and made a reservation not only to live in the funky hotel, but to join the ranks of young women like me. I thought I was unbelievably brave, but the step I was taking was in no way unique or even unusual for a young woman of my generation. All that made me different was having the inheritance I'd come into at twenty-one, which made it easy for me to afford the then exorbitant rent of $250 a month. I was twenty-three, the age my mother was when she moved with my father and me to 447 West 21st Street. It was a 10-minute walk from where I now planned to begin my life as a writer.

VIII

Our Revolution

1.

MY MOTHER IS STANDING ON THE PORCH IN THE ADIRONDACKS, HER BACK to the lake.

The family place here is an old-fashioned camp, which my father's father and a group of his friends purchased for hunting and fishing in 1923. There are several cabins, a big kitchen building, and a living-room building with this porch outside it. Below that are a boathouse and docks that give onto a lake encircled by small mountains named for minerals—Copper, Silver, Iron. The other families are long gone now; for us it's a summer vacation place where we share and divide the time with cousins. My father came here every summer of his life, and my mother, every summer since I was born. It was the place where we marked the progress of our childhoods—where we swam and rowed, learned Liar's Dice and Scrabble, climbed mountains and played prisoner's base. Other than playing tennis on the dilapidated court, my mother didn't like being there much—too isolated; she looked awkward on hikes, but right at home lying on this porch reading. Once in a while though, she'd initiate "a new phase"—as when she conspired with my most mechanically minded cousin to purchase a motor boat (long forbidden by Gramps, now dead). The purpose was not to replace the old guide boats and canoes, but to institute water-skiing: Really, what's the point of the lake? She took up waterskiing with a competitor's panache, skimming the sparkling surface, one of my brothers steering the boat in fast, wide loops until she wiped out and rose amid our cheers to begin again.

Just now, with a friend, I'm setting up writing space in the dining room. We push the long table to make room, and as I turn, I feel my mother so powerfully I say, "My God, she's actually here." It's the end of August 1969, and I am walking toward her, along the boardwalk. The day is cloudy and she's wearing long pants and a crookedly buttoned cardigan. In my memory, what was meant to be a small goodbye before I left the camp became momentous; but at the time, I was simply leaving in half an hour for my new life. I think we must have talked a bit before she said it.

"I'm having some problems with my marriage."

I'm sure she thought she was confiding; I'm sure she needed to tell someone. I know now that for her to admit such a feeling to anyone was, at the time, brand new—part of what she was talking about when she told the oral historian she wanted to be more honest. But as with many revolutionary acts, there were unforeseen consequences.

I am having some problems with my marriage, said the mother. The daughter was so shocked she hardly understood what the mother was saying.

I don't remember what I said, but I do remember what I would have said if I'd had any idea what she was talking about. Didn't she know that this marriage belonged not only to her but to my father and to me and to my eight brothers and sisters? She looked so helpless there in her strange sweater, crooked because the wrong button was in the wrong hole.

I have the letter I wrote her two days later, and I remember writing it, sitting on a bed in Gordon and Masha's apartment in Cambridge—they were the couple who had taken care of me after the abortion, and now they were taking care of me again. I liked the way they lived, eating vegetables and brown rice, an apartment with no doors between rooms, calm, quiet voices. "Why don't you write your mother a letter?" Gordon may have said.

I wrote in turquoise felt tip on onionskin paper. What I had to say roared out of me:

September 4, 1969
Dear Mommy,
I'm sorry I was rude on the phone this morning, but I can't help
the fact that my feelings about you are extremely ambivalent at the
moment. I would have thought you might have gathered that my
decision not to go to Chicago to live with Arnold was not entirely a
happy one—

As I read it now, thinking of myself at twenty-three, I think that I must have wanted her, miraculously, to understand everything and make everything all right. What I said was that there was a lot she didn't know about me: "I want to know you as a person," I wrote, "but the mother-daughter thing confuses it a lot."

The anger that you have gotten & are beginning to get again now has
to do with my not having felt known & taken care of as your daughter, as a child & adolescent. I did try and make my terror of my plans
clear & my general unsteadiness must have been obvious—so then
you say (just ½ hour before I leave), "I am having some problems
with my marriage." Now, are you being a mother or a friend? And if
you are being the latter, do you have the right to be, to your daughter,
about the marriage that produced her? And as the mother, wouldn't

you have been more sensitive to her state of mind or something?" (It would have been different if you had said "Poppy & I are having a few problems with <u>our</u> marriage" for instance).

After I left her, I went straight to the Berkshires to pack up after the summer and managed to see a psychiatrist. I wanted her to imagine the worst, that I was turning into her manic-depressive, distressed mother and it was all her fault. How could she not know that everything in my life was falling apart: "Arnold, you, the end of school, the terror of beginning a new life."

At the end of the letter, I am merciful and proud: she should know that "I am very excited, happy & on the upswing" (the phrase she often used to describe the better phases of Margarett's psychological condition).

A week later, I got a letter from my father: "Sorry you have had such a rough time Chicago-wise etc. Things are a little bumpy here as I guess Mom indicated." Neither revealed any details: that she actually wanted to leave the marriage, that he was—"Very angry. Hurt . . . sometimes inside my spirit & sort of in my mind, and sometimes in my chest, hurting hurting hurting." The likelihood that he would be elected bishop of New York had precipitated a crisis. He could turn down the job, he reported my mother saying, "knowing I couldn't accept the suggestion." What if she wanted to stay in Washington? Nothing formal, rather living separate lives "sort of indefinitely until one of us wants to get married." At the time, canon law of the Episcopal church forbade divorce even among laypeople and priests, except with special permission—in practice, a divorced man could not be bishop. "I think I will put it to her," my father mused in a notebook, "would you want to leave the house if it meant leaving the children?" Of course there was always the chance he would not be elected.

Years later, I asked my sister Rosemary about that summer, and she reminded me it was the summer she and one of my brothers went to Europe with my parents, as Paul and Adelia and I had in 1960. They visited a friend on the Greek island of Hydra and then went on to Athens. My mother had an almost disabling toothache, Rosie remembered. Talking one day about those years, my aunt Margie remembered the toothache, and another story Jenny told her about that trip: that they were joined at the last minute one night at a restaurant by a younger Episcopal priest "and some other people." Such a coincidence that they were all in Athens at the same time! My mother did not consider it a coincidence, she told Margie. She felt, she said, "a frisson" between my father and the priest. Margie did not remember this detail until decades after my mother died: "I blocked it," she said.

Writing history requires putting one thing next to another thing. When my mother told me that morning in the Adirondacks that she was *having some problems* with her marriage, I could not imagine what was wrong because I had no other thing to put next to what she said. At the time, what my mother witnessed—a sexual moment between her husband and another man—had the disorienting power of an unexpected assault. How could she not have known this? And she had thought their sexual problems had been hers! "She told me she thought he was the unhappiest man she'd ever known and that he was homosexual," said one of the three women with whom I talked about my father's secret. "And so it was true," said Margie, "and I never believed her."

"Please go carefully if you write about it," said the third friend. "She did love him, and you owe it to your father." When I learned about his hidden life twenty years later, I had no judgment of my father—rather, a complicated blend of shock, sadness, and betrayal. Toward my mother, by then long dead, I felt a new mother-bear protectiveness.

In light of the incident at the café in Athens, what my mother had said to me that morning on the porch was a drastic understatement: *I am having some problems with my marriage.* Even though a sequence of moments had built to her conclusion, the actual realization must have seemed to come out of the blue, as if a cataclysmic storm could descend when the sky was pure blue and the sun was out. That she did not ever confront my father or reveal to any of her children her suspicions was certainly self-protective, but it was also an act of extraordinary generosity. My father was at the height of his heroism, about to enter the triumphant chapter of his life. *I thought I had to be ambitious for him, & I was:* that is her surviving statement on the matter. Her continuing silence was a choice—I found no mention of my father's sexual conflicts in any of her papers. If she ever wrote about it, she must have destroyed those pages before her death. I wonder when or if we would ever have talked about it.

Eighteen months after our moment on the porch, my mother will write me about *the play that is in my head "women, Mothers and Daughters"—I want to deal with who has a right to "hurt" whom? Can daughters "hurt" mothers or is that something else, like "acting out"? My thought of yesterday: set will be a lot of mirrors (among other things) some mirrors may get broken, etc. etc.* At my suggestion, she was reading *The Golden Notebook* by Doris Lessing, in 1970 the only novel around about contemporary women trying to hack out independent lives. Lessing used the phrase, "Free Women." And so, my mother and I began to stumble toward new terms of engagement—as *free women*.

2.

As I stood at the entrance of the Chelsea Hotel with my suitcases, I couldn't help noticing that all the writers commemorated there by bronze plaques were men and now dead—often of suicide—and that, like those men, I'd come here to write. In the lobby hung paintings by Arnold's best friend Larry Rivers, and in the elevator women my age with sunken eyes and dull blond hair looked up at the ceiling and scratched their forearms. That final spring at Yale, I'd fallen in with a group of people who wanted to be "brilliant writers," who were in graduate school solely to avoid the draft. My friend Bob Mandel had quit the school anyway, beginning years of changing his address—"I'd move before I got any mail from the draft board and send them a change of address form; eventually they gave up on me." Now he was in Massachusetts writing a novel, and he thought I should write one too, so I set myself up, turning my desk to face a pair of French windows that looked out on 23d Street. A few days a week, I went uptown to an office where I was raising money for the play I was coproducing with my friend Ann—we had hired a director and were looking for a theater.

What do I remember from that fall? For the first time, I ate Häagen-Dazs ice cream, which then had only three flavors: vanilla, chocolate, and boysenberry sherbet (sorbet but not yet called that). My first night in town, Ann and I had supper at a Japanese restaurant on Eighth Street, and an actor who had made his name off Broadway sat down with us. He had just turned down a part in a film, he was proud to tell us. Later he would become a movie star named Al Pacino. That summer, in the Berkshires, I'd met a writer named Venable, a playwright and screenwriter who had written a movie called *Alice's Restaurant*, about the draft and people I sort of knew in Stockbridge. I had a crush on him so I invited him to a party at my Berkshire rental; late in the evening, I asked to kiss him. He said no, he was living with someone. Couldn't we just have lunch? No. I talked to Ann about him all the time, shocked at the plots she devised to help me steal him from the girlfriend he was living with in Los Angeles. Once a week I went uptown to see my new psychiatrist.

And then one night, Arnold called from Chicago. He was coming into the city, did I want to have a drink? I hesitated, but within seconds acquiesced. We had dinner, and afterward, he came back to the Chelsea with me and we took the elevator to my room—lovers again, it seemed. He would be in town for several weeks, he said. He was translating the Bertolt Brecht–Kurt Weill opera *Mahagonny* for the man who had produced their legendary *Threepenny Opera*, which had run forever off-Broadway. Having Arnold in my bed put an end to my novel; again he ranted and raved about the irrelevance of anything I might write. I didn't have the strength to tell him I didn't want him to move in; and anyway, maybe now we would be together again and that awful brokenness I was still feeling would dissolve.

Soon all my hours were for him, listening to him on the phone with Larry Rivers or the producer called Carmen—an odd name for a man, I thought—or a poet named Kenneth (Koch, I learned when we had dinner with him) I took a break from coproducing the play, which was, I wrote my mother, "very funny, a panic" by a woman just five years older than me, a comedy about three women roommates in New York. I told my psychiatrist I couldn't be sure Arnold and I wouldn't get married. I don't remember if I typed up his translations of Kurt Weill's lyrics, but I might have. I would go with him to the producer's high-ceilinged apartment on West 10th Street, sit and wait for hours while they worked out the translation of another song (the producer played the piano). Then Arnold and I would have late supper at a place called Casey's—Casey was Japanese, and the restaurant was French and delicious; an expensive meal was $10. Afterward maybe we would go to Bradley's, the jazz bar a friend of Arnold's had opened on University Place. Though I considered myself barely corporeal as I sat through those smoky evenings, most of the people I met in those days remembered me when I met them later in New York. Others I read about in the *New York Times* decades later when they died: Paul Desmond, Elvin Jones, Iris Owens, Bradley Cunningham. Some of the poets I met then, I got to know later: John Ashbery, Kenneth Koch, Anne Waldman, Harry Mathews. All of them were still talking about someone named Frank—a poet named Frank O'Hara who had died in 1966.

It took only days for the romantic idyll to end, and a week for the sex to wind down, but Arnold stayed on. "I'm at the Chelsea," I'd hear him say on the phone, at night find myself in bed alone after midnight waiting for the sound of his key in the lock. "I've got to work late on a song," he'd say, calling at 2 a.m. "I'll be home in no time, Pussy." (How I hated to be called that.) My psychiatrist declared Arnold "exploitative" and advised that I ask him to move out.

I didn't need to; he soon left abruptly for Chicago, and in November I visited him there for a long weekend. Pam and Jim Morton lived there now, and I had tea with Pam while Arnold was teaching a class. It felt comforting to talk to someone I had always known, since Arnold was, as usual, barely present. The only letter I have from Pam to my mother is about that visit: "He sounds brilliant, but I can certainly get the picture of how complicated it all is, as Honor herself was the first to say. I think that the visit was really hard for her—not entirely sure why, but his preoccupation with the job + her having to pitch in + be supportive when she felt like being supported (how's that for a marriage in-spite-of-itself situation) had something to do with it, I gather."

Pam's take on the situation was pitch perfect. I was using every bit of my imagination to act as if I was not unhappy the entire time I was there. Arnold was not affectionate, he did not take me with him to rehearsals, and he kept saying that I didn't "help" enough. I didn't know quite what he meant since I had unpacked all the books and records, including my full set of the Beatles, bought bookshelves and put all the books away, and scoured the kitchen, scrubbing and arranging, while he went off to teach, only to return hours late and fall immediately asleep. Soon I was back in New York, having agreed to sublet his apartment on 13th Street. Actually, I wanted to stay at the Chelsea, but I couldn't bear the thought of separating from Arnold so I rented his "great place" for $150 a month.

It was a bit ratty—uncomfortable battered furniture, his books, tired dishtowels, his paintings: a small Jane Freilicher landscape, an Andy Warhol silk screen of the exploding atom bomb—black on brown paper—that I rolled up and stowed beneath the desk. The apartment was a floor-through. In the room you entered, there was a round table— "Moroccan," Arnold said—and a small kitchenette off to one side. "Isn't the terrace great!" he exclaimed the first time he called. I never used the terrace, which was the tarred roof of the Italian restaurant beneath—it got sticky when it was hot outside. I was used to terraces of flagstone, like the one at Hollow Hill that was shaded by espaliered apple trees.

Soon, Arnold promised, he'd be back for rehearsals of *Mahagonny* and my certain reign at his side, girlfriend to genius. One day late that fall, I was visiting friends on the Upper West Side when another friend turned up from Chicago with the news that Arnold had married a woman named Suzanne. Could this be true? Yes. Wasn't I living in his apartment, waiting for his return? Hadn't he called me just last week, the same sexy endearments? Now it was all I could do to keep myself from weeping in front of my former teacher, his lover, and my classmate who had delivered the news. How could I have been so stupid? Those long nights "teaching," he'd been with Suzanne!

Do you have fantasies, my psychiatrist asked? I said I could see myself with a gun, pointing it at Arnold from a vantage point on my bed. Is that a fantasy? The psychiatrist smiled and nodded. I also had fantasies about Arnold and his new wife, which I tried to banish. Once I was finished crying, I began to write enraged fragments that wished to be poems and piled them on the Moroccan table. Some days that fall I'd go downtown to Wooster Street and sit in on rehearsals of a dramatization of *Naked Lunch* that some fellow drama school dropouts were putting on. It was one day that fall that I drove a bunch of us up to Vassar to see the Open Theater and first heard of a movement called women's liberation—it turned up soon after in the *Village Voice*—a long article about something called an abortion speakout.

My abortion had been safe, and I hadn't died; I couldn't possibly belong at such an event. I was too embarrassed by my clearly retro connection to Arnold to seek out the feminists, but I did once meet a lawyer named Flo Kennedy—later she said that because I'd asked her where to find the Black Panthers, she thought I was an informer. I tried to put my heart-break behind me as I did my work on the play, brightly optimistic. My mother had sent in a $750 investment toward the $4,000 I had to raise. For comfort, I went to New Haven to visit my friend Lily, an African American woman whose Black Panther husband was in jail; I had helped her financially after their son was born. I showed her my poems and she took me to a poetry reading in a bar where there was an open mic—there I stood and read my own poems for the first time, brittle and furi-ous. When I finished, Lily clapped loudly and assured me that someday Arnold would regret losing me. Decades later she was proved correct; but at the time, I believed that I was a failure as a radical and a woman and that my writing was nothing Arnold would ever appreciate. "You're not writing for him," Lily would say. "You're doing it for yourself." A good idea, I thought; why couldn't I feel it?

It took decades, but Arnold and I cautiously became a version of friends, and he'd tell me repeatedly what a terrible mistake he'd made all those years ago. When his translation of *Mahagonny* was finally performed at the Metropolitan Opera sometime in the 1990s, I went to the opening, the old sorrow washed away when, weeping, he took a tuxedoed bow on the stage with the conductor. By then in his seventies, he could still make me laugh in that old particular way. Years later, months before he died, I ran into him on the street, and he insisted I sit down with him for a cup of coffee. I had only 15 minutes before an appointment, but I happened to have a galley proof of a new book of my poems, which I gave to him.

"I love you and I have always loved you," he said, taking my hands. "I'm so sorry I hurt you so much, and I'm very happy you found your way to poetry." It was the last time I saw him. How had this man, so old and tired, ever caused me such pain? In that moment, I was much closer to how he had inspired my writing than I was to the great heartbreak that defined my first years in New York.

3.

Living in Arnold's apartment on 13th Street, I was now reading everything I could about women's liberation. My favorite periodical, which felt as forbidden as pornography, was a Boston journal called *No More Fun and Games*: one article I read there advocated doing away with men altogether—"On Celibacy," it was called. Soon after, a friend from Radcliffe took me to a meeting of a group of radical journalists, and some of the women I met there invited me to join a "small group"—as consciousness-raising groups were then called. My poems were getting angrier, and I was beginning to think about women in relationship to their own power. "What about Queen Victoria?" one of my Yale professors asked when I announced I was part of women's liberation. "Well," I said, surprised when he actually listened, "the power wasn't really hers; she was an instrument of patriarchy."

I understood that my father was also an instrument of patriarchy; but to me, he was of course an exception. Now the news came that he really might be elected Episcopal bishop of New York—he was one of three finalists, and we would know in December. Now, on the actual day of a huge peace demonstration in Washington, he was turning fifty, and my mother was putting on a big party. The house was the unofficial political headquarters for anyone who knew anyone in our family. Yes, my mother said, of course, bring as many friends as you want. Sleeping bags and neighbors' houses were commandeered. She was in her element, her highly organized, excellent motherhood fused with her politics. I remember the energy of her welcome and excitement as I came into the house. Did I drive down? My former writing teacher and his partner were with me. Did we stay in sleeping bags in the house? Early Saturday morning, on foot, we solemnly headed out to the march, walking along the Mall toward the Washington Monument, the Capitol, the White House. Just three days before, on November 12, an article by the reporter Seymour Hersch broke in the *St. Louis Post-Dispatch* with news of what came to be called the My Lai Massacre; the peace talks in Paris were stalled over procedure; and the United States, under the leadership of now President Nixon, was bombing the Ho Chi Minh supply trail in Laos. Half a million of us marched that day, which I remember as crisp and sunny.

The door was wide open at Newark Street when we returned from the march. The demonstration had been the largest since the civil rights march five years earlier, and there was a new sense of hope. The house filled, the crowd directed by handwritten signs my siblings had posted everywhere: "Don't let the dog out"; "Downstairs WC here," with a red arrow pointing upstairs. My father looked sweet and dazed, and my mother had her smile on. Supper took place in the big kitchen with the black-and-white floor, the German beer table, extra chairs, people sitting on the floor on pillows; I think we had spaghetti and a big salad. "No Bob Dylan," said one of the signs—my mother's humor. The song of the hour, "Give Peace a Chance," had just been recorded by John Lennon and Yoko Ono. There was plenty to eat despite the crowd, the birthday cake ordered from University Pastry, which also had the best vanilla ice cream ever. On the cake, HAPPY BIRTHDAY POPPY, with fifty candles and one to grow on—hilarious because he was already so tall. Two weeks after the demonstration, the Selective Service instituted a lottery system to choose recruits, and my brother Paul drew a number that kept him at home. American dead numbered 9,400 for the year 1969, and 475,000 American troops were still in Vietnam.

On December 10, the Diocese of New York, the largest and most urban in the Episcopal Church, elected my fifty-year-old father its new bishop. Days afterward the Potters threw a party at their apartment on East End Avenue, the East River right out the window, blinking lights reflected, the gray water. The Potters had been friends of my parents for so long, they were like family. I remember bursting through the door: Mrs. Potter, blond and fast-talking, and Mr. Potter, with a proud expression befitting the occasion, hugging me; my mother and father together and all smiles. I was excited for my father, and I was also relieved—it didn't look like a divorce or even a separation was underway. I thought this would be a new beginning, and so did my mother, she wrote later. I watched her in the room, all laughter and greeting, moving among old friends. She was excited about what the life of the family could be here, and she was starting to think about a new book. My father was happy but also solemn—or had my sense of him changed? He'd hardly seemed majestic in Washington— more a dashing man on the rise—but now he would be "diocesan," which meant bishop in charge: "The greatest fulfillment for one who had devoted his life to the work of the church in the city," he wrote later. His home church would now be St. John the Divine, unfinished at 112th and Amsterdam and the largest Gothic structure in the world.

I felt important being this father's daughter, but again I felt caught in a contradiction. Surely being pleased about my father's ascension in the patriarchy was against the rules of the movement I was becoming part of. On the other hand, despite joking to my friends that my enormous family's arrival in New York would cramp my new independence, I was happy they were coming. Gone from my mind was *I'm having some problems with my marriage*. What would it be like to go uptown for supper once in a while? I would tell my mother about the women's movement, what my consciousness group was like; and we could talk about *The Second Sex* by Simone de Beauvoir, which I was finally reading. The siblings who'd been so little when I left home six years before were now growing into people—my sister Marian was almost fifteen, my brother Danny twelve, the little girls eight and ten! I'd get to know them.

My mother wound herself up. She was of course sad about leaving Washington, but if she was seriously ambivalent, she did not reveal it to me. She went into gear, writing letters to me about who would sleep in what room, the colors of curtains and carpets and rugs. Since my father would be coadjutor—assistant bishop with the right of succession in a year—the family would not yet live in the bishop's house behind the cathedral, but in three floors of a mansion at the center of the close; the first floor was offices. In square footage, the apartment was by far the largest place my mother had ever moved the family into, but it was also a little on the gloomy, looming side—she'd paint the dark paneling white and the kitchen orange. There was no good public school if you lived at 110th and Amsterdam, so my mother asked around and made a list of possibilities. One day, with Marian, Danny, and George, she took the train to New York to investigate: Elizabeth Irwin; Little Red Schoolhouse; Dalton, which Marian remembered had carpets; and New Lincoln, which was, by contrast, "in flux" and conveniently located on 110th Street and 5th Avenue. The student body was 30 percent black and 60 percent Jewish. The white WASP Moores would be in a minority.

Thursday, the children went back to Washington on the train, and my mother flew to Boston to visit her mother. She was now living in an apartment jammed with paintings and sculpture—hers and those she had collected—above the Public Garden, close to where she'd lived as a child. Three strokes had confined Margarett to a wheelchair, and she could no longer manage Prides; but after years spent in and out of private mental hospitals, she had a home again—she could have parties, hold court. Margie was in charge of her care, and my mother visited once every few months. Shaw telephoned every Sunday, and Harry visited when he came to Boston from where he now lived, in Jamaica. The siblings had periodic conversations: Was the chauffeur working out? (He was a retired Episcopal priest.) How could they get her to stop shouting at the nurses? Spending so much money? But the situation was becoming manageable;

there was a new doctor, and finally drugs for manic-depressive illness. My mother reported occasional good news, but her mother could still infuriate her—as when she ordered fifty copies of *The People on Second Street*, inscribed them as if she were the author, and sent them to friends. *Can you believe it! It was MY book!* my mother fumed, though at Margarett's bedside, she bit her lip and said nothing.

My mother's two-hour flight back to Washington was easy, and it was a Saturday. Bob Amory, an old friend, was on the plane. She couldn't wait to get home; she was 20,000 words into writing a novel, racing to get *something down* before the move—it's the only entity among her papers that was lost. Did she write on the plane, or did she talk to Bob Amory? He was from Boston, had been in the CIA, and must have known Cord Meyer. He had his car at the airport, and he said, he could give her a ride home.

It was January 10, 1970, and I was standing in my apartment on 13th Street.

At a four-way stop, a car had run a stop sign and hit Bob Amory's Volkswagen. My mother was thrown forward onto the gearshift stick; Mr. Amory was okay, and she wasn't hurt either, just a little pain in her lower gut. The police drove her home; my father was waiting at the door and they were going out to supper. Yes, of course she wanted to go; she felt fine. But while getting dressed, she fell across the bed in sudden enormous pain. She'd be *fine* in just a second. But she couldn't stand up. My father called an ambulance.

In my apartment on 13th Street, the telephone rang. It was my father. He said it wasn't clear if she would live.

In that split second, everything changed.

My mother had a phrase for it: *the end of an era.*

4.

A few unchangeables in hosp: jello cut in squares stays in squares—tastes like melted lollipops but may be picked up like a shrimp on a toothpick after long hours. It's ten days after the surgery: *Do you like hospital work?"* she asks a nurse. *I don't like it, I love it. How many children do you have? Nine. My mother had nine,* the nurse says, *5 girls, 4 boys.*

She will always say that Dr. Bremer saved her life when the odds were almost entirely against her. The surgery involved cutting away the ruptured and damaged liver and leaving the healthy three-tenths to regenerate. "It is the only human organ that can," is a fact I saved in a poem.

For days it was almost certain she would die, and my father and I, and others of the children, visited her in intensive care.

But she didn't plan to die: *I never doubted I would get well. I never for one instant believed that my strength would be permanently impaired or that in my weakened condition the seeds of future illness might find a growing space.*

In a letter from her lover, now returned to her life, I find that by January 14, she is "out of danger." When she was out of intensive care, I flew down again—so happy to see her there, lying in a hospital bed, surrounded by flowers, thin and only intermittently present but certainly alive. I don't remember how many times I flew to Washington, but she seemed better on each visit, even starting to talk about plans for New York, what the children would do there, how she would work into her new life the time for writing.

Day after day in a hospital bed in a big room, windows, color television—so luxurious I'm thinking there was even a fireplace. Many visitors, the children rushing in and out, the older ones visiting from out of town, friends, priests, my father back and forth from New York and St. John the Divine, where he was intensely involved in meetings for his new job.

And there were hours of solitude, long stretches of time that she didn't have energy to read or even watch television, hours to consider her life, her close call with death. *I knew always the boundaries of emotional frailty, but until then I drew those lines on a different page from physical confidence, with a kind of arrogance.*

Or courage? And why should she not have physical confidence? Her lover wrote her the letters she later destroyed.

Over and over, she took inventory of her marriage, but whenever she worked out a way she might leave my father while holding onto a situation in which the children would have both parents, she saw that it couldn't work and put it aside. *I thought I had to be ambitious for him, & I was.* Also, she didn't want to hurt him.

Ten weeks she stayed there, and sometime in May it was time to go home.

I left the hospital with 80% of my liver newly regenerated, weak, but assured that each day I would feel better.

It seems mad now, the idea of moving a household and five children less than a year after almost dying.

The lover came to visit, and after she left the hospital, there came the *great resurgence* in their relationship.

On March 10, 1970, a Federal-era rowhouse on West 11th street in Manhattan was destroyed by a bomb, and two of three SDS Weatherman bombers were killed. It was an accident, the bombs planned for other locations—a servicemen's dance at Fort Dix, an administration building at Columbia. The Weatherman slogan was "Bring the War Home." The bombed house was less than three blocks from where I lived. Two of the bombers were friends of a close friend of mine at Yale, and one of the women had gone to Madeira, the same boarding school as my mother. I was becoming friends with a woman my age who had gone to Swarthmore and was out on bail, indicted in another bombing conspiracy. She had been a classics major; wanting to write was what we had in common. The idea of making or planting a bomb was completely outside what I believed in, though at the time, the radical commitment of my new friend and of those who had died seemed admirably pure.

That April 10, the play I coproduced off Broadway opened and closed in one night. Its author Tina Howe wasn't present at the opening, because she was giving birth to her first child. I remember a friend from Yale passing me in the lobby after the show: "You guys are nuts," she said, leaving very quickly. She did not believe the critics would respond to a play in which two men licked whipped cream off a naked woman while her roommates watched, even if the play was a satire of Upper East Side dating life. She was correct, but I had an explanation that fit into my evolving women's liberation critique of power relations: it was a play by a woman and the critics were male. Even now, I believe their reviews were gratuitously hostile; but I also remember having a sinking sensation, when performances began, that the production did not represent the wild absurdist feminism that had attracted me to the play.

My mother was still in the hospital, and now my brother Paul, who was living in Berkeley, was in the hospital too; he had collapsed with a serious case of tuberculosis. My father flew to California and got him settled in a TB ward in Marin County; my mother would visit in June. I was planning a trip to visit him that summer; but one afternoon, Venable Herndon called—my crush from the Berkshires. The success of his movie *Alice's Restaurant*, based on the anti-draft song by Arlo Guthrie and directed by Arthur Penn (whose previous film was *Bonnie and Clyde*), meant he had lots of screenwriting opportunities. But he hated Los Angeles and had moved back to New York—would I like to have dinner? We went to a Spanish restaurant in the Village and he told me about everything: his work in advertising, his early marriage to a much older woman, the daughter he'd recently discovered was his, the successful play that had led to his writing *Alice's Restaurant*. Afterward, in his loft on 14th Street, we made love all night in a bed surrounded by white organza curtains. He'd be in touch, he said when we parted. He was breaking up with his girlfriend; it wouldn't be long. I was blasé—I was used to waiting for love.

I flew to California a week later to visit Paul, stopping first in Los Angeles to visit an actress friend from Yale. During the day, while she was in rehearsal, I read *Living My Life*, the two-volume autobiography of Emma Goldman—a feminist who was a revolutionary anarchist. I recognized some names in the cast of characters, among them Henry Frick, the steel tycoon whose house on the North Shore in Massachusetts was next door to Rockmarge, my father's grandparents' house. Emma Goldman's reading of the twentieth century was new to me; I could now clearly see that I was a daughter of what my friends called the ruling class. I couldn't put the book down; her thinking was closer to what I believed than anything I had yet read. Emma Goldman was a revolutionary who cared about women, about birth control, and her lover was her equal and comrade. I read all day out by the pool, as sun poisoning scarred my chest.

I carried Red Emma with me to Berkeley—did I stay in my brother's apartment there? Every day for two weeks, I drove across the Richmond Bridge to sit by his bed in the tuberculosis ward. He was very skinny, but he was in less pain now and less scared than when I'd first talked to him on the phone. He was sweetly welcoming, and newly in love with Debra Busta—also present at his bedside—whom he would marry. But also, I soon learned, he was very angry. He was angry about the war, and his political differences with my father had intensified, becoming a fury that scared me. Somehow I was too frightened to identify with him. In that moment, it didn't occur to me that I'd been just as angry at our mother, had wanted from her the same thing Paul now wanted from both our parents—more attention, more care, more presence. His future was in shambles. He had loved his work for McCarthy and McGovern and planned to continue, at least for a while, in politics. But his body had betrayed him. The day he received his TB diagnosis, Senator McGovern himself called to offer him a senior staff position in his 1972 presidential primary campaign, and of course he'd had to refuse. Was I really going to write? It was the era of seeing who could be more radical, and my brother's political passion and his judgment of our parents made me feel guilty, fraudulent about my politics.

After leaving Berkeley, I stopped in Colorado to visit some radical movement friends from New York who were moving to St. Louis that fall to start a collective, taking jobs and organizing workers. I had purposely not given my mother my itinerary, but finally I did call her. She wrote me right back: *I always panic when I don't know how to get hold of you. I asked Paul two or three times and finally he said, "I think it's General Delivery, Evergreen," and at that point, you called.* I remember sunbathing topless with the other women there—we were no longer girls—talking about a new book that had just come out: *Sexual Politics*, by Kate Millet, and insisting the men also cook and wash dishes.

Have you read Millet? asked my mother's next letter.

I'd sent Venable some of my poems, and when I got back to New York there was a formal note: "Your poems bring to mind Pablo Neruda," or words to that effect. I knew he was overpraising, but he was taking my writing seriously. I immediately read Neruda. I couldn't quite see what Venable meant except that my lines were also short, but I wanted to learn what he had to teach me about writing poems. He'd once been an editor of a literary magazine called *Chelsea Review,* I remembered. It seemed foretold that I would spend another night making love with this man with ruffly dark brown hair and blue eyes who was so kind and seemed to know about everything. I assumed he was significantly younger than Arnold, but his dark shiny hair and unlined face had deceived me. I'd sworn to stay away from older men, but by the time Venable told me he was exactly Arnold's age, I had fallen for his attentiveness, his ability to read and speak Russian and French, his skill as a screenwriter with a hit movie, and his expertise about poetry. I couldn't wait to introduce him to my parents.

5.

It was ghastly leaving the house on Newark St., my mother wrote Pam. Georgia Borum, who had been our housekeeper all the years we lived there, *came to say goodbye stoned, and that was depressing if understandable. Patience commented that it must have made it easier for her.* And Mrs. Gill, the mother of our babysitters Gloria Gill and Dorothy Waddell, *drove up from South Carolina to pick up a rug & some other things I gave her & said she never expected a white woman would be a mother to her daughters*—my mother loved the compliment—*it set me up for a week.*

Four months earlier she had been close to death; three months earlier, still in the hospital. No one suggested it was too soon for her to undertake a move.

Mr. Dudman drove her to the airport. It seemed so odd, meeting moving trucks again, on a hot street in a part of New York City that was so alien. *The move was pretty grueling but accomplished, in that week of 93°, smog, squatters hurling human you-know-what at the cathedral doors etc.* My father had heard news of the demonstration on the radio while still driving north on the New Jersey Turnpike; until he learned that the buildings in question were at 112th and Amsterdam, he thought it was John Lindsay's problem. Just arrived, my father was deep into his first New York City crisis. Apparently, when the diocese considered tearing down two tenements to build elderly housing, they hadn't considered the present occupants.

My mother, meanwhile, was greeting the movers—*hopelessly muddled, walking up 2 flights of stairs with one bed slat*—*"Where does this go, lady?"* She managed to get through the first day; she was now, she wrote Pam, at a *plateau where one night of sleep cures the day's fatigue as opposed to 3 days of hysteria*—meaning weeping from exhaustion?—*The rooms are all bright Moore colors, and our bulky furniture looks well in the high-stud room. The kitchen is pretty grim but yellow and orange plus a few of the old mementos—* the Jersey City sugar bowl—*cheered it up.* She was writing at the end of July; after the move they'd gone to the Adirondacks. My mother, barely recovered herself, was concerned, she wrote Pam, that Paul was already working too hard—the old fatigue. As for the children:

> *At this moment I feel good about all nine. George has been in England & Ireland with a friend, winding up at a work camp in Wales. Rosie has been on a kibbutz in Israel—adores the physical labor. Classic comment in one letter: "I am going to hitchhike to Jerusalem in a few weeks. Mommy, in your next letter, will you tell me the name of the hill where Jesus was crucified, the streets where they threw the palms at him & other points of interest?"*

Adelia (no longer "Dee") was just back from Cuba, where she had spent ten weeks cutting sugarcane with the Venceremos Brigade: *a really freeing experience*, my mother wrote Pam—*she is lovely, soft, understanding of others*—living in Boston now with Tom, whom she would marry two years later: *2 pots, an orange crate for a bureau & about 3 garments.* My brother Paul, out of the TB ward, was also living with the person he would marry—Debra—*in Berkeley, working in a TV research group and studying. Honor is freer and tougher than I've ever seen her. A little overboard (I think) on Women's Lib & Black Panther fund-raising, but who knows?*

I was working with a group of women to free one of the two women in the Panther 21—members of the Black Panthers who had been arrested, falsely it would turn out, for conspiracy to bomb targets in New York. Joan Bird was a nursing student, younger than we were, just a girl, nothing like the other woman of the 21: Afeni Shakur was a natural star, intellectually sophisticated, articulate, charismatic—and pregnant with the future rapper, Tupac Shakur. Our goal was to integrate more consciousness of racism into the growing women's movement. We published a beautiful brochure and distributed it around the city, and every day a few of us monitored the trial. We were there especially for Joan and her family, but we soon knew all the lawyers, everyone "at court"—even the glamorous Panthers themselves. I was chosen to visit Joan in the Women's House of Detention, which I did two or three times. When we finally raised money for her bail, I was chosen to accompany Joan's parents to her release—reporters and photographers gathered as we pushed through. Behind Joan, in the *Time* magazine photograph, you can see half of me—very long hair, very short Marimekko dress.

There's a photograph of me in sunglasses on the porch in the Adirondacks, taken that summer, a copy of *The Second Sex* on my lap. I seem happy, a different creature than I'd been the previous August when my mother made the dire announcement about her marriage. The family stayed on for Labor Day weekend, but I was in Philadelphia at the Revolutionary People's Convention called by the Black Panther Party. Their "minister of defense" Huey P. Newton had been released from prison, and soon after had made a declaration declaring gay and women's liberation in line with the party's program. I wanted so much for it to be true that the movement I was part of was opening up, that it might be possible to draft a constitution that would secure economic justice and rights for everyone.

The arena was filled with movement people, black and white, men and women—some older people, but mostly people more or less my age. A crackle of excitement cut the humid summer air with the tiny hope that people might come together; I ran into a friend from Harvard and a woman from my camp counseling days. I see now that I have always been a romantic, expecting reality to manifest exactly as I imagine it—this inclination applied to politics as well as love. Having gazed for months at the iconic poster of Huey Newton in the peacock wicker chair that hung in every movement office, I imagined a god; but Huey was quite small in stature and seemed fragile, weakened I was sure by prison. I have a vague memory of his speaking, but not of what he said. And I have only a hazy sense of the workshop room where I must have sat, trying to work out a passage for the new constitution, detailing women's rights.

Back from Philadelphia Sunday night, I spent Labor Day lying on my bed on 13th Street. The room was hot and tiny, the bed just a mattress on a piece of plywood raised from the floor I don't remember how. I had lost touch with myself, I would have said then—even in the consciousness-raising group, which I faithfully attended, I didn't seem myself. My psychiatrist was on his August break, and in any case I never called him. I could feel myself breaking apart. Where were my friends? I don't know who I would have called right then. *Tougher and freer than I've ever seen her,* my mother had written—that wasn't how I felt. I'd left home for college six years earlier, and now, abruptly, my family was about to be very present. I thought I wanted to get to know them, but was that lovely sentiment really how I felt? The problem wasn't my family, though; it was that I didn't know what I was doing.

In movement meetings, we were always talking about the idea of collective action. The gathering in Philadelphia, so thrilling in my imagination, had in reality confirmed my uneasy feeling that in political meetings I too often conformed what I said and thought to a particular "line." I had grown up reciting prayers from the prayer book with the rest of a congregation, but when my mind wandered in church, no one judged me, and I came to accept my imagining as part of the experience of praying. All those lives of saints my mother read to me had remained with me, their individual acts of courage and faith vivid touchstones. Shyly, I began to suggest in meetings that collectivity might not mean that all of us should believe the same thing, that more durable power would come when each member contributed individual thinking. "All power to the imagination," students had shouted in Paris; it was the first slogan I ever really loved, inspiring what was truly individual in each of us. But I wanted to be the perfect radical, so I rarely insisted.

That fall a thick engraved invitation arrived on 13th Street—Mayor John Lindsay and his wife Mary were giving a formal welcome dinner for my father and mother. I felt a surge of excitement—Gracie Mansion!—then a sinking feeling: the invitation was evidence that I was part of the "ruling class," and anyway, wasn't I supposed to think of the mayor as "a pig" even though he was trying to do good things? I was in tears when I confessed the invitation to a woman in my consciousness-raising group—she had grown up poor; certainly she would judge me. "Of course, go," she tenderly said; "I[t will be wonderful!" I remember the candlelit dining table, my mother glamorous on my father's arm, a diverse two dozen of my parents' friends, all of us sitting outdoors on the lawn afterward, lights of boats passing on the East River. The roar of traffic on FDR Drive beneath us was muted, it seemed, by the balmy air and a romantic starry sky.

For decades after we left Washington, I would meet people I didn't know who told me they had "lived with your family" during the McCarthy campaign; for a semester of graduate school; for "a month after dropping out of college when I was hardly speaking to my parents." The cathedral apartment seemed so empty. Unaccountably, my mother had hired a Chinese couple *to do everything*, as she put it to Pam. The two lived in a separate apartment off the kitchen. Mrs. Chang barely spoke, and Mr. Chang was *a jolly, warm, father-figure type, thrilled to come to NY & has a car he can keep on the Close.* She closed the letter to Pam with news from Newark Street: *The Diocese had some men come by and rip from my side porch all the ivy that I had nurtured all those years, so that put me in a temporary fury.*

I had lunch from time to time with my mother, and that fall, she announced she wanted to give me a party for my twenty-fifth birthday in the high-ceilinged living room. I was to invite anyone I wanted to. All women, I decided—she loved the idea. I invited my consciousness-raising group, and my mother invited a young writer she wanted me to meet—the daughter of Mrs. Cade, who'd taught arts and crafts at Grace Church. Her daughter's name was Toni; and soon, as Toni Cade Bambara, she edited an anthology of black feminist writing and began to publish short stories—that day she gave me a teak cigarette box. Everyone sang happy birthday, and after the cake, I opened my mother's present—four leather scrapbooks, each a different color. She'd enlarged and copied photographs from the family scrapbooks: of Margarett young and beautiful, myself on a pony at Hollow Hill, my father's portrait of me at ten in Kent, herself in riding clothes sitting with her sister on a stone wall. She was offering a version of where I had come from. On the inside back cover of the yellow book—the others were green and blue and orange—she'd pasted half a page from snipped from a copy of *The Scarlet Letter*.

> Women, more especially, in the continually recurring trials of wounded, wasted, wronged, misplaced, or erring and sinful passion—or with the dreary burden of a heart unyielded because unvalued and unsought—came to Hester's cottage demanding why they were so wretched, and what the remedy. Hester comforted and counseled them as best she might and she assured them too of her firm belief that, at some brighter period, when the world should have grown ripe for it, in Heaven's own time, a new truth would be revealed, in order to establish the whole relation between men and women on a surer ground of mutual happiness.

To find this, written a hundred years earlier by Nathaniel Hawthorne! And to know how much my mother understood. I was overwhelmed. This mother was new, reaching toward me out of some long-ago moment in imagination and a shared history that, in my young womanhood, I had yet to reckon with. Was it possible that a mother and a daughter might move together into a brave and untried future? At twenty-five, I had no inkling of the resonance these ideas already had for my mother. My thinking about women's freedom had not been tested, but she'd had twenty-six years of marriage, nine children, and an encounter with mortality. I did not see that she was already wrestling with the possibility of a drastic change in her life, or that she was aware of the risks of staying the established course: *My own sense of obligation,* she wrote of this time, *that my husband's job came first, the long accepted assumption that moving from city to city was part of my life, and a belief that somehow New York as a new home would sew together some of the frayed edges of my life—writing projects had been interrupted by my accident; children were growing older; and in middle age, marital problems were more acute. Somehow, I rationalized, New York City, even a third floor apartment in a palatial church building at 110th and Amsterdam Avenue, could represent a new start. But I had all too willingly pushed myself too far.*

6.

My new psychiatrist had met my mother somewhere and said she was "very seductive." She called me and said, "I met Doctor G. He's very nice." What does *seductive* mean, I asked myself? I was trying to keep from getting angry at her again. I ignored it when she told me she hated living in the cathedral close even though I knew what she meant; it was a little like living in a monastery—"patriarchal," I might say later; "gyno-phobic," I would say even later. There were priests all over, all men, often sweeping around in black or purple cassocks that almost touched the ground. There were no women priests, of course. I wasn't even thinking of the possibility—my psyche still held to a wacky patriarchal assumption: the fewer women there were in a place, the closer it was to God.

One of the priests who lived on the close had a Doberman pinscher, and one day my mother watched from the window as the Doberman attacked a smaller dog and killed it. For hours, she couldn't stop crying. She believed it was *a sign.* She began to wear a sleep mask. "A sleep mask?" I asked Marian. "Yes, she couldn't sleep, and white gloves so she wouldn't bite her nails." An unthinkable idea took root: She'd take the children back to Washington; she could have a garden there; my father could commute. She and my father began to talk about it, fight about it. *I have been so desperately unhappy here that I know I can't cope*, she wrote him, comparing how she felt to his exhaustion at the end of Jersey City. My father, too, seemed lost, dazed. What about living elsewhere in Manhattan? He found a realtor and began to look on Park Avenue, not far from where she had lived awaiting my birth.

No matter how she tried to make it clear, didn't really understand what she was feeling, that it was herself she felt slipping away. She wrote about it later.

> *New York frightened her, but everyone said New York was frightening. "You just have to find your own thing and you'll like it." Her children were unhappy and homesick for Washington which had been home for so long (it's not geography people would tell her later). And they were afraid of the bus, that it would not stop at their corner, offended by the dirt, touched to their core by the suffering they saw on 110th Street and had only heard about before.*
>
> *They will adjust, children always do, people said.*

The truth was, Susanna and Patience loved their school, and the other three liked theirs well enough. Rosemary was at boarding school in Arizona. The problem was not school or 110th Street. The problem was that our mother wasn't herself; she knew that, she wrote later, but we didn't: *New York—everything—physical strength, "home," beauty of nature in Washington, street life & friendships, faith, relationship—was taken away in one big wrench.* The belief in God that had always sustained her was dissolving. Was this a response to the sequence of losses, or was she actually losing her faith?

She began to see an older woman psychoanalyst on East 91st Street and old friends for lunch. Women friends, especially became newly important. Her editor introduced her to Jane Howard, the writer from *Life* magazine: "Fascinating," she told me; and a friend put her in touch with Barbara Epstein, co-editor of the *New York Review of Books*—"I liked her so much." But there was no one, not even the psychiatrist, to whom she believed she could reveal everything. She barely had language for it: "I always thought your mother was going to tell me something," Polly Kraft, a friend from Washington, said, "but she never did." "I know what a private person you are," another friend wrote; "There was so much I was afraid to ask."

She found a group of radical Episcopalians who met on the Upper West Side, but after a few meetings she stopped going. She went on a gestalt therapy weekend, which she liked so much that she sent Marian (aged fourteen) and George (sixteen) to the next one; maybe if they learned early about their inner lives: *Desperate last-ditch attempts at instant salvation from outside—a new psychiatrist, an encounter group weekend, an evening with some Jesus people, contract for a book I didn't want to write, a three day affair with someone I didn't care about and knew was involved with someone else.* Why did nothing take away the feeling—somewhere between sadness and dread—that felt like a physical weight? She needed to find a way that made it possible for her to stay with my father whatever their differences; he had now realized his life's ambition—how could she deny him that? A bishop's wife! Easy enough to joke about all those years ago in Indianapolis. Things had been so different then—coherent.

I had lunch with her one day at the Plaza Hotel, and in my memory she is looking down at her plate. My motorcyclist boyfriend of a few weeks had disappeared into thin air—I was trying to replace Venable, who still hadn't called. My mother barely spoke. I wanted to ask her advice, but she had little to say except what she'd said when I was in high school: "Play hard to get." I did not know that she was unbearably sad, that she and her important lover had broken up; I was too involved in my own life. Instead of having compassion, instead of pushing at her silence, I felt rejected.

Even her participation in my father's work, their partnership, was a thing of the past. She no longer had a voice in any of his decisions, though, as always, she had strong opinions. The diocese with its 202 parishes seemed like a corporation, and she began to feel that my father was *selling out to power.* Inevitably when they disagreed, he took what she considered the more conventional path. *Church per se has fallen by the wayside: my communities are elsewhere: and I am far too aware of self-deception. I have*

some regard for the "gospel story," but for me, the code as it vibrates in con-
temporary church life—liberated, renewed or whatever—comes across as too
demanding—and I feel torn apart.

My father kept saying that if she found something to do, she'd feel
better. She was offered a job in the New York office of McGovern's 1972
campaign, but she turned it down: *I didn't think it was my slot.* For a while
that fall, she and my sister Marian went to yoga sessions in a big West End
Avenue apartment. Adelia had suggested it; yoga was then strictly part
of the "counterculture," its wide acceptance decades in the future. One
day I went with them. As, in half-dark, I awkwardly stretched, my mother's presence bled into my concentration, her familiar body moving with
effort into alien positions, at the end of the hour both of us resting on the
floor and breathing through the final chant. "I find it too religious," she
said as we left. After a while she quit—"I prefer tennis," she told Marian.

Sometime in November, Venable came back to New York. Within days,
we were spending every night together, though some nights when I came
over, he'd spend as much as an hour on the telephone—he was still breaking up with his girlfriend. (Q: Why didn't I go back to my apartment, tell
him to call when he was free? A: I was used to lining up for love.) Soon
I was bringing Venable along to supper at the Manse, as we now called
the cathedral apartment, and he would spend after-dinner hours spouting
Jung and Freud as my brothers and sisters did acrobatics on the carpet and
my mother sat in a rocking chair watching. A friend soon started calling
Venable the "theory of the month club." I don't remember my father at
those dinners—just Venable, filling the silence with his unending talk, as
if to keep everyone's fear and sadness at bay.

It was like a huge bottle of soda water with the lid gently inexorably pried open,
she later wrote. *They* [the psychiatrist] *said that was a good thing, that she'd*
been too controlled for too long. But understanding didn't help, *so she went*
to the doctor, the tests were fine, blood fine, liver fine—"You're a miracle,"
he told her—"Don't think about yourself too much." Her husband loved his
new job and worried about her when he came home in the evening. Her editor
thought up a subject for her next book—*"problems of the ageing"—"You're*

good with people." She started to read and interview, but she never signed the contract.

The success of *The People on Second Street*, the scores of marvelous reviews, TV appearances, speeches all over the country, a possible movie, new literary friendships, the continuing friendship of people from the McCarthy campaign: all of it had vanished along with that new sense of self she had so cherished. What was wrong?

"Well," I remember saying, "you almost died. It will take a while to recover." I didn't yet know to reassure her that many writers have post-book depressions. In a letter of encouragement, Mary McGrory quoted Emily Dickinson, writing in a letter after a move from one house to another in Amherst: "A year of earthquakes; I am out with lanterns looking for myself."

"Your mother was spent," says my friend the psychoanalyst, a woman in her eighties. "Depression from being spent. It seems so obvious."

Not obvious to Jenny Moore. My younger brothers and sisters remember these weeks as the time when things "got weird." Why had she put the little girls' bedroom on the third floor? At the farthest possible distance from the master bedroom? What was she thinking? She wasn't thinking. *She began to make dates and cancel them—("You're so wise to take it easy," friends said when she called them,")—began not to sleep and to try to smoke away the insomnia. And then she couldn't read the newspapers ("That's the first REAL sign," they told her later.) She remembered the times in the hospital after the accident when all she could do was watch two goldfish in a bowl and how that was spoiled when a clergyman she loathed said to her about the goldfish, "Isn't it glorious, they give to you and ask nothing in return."*

I wasn't home for Thanksgiving, but apparently there was an epic battle—"Right in front of everyone," Marian remembered. Adelia offered to take the little girls to the kitchen to make cookies, and my mother flew into a rage, things unsaid rising to the surface: *"You're always trying to be the little mother!"* My father began to be afraid, as he always did when my mother lost her temper—an angry woman was a crazy woman, and besides her mother was crazy, so . . . I had no sense of a crisis. I was at another Thanksgiving table—that of a friend from my consciousness-raising group, Leslie Cagan, and her family in their big apartment on the Grand Concourse in the Bronx. I remember plenty of food and laughing, and after supper lying on the floor listening to an album called *Sweet Baby James* and sighing. Why had none of us found a boyfriend as kind and sensitive as James Taylor? Why was I living with a man who was not my own age? Why wasn't Venable with me on Thanksgiving? (I don't remember why.) I loved the Cagans—warm and funny and very kind. They often came to court during the Panther 21 trial, which was dragging on and on. I couldn't admit that I was getting bored with the trial, even politics. I wanted to write, but I felt guilty that I didn't need a job. I was always giving away money, but could I really spend it on becoming a writer? "You have your own grant," my psychiatrist kept saying, trying to change my perspective, but he was a white man. How could he understand how I felt about what my friends called ruling-class privilege? I wanted to study poems by other women. I don't think I explained that night my idea that if I could write as a woman—further investigate my existence as a woman—that my poems might become more original.

I don't know how I got up the courage that day at Thanksgiving dinner. Were we going around the table talking about what we were thankful for? I somehow managed to say that I wanted to leave the movement and write, that I didn't feel I could do organizing work and write at the same time. Clear in my mind still is what Jessie, Leslie's mother, said: I will support you entirely if you actually write, "because I know you will put what you believe into your writing, and that will help the movement."

Of course I would put what I believed into my writing—but I sensed it would take a long time to discover who I was and what I believed and knew. I remember one day, sitting in Venable's apartment with a pen and paper; another day, with my new electric portable typewriter. I felt entirely fraudulent, but no matter what I laboriously typed out and showed to him, Venable told me to keep writing. At night we went out to restaurants where he seemed always to know the proprietor—French, Italian, Spanish—and then came home to bed. I bought bright red and green patent leather platform shoes, grew my hair, and went to a salon called Louis-Guy D that specialized in the care and feeding of ever longer hair. One day I saw my Radcliffe friend Susan Channing in a big photograph on the cover of the *New York Times* Sunday entertainment section—she was in an off-Broadway play. The name under her photograph was "Stockard" Channing. I located her finally and one day asked why she'd changed her name. "It's more memorable," she said. Where did she get all that confidence?

My mother was now so tired she could hardly move, and one day my father took her to Mount Sinai Hospital for another round of tests. Was there some new problem with her liver? She did look kind of yellow. Venable and I went to visit—she seemed so small on the hospital bed, the room dark and shadowy. Again, nothing was physically wrong, and so she went to a new psychiatrist. He didn't understand why she was depressed: *"Think of all you have, all those wonderful children! I think you must be competing with your husband."* She repeated that exchange on the phone one day, outraged. By then all she wanted was to leave my father to his happy job in New York and move back to Washington, an idea which I found as impossibly threatening as her speech about *my marriage* on the porch in the Adirondacks. My father had closed a $27,000 contract on a huge Park Avenue apartment, but my mother barely looked at it. She wanted to go back to Cleveland Park, a street with trees, a house that was her own, a garden. . . . Lilacs, she imagined. Delphiniums, and roses.

7.

Unthinkable, repeated my father. What about the children? Unthinkable, agreed the psychiatrist. An impasse. When she writes about it, she uses the third person.

> *So finally she said, "I want to go somewhere and sleep for two weeks."*
> *"Yes," the doctor said in a relieved voice. "I know a place where there*

are flowers and places to walk—and they have rich experience with drugs." "Is it a hospital?" she asked.

Surely, she had told the psychiatrist about her mother's years in mental hospitals, the impact on Margarett's memory and cognition of all those shock treatments. Ending up like that was my mother's worst fear.

"Is it a hospital?" she repeated.

"There is no reason for me to tell you what or where it is," the doctor said. She answered, "I want to be in the city near my family, and I have a right to know what the place is." "They have rich experience in drugs," the doctor repeated.

So she went in a taxi to the hospital near the East River—and the taxi kept stopping and starting in the traffic, "Every face I see looks happy," she said—knowing it was not true. "I understand," said her husband, knowing he didn't. "I'm so proud of you," said her husband. "Oh for Christ's sake," she said.

The Payne Whitney Clinic was part of New York Hospital, located on East 68th Street, near the East River.

The door to the office of the receiving psychiatrist was locked. "Why are you here?" he inquired. "Because I need shelter from the outside and I am afraid," she answered. "How good of you to be so honest . . . but you are the type who is going to want to leave to soon," the receiving psychiatrist said. "Why don't you try and surprise me?" "Why am I the type to leave?" she asked, genuinely curious. "You're the type," he said, not unkindly. "Wait and see."

Her husband left, his face more scared than she felt hers was.

When my father got back to his office at the cathedral, he began to make phone calls. Venable and I were just home from lunch when the telephone rang. I remember I was was wearing a suit I had just bought—it was beige and maroon with a cinched waistline and a gored skirt. "Jenny is going into a place called Payne Whitney for a while." It was my father. He always used her name when things were really serious, when she was no longer functioning as a mother. Margarett and her shock treatments came into my mind, my mother tapping her head when she described her mother's mental illness to me when I was a child. Jenny, my father said, had decided to go to a place to work things out. I hung up after a few more exchanges and slept for eighteen hours. Had my mother told my father what she wrote later, that she couldn't stop having *suicidal thoughts & obsessions?*

"Suicide," the poet Muriel Rukeyeser wrote, "is a lazy wish for rebirth." When I was about ten and we still lived in Jersey City, I'd think about Annabel Herter, the Vassar friend of my mother's who killed herself after the war—and I would see a big trunk. What was inside it? If I killed myself, I would never know. When I turned eighteen, my parents gave me a beautiful Chinese chest of camphor wood. "A hope chest," my mother said. How far away she was now, that mother.

> *"This is your room," a brown-eyed, brown-haired nurse said, reclining college-dorm-style on the bed. "My God, it is a movie," the woman thought. "Everyone here wants to know you," the nurse said. "We are a community—talk to the patients, the aides, the nurses, the doctors about yourself." "My God," the woman thought, "Where is the sleep? The drugs, the white pillow?"*
>
> *"Now take a shower while we go through your luggage—turn in your scissors—I have to watch you undress and shower. It's because we don' want you to do anything to yourself—and we can't be responsible for any scars you have on your body." She undressed and showered—meek and silent. "Well, we certainly aren't responsible for that," the nurse commented, again kindly, observing the long red scar the length of the woman's body, tracing it with a gentle index finger. "I trust you . . . the gong will sound for supper soon."*

It was the scar from the liver surgery, and on the menu that night in the dining room was broiled liver.

The woman sat at one of the two tables—Next summer I'm going skating on the South Pole—I hate liver, do you? said Arlene, shrill, warmly welcoming. Let me tell you about my dog Rusty. He's a golden spaniel. I get passes now, and go home to see him. I really love him." (It's not possible that I am here, the woman thought to herself.)

An emaciated boy of about 20 is helped to her table by a huge black male aide. The boy slumps in a chair and half falls. "Eat, David," says the aide. "He won't eat," Arlene informs the woman. "That's why he's here." The woman goes to her room thinking, Liver—I said I'd never be able to eat liver again after my own liver was removed—the doctors said I would, but tonight they cut it too thick.

She pulls back the spread, which is olive green and uncrushable. The brown-eyed, brown-haired nurse comes to the door—head cranes around college-dorm style, "Charades in a few minutes—come to the center lounge when you hear the gong." Charades, the woman thought to herself, this is too much. "I don't think I'll come tonight," she said politely.

"We all do—staff and patients—this is a community—besides we don't let you go to sleep until after 10:30—and relating to patients and staff is part of the therapy," she said. "May I knit?" asked the woman. "As long as you participate," the nurse answered. She went to the center lounge and knitted—the stitches were first too loose and then too tight.

"Hell," she thought to herself, "I'll just knit."

A nurse in clogs and a white uniform dances in. "I'm Bobby Frances," she says gaily. "God, one of those," thinks the woman. "And here's Bob—you must be Jenny." She pats the woman. Bob is tall, bloodhound-sad, three-day beard, heavy black hair. He looks at Jenny. "I'm going bald, aren't I?" "No," the woman says, startled. "You have a lot of hair."

Bob thumps down to a kneeling position in front of her. "You mean it? No, you're lying—I'm going bald," he weeps.

"It's a virility problem—that's the way it comes out," shrills Arlene. A gong rings. "Medication time," Arlene shrills.

"None for you," the nurse informs the woman. "We want to observe you without anything." The woman lies awake and smokes all night but feels safer.

The next day, she met her therapist for the first time.

A youthful gray curly-headed handsome doctor with a vermilion necktie: "Let's try and find an empty room. He walks down the hall, she follows him. "Why do you walk six steps behind me?" he says. Because I feel six steps behind you, she thinks but doesn't say. "I understand you're not participating," he says when they sit down. "You knitted at game-night."

"I feel as if I am at a movie," she answers.

"It takes a while," he says. "Now what about your sexual life?— we must go into things, you know."

"It hardly seems on the top of the agenda," she replies with some spirit. "May I have something to help me sleep?

"No, we want to watch what you do without anything," he says. "I'll be seeing you thirty minutes twice a week."

When she writes this account, she does not go into detail about the content of her therapy, nor does she mention any drugs. In use at the time were a class of drugs called tricyclic; the name for the one then in general use was Elavil, which was an amitriptyline.

Bob, in pajamas, is staring from the depths of a burgundy red leather armchair; he taps her arm. She stops. "Am I going bald" I'm losing my hair," he begins to sob. "Do you have an obsession?" He knots the already knotted pale-blue terry cloth bathrobe around him.

She wants to go back to Washington—that's her obsession," shrills Arlene from a nearby ping-pong table.

Letters came from the lover, from Mary McGrory. Art Buchwald, the columnist, wrote her a sheaf of them and came to visit—*he had put a pistol to his head—and cried in a hospital for three months without stopping,* he told her: testimony and secrets from old friends and friends of friends.

"It seems to me you're in the midpoint-of-life crisis," said the hand-
some vermilion-tied doctor. "The crying will stop, Mrs. Moore,"
"But there are times when I have to pant, it's so painful," she
answers.
"And you think you're going to die," he says calmly. "That's very
typical."

On her first day pass, Gene McCarthy took her out to lunch. *He gave her*
tiger lilies in white paper and told her the only thing she had control over was
her own life.

I visited only once, such a shock, the locked ward, my mother's tiny
monastery-like room.

"You've got to go the end of the tunnel before you get out of the tunnel," Art
Buchwald wrote her.

And Mayor Lindsay telephoned. *He told her the outside was one hell of a*
lot worse than the inside.

She came out once that May for a family supper—the kids living at
home, my father—at Molfetas, a Greek restaurant near Times Square.
When I ordered cake for dessert, she pointedly told a story she'd heard
from a mutual friend about the poet Muriel Rukeyser (who was diabetic,
I learned later) eating an entire chocolate cake. Because I was starting to
write poems, I took the anecdote as an attack on my new life, an inter-
pretation my psychiatrist encouraged: "You'll get more of that," he said,
which made me feel disloyal—I wanted a way to be compassionate. On
my way out of the psychiatrist's office, I saw my mother's friend Roger
Wilkins. Later I learned he'd been to see my mother.

When he rings the bell at the locked door, the staff mistake him for a
maintenance man because he's black. She weeps when he comes into
her room. He kisses and holds her. "Roger, for God's sake," she says,
"if someone comes in, I'll get kicked out of here."
"Well, I'm not screwing you," he says. "What is this place, a
convent?" And he stays for an hour which is all that is allowed one
person—and he asks tough questions, and says tough things in his

tough way. And she listens because she knows he cares, and she knows
he's on the edge of the abyss himself.

The gong rings. She walks him to the locked door at the end of
the hall. "What's that?" he asks, looking into a room containing one
plastic-covered mattress on the floor. "Stay out of here, baby," he
says, hugging her shoulders.

She remains at Payne Whitney for two months as I simply go on; my
life has a new strain that weaves through it like a jazz line for a wind
instrument—the swish of a key turning in a lock, my grandmother in
those places for decades and now my mother. I stay away from Anne Sexton's poems about her nervous breakdown. When I can't write, the strain
intensifies: Locked ward. Snake Pit. Insane asylum. Baldpate, the name of
the place Margarett was for years. Therapy was not then considered treatment for a sane person, and being hospitalized like my mother now was
required a whisper: *Women and Madness.* Phyllis Chesler's book was not
yet published, but its ideas were in the air: women were often incarcerated
not for mental illness but for what they knew; soon the entire discipline of
psychotherapy would be revolutionized to account for the lives of women.
My own psychiatrist debated this thinking with me. One night, out with
Venable, I met a man named Whitey Lutz and learned he had sculpted
the plaster angel with the broken-off wing I later found in the dump near
Prides Crossing. "You come from a fine line of fillies," he said. What did
that mean about my future? Even my psychiatrist couldn't tell me.

One day, after about 3 weeks, inexplicably, she was no longer at the
movies and no longer knitted. Instead she wept; she wept playing
volleyball which was required every morning—and Barbara, who
loved her dog Rusty, propelled her around the volleyball court—and
she cried making ashtrays in occupational therapy and shrill Arlene
sat with her and didn't say anything and Bob asked her at every
meal to reassure him he wasn't bald. Charades rolled around each
Friday—and the nurse with clogs danced around, organizing teams.
Emaciated David came and slept on the sofa and Bob wept. One

night, Michael, the intellectual, acted a charade and David opened his eyes and said almost inaudibly, "Man . . . and . . . Superman." "He guessed it! He guessed it," the woman cried. She was sitting next to him on the sofa. "Did you hear—did you hear what Jenny said?" chirped the nurse. "David guessed it," and then David ate one cookie and drank a glass of milk for the first time.

Recently, I sought out a friend who spent months in Payne Whitney a few years before my mother. "I was lying all the time," he said. "Halfway through my stay, the staff discovered something I had done and I couldn't deny it. I began to cry. That's when I started to get better." My mother's lies were not a young man's lies, but without knowing exactly what she revealed to the doctor with the vermilion tie, I know that she stopped lying to herself. What she now understood was stark: Her marriage was over, she had understood certain things about her relationship with her husband, she had to change her life. The locked room had not kept her a prisoner, it had given her refuge—privacy and mental freedom. And the sixth-floor community had embraced her. Time and space away, I am thinking—a liberation zone.

And slowly, precariously, my mother wrote, *there was the end of the tunnel—and the fear she had gulped so deeply was gone.*

8.

WE. ARE. MOVING. BACK. TO. WASHINGTON.

One large word in magic marker on each eight-by-ten sheet of white cardboard; she pulled them slowly from her purse like rabbits from a magician's hat. Magic, it seemed to her, and to the children who had longed to go back to Washington. "I will have my life back," Marian, just fifteen, recalled thinking. They were gathered: Jenny, my father, the children living at home, in Gami's apartment at 825 Fifth Avenue—the same midnight blue carpet and comfortable chintz covered sofas.

Marian remembered that everyone cheered.

"After consultation with the doctor," my father wrote in a public letter that went to all 202 parishes in the diocese, "we have concluded that Jenny should be in a quiet familiar place where she can regain her strength and where it is easier to take care of the children."

The new house was also on the corner of 34th and Newark but diagonally across from the old one. *We bought a house, & you can't imagine what security it gives me to have my own pad! Never before (& that of course was a mistake),* she wrote an Indianapolis friend the summer of 1971 just after the move: *It's hard on Paul—who really loves his job—but there seemed no other alternative for the moment. I really could have gone through all this at home, but it was too much for the children, bewildered Paul, and would have taken longer to hack out.*

I was bewildered too, but I didn't have all the information. My father was "bewildered" because my mother had not, and never would, confront him with her reasons for wanting to leave him, her certain knowledge of his hidden bisexual life. Nor did she ever reveal those suspicions to any one of her children. Knowing the entire story now, I consider her heroic. Despite a significant chill from some of their old friends, women who disapproved of her "abandoning" her husband, she took the move smoothly in stride: *Having always cared too much what "people" thought, I really don't give a shit what "they" say about this.*

As for our relationship, without telling me the central fact of my father's infidelity and bisexuality, she pushed, often being more intimate with me than I expected or wanted: thus when she revealed to me that she hadn't had an orgasm until she was forty. She might also report some of my father's "sexist" mistakes, or some resentment of the church. But more often she also wrote about the pleasures of her new life: *My life alone—and relationship with Poppy are reconstructed in a way I never dreamed possible— albeit somewhat Jamesian and I feel an inner joy and clarity.* The friends that really mattered embraced her: the Harrisons, the Whittemores, the Dudmans, the Bradlees. She also renewed other Washington friendships, chief among them the columnist Mary McGrory, whose letters to her in Payne Whitney had been such a solace. Once in a while my mother's new feminism broke silences she'd always observed: when her old friend Ben Bradlee asked her whom she'd put forth for a Pulitzer in the columnist category and she said Mary McGrory, he dismissed the idea: "But she's a woman!" (McGrory did win in 1975.)

After the children were settled in bedrooms, curtains and bedspreads chosen, she worked with an architect on what came to be called "the new room." The garage at the back of the house was converted and linked by a stairway and French doors to the prior tiny living room. And she began planting—a rose garden, lilacs. I was home the day she unpacked boxes of ruby glasses that I had never seen, once used for dinner parties at my grandparents' house in Palm Beach (now sold). I stood mesmerized as she placed them one by one on a shelf painted bright white—bold deep red is to me an image for my mother's dreams. Of twenty place settings, she kept fourteen: large tumblers, small tumblers, water goblets and three kinds of wine glasses, finger bowls, liqueur glasses, some so tiny they seemed doll-size. She was both back at home and in a new place. Susan Willens, who moved to Newark Street after "the Moores" left for New York, remembered when Jenny Moore returned to the neighborhood: "We were a pretty young, energetic group in Cleveland Park, but no one held a candle to her, in terms of beauty."

She resumed gathering honorary children. Joel, the youngest Harrison child, who later became a jazz composer, remembered her taking his mother and a gang of boys, including him, to a Stevie Wonder concert, and she had long conversations with Jeff Kampelman, a friend of Danny's who had always been very quiet. He recalls now that the friendship was "cemented" when she asked him to name his favorite playwright and he said, "Eugene O'Neill and Noel Coward." Self-consciously she set about making a new set of friends. Cleveland Park at the time was populated by a number of women, slightly younger than she was, who were making careers. Ruth Pollak, the mother of Patience's best friend and a filmmaker, had her over for coffee with some of them. "I'd known who she was," Faye Moskowitz said, "but I hadn't actually met her. I have to admit that I was prejudiced—did I really need to meet another rich WASP woman?"

"When did you start to like her?" I asked, fifty years later.

"Right away." Faye said.

"What was it about her?"

"I could tell she was hungry for something." Faye took writing classes with a brilliant teacher at George Washington University whose name was Astere Claeyssens: "I told her all about him."

My mother had read *Sexual Politics* before she got sick, and she and I both promptly subscribed to *Ms.*, when its first issue came out in January 1972. I remember her calling me to talk about a piece called "Combat in the Erogenous Zone," from the book by a young writer named Ingrid Bengis—radical and open about sex, the book was a memoir, the as yet unnamed genre in which my mother had written *The People on Second Street*. In sensual language laced with anger, Bengis addressed "Manhating" and "Lesbianism." My mother's ideas were changing. There was no question about her children and their "significant others" sleeping in the same room; instead of saying *Don't come home pregnant*, she offered advice about birth control, and when she lost her temper with one of us she might apologize and explain. On her bed one day, my sister Rosemary, then twenty and living at home, found a note.

My mother had returned home at seven and found that despite promises, *Nothing is started for supper*. The casserole was out but no one had put it in the oven: that was why *My voice got strident*, she explained. She was not going to stop employing help, she wrote, addressing an ongoing family controversy at the time. None of the children" took up the slack" and neither did Poppy when he was in Washington. She was not going to change in asking for help, she wrote. *The creativity and strength are bubbling up in me like two great springs, and I will not use them up on the vacuum cleaner. When you die in the flesh (almost) and die in the spirit (almost) as I did you are very conscious (to the point of absurdity perhaps) of each of the moments of the rest of your life. I have no fear and therefore no depression of that nature—that's why I say I'm different—and sometimes, it comes out like insufferable arrogance.* New was the atmosphere, her new freedom manifest in the bright Sister Mary Corita silk screens that seemed to hang everywhere. My mother loved that the artist was a woman and a nun, how she reclaimed commercial language in blasts of color. "Turn, turn, turn" from the New Testament in huge type, yellow and orange tilted into each other as if acknowledging such turning involved fragility; the trademark *LIFE* of the magazine two feet long, silk-screened orange and blue vibrating, to declare a simple message.

One day in New York, I was at my desk in my study on the top floor of the Federal rowhouse on 22d Street, which Venable and I bought with a friend. The house had belonged to the avant garde publisher of Something Else Press, and small-press magazines and books, often by women, ceaselessly poured through the brass mail slot in the front door; I hardly understood them—pamphlets by Kathy Acker, a series of boots on postcards by Eleanor Antin. From the third floor, I heard the mail land and ran down the three flights. There was a letter from my mother; I ripped open the envelope. The handwriting was familiar but not the contents. She had a lover, she wrote, and she was happy. Oddly this revelation did not make me angry, and I wrote her right back. I was beginning to understand, finally, that she and I were in this together:

I am really glad you told me. Please believe that and don't be frightened, even though it is frightening for women (maybe any two people of the same sex) to try really to relate even if they're not mother and daughter. When I said, Don't be frightened what I meant was: of me breaking your confidence / or / of me not believing things you say / or of me not understanding that you acting in your own interest is morally correct. But don't let the fact that you are in a position of high risk destroy your pleasure in it or in the freedom from nuclear familial constraint it gives you.

Her reply was immediate:

I loved your letter a) because it was so clear and intelligent—it would never occur to me that you would be indiscreet, & on the "high risk" we are very careful—never have dinner in town etc. etc. Also he has an apt. so no motel-life is needed.

As was my next reply to her:

> I am nervous about my relationship with you anyway. I will probably
> stay nervous about it until I am sure that I will never be hurt by you
> again / or / until I am sure that nothing you do will hurt me in that
> mother/child way again. The other reason our relationship makes
> me nervous is because it is an experiment. It is almost too good to be
> true. So I am nervous in case I am deluding myself about how good it
> is / and / worry about whether or not it's so good for me it's bad for
> me, as the Cole Porter song goes. SO anything you reveal to me only
> makes it less possible that you will hurt me because surprise is what
> hurts, not quiet revelation.

I remember typing the letter and keeping a carbon, but reading now what I was able to say stuns me: 'Until I am sure that nothing you do will hurt me in that mother/child way again." Now I remember that it was to this letter of mine that she replied with her plans for a play called *"Women, Mothers and Daughters"*—in which she would explore *who has a right to "hurt" whom? Can daughters "hurt" mothers or is that something else like "acting out"? My thought of yesterday: set will be a lot of mirrors (among other things) some mirrors may get broken, etc. etc.*

Despite my dreams that we might one day communicate, I never imagined that she would write me such a letter. I began to think of her fragility in different terms, more as delicacy. I began to honor her in my imagination, to hold her very dear.

9.

In the spring of 1972, she began to study with Astere Claeyssens at George Washington University, resuming in a class of undergraduates the study Claeyssens, as he was called, literature she had left off when she and my father became engaged almost thirty years earlier. He was one of those extraordinary teachers—charismatic, in his soul a poet but in his life a teacher. My mother wrote me with excitement about her "fascinating" professor: he was a playwright who had also written reviews in the *Village Voice*—the name was Welsh, pronounced "clay-sense." He wore plaid jackets. He had dancing, shining eyes. In his American literature class, she read James Agee, Nabokov, and *Losing Battles*, by Eudora Welty. I have found papers on Thoreau and *The Wings of the Dove* in the cartons, along with my favorite, in which she compares her beloved St. Thérèse and Emily Dickinson. She finds this by Thérèse: "When I was ill, I couldn't bear people sitting on my bed like a great string of onions looking at me as if I were some strange beast"; and this, rare for the saint, about mortal love: "I might have squandered my affections on other people if I'd found anybody who could appreciate the depth of my feelings." It's the idea of eternity in each that for my mother brings them closest; St. Thérèse's "little way—each instant a treasure" approaching Dickinson's "the Blunder is in Estimate / Eternity is there" While Dickinson throws her uncertainties at her readers, Thérèse has her Roman Catholic God, my mother writes; these conclusions seem to harken back to her long hours of contemplation in the hospital, as each woman offers a use for silence—*the equivalent of solitude rather than loneliness.*

Her new friends were literary—Susan Willens and Faye Moskowitz were getting doctorates in English Literature at George Washington— and she connected in a new way with old friends who were artists. Polly Kraft was a painter, Ben's wife Tony Bradlee was a sculptor, and Tony's friend Ann Truitt made stark minimalist constructions. She also took particular interest in women who were moving forward by themselves or trying to work out relationships with husbands with whom conventional marriages had come to an end. How was one to be independent while keeping the children happy and secure?

That fall, she took her first writing class with Claeyssens, and by winter, my mother and her teacher had fallen into a kind of love. It had been a year since she had written me about her happy love affair, which I later learned was with Joe Walker, the man she would have married "if it hadn't been for your father." I'd thought the relationship with Claeyssens a mentorship, but in the boxes I found amorous, delicate, even desperate letters to and from him—I remembered then that it was him she wanted Venable and me to meet when we were in Washington, and once, she wrote me, he'd come with her to the Bach Festival in Pennsylvania.

I don't have her account of this change in her feeling for her teacher, but I have stories two women told me decades later. One was a young publisher I met in the 1990s in Connecticut—I have been wanting to meet you, she said, as I took in her black hair, dark eyes. "Really?" I asked. "Claeyssens," she said.

She had been his student, taken every course he taught, including his creative writing courses. She had fallen "madly in love" with him, and finally, after she graduated, finagled staying with him once when she visited Washington on business. "Finally, I thought," she said; "finally it's going to happen." But when he sat on her bed to say goodnight, he did not take her in his arms. Instead, he told her about a woman he'd been in love with, a woman who'd been his student, a very gifted writer, who had died in the early 1970s. He was just not over her.

"It was your mother," the woman said; "I just wanted to tell you that."

Twenty years after that encounter, I walked into a cocktail party for an artist friend on Martha's Vineyard and was introduced to the hostess, who said, immediately, "I know all about you. I know all about your mother, and I know all about Claeyssens." She had been a premed student at GW in the early 2000s and had taken his American literature class. After the first snap exam, a stack of them on his desk, Claeyssens announced that he had never read "a more dismal" group of blue books! "The only one worth anything is by a premed student, and I'm going to read it to you in full." "I couldn't believe my ears," my hostess said. "I just sat there, frozen, paralyzed as he read the entire thing." "You are a writer," he said right then. "You have to take this seriously."

I don't believe that my mother's romance with her teacher became an affair. The letters are anguished on the subject of what kind of a relationship they might have, but the last year of her life she never took off the ring he gave her, beautiful despite its humble materials—a forget-me-not blossom suspended in plexiglass.

Under the guidance of Claeyssens, my mother resumed her writing. She was back at the Dudmans, this time in their dining room. She wrote the story of the mental hospital, and she wrote pages of autobiography that I have quoted. She wrote a bold narrative about going to the Carlyle on the arm of a handsome black man, her friend Roger Wilkins. While at Barnard, she'd turned down a black man's invitation to Paul Robeson in *Othello* for fear of a Boston dowager turning up at the theater; now, at the Carlyle, when she saw a white female acquaintance in a Chanel suit, she and Roger just changed tables. She wrote on airplanes and she wrote letters. She started a play called *The Job* about a Ben Bradlee–like character who plans to fire a managing editor, covering his jealousy with an ethical excuse, some details of his marriage inspired by her own.

She was beginning to think about different kinds of power, and was taping conversations with journalists and friends from the neighborhood, even with my brother Paul, asking questions about the relationship between public and private morality. My sister Rosemary dropped out of Antioch and came home for a semester: "She asked me if I wanted to take a writing class with her at GW. Of course I said yes." My mother was repairing, recreating relationships with her children to fit her new life—trips alone with her, a family trip to a dude ranch in Wyoming, a visit to Paul in California, visits to Adelia to plan for her wedding the coming October. Early that summer of 1972, first reports of what came to be called the Watergate scandal broke in the *Washington Post*: a burglary at the Democratic Party headquarters; Ben Bradlee was overseeing two young reporters, Bob Woodward and Carl Bernstein. At my parents' house in Kent, Venable and I watched the July Democratic Convention. Later that summer, we were in the Adirondacks when the news came that my mother's father, my Grandpa Kean, had died. It was a dark rainy day, common there in mid-August. I remember footsteps along the boardwalk, my mother banging through the screen door of my cabin.

As soon as she told me the news—"my father died"—I realized her tears expressed more than simple grief; he was only eighty-one, and Margie had just told her we children weren't welcome at the funeral—it was to be small, intimate. Was this a criticism of her separation from my father?

Defiant, she took us all to Massachusetts, but went to the service with just my father. That night I learned that my mother had been left only a token inheritance, hundreds of thousands less than Margie and her brothers and half-brothers. "He was sure you were taken care of," Margie said. Of course, in some way she was, but my mother was weeping again—her father had known she was now living on her own—a bequest like her siblings had received would have given her financial independence. He had always taken care of her; why had he abandoned her now?

She turned herself immediately to Adelia's wedding, to take place in just two months. My sister and Tom were of our generation, buoyantly antiestablishment. They didn't want a caterer—nothing "fancy"—so cooking the vegetarian brown rice and ratatouille wedding banquet for a hundred guests in the Adirondacks fell to my mother. For the cake, she bought tins for a layered wedding cake, tested the carrot cake recipe at home on Newark Street. Often she called me, weeping—she was "exhausted" she'd say, or hurt by another misunderstanding about the wedding arrangements. She tried gamely to intuit what would be right; instead of ordering a new set of monogrammed silver for Adelia, she'd collect disparate pieces from antique shops. She'd do that next for me, she said. Why should marriage be given preferential treatment? With a principled feminist critique, I rationalized my envy of my younger sister marrying first. A secure relationship—marriage or not—is what you need, my forty-two-year-old, white male, married-with-children, supremely rational psychiatrist kept gently insisting.

Wearing homemade long dark-green velvet skirts and white blouses—for the boys, trousers and coordinated tops—we were called "brides persons" and "grooms persons." It rained the wedding day; my wedding present would be a suite of photographs. Venable had encouraged me to take pictures, and I was using a Nikon. I took a black and white sequence—the romantic entrance of the bridal couple in a canoe across the lake in the near-rain; my mother and Adelia in intense conversation in the kitchen; my parents, standing together, watching the ceremony performed by the Yale chaplain William Sloane Coffin, who had counseled both Tom and my brother Paul about the draft. In the photograph, my parents look both proud and sad. Proud of their daughter, their children; resigned and sad about their own marriage. I knew I should have been happy for my sister, but in hindsight I understand that my inability to do so had little to do with her. I could not overcome a sadness that was purely my own—my family was ending as the first of us cut loose to form her own.

I dove back into the past. The family friends who had lived in the house in Kent since we left for Indianapolis were moving on, and Venable and I took it over as a weekend and summer retreat. Three weeks after the wedding, my mother came for my birthday; I was turning twenty-seven. My father had come weekends that summer to help clear away brush, but this was my mother's first visit, and her first to a household of mine. Having flown to Hartford from Washington, she arrived in a white rented car. "I like what you've done here," she said with shy formality, as if I had done anything at all to the easy chairs that had been Uncle Leonard's wedding present, the ugly Victorian sofa that had always been in the house. She had brought a square tin box, which she put in the refrigerator. "What is it?" I asked. "A surprise," she answered, with that old Christmas-present laugh. For supper, I made leg of lamb from a recipe in the newsletter Craig Claiborne started when he left the *Times*—she'd given me a subscription—and I spun the lettuce in the odd plastic gadget she'd sent; the now common salad spinner was a new invention that year. "It makes *all* the difference," my mother said. "Trust the French!" It was orange, made by Peugeot, and lasted until I sold the house in Kent thirty years later.

At dessert she disappeared into the kitchen. In the tin box was a walnut torte she'd baked in Washington; she and Venable had conspired— "You'll get a half pint of heavy cream and hide it behind the milk." After the singing of "Happy Birthday," we sat in the living room and she gave me presents. I remember only one: a magenta plastic notebook, color photos of roses cut from a garden catalogue, their romantic names: Garden Party white with pink edges, Queen Elizabeth, pure pink; Mr. Lincoln, deep red. "They will arrive in the spring," she proclaimed, "and darling Venable will dig the holes."

My mother was turning fifty on March 12, and she was planning a party. A gathering of friends, old and new, at the F Street Club in Washington. Bradlees, Harrisons, Dudmans, her editor Bill McPherson, and Claeyssens of course. Venable and I planned to fly down. I rewrote the Kurt Weill—Ira Gershwin song "The Saga of Jenny"—I'd sing my new lyrics as a toast. My father was in Washington, and they had planned the evening together. It was just like old times, and her old expression returns to me: so *pre-war.* White damask tablecloth, napkins, silver sparkling in candlelight—about thirty people at a long table. I remember rising to sing: "Jenny made her mind up. . . ." My nerves set me only a little off-key. There was a small combo and music after supper; at the very end of the party, my parents danced together to some old standard; in spite of myself, I dared imagine they might get back together. "I saw it!" Marian said (so I wasn't crazy), "the way she touched his hand once, leaving the kitchen."

With royalties from *The People on Second Street*—the 25,000 copies— and her father's small legacy, my mother bought herself a small house in the Virginia countryside—a place to write, a place to celebrate her new independent life. She and my father were spending a few days there after the party. "Working things out," my mother said.

I can't resist one of the best stories about the new house at 3319 Newark Street, even though I wasn't there—it happened on the spur of the moment. Because of his peace activism with Yoko Ono, John Lennon, on the basis of an arrest for marijuana possession in London in 1968, had been denied a residency visa. Somehow my father had posted bail for Lennon after his original bust for the offense, and now the most famous couple in the world—or at least in our world then—was coming to Washington for a press conference at which my father would testify in support of their visa. "What are you doing tomorrow?" my father asked Marian and Danny. "Would you like to meet John Lennon?" Wow!

They raced to the car, zipped to the Hay-Adams hotel, and before they knew it, Yoko Ono was opening a hotel room door and John Lennon, sitting on a sofa, was patting the cushion next to him and summoning Marian: "Come sit over here, luv." Later, after he testified, my father invited

John and Yoko to Newark Street. A couple of hours later, in my mother's new living room, John was wildly acting out the bust; "for "Mom, Pop, Danny, me," Marian said, "and a line-up of kids, our friends." My parents invited John and Yoko to come back that evening: "We're having a party tonight for friends moving to the neighborhood—there will be lots of press people." As word burned through Cleveland Park, the party over-flowed, teenagers gawped, and the honorees were eclipsed as kids lined up for John to autograph their record albums and forearms. There were reporters at the party, including Sy Hersch, then of the *New York Times*—he had been my mother's comrade in the McCarthy campaign and lived in the neighborhood. Years later, he remembered himself deep in conversa-tion with "a Japanese lady" as my sister's friend Laura, madly gesturing, mouthed her name: "Yoko Ono! Yoko Ono!"

"I think your parents thought I might write a piece about the visa prob-lem," Sy told me;

"I did write a piece for the *New York Times*, and the visa problem was solved."

Among my photographs of Adelia and Tom's wedding is a portrait of my mother I took that day. She looks radiant and utterly content, cat-swallowed-a-canary content. She had her own home, she was working out a new kind of relationship with her husband that maintained the life of the family, and she had managed the wedding of one of her daughters. Just after Thanksgiving, the family was photographed for *Newsweek*—my father would be on the cover of the Christmas issue in bright red rega-lia; a wag said he looked like St. Patrick. The article quoted my mother saying that "life in New York with five kids under 17" was "too big a burden to carry." Concerning the move my mother had fought so hard for, the journalist shifted all agency to my father: "To lighten the load, Moore moved his wife and the younger children back to Washington." My mother had joined a consciousness-raising group, and she was *on at the meeting about Newsweek article*. She was living her own version of the narrative. She was writing stories and close to finishing a play, and she had been accepted for the following fall, 1973, in the master's fiction pro-gram at the Johns Hopkins Writing Workshops.

10.

Venable and I were asleep in Kent when the phone rang. I stumbled out to the phone in the hallway and answered. It was my father. Jenny had gone to the hospital for tests, and they had found cancer in both her colon and her liver. "I wish I had never met you," Dr. Bremer said to her when he gave her the diagnosis. I flew down before the surgery. "The liver regenerates," I wrote in a poem. "It is the only human organ that can." But she was vulnerable because of the accident, and cancer beginning in the colon had spread there; Dr. Bremer would remove most of her liver. *Finally there was the black out of surgery, followed by brief visions of Paul and the children riding opiated puffs of my consciousness.* I sat in the hospital room by her bed, her little girl daughter again, all shy. I was afraid that if I spoke what was true—that she might die—that I'd hurt her feelings. We stayed off the subject.

She asked about my poems. I'd had one called "My Mother's Moustache" accepted by the *American Review* by Pulitzer Prize–winning poet Richard Howard. It was a poem about her, and she loved it: "My mother said I'd inherit a moustache, and I did. / Hers she removed with green wax . . ." When would it be published? January, I said. She asked me if I planned to have children, and when I said I didn't know, she surprised me: "You'd be crazy to have children," she said. "You love your independence too much."

She didn't go home after the operation. She went to the Dudmans, not to the dining room, but to Martha Dudman's bedroom. She needed to be away from the noise, the chaos of the household that had so delighted her. I think now that she couldn't bear it, couldn't bear the thought of being all broken in the place she had worked so hard to put together. In her memoir pages: *The hospital bed had its hiding places. Here I could sweat silently my rage that my beloved friends were not screaming their thanks to the heavens that they could even walk. Would I ever see my ten-year-old daughter with breasts? Could anyone else love her as I did?*

I flew down to help the day after she got out of the hospital, and found my father alone in the Dudmans' kitchen. Did I want some instant coffee? My mind turned his question into a metaphor. Nothing was the real thing anymore; nothing would be the real thing, ever again. "She's asleep," he said. Then we heard her shout and went upstairs.

"She is like a cat gone mad, hissing from fear," I wrote; "I don't know where the wound is." There was no place to touch her. Her pain had such force—like the opposite of a magnet, it pushed you away.

She decided not to have chemotherapy. "I want the little ones to remember me as me," my poem said, in her voice, "not as some charred, alienated vegetable. They can't know." Treatment for liver cancer is still, fifty years later, not a certain cure, and in 1973 it was quite primitive. Even Doctor Bremer advised against it. About a week later, she was back in the house with her new living room, her garden, and the Sister Marie Corita silk screens on the wall: "APPLES ARE BASIC" in magenta acid green.

My father began to investigate cancer cures—trips to faith healers in Arizona, cancer healers in New Mexico; his old friend John Wing went with him. Eventually they chose a Washington doctor; Frank Woidich and his wife Carmen became part of our daily life. He prescribed supplements, whose effectiveness he gauged each day by looking into my mother's eyes and scrutinizing her irises. He used alternative techniques, but he was an MD who had cured himself of cancer. Vegetable juices, wheat grass juice, so many vitamins. Trays of wheat grass were put under cultivation on the back terrace, beyond which flourished my mother's new roses and delphiniums, the tiny lilac bushes. The family became a legion of care, and my father took a leave from the diocese. All that early summer we believed a miracle was in the works.

There was a remedy Woidich wanted to add to her regimen. Did she have a friend who could easily travel to France? Evans Woollen picked up the phone in Indianapolis. *You are the ONE,* my mother declared. Evans, giggling, imitated her tone of voice that day when we had lunch at the Museum of Modern Art forty years later. He flew to Nice, made the "connection"—more giggles—and packed the suitcase, laying the white powder in plastic bags beneath his clothing. "It definitely looked criminal," he said, but customs waved him through, and he arrived safely at Dulles with the drug, taking a cab straight to Newark Street. Because laetrile was illegal, we called it lemon drops.

My mother wrote and rewrote her will with Steve Pollak, the father of Patience's best friend. "What will she leave me?" said my poem, "except alone by myself?" Claeyssens encouraged her to write the memoir she had been thinking about; as soon as she could, she began to dictate the passages from which I drew those details of her childhood—*so I would ride my brown horse through the woods*. Between writing bouts, she had the secretary help her destroy private correspondence. When August came, she dispatched my father to the Adirondacks with the children and a gang of teenage friends. He could hardly bear it, but she was adamant. She wanted the solitude she had learned from Emily Dickinson: time with herself. There were several people she wouldn't allow to visit—Gagy, for instance, who had taken care of all of her children as infants. I think she couldn't bear to think about past happiness; that was what I said when Gagy called me in tears.

Often I flew down, bringing roses from the garden she had given me for my birthday the previous fall. The bare roots had become enormously tall bushes with huge blooms. I couldn't stop fertilizing them. Margarett had been sending presents all spring, furniture from Prides for her new room, works of art from her collection—a Mary Cassatt monoprint of a dark-haired mother holding a blond child, a yellow dress, on a very green lawn.

My favorite evenings that summer were when some of the men she called her boyfriends arrived, and we sat on the front porch into the night, laughing and joking. Roger Wilkins; Bill McPherson, her editor, now book review editor at the *Post*; and Ben Bradlee, who teased her with what Woodward and Bernstein would report about the Watergate cover-up in the next day in the *Post*—but only if she promised not to tell. He knew she'd keep it to herself because he'd already confided that he and Tony were divorcing and that he was engaged to the journalist Sally Quinn. My mother loved being part of the story, and she did keep quiet; she wouldn't even tell me. It was a different kind of evening when some of her women friends came. One afternoon Mary brought Daniel Ellsberg to visit—he'd been responsible for the release of the Pentagon Papers, which had been published in 1971. Is that encounter what got her on President Nixon's enemies list, published two months after she died?

It was the summer of Billie Jean King and Bobby Riggs. We watched the match together, my mother in bed.

Late August and the heat, and now she was in and out of the hospital. Her abdomen would fill with liquid and she'd need to get it tapped, so she'd be admitted for a day and then come home. I came and left, but Rosie stayed; she and her boyfriend, as my mother put it, "holding down the fort." Adelia and her husband Tom were in Europe for the year, and Paul came, but not until September. She summoned particular friends each to come for a week and help—her old best friend Sylvia; Pam Morton; her sister Margie; Gay, who had been a younger staff member in Jersey City. She was starting to plan the funeral, making lists of prayers and hymns. She called Bill Wendt—would he come to discuss her coffin? She didn't want one of those awful mahogany satin-lined things, she said. She wanted plain pine, unadorned. Of course, he assured her. He found a way to have one made for her—beginning a small business that benefited St. Stephens for years.

"I love you, sweetie," she'd say, as I sat there. Claeyssens was bringing edits, but she no longer had the strength to dictate. She'd hold her arms up and rub her fingers against each other with a soft swishing sound. Roberta Flack had just recorded "Killing Me Softly," and my mother couldn't get enough of it. This was when I began to scrutinize the Currier and Ives print of *Life and Age of Woman*—where in woman's passage was my extraordinary mother? My father and the children got home from the Adirondacks and then, in mid-September, she went into the hospital again, and it didn't seem that she'd get back to Newark Street.

Now, when I came to Washington, I stayed at the Dudmans—no room at home. One day I came with a larger suitcase and brought a black dress, and soon Venable joined me. We had accepted the reality that she would not recover.

Gradually, all the older children arrived from their lives, so that all nine of us were there. And Aunt Margie, who planned to stay just a week, had decided to remain "for the duration." This was when she became our second mother; she had six children of her own, but she sent Christmas presents to all nine of us until she died at ninety-two.

I visited the hospital every day, and driving home late at night, passed again and again the small brick rowhouses that somehow consoled me. Once, as I was driving through Adams Morgan, the Helen Reddy song—popular that fall—came over the radio: "Yes, I am Woman, hear me roar."

My mother was starting to say things that were preternatural. "Will it be bumpy on the way to the cemetery?" "No, Mom, of course not. We'll get you the smoothest limousine possible." A lot of her friends were visiting the hospital now, and one afternoon all nine children and my father surrounded her and sang, without lyrics, "Jesu, Joy of Man's Desiring."

I had decided to go to New York for the day on October 4—she didn't seem to be dying, and I was frustrated. I wanted to check in on my life. Venable had left a few days earlier. On October 3, I went to bed early. I was staying this time at the Moskowitzes. I was in deep sleep when Faye woke me, handing me the telephone.

"Jenny died a few minutes ago," my father said. "Perhaps you want to come to the hospital."

11.

There is so much I've left out, so much more about her that I could tell you, but I think of one of my mother's expressions: "Don't overdo it." There were obituaries in the *Washington Post* and the *New York Times* and in papers across the country. When Betty Medsger, a D.C. reporter, got the call to write the *Times* obit, she would accept the assignment only on the condition that she not be required to write a lede that had my mother as the bishop's wife—she knew of my mother's struggle. The editors agreed. My father and Rosie and I stepped into organizing mode, and Marian was given the task of calling the men my mother had named her pallbearers: Gene McCarthy, Joe Walker, Ben Bradlee, Bobby Potter, Bill McPherson, Roger Wilkins, Alan Nolan, Steve Pollak, Thaddeus Beal, and Claeyssens.

We thought it was amazing that she had planned the funeral, the hymns, that bread and wine would be passed by her children, the feast an Agape rather than Communion and therefore open to all. Rosie and I bought huge baskets and red and blue linen napkins, peasant bread, and an abundance of plastic cups. Six hundred filled the nave of the National Cathedral, people from Washington, Jersey City, New York. Dorothy Day came, and Margarett arrived late in a wheelchair, swathed in black lace. My father couldn't believe it: "Upstaging her own daughter's funeral!"

The night before the funeral, we had all gathered in the living room to hear the will. Steve Pollak, slowly reading, had gotten through the paintings and jewelry, but just as he was reading the sentence in which my mother leaves the balance of her money including royalties of her book to support young writers, the raucous celebratory mood was broken as Patience, still a little girl at eleven, ran into the room crying, screaming with something that sounded like terror. Lucy, the yellow lab, had just given birth on her beautiful sheets and coverlet, my mother's final present to her. There was blood everywhere, three puppies, and we hadn't known she was pregnant. "Never a dull moment," I could hear my mother saying, her laugh vibrating, her gorgeous smile. I promised Patience I would buy her another set of sheets exactly the same the next day, and I did.

Someone comforted Patience, and the reading resumed. Mr. Pollak soon reached the passage in which my mother leaves me her writing. It seems that I misremembered—I was not alone in the bequest. Claeyssens and I were meant to work together. But, though we swore to for years, we could never bear to talk about it; we lived in different cities, and then he died in his sixties. What I found when at last I went systematically through the papers was that there was no manuscript that could make a complete book. Nor was her play quite finished. Maybe I hadn't really been resisting all those years, just trying to figure out what to do. What I had done, dear reader, dear Mom, was first to become a writer myself.

Wasn't that what you wanted for me? As for your writing, I never stopped thinking about it. When I started this book, your book, I asked for your help, and you gave it to me, in the papers confiding everything I wanted to know. And as I wrote, I felt you falling away from my old ideas of you, my overemphasis on your sadness and discouragement, my loss of you releasing itself like an old skin.

Isn't it strange that it's taken so long, all the way into my seventies, for me to feel that I am finally your daughter: prepared to inherit what you offered, stumbling as you did toward what I so awkwardly wanted all these years, to accept how you lived, how you kept changing, to understand that each new phase of your life was not a static place like a step on the Currier and Ives *Life and Age of Woman*, but one chrysalis of many, from which you kept emerging.

I was always going to call the last portion of the book "Revolution," but like you with *The People on Second Street*, a title for the book kept eluding me. I was writing in a room in the Adirondacks with a fire going, in September 2018, entirely off the grid, and my consciousness was fully with you. I was in the room where I remember you most vividly at cocktails before supper, the very interesting chatter, cheese and crackers and decoratively cut radishes. After supper there would be Scrabble or Liar's Dice, charades or conversation—how in the *New York Times*, this or that had happened and how did we think that would affect . . . Now, in the present, it was before lunch, and one of my guests, also a writer, came into the room. I looked down at the typed word *Revolution*, and saw that I'd scribbled *Our* above it. What do you think? I asked my friend, repeating the phrase. She was smiling at me. I would call the final section "Our Revolution" to allow for the changes of those years. And then I knew it was also the title of the book. I'd suddenly understood that I wanted to account for you continually changing, encouraging others to keep moving and noticing; how alive you were, how you were not alone in your revolution—your turning—but part of a generation, a generation of mothers, a generation of women. And then I draw in to focus on you, a white privileged woman in a century of change, who sought to take her place in movement forward; you gave me that, a kind of force within that never allows me to stay still.

—October 7, 2018

ACKNOWLEDGMENTS

TK

NOTES

All quotations from the writings and speech (author memory) of Jenny McKean
  Moore appear in italics.
All Jenny McKean Moore scrapbooks are in family collections.
All quotes are from the following sources.

Since an aspect of the book is the weaving of Jenny Moore's unpublished writing
through the text, I have noted at the beginning of the notes for each chapter where
most of the italicized Jenny Moore text is from, and specified only when a quote is
from another source, published or unpublished.

2d St   *The People on Second Street*, by Jenny Moore (New York: William Mor-
          row, 1968)

BCA   Barnard College Archives

ECA   The Episcopal Church Archives, Seminary of the Southwest, Austin, TX

FC   Family collection. Jenny kept scrapbooks all her married life, so when I refer to *scrapbook* the reference is to them—about thirty volumes, which are in the family collection.

HM   Author collection

LG   Lewis Galantière papers, Columbia University. Mark Lurie, *Galantière: The Lost Generation's Forgotten Man* (West Palm Beach, FL: Overlook Press, 2017). Courtesy of the author.

M   Author memory

Mad   Paula Skallerup Osborn, ed., *Strong in Her Girls: The Madeira School Centennial History, 1906–2006* (McLean, VA: Madeira School, 2005)

McC   Historical Project, Oral History Interview Series, *Jenny Moore*

MP   *Mourning Pictures*, play by Honor Moore about Jenny McKean Moore's death; *The New Women's Theatre: Ten Plays by Contemporary American Women*, ed. Honor Moore (New York: Random House, 1977). Quotations from Jenny ("Maggie") in the play are from the author's 1973 diaries and memory at the time of writing, 1974. *Mourning Pictures* began as poems and became a play composed of poems and prose when Lyn Austin asked to see the poems. She and Mary Silverman produced the play, with music by Nöa Ain, at the Lenox Arts Center (at Wheatleigh in Lenox, Massachusetts) and on Broadway (the Lyceum Theatre) in 1974.

PTM   Letters from Jenny Moore to Pamela Morton, FC

Sch   Honor Moore papers, Schlesinger Library of Women's History, Radcliffe Institute, Harvard University. Includes papers from *The White Blackbird* and much of the material left to the author by Jenny Moore in her will.

TBD   *The Bishop's Daughter*, by Honor Moore

VCA   Vassar College Archives

WAR   Wartime correspondence, Jenny McKean and Paul Moore, 1942–1946, FC

WBB   *The White Blackbird*, by Honor Moore

PROLOGUE

All Jenny Moore quotations in this section are from memoir pages (Sch) unless noted below.

000   *Everything was . . .*: MP, p. 197.

I. FRETWORK

All quotations in this section are from Jenny McKean Moore's memoir and memoir pages (Sch), unless noted below.

000   *"At a dinner party"*: All quotes from Evans Woollen from author interview, 2009.

000   *"Can you believe it?"*: From a telephone call, c. 1971; M.

000   *I was going to*: Sch., McKean scrapbooks.

000   *"turned to horticulture"*: WBB, p. 247.

000   *Margarett Sargent took up*: Sch, McKean scrapbooks.

000   "A good costume": Sch, McKean scrapbooks.

000   *My hard hard work*: Sch, McKean scrapbooks.

000   *Laetae Sumus*: Sch, McKean scrapbooks.

000   *Jen's [poems]*: Sch, scrapbooks.

000   *Horrible shouting*: M.

000   *she was a lush*: Sch, Margie interviews for WBB.

000   *Color of envy*: Sch, McKean scrapbooks.

000   *I adore you*: Sch, scrapbooks.

000   "flowers came in like a snowstorm": LG; Butler Library Rare Books and Manuscripts, Columbia University, Galantière Collection, box 2–00; courtesy of Mark Lurie.

000   I can't live for things: Sch, McKean scrapbooks.

000   Attractive to women: WBB, p. 230; from Daniel Sargent interviews Honor Moore.

000   Can you imagine: WBB, p. 230.

000   *I'm sorry that I had so little time*: letter to Honor Moore, HM.

000   *I was twelve*: notes, class at Union Seminary, 1946; HM.

000   for lunch and supper: Sch, McKean scrapbooks.

000   Mama and Jenny came home: Sch, McKean scrapbooks.

II. THE DIANA CUP

All Jenny McKean Moore italicized quotes in this section, unless otherwise noted, are from memoir pages in Sch.

000   an old clipping: HM, possibly *Boston Globe*.

000   "strong in her girls": Mad; title page, centennial book.

000   "lack of material things never dampened Lucy's spirits": Mad, p. 11.

000   "separate lives": Sch, Margie interviews.

000   *most glamorous . . . smoothie*: Mad, 1940 yearbook.

000 "pathetic" . . . "desperate": with Deborah Solbert, New York City, 2014.

000 one of 370 freshmen: VCA—*Vassar Miscellany News*, Sept. 21, 1940, p. 1.

000 "the world stands out": "Renascence," Edna St. Vincent Millay.

000 "sound of an ax": Untermeyer quote and Millay details are from Nancy Milford, *Savage Beauty: The Life of Edna St. Vincent Millay* (New York: Random House, 2001), p. 94.

000 "to startle": Elizabeth Bishop, quoted in the *Vassar Encyclopedia*, http://vcencyclopedia.vassar.edu.

000 "unsigned, on a wooden chair": Mary McCarthy, *How I Grew* (San Diego, CA: Harcourt Brace Jovanovich, 1987), p. 258.

000 "treason against poetic tradition": VCA. "New World Reporter Rukeyser Speaks to the Problem of Communication in Poetry," *Vassar Miscellany News*, Oct. 23, 1940, p. 1.

000 *There is sweat and stubble*: Jenny McKean Vassar paper, HM.

000 *Tiny and rather squat . . . throats*: Jenny McKean Vassar paper, HM.

000 *wonderful furs . . . all the way down*: Sch, Jenny McKean short story.

000 "Potter's girl": Sch, Ruth Robb interview for WBB.

000 *The thing with Potter*: WAR.

000 *since I saw you . . . Phillips House*: WAR.

000 "Withdrew, September 1941": Registrar, Vassar College.

000 *wrong with my eyes . . . read too much*: M.

000 "the ark at Prides": Harry Fowler letter, HM.

000 *Contrary to . . . always pro-wholesome*: WAR.

000 "on the Negro problem and on Peace": *Barnard Mortarboard* (yearbook), 1942, unpaged; BCA.

000 "what to feed . . . kitchen units": *Barnard Motorboard*, 1942; BCA.

000 "new engagement ring": *Barnard Motorboard*, 1942.

000 "Frankly": *Barnard Mortarboard*, 1946, unpaged.

000 *In the early forties*: Sch, Jenny Moore memoir pages.

000 "sports, games, dancing": Barnard Catalogue 1941, BCA.

000 "for women of every class": Rosalind Rosenberg, *Changing the Subject: How the Women of Columbia Shaped the Way We Think About Sexual Politics* (New York: Columbia University Press, 2004), p. 58.

000 "problems of race": BCA, "comparative anthropology," Barnard catalogue, 1941.

000 "The peoples of the earth": Ruth Benedict, *Barnard Bulletin*, 1941, p. 1.

000 "a wilderness of smashed plate glass": James Baldwin, "Notes of a Native Son" (Boston: Beacon Press, 1984), 57.

000 "different kinds of people": M.

000 "I realized I was an intellectual . . . Technological monsters": BCA, Thorndike interview, *Barnard Bulletin*, Oct. 5, 1940; p. 1.

000   *The stairs were bare*: Sch, Jenny McKean short story.

000   **When and if Moore comes back**: WAR.

000   *at factories*: 2d S, p. 27.

000   **We all went out**: WAR.

000   *college gingham*: WAR.

000   **"I hang around the phone"**: Cole Porter, "I'm in Love with a Soldier Boy."

000   *Everything so false*: WAR.

000   *He was terribly tall . . . understood*: 2d St, pp. 28–29.

000   *Electricity*: HM conversations with PM Jr.

000   *This is happening*: WAR.

000   *Paul understood . . . how dishonest*: 2d St, p. 28.

000   *went to parties*: ibid.

000   *"Moore's sanctification"*: Cord Meyer to Jenny McKean, HM.

000   *fifty thousand teachers . . . made practical*: Jenny McKean Barnard Paper, HM.

000   *My shell was gone . . . headboard*: WAR.

000   *We fell in love*: 2d St, p. 28.

000   *too available . . . bloody murder*: WAR.

000   "Propinquity; fun": WAR.

000   *steer away . . . in circles*: WAR.

000   "Please write. The relationship": WAR.

000   *embarrassed to say . . . so pre-war*: WAR.

000   "sort of subjective": WAR.

000   *emotionée . . . buttons*: WAR.

000   "I'm curious": WAR.

000   *"WASP Catholic"*: David Challinor interview, Washington, D.C., 1993.

000   *I'll meet you*: Jenny McKean letter to David Challinor, HM; gift of David Challinor.

000   *He didn't do no more. . . . flung herself*: Sch, Jenny McKean short story.

000   *I love to hear him talk*: WAR.

III. PERSUASION

All quotes in this section, unless otherwise noted, are from the wartime correspondence of Jenny McKean (italics) and Paul Moore Jr. (roman, in quotes); FC.

000   "from all reports": Harry Fowler; HM.

000   "I had heard rumors": Cord Myer to Jenny McKean Moore; HM.

000   "out of the ranks of starved": Emma Goldman, *Living My Life* (New York: Knopf, 1931), Vol. 2, p. 17.

000   *the tremendous happenings*: Jenny McKean Barnard paper.

000   **"I could hardly lift my head"**: Margie interviews for WBB 1990–95.

000   **"I shall never forget"**: Gordon Wadhams, letter to Jenny McKean, Nov. 28, 1945, HM.

IV. SIZE OF A COCONUT

All Jenny McKean and Paul Moore Jr. quotes in this section are from WAR, unless otherwise noted.

000   *surrounded by ploughed fields*: 2d St, p 28.

000   **"on the move to the box planting"**: Sch, Margarett Sargent McKean letter.

000   **"Lady Reading"**: Harry McKean letters, HM.

000   **"I remember Len Hanna"**: Tab Hunter, e-mail communication with Honor Moore, 2016.

000   **"Christmas night had several"**: Leonard Hanna letter, HM.

000   **"his own table"**: *Life*, Sept. 13, 1968, pp. 51–54.

000   **"Your letter came"**: Letter, Fanny Hanna Moore; HM.

V. A BABY UNDER ONE ARM, A CABBAGE IN THE OTHER

All quotations in this section, unless otherwise noted, are from *The People On Second Street*, by Jenny Moore (New York: William Morrow, 1968).

000   *It was so wonderful*: WAR.

000   **"I was surprised myself"**: Dorothy Day, *The Long Loneliness* (New York: Harper Brothers, 1952), p. 56.

000   *without crying out*: *The Long Loneliness*, p. 83.

000   **"fine gifts as a writer"**: Dorothy Day, *The Catholic Worker*, November 1973.

000   *The soul must . . . self-appraisal*: Jenny McKean Moore Union Seminary class notes, HM.

000   *a sad poor parish*: WAR, Jenny, HM.

000   **"She thought it was ridiculous"**: Interview with Laine Dickerman, 2016.

000   **"I don't remember much about your mother . . . I didn't know you could dance"**: Interview with Catherine Skipper, 2014.

000   *I remember we made coffee cake*: Jenny McKean Moore letter to Honor Moore, HM.

000   *imbalance lying down*: "Palms on 14th Street: Urban Crisis Report," clipping; HM. (Probably a publication of Episcopal Diocese of Washington, DC, April 1967, but no date and unpaged.)

000   **"The ungodly have drawn out"**: *The Book of Common Prayer*, 1940, Psalm 37.

000   **"CREMATORY HORROR"**: *Jersey Journal*, clipping in scrapbook.

VI. AN INSTITUTION

All quotes from Jenny Moore in this section, unless otherwise noted, are from her correspondence with Pamela Taylor Morton, a gift of Mrs. Morton to the author.

000 **"I want to ride to the ridge":** "Don't Fence Me In," lyrics by Robert Fletcher and Cole Porter, music by Cole Porter, 1934.

000 **"Take, eat, this is my body":** *The Book of Common Prayer*, 1940, pp. 82–83.

000 **"Let all mortal flesh keep silence":** *The Hymnal* (New York: Episcopal Church Pension Fund, 1982), p. 324.

000 *Rest awhile:* Scrapbook.

000 *Tell her that I had one:* Jenny McKean Moore to Dorothy Day, Dorothy Day–Catholic Worker Collection, Series D-1. Box 30. Marquette University, Milwaukee, WI.

000 **"I have a war with my mother":** Unpublished poem, recited in *Girlfriends*, the film by Claudia Well, 1978. Text, Sch.

000 **"Horrible—although beautiful:** Honor Moore from her diary, 1960; HM.

000 *Idlewild for a couple of hours . . . slippery places:* Jenny McKean Moore diary, 1960; HM.

000 **"I can't get used to the turbaned men . . . girl before":** Honor Moore from her letters home, which Jenny McKean Moore had typed and bound for her birthday, 1962.

000 *"glass bangles of every color":* Honor Moore, "The Mogul Gardens Near Mah, 1962," poem, *Freeman's: Arrival* (New York: Grove Press, 2015).

VII. FIRST-PERSON SINGULAR

000 **"The needs of the Moores":** Scrapbook, FC.

000 *six burners:* Jenny McKean Moore letter to Honor Moore, HM.

000 *We feel a twinge of guilt:* Jenny Moore, "Bishop Paul Moore's Wife Looks Back at Six Years in Washington with Confusion and Love," *Potomac Magazine, The Washington Post*, Sept. 20, 1970.

000 **"Cautious, sherry-serving":** Claude Spillman letter, scrapbooks, FC.

000 *She says she wants: Washington Diocese*, March 1965, p. 10.

000 *some furniture:* PTM.

000 *I was almost always we:* Sch memoir pages.

000 *to Paul, who has led a life:* dedication, unpaged; 2d St.

000 *For my husband Paul:* 2d St., p. 17.

000 *I was in that cast-a-glazed-eye:* 2d St, p. 39.

000 *a matter of being impregnated:* PTM.

000 *I'm working hard:* Jenny McKean Moore diary, 1964–1967; HM.

000   *Went to Georgetown . . . killer approached:* Jenny McKean Moore diary, HM.

000   *a late dinner . . . fond of them:* Letter to Honor Moore, HM.

000   *I am going to have to revise:* PTM.

000   *You have been:* Letter to Honor Moore; HM.

000   *Sat next to. . . . for a hick:* Jenny McKean Moore diary 1964–1967, HM.

000   *Jackie, surprisingly tall:* Jenny McKean Moore diary; HM.

000   *African parrot:* Jenny McKean Moore diary; HM.

000   *ignorance of where the suffragan:* Potomac Magazine, Sept. 20, 1970.

000   *George Lincoln Rockwell:* Letter to Honor Moore, HM.

000   **"I wanted my life to be a credit":** Paul Moore, III, class of 1969 Yale 50th Reunion Book, 2019.

000   *I can't wait:* Letter to Honor Moore, HM.

000   **"DC CITIZENS":** Scrapbook.

000   *splitting apart forever:* Jenny Moore diary; HM.

000   **"TRY TO COME":** Telegram to Honor Moore; HM.

000   *talked for seventy minutes:* Letter to Honor Moore, HM.

000   *beating readers over the head:* PTM.

000   *Yet I was also aware:* 2d St.

000   *Often, surrounded:* 2d St.

000   *identification with . . . whatcha-call-it:* 2d St.

000   *have perspective:* Letter to Honor Moore, HM.

000   *plus Leroi Jones (!) . . . new ideas:* PTM.

000   *that Monday in late June:* 2d Street, p. 17.

000   *but the hard avoidable fact . . . pin them down:* 2d St, p. 218.

000   *The children are all well. . . . mother figure:* PTM.

000   *huge emotional investment:* Memoir pages, Sch.

000   *not making the public and the private:* McC, p. 9.

000   **"devastating ostracism . . . in tears":** Taylor Branch, quoted in Lawrence Rosenwald, ed., *War No More: Three Centuries of American Antiwar Peace Writing* (New York: Library of America, 2016), p. 407.

000   **"stump limbs":** *Ramparts*, January 1967.

000   **"I could never again raise":** Martin Luther King, quoted in War No More, p. 411.

000   *selling out to power:* Memoir pages, Sch.

000   *The train ride . . . peak hour:* Jenny Moore, unable to locate clipping; *The Washington Post*, Typescript; HM.

000   *Really everyone:* Jenny Moore diary, Sch.

000   *I believe the Dudmans . . . nut in his cheek:* McC, p. 1.

000   **"I felt the spirt of the campaign":** Eugene McCarthy, *The Year of the People* (New York: Doubleday, 1969), p. 98.

000   *Gene McCarthy is the only:* PTM.

000   *Father Wendt was having . . . overcome someday:* "Palms on 14th Street: Urban Crisis Report," clipping; HM. (Probably a publication of Episcopal Diocese of Washington, DC, April 1967, but no date and unpaged.)

000   *I felt so proud:* PTM.

000   *They were all so enthusiastic . . . hung-up boy:* PTM.

000   *Long relationship:* Memoir pages, Sch.

000   *his need for me . . . final break-off:* Memoir pages, Sch.

000   "The marriage was over": E-mail exchange, Honor Moore and Paul Moore, Summer 2018.

000   "The erotic is a resource": Audre Lorde, Berkshire Conference on the History of Women, August 25, 1978; in *Sister Outsider* (San Francisco: Crossing Press, 2007), p. 53.

000   *I feel differently . . . as possible:* Memoir pages, Sch.

000   *racing all over:* PTM.

000   *sniffling and holding . . . I was a mother:* McC, pp. 9–10b.

000   *We would be stopped . . . being there:* "Magnificat in Chicago," by Jennie [*sic*] Moore; *Catholic Worker*, September 1968, p. 1.

000   *thinking there were troops or crowds . . . a different person:* McC, p. 10.

000   "hated its words . . . amazement grew": C. Kilmer Myers, "A Wondrously Beautiful Web of Relationship," LIFE, Sept. 13, 1968, p 54.

000   "a privileged, highly educated . . .": Mary McGrory, *Washington Star*, Sept. 1967; clipping date Sept. 15, 1968.

000   "Jenny Moore's triumph": Robert Coles, *New Republic*, Dec. 1968.

000   "the Duke of Edinburgh": "Bishop to Duke," "Personalities," compiled by Michael Kerman and Marie Smith, *Washington Post*, Feb. 9, 1969, p. B3.

VIII. OUR REVOLUTION

All Jenny Moore quotations in this section, unless otherwise noted, come from memoir pages; Sch.

000   "September 4, 1969, Dear Mommy" . . . "The upswing": Honor Moore letter to Jenny McKean Moore; HM.

000   "such a rough time": Paul Moore Jr. to Honor Moore; HM.

000   "Very angry . . . children": Paul Moore Jr.; ECA.

000   "very funny, a panic": Honor Moore letter to Jenny McKean Moore; HM.

000   "He sounds brilliant . . . I gather": Pamela T. Morton to Jenny McKean Moore.

000   "On Celibacy": By Dana Densmore; widely anthologized.

000   "the greatest fulfillment": Paul Moore, *Presences: A Bishop's Life in the City* (New York: Farrar Strauss & Giroux, 1997), p. 211.

000   *something down:* Jenny McKean Moore letter to Honor Moore, HM.

000   *it was ghastly . . . temporary fury:* Pamela T. Morton correspondence.

000   **"Women, more especially. . . . happiness":** Nathaniel Hawthorne, *The Scarlet Letter* (Boston: Ticknor, Read, and Fields, 1850), final page.

000   *I have been so desperately:* Jenny Moore letter to Paul Moore Jr., ECA.

000   **"but she never did":** Polly Kraft interview with HM.

000   *We bought a house:* Letter to Rachel Beck; HM.

000   *My life alone:* Letter to Honor Moore, HM.

000   **"I am really glad":** Honor Moore to Jenny McKean Moore; HM.

000   *I loved your letter:* Jenny McKean Moore to Honor Moore; HM.

000   I am nervous . . . : Honor Moore to Jenny McKean Moore; HM.

000   *who has a right:* Jenny McKean Moore to Honor Moore; HM.

000   *the equivalent of solitude:* Jenny McKean Moore, English paper, George Washington University; HM.

000   **"life in New York . . . to Washington":** *Newsweek*, Dec. 10, 1972, p. 58.

000   *about Newsweek article:* Letter from Jenny McKean Moore to Honor Moore, Dec. 1972; HM.

000   **"It is the only human organ":** *Mourning Pictures*, by Honor Moore, p. 206.

000   **"My mother said":** "My Mother's Moustache," poem, in *American Review* 19 (1974), p. 20; also in Honor Moore, *Memoir*, poems (Goshen, CT: Chicory Blue Press, 1988; Pittsburgh, PA: Carnegie Mellon Press, 2020 reprint), p. 70.

000   **"cat gone mad":** *Mourning Pictures*, p. 210.

000   **"charred, alienated vegetable":** Honor Moore, *Mourning Pictures*, p. 210.

000   **President Nixon's enemies list":** Staff of the Joint Committee on Internal Revenue Taxation, "Investigation into Certain Charges of the Use of the Internal Revenue Service for Political Purposes" (Washington, DC: U.S. Government Printing Office, 1978), p. 26.

000   **support young writers:** The bequest, well invested since 1975, as of 2019 still funds the Jenny Moore Writer in Washington position at George Washington University.

PHOTOGRAPHS

Susanna, Rosemary, Jenny, Patience; front: Daniel. Credit: Photograph by Judith Gellert.

PART VII: FIRST-PERSON SINGULAR: p. 000

Jenny back in Jersey City for the publication of *The People on Second Street*, 1968. Credit: Photograph by William Albert Allard.

PART VIII: OUR REVOLUTION: p. 000

Jenny in Washington, 1968. Credit: Photograph by William Albert Allard.

ACKNOWLEDGMENTS: p. 000

Jenny and Paul at Adelia's wedding, October 1972.

NOTES: p. 000

Jenny and (from left) Paul, Rosemary, Adelia, George, and Honor in the Adirondacks. Credit: Photograph by Paul Moore.